SPY FICTION

A Connoisseur's Guide

SPY FICTION

A Connoisseur's Guide

Donald McCormick

&

Katy Fletcher

Facts On File

New York • Oxford • Sydney

SPY FICTION: A CONNOISSEUR'S GUIDE

Facts On File Limited
Collins Street , Oxford OX4 1XJ
United Kingdom
or
Facts On File Inc.
460 Park Avenue South, New York NY 10016
USA
or
Facts On File Pty Ltd
Talavera & Kartoum Rds, North Ryde NSW 2113
Australia

British Library Cataloguing in Publication Data
Spy Fiction: A Connoisseur's Guide
McCormick, Donald
Fletcher, Katy
I. Title. II. Spy thrillers
1245'389.67

ISBN 0 - 8160 - 2098 - 1

Library of Congress Cataloging-in-Publication Data
McCormick, Donald, 1911-
Spy fiction: a connoisseur's guide / Donald McCormick and
Katy Fletcher
p. cm.
Expanded version of the author's Who's who in spy fiction.
ISBN 0-8160-2098-1
1. Spy stories—Bio-bibliography. 2. Authors—Biography.
I. Fletcher, Katy, 1958- . II. McCormick, Donald, 1911- Who's
who in spy fiction. III. Title. IV. Title: Spy fiction.
PN3448.S66M3 1990
809.3'872—dc20
[B]

Australian CIP data available on request from Facts On File

Facts On File books are available at special discounts when purchased in bulk quantities
for businesses, associations, institutions or sales promotion.
Please contact the Special Sales Department of our Oxford office
at 0865 728399 or our New York office at 212/683 - 2244
(dial 800/322 - 8755 except in New York, AK or HI)

Text design and processing by *P i* c A Publishing Services, Abingdon, Oxon
Jacket design by Richard Garratt Design
Jacket illustration by Colin Robson
Printed and bound in Great Britain by
Biddles Ltd, Guildford and King's Lynn

10 9 8 7 6 5 4 3 2 1

This book is printed on acid-free paper

Contents

Introduction

Espionage has fascinated a large number of people whether in the form of a spy novel, a film, or a newspaper story. The world of Intelligence is shrouded in mystery and secrecy and this accounts for some of the attraction. Also, only those who have had experience in the business can know exactly what espionage involves, which has invited speculation and sensationalism amongst us lesser mortals. In the past, many people have based their views of espionage upon the spy novels they had read or the James Bond films they had seen. Where little alternative information was available these sensational impressions filled the vacuum. Nowadays more information about Intelligence services is obtainable, but a great deal of this information can be confusing and deceptive. Spy fiction has coloured the public's view of Intelligence in the past and may continue to influence their opinions in the future, despite the lack of realism in most spy fiction. Indeed, spy novels may become more influential as the real world of Intelligence grows in complexity — it can offer simple explanations in an increasingly complicated world. Because of its effects in the past and its potential influence in the future, it is important to look at spy ficiton, not just as an enjoyable form of entertainment, but also as a reflection of the social and political values of our time.

All forms of literature reflect the social and political attitudes of the author and the culture of the country in which he or she lives. Spy fiction is no exception, and in some cases this can add to our knowledge of espionage. John le Carré once wrote that the British secret services were "microcosms of the British condition, of our social attitudes and vanities". This statement can be applied to the spy fiction of any country, the background of which is the real world of politics and international intrigue; moreover it is this reality that provides the stories and events of the modern spy novel.

The word "spy", for which there is a single character in the Chinese language, had as its original meaning in ancient China that of "a chink", "a crack" or "crevice". From any of these meanings one can derive the sense of a peep-hole, so it would seem that the earliest Chinese conception of a spy is very simply one who peeps through a crack.

It is worthwhile turning to ancient China for some background to spy fiction. As far back as 510 BC the earliest textbook, not only on the arts of war, but on espionage and the organisation of a secret service, was written. This was the *Ping Fa* of Sun Tzu. It has not only been respected as a valuable guide to the arts of espionage down the ages in China, but an abbreviated, simplified version of the book in English was issued to the RAF in Ceylon during the Second World War.

One of the attractions of spy fiction is that, unlike a history book or a newspaper story, it dramatises events and gives us an insight into human behaviour in different situations. It not only provides us with a glimpse into a secret world, but a glimpse that changes in its images from age to age, from generation to generation. In the early 1900s spy fiction focused mainly on German spies as seen on the Riviera, in Vienna and Paris (actually the Germans' real spying then was done in Portsmouth, Chatham, Devonport and Marseilles); in the 1920s it switched to watching Chinese and Russian spies. At one time it was essentially high-life espionage, telling how the butler in a country house saw the black-velveted seductress stealing the plans of a new submarine. Today spy fiction is much more likely to feature a rather scruffy, pimply student of electronics working out how to infiltrate the computer which contains the secrets of the round-the-clock anti-sub-marine warfare watch. Changes in spy fiction are also reflected in the development of the spy hero, who has moved on from the early amateur spy involved by accident, to the professional intelligence officer employed by a secret organisation, to the professional "rogue" agent, who at one time was employed by an organisation but now works alone.

One of the difficulties in compiling a guide to spy fiction is that it is far from easy either to pin-point the beginning of the genre, or to define who is and who is not of this particular Band of Brothers. Therefore one can only try to give a brief history of the development of spy fiction in Britain; the origins of the spy novel in America can be found in an article in Section 2.

To define spy fiction is not as easy as to define detective literature. The latter can be described in precise terms and has therefore come to be accepted as a branch of literature. But not so the spy story, which has been much more the subject of sneers and derision. Many authors object, sometimes with justice, to the labelling of their novels as "spy stories". Even some of the authors included in this book have registered this objection, insisting that their books are novels first and foremost and only incidentally spy stories. As one of them points out, "once you start pigeon-holing novels and plays I suppose you reach the point where King Lear is defined as 'regal fiction— Drama'". The purpose of compiling this guide to spy fiction is not to trap the authors into a definite category but to show the variety and scope of the spy story as practised by a number of writers.

Some of the practitioners of the spy story are authors of great distinction in the broader world of literature; Conrad, Chesterton and Maugham among them. It cannot, however, be denied that some of the best-known and most prolific writers of this genre have given the spy story a bad name. Indeed, as will be seen in this book, it is sometimes impossible not to give them more space than some of the better writers, if only because in their clumsy and rodomontade manner they have been trend-setters. Curiously, not one of their characters is likely to become one of the immortals of literature. So far there has been no spy fiction hero to vie with Sherlock Holmes for longevity of fame. This may be due to the fact that "spy story" is in itself a misnomer. A detective story is built entirely around the character of the detective. Without him there would be no story, and he can survive indefinitely. But the main figure in a spy story, if he is technically a spy, cannot be expected to have too long a life: sooner or later he must be "blown", or "taken to the cleaners". But he may not be a spy at all: he may be a counter-espionage agent like James Bond, or an Intelligence Chief sitting at a desk in London, Washington or Moscow, controlling a network of spies, but not doing any spying himself. In fact, when we speak of the spy story we are talking of spy-catchers as well as spies, of double and treble-agents as well as agents, of hired killers, planters of misinformation, or sometimes even of that unassuming little man at the corner shop who operates a kind of letter-box for agents.

Yet for very many years, in the Western world, there was another reason why the pure spy story was, if not derided, at least ignored. Spying was regarded as something despicable and no spy could be considered as a hero. Nor was it even considered desirable that the chief villain of a story should be a spy. A thief, yes; a murderer, most certainly; but a spy was the nineteenth-century equivalent of the sexual pervert hero or villain of the pre-1939 period — the most ostracised character in literature. Unlike the Chinese, who have shown a remarkable taste for their own spy literature and have even made this part of their education, the Western world has only belatedly learned some of the lessons of ancient espionage. Shakespeare introduced an espionage trick in *Macbeth*, when Malcolm ordered:

> Let every soldier hew him down a bough,
> And bear't before him; thereby shall we shadow
> The numbers of our host, and make discovery
> Err in report of us.

But it was centuries later before this lesson in camouflage was scientifically adopted by military strategists.

Many authors embraced the spy story at their peril, as shown by the example of Joseph Conrad's *The Secret Agent*. This novel was published in 1907, and like many modern spy novelists Conrad based his story upon a real event — the strange incident in 1894 which became known as the Greenwich Bomb Outrage. An anarchist called Martial Bourdin was killed by a bomb he was carrying towards the Observatory at Greenwich. The event was mysterious and seemed to be pointless but it attracted the attention of Conrad, who had suffered from the extremes of revolution and repression in his childhood. The novel was European in its outlook as it embraced many current revolutionary philosophies which were affecting the political status quo in a number of European countries. Conrad suffered as a writer when he embraced the themes of betrayal, treachery and anarchy in this story, themes seen all the more violently when juxtaposed to the economic prosperity and political stability of England. When *The Secret Agent* did not become the great success that he hoped for, he explained it by saying: "Foreignness, I suppose." To a great extent Conrad was ahead of his time in writing of the machinations of the agent prova-cateur, and the grey picture he painted of the world in which these people lived. His reading public were not ready to accept these morally dubious subjects, despite the fact that the book was a fine piece of literature.

Malcolm Bradbury, in his essay on Joseph Conrad in *The Modern World — Ten Great Writers* (London, Penguin, 1989), declared that with *The Secret Agent*: "Conrad had hoped that the serious melodrama, the thriller that constituted a full vision of modern life, would make him a popular writer, something he craved. It did not happen with the book, and Conrad finally pronounced it 'an honorable failure. It brought me neither love nor the promise of literary success. I own that I am cast down.' " This book is a fascinating example of a story, well written by a great writer, but unaccept-able to the majority of his audience because it incorporated many ingredi-ents related to the spy story. This novel had to await a later generation of readers before it was appreciated.

Antipathy to the spy story was presumably as marked in the seventeenth and eighteenth centuries as it was in the nineteenth. One would have expected both Mrs Aphra Behn and Daniel Defoe to have contributed to this form of literature. Defoe admitted that he had been employed by Queen Anne "in several honourable, though secret services", yet he never drew on his experiences in his writing either in fiction or in fact. Like Aphra Behn, he was more interested in the antics of the bedroom than in those of the informer travelling from tavern to tavern. Aphra Behn was probably the first really effective professional female secret agent in Britain as well as being the first Englishwoman to write plays. She, too, avoided the theme of the spy story.

Yet the links between literature and espionage are considerable, and this applies more to Britain than to any other country. The Americans can fairly claim to have produced the first writer of a spy fiction book — Fenimore Cooper. Probably this was due to an aroused interest in espionage as a patriotic duty during the War of Independence. The spy was much more of a hero in America in this period than he was elsewhere. But American writers did not follow up this trend in the early part of the twentieth century to the extent to which the British did. The French, surprisingly, have produced few spy fiction writers, even though their talent for espio-nage can probably be rated higher than that of most nations. Like the Germans and the Spanish, the French seem quite content to read trans-lations of Anglo-Saxon espionage stories.

There is a long list of authors in Britain who have been engaged in Intelligence and have also written spy stories, including Somerset Maugham,

Graham Greene and John le Carré. This tradition is also growing in America, where a number of people who have worked for the CIA at some time in their careers, have turned to writing spy fiction. The connection between British writers and the world of Intelligence is explored in an article in the second section of this book (pages 297–305).

After Fenimore Cooper there is a long gap before discovering the next real spy story, *The Riddle of the Sands* (1903), by Erskine Childers. He based the tale on his own yachting voyages in the vicinity of the Frisian Islands. Intended as an awful warning of the threat of Prussian militarism, his novel revealed that the Admiralty charts of the area were not up to date. The NID then sanctioned a real-life spy trip to the Frisian Islands.

The most prolific period of the spy story was between 1914 and 1939, but it was very far from being a golden age of espionage fiction. Hundreds of authors of this genre produced thousands of stories, short and long, during that quarter of a century. The advent of the First World War whetted the appetite of the reading public for this kind of writing, and the spy story became a habit rather than a cult. Some of the stories were competent, one or two like Maugham's *Ashenden* were first class, but the vast majority was mediocre and many were appallingly bad both as credible plots and as examples of the written word.

These novels provided entertainment on a grand scale and exploited the desire for escapism into the exotic high-life of the 1920s. It was in some ways magnificent in its uninhibited flamboyance and flaunted grandiloquence, but it was not literature until the advent of Eric Ambler at the tail end of the 1930s. Maugham had struck his own warning much earlier, but this message had not yet penetrated to the masses who still lapped up the offerings of Horler, Le Queux, Beeding and "Sapper". They were not ready to appreciate the "new look" at the spy as provided by such a realist as Maugham when he made his character Ashenden ruefully comment that: "the great chiefs of the secret service in their London offices, their hands on the throttle of this great machine, led a life full of excitement; they moved their pieces here and there, they saw the pattern woven by the multitudinous threads ... but it must be confessed that for the small fry like himself to be a member of the secret service was not as adventurous an affair as the public thought."

It was Ambler who really put over the Maugham message to a wider readership, who successfully changed the pattern of the spy story and paved the way to the emergence of something more adult and realistic. And it was Ambler, paradoxically the one man who had not been mixed up in the Intelligence game, who first produced the most factual, authentic spy stories of the century. He achieved this simply by patient, meticulous attention to detail, by checking and cross-checking on his facts.

Ambler pointed the way towards a golden age for the spy story, at least to a standard far higher than previously — a genre to which a serious, highly skilled novelist such as Graham Greene could at least contribute.

From Ambler onwards the emphasis was on authentic detail and diligent, accurate research.

It was possible in 1925 for a writer who had never travelled more than six miles from, say, Pudsey, to produce a spy novel that would be acceptable. Today not only does it require the author to be widely travelled, highly sophisticated, knowledgeable about the technology of espionage and to have some first-hand knowledge of how Secret Services operate, but he (or she) probably needs to spend a holiday in the actual setting chosen for the book, not to mention taking a crash course in electronics and spending an afternoon learning how debugging devices work. Fleming not only travelled far afield in quest of more exotic settings for his stories, but employed a number of people to undertake research for him. Even so, it is doubtful if his books were as realistic as those of Len Deighton, and his readers frequently delighted in catching him out in some tiny detail. John Dee, Queen Elizabeth I's astrologer and secret agent, signed himself "007" but nobody seems to have pointed this out to Fleming. It also happens to have been the number of the door of the ladies' lavatory at the old Commonwealth Relations Office, now incorporated into the Foreign Office. (In conversation Fleming once said that he took the code-name from the zip code for the Georgetown area of Washington, DC, where many CIA agents live - 20007.)

So the new "in" thing in spy fiction became a passion for detail. At first it was "fun finding out" (which, incidentally, was the title of a regular column in the *Daily Express* in the immediate post-war years when people began to yearn for all they had missed learning in those six years of war). But Fleming erred in writing the kind of detail that interested him rather than what might appeal to his readers. At first it did not matter because the reader was flattered that the author should appear to think that he appreciated these things and wanted to know more about them. This was particularly true of food and drink in the mid-1950s after years of wartime austerity, and possibly Fleming did more than anyone to make vodka popular in suburbia. But, as Kingsley Amis has pointed out, this tendency began to reach an extreme point "... the identifying of a Soviet agent in London is the merest peg for a great lump of information about Faberge jewellery [Fleming's "The Property of a Lady", *Playboy*, January 1964], Wartski's shop and Sotheby's auction rooms. Mr Fleming lectures as well in fiction as any writer I know, but one expected at least a more energetic pretence that the facts are doing some honest work instead of merely hanging about asking to be admired."

It was the brief age of the "super"-figure — "SuperMac", "Super-Bond" — and there was bound to be a reaction to it. James Bond was grossly oversold as the man who never failed to lay a girl. Statistics show that only twice in thirteen books did Bond fail to seduce the girl he fancied. One wonders whether Fleming acted out his own sexual fantasies in Bond. Not only did the sex-bomb Bond lure a lesbian to change her allegiance to his side, and his bed, but in *From Russia With Love*, the dedicated Soviet agent, Tatiana Romanova, becomes so enamoured with Bond's photograph that she decides to double-cross her bosses and bring information with her, if only the irresistible James will enable her to escape with him from Istanbul.

Fleming forgot the lessons of Ambler: he tended to make Bond and his enemies less credible figures in his later books. When the reaction set in the demise of Bond was swift, even among his most fervent admirers. But the reaction of other up-and-coming writers was even more pronounced. A new school emerged: these writers actually loathed Bond, seeing him as a neo-Fascist, a propagandist of the Cold War and an awful reminder of the nadir of racialist, right-wing "Bulldog" Drummondism. Some of them felt this instinctively on aesthetic grounds, while others reacted morally and politically. The Communist *Morning Star* gave quite a lot of space to a write-up of an interview with John Gardner. In the United States there was *Alligator*, the Harvard *Lampoon* parody of an Ian Fleming book, while in *The London Magazine* Cyril Connolly concocted his satirical extravaganza, *Bond Strikes Camp*.

Thus by the mid-1960s the spy story had become the target of the satirists. For a while the John Gardner approach of "sending-up" espionage fiction was highly popular. But by the early 1970s the pendulum had swung again: this time it settled down to something like a happy mean, an almost imperceptible movement around sober realism. The stories eschewed the melodramatic, the ultra-heroic, the extravagant; the characters were much more like the gentle old man in the antiquarian bookshop, the girl teacher who takes a package-tour holiday to Yugoslavia; the settings for the stories were changed to more distant places and in many instances, in order to heighten the effect of realism, real-life stories were taken as the subjects for fiction. Alan Williams made Kim Philby an important figure in one of his books, while R Wright Campbell took the incidents surrounding the sinking of the *Royal Oak* in the Second World War as the theme for his *The Spy Who Sat and Waited*.

In retrospect, it may now appear that the Ambler–Greene–Fleming–le Carré–Deighton period was the golden age of spy fiction, say from 1939 to 1969, though most of these books were published after 1955. This era covered a wide range of trends from the Bulldog Drummond Mark II of the 1950s (Bond) to the Ashenden Mark II of the 1960s (Leamas and Boysie Oakes), though Maugham might wince at the thought of Boysie Oakes being linked to Ashenden. Spy fiction had long been regarded as excellent material for films, but the golden age of this genre brought the spy story into the living-room via the television screen. Here was a new medium for the writer of this type of book and the character of Callan, the agent with a chip on his shoulder, became almost one of the family, a favourite erring son who popped back into the sitting-room of an evening.

One of the characteristics of the modern spy novel has been this quest for ultra-realism, for accurate mirroring of contemporary trends in espionage and counter-espionage, which has become so general on both sides of the Atlantic that it is bound to have some political influence. In America the revelations of Watergate in the 1970s provoked a spate of such spy stories and, whereas previously a man like E Howard Hunt was able to get away with no less than 43 atrociously written specimens of the genre before he was jailed for his part in the "plumbers' raid", more recent authors of successful and extremely well-written spy stories have been ex-CIA or Secret Service men — Victor Marchetti, Charles McCarry and Wilson Mc-Carthy among them. Their novels, and those of Brian Garfield and James Grady with their investigative approach, have probably done as much as the media to put the spotlight on CIA methods and force the nation as a whole to take a more critical look at the business of "dirty tricks". Similarly in Europe there is the gradual development of a highly intelligent new type of spy story that often has a political and even moral message. Douglas Hurd, Andrew Osmond, and Robert Rostand are all in their different ways highly articulate practitioners of this art: they are didactic without being propagandist or "factionist".

One of the reasons why the spy novel is so hard to define is because it is so flexible — it can incorporate elements from the adventure novel, the romance and the detective story: it may even include them all. As a result the spy story has engendered a number of sub-genres, such as the conspir-acy-assassination story, an example of which is examined on pages 279–86. Instead of a straight spy story, new novels are often now described as "techno-thrillers" or other such names, which contain increasingly compli-cated plots involving the intricacies of military weaponry or computer technology. Far from simplifying the definition of the spy story, they serve only to further confuse the issue.

Increasingly, too, the reader of espionage tales of the future must be on his guard against blatant propaganda heavily disguised as spy fiction. The Russians have paved the way with this in recent years, but the Americans have not lagged far behind. The *Penkovsky Papers* are still the subject of much argument as to whether they are fact or fiction, faked by the CIA, as Mr Victor Zorza seems to suggest, or "a last message and testament from the brave and intelligent man", as Robert Conquest avers.

The list of authors included in this book is, inevitably, a selective one. Some of the writers who in our opinion should have had an entry have been omitted because they have declined to give information about themselves; sometimes their reluctance has been due to a dislike or fear of being dubbed spy fiction authors, which should bear no relation to their ability to write. In other cases we have still included them, even if the available material is scanty.

There is a vast number of authors who could have been included in this work. We make no claims that it is a complete or definitive guide, and no doubt some omissions will be regarded as negligent, while others who have been included may well cause objection. What we have tried to do throughout is to cover as wide a range of styles and types (both past and present) and to stress especially all links between fact and fiction and fiction and fact, because, unless this link is perceived, the modern spy story loses much of its vitality and purpose. A novel by Nicholas Luard can be regarded as a salutary firing of a warning shot across the bows of the CIA or the KGB. Sometimes an author who has written only one spy story can be of greater interest than another who has written thirty. Some young and little known contemporary authors who have not yet written much seem to have things of importance to say, while other tired old scribes past and present have produced a score or more novels and do not seem to warrant a mention. Choice is always difficult, and because it is so personal we cannot hope to please everyone.

The topography and the secret language of the spy story are separate and yet inseparable subjects. So, too, is the game of spotting the real-life characters behind such people as Richard Hannay, Bulldog Drummond, Ashenden and James Bond. It is because there really are thirty-nine steps near Broadstairs that Buchan's novel can become an excuse for an after-noon's exploration. Similarly, it is a positive delight to discover that the improbably named Pett Bottom in Fleming's novels actually exists in East Kent and that one can have a splendid dinner at the Duck Inn, opposite the cottage where James Bond lived as a boy. And the thought of Somerset Maugham having personally directed British Secret Service activities in-side Russia in the First World War (with quotations from authenticated documents to prove it) makes *Ashenden* that much more credible. It is known that the KGB go through Len Deighton's novels with great dili-gence and that they spent some time checking on STUCEN and the island mentioned in *Spy Story* where anthrax experiments were carried out in the Second World War (yes, that island actually exists: its name is Gruinard, two miles north of Ross and Cromarty, and is still banned to the public).

This guide is arranged in two sections, the first of which is a compilation of over two hundred authors, mostly British and American. The author entries consist of personal details where available, publication details, short biographies and a critical analysis of their published works. These entries vary in length according to the contribution of the author to this form of fiction and also to the amount of information available. The second part of this book is divided into eight short articles about various themes and topics covered in these spy novels. Most of the authors mentioned in these articles can be found in Section 1.

At the end of this book we have included a glossary of abbreviations, terms, places, phrases and jargon used in the twilight world of Intelligence. This has become important for two reasons: first, because increasingly in spy fiction a great many such abbreviations and phrases are picked from real life, while others are invented; secondly, the readership of people who are actually in the spy game has risen enormously in the past twenty years. Indeed, any author who can sell to the personnel of his own and rival Secret

Services can be a bestseller. The American author who writes under the pseudonym of Trevanian, creates characters so true to life in the Intelligence world that they frequently make "in" jokes to tell readers among professional spooks that they know what it is all about. It is useful to have a glossary to refer to when reading and studying spy fiction and this is being added to every day.

"Factional" is a horrible word, but how else can one describe the increasing number of spy stories which, according to Jonathan Green's *Newspeak: A Dictionary of Jargon*, can be described as works of "fiction that is taken with only minimal alterations from events that have actually happened"? It is partly because of the factional spy novel that Intelligence services all over the world eagerly study spy fiction as new books come out if only to see whether they have been compromised in some way, or if there are any worthwhile facts to be picked up. On occasion, Intelligence services in recent times have actually used novelists to work into their books either facts or suggestions which they feel might help their own cause.

Not surprisingly this has caused questions to be asked in political circles. There was a debate on this very subject in Britain's House of Commons in 1989 when Mr Patten, a Home Office Minister, sought to allay anxieties on both sides of the House of Commons, that writers such as John le Carré might be open to prosecution under provisions of the proposed new Official Secrets Bill concerning unauthorised disclosure of secret information. Mr Patten's reply was "that it would be absurd if a former member of the security service writing a spy novel were in danger of prosecution simply because some people took his fiction as truth. The bill did not inhibit the writing of a genuine spy novel, but *would prevent the use of fiction where the real purpose was to disclose facts.*"

The main reason for the factional spy novel has been, of course, a reaction against the romantic and outdated novels of Hannay and Bond, from an era of an heroic world where secret agents struggled against spies in noble and patriotic conflicts across the globe to an awareness that in real life there were traitors and moles within the protagonist's own national agency. Nigel West, whose real name is Rupert Allason, Conservative MP for Torbay, believes that spy novelists who turn to domestic espionage are likely to clash in the future with the government. He believes that the proposed new Official Secrets Act in Britain will turn the spy novel into an object of government suspicion. He made this suggestion at the time when he was working on this first spy novel, *The Blue List*, which, he said, would "unquestioningly" fall foul of the new Bill. "The book is full of details about a secret detention centre in Scotland, called Inverlair, which actually exists", he told the London *Daily Telegraph*.

As John G Cawelti and Bruce A Rosenberg have pointed out in their book, *The Spy Story*, in recent times spy fiction can be seen "as a major expressive phenomenon of modern culture" and they devote a whole chapter to the cultural and psychological significance of the spy story.

Will *glasnost* put an end to spy fiction? It is hard to imagine and seems highly unlikely. The most enduring feature of the spy novel is precisely its flexibility as far as political change is concerned. It has survived many social and political upheavals in the past and will continue to thrive in the future. New political developments can only give authors more material for their fiction. No matter what shape the world is in people wil l continue to spy on each other for whatever reasons.

John le Carré commented recently with the publication of *The Russia House*, "the spy story wasn't invented by the Cold War, and it won't be finished off by the end of it. On the contrary, this is a new springtime for espionage writing. Spying will take a more benign form in the future, but we haven't deloused the earth quite yet. We haven't got rid of the mutual suspicion and hostility between the powers. We are still poised to destroy each other. For a writer it's a great opportunity. I feel as if I've been given a whole new pack of cards to play with ...". So perhaps if other writers see the situation in the same light we may look forward to a new golden age of spy fiction in the near future.

A-Z AUTHOR ENTRIES

DAVID AARON
American.

Titles
State Scarlet. New York, Putnam, 1987; London, Macmillan, 1987.
Agent of Influence. New York, Putnam, 1989.

Biography
David Aaron has served on the National Security Council in both Republican and Democratic administrations from 1972 to 1974 as senior staff member and, from 1977 to 1981, as Deputy Assistant to the President for National Security Affairs. From 1974 to 1976 he headed an investigative task force for the Senate Intelligence Committee. He has been sent on sensitive presidential missions to Europe, Africa, China and Latin America, and in 1981 won the National Defense Medal, the Pentagon's highest civilian award. He is on the board of Oppenheimer & Co. QFV fund, and was formerly Vice-President for mergers at Oppenheimer & Co. and on the board of Oppenheimer International.

Critical Analysis
State Scarlet is the story of terrorism which brings the world to the brink of nuclear holocaust. It begins with a phone call to the White House in which the caller says that he has stolen an American nuclear device and will set it off in a European city. It is presumed to be a hoax, but nevertheless provides them with an opportunity to check the security of the nuclear weapons system. But it is not a crank call — a nuclear device has been stolen and everyone panics, with the Russians and the Americans blaming each other. As time gets shorter the Americans' strategy of defence turns to plans of a pre-emptive strike...

State Scarlet became a national bestseller. The *New York Times Book Review* wrote: "Aaron skilfully interweaves his characterizations with insights into the power plays and paranoia of government bureaucracy. Thought-provoking entertainment." The author used his experience of years in the White House to convey the reality of power politics.

Again Aaron draws on his experience of Wall Street in his latest novel, *Agent of Influence*. The story is about a young Wall Street deal-maker, Jason Lyman, who gets an assignment. *News/Worldweek*, the media conglomerate that controls many of the nation's top newspapers, magazines and television stations, has been targeted for a takeover by French magnate Marcel Bresson. Lyman is ordered to investigate Bresson and prevent this foreigner from controlling the American Press.

Lyman starts his investigation of this shadowy figure, but learns little about him until he meets Heidi Bruce, deputy director of the Senate Intelligence Committee, who is trying to convince the American government that the Soviets are using advanced intelligence technology to manipulate Western financial market — and so control Western governments.

With the help of Sean Gordon, a maverick CIA agent, the three of them race across Europe, following a trail of deception and death to find Bresson's true identity. Convinced that Bresson is under Soviet control, their investigation alarms the CIA, the KGB and the French Deuxième Bureau.

EDWARD SIDNEY AARONS
Pseudonyms: PAUL AYRES, EDWARD RONNS
American. Born in Philadelphia, 1916. Died 16 June 1975.

Titles
[Major character: Sam Durell]
Assignment to Disaster. New York, Fawcett, 1955; London, Fawcett, 1956.
Assignment — Suicide. New York, Fawcett, 1956; London, Fawcett, 1958.
Assignment — Treason. New York, Fawcett, 1956; London, Fawcett, 1957.
Assignment — Budapest. New York, Fawcett, 1957; London, Fawcett, 1959.
Assignment — Stella Marni. New York, Fawcett, 1957; London, Fawcett, 1958.
Assignment — Angelina. New York, Fawcett, 1958; London, Fawcett, 1959.
Assignment — Madeleine. New York, Fawcett, 1958; London, Muller, 1960.
Assignment — Carlotta Cortez. New York, Fawcett, 1959; London, Muller, 1960.
Assignment — Helene. New York, Fawcett, 1959; London, Muller, 1960.
Assignment — Lili Lamaris. New York, Fawcett, 1959; London, Muller, 1960.
Assignment — Mara Tirana. New York, Fawcett, 1960; London, Fawcett, 1962.
Assignment — Zoraya. New York, Fawcett, 1960; London, Muller, 1960.
Assignment — Ankara. New York, Fawcett, 1960; London, Muller, 1962.
Assignment — Lowlands. New York, Fawcett, 1961; London, Muller, 1962.
Assignment — Burma Girl. New York, Fawcett, 1961; London, Muller, 1962.
(26 further titles in the series featuring Durell)

Biography
Edward S Aarons was educated at Columbia University, New York, where he obtained degrees in Ancient History and Literature. During the Second World War he served in the US Coast Guard between 1941 and 1945. After the war he worked as a millhand, salesman, fisherman, and as a reporter on a Philadelphia newspaper. He became a full-time writer from 1945.

Critical Analysis
Aarons was certainly a prolific writer — he produced over 40 stories for the *Assignment* series, which continued to be published posthumously until 1979. He wrote other mystery novels before he started the series which made him internationally known. The series was so popular that his son, Will Aarons, continued with the stories after his father's death.

The hero of the Assignment series is Sam Durell — a field operative of the CIA's "K" section. The novels are concerned with action — plot, characterization, locale and romance take a second place.

As one critic, David K Jeffrey, in *Twentieth Century Crime and Mystery Writers* (1985), has described them: "The novels are generally as topical as yesterday's newspaper. Aarons wrote, for example, of the Algerian conflict, Cold War tensions, the Chinese influence in Albania, spy satellites, the Indochina wars, and the oil crisis. His formula was to open each novel with a chapter of violence and mystery, introduce Durell, situate him in a foreign country and direct him through a series of false leads and traitors until he meets the arch-villain and emerges triumphantly from his confrontation with a shaky peace and the lady."

In Durell's first mission in *Assignment to Disaster* he is sent to find a man who has disappeared from a missile base in the New Mexico desert — and to kill him if he has leaked any information about a top-secret atomic project.

At one point in *Assignment — School for Spies* (1966), Durell reflects on his job — despite its dangers, it is better than some occupations: "As a sub-chief for K Section of the Central Intelligence Agency, he had been in field operations longer than his survival factor permitted. But he would not transfer to a Washington desk, in *Synthesis and Analysis*, for example, to spend his days in preparing extrapolative reports for Joint Chief and the White House. He had journeyed too far into the shadows of the secret war, and could never go back to the apparent normality of suburban boxes, commuter schedules, ulcers, and interoffice back-scratching."

Durell was a contemporary of Donald Hamilton's Matt Helm; although both secret agents, Durell is tough on the outside, but softer on the inside, especially when it comes to protecting women. Despite their differences, both these characters contributed to the popularity of the spy hero in the 1960s.

WARREN ADLER

American. Born in Brooklyn, New York, 16 December 1927.

Titles

Options. New York, Whitman Publishing, 1974.
Banquet before Dawn. New York, Putnam, 1976.
The Henderson Equations. New York, Putnam, 1976.
Trans-Siberian Express. New York, Putnam, 1977.
The Sunset Gang. New York, Viking, 1978.
The Casanova Embrace. New York, Putnam, 1978.
Blood Ties. New York, Putnam, 1979.
Natural Enemies. New York, Pocket Books, 1980.
The War of the Roses. New York, Warner Books, 1981.
American Quartet. New York, Arbor House, 1982.
American Sextet. New York, Arbor House, 1983.

Biography

Warren Adler was educated at the University of New York from where he received a BA in 1947. He has worked as a journalist for the *New York Daily News*, and was also the former editor of *Queens Post*, Forest Hills, New York. President of an advertising and public relations agency in Washington DC 1959–78, he has been a full-time writer since 1978.

Critical Analysis

In the *Trans-Siberian Express* American physician, Alex Cousins, is sent to the Soviet Union to treat the ailing Secretary of the Communist Party, and is then followed by the KGB as he returns to the West, travelling on the famous train of the title across the Soviet states.

The Casanova Embrace is about a CIA maverick agent who must search into the past of a prominent Chilean exile to discover why he was murdered.

MARTHA ALBRAND

Pseudonyms: KATRIN HOLLAND, CHRISTINE LAMBERT
American. Born in Rostock, Germany, 8 September 1914. Died 24 June 1981.

Titles

No Surrender. London, Chatto and Windus, 1943; Boston, Little Brown, 1942.
The Hunted Woman. London, Hodder & Stoughton, 1953; New York, Random House, 1952.
Nightmare in Copenhagen. London, Hodder & Stoughton, 1954; New York, Random House, 1954.
The Story That Could Not be Told. London, Hodder & Stoughton, 1956; as *The Linden Affair*. New York, Random House, 1956.
Meet Me Tonight. London, Hodder & Stoughton, 1961; New York, Random House, 1960.
A Door Fell Shut. London, Hodder & Stoughton, 1966; New York, New American Library, 1966.

Biography

Born Heidi Huberta Freybe, Martha Albrand was educated privately under tutors in Germany and later at schools in Switzerland, Italy, France and England. She had a Lutheran upbringing, and this was linked with a strong sense of internationalism. Starting her career as a journalist in Europe, she had her first book published in German at the age of seventeen, using the pseudonym of Katrin Holland. Later she used another pen-name, Christine Lambert, but her best work has undoubtedly been done under the name of Martha Albrand.

Martha Albrand went to the United States in 1937 and in 1947 was naturalised as an American citizen. Her mystery and crime stories have met with much success. Most were serialised before publication in the now defunct *Saturday Evening Post*, and many of them have been translated into German, Danish, Italian, French, Swedish and even Arabic. Martha Albrand received Le Grand Prix de Littérature Policière in 1950.

Martha Albrand is quoted as saying in the *Twentieth Century Crime and Mystery Writers*: "My early novels published in Germany reflect the interest and concern of a young female writer with the romantic influences of that period. They were successful because the reading public in Germany wanted, besides a good story, a plot with which they could temporarily exit from reality.

But my first book published in America, *No Surrender*, changed my writing wittingly and unwittingly. It was a story of the Dutch underground fictionalized but basically as I'd known it firsthand. I considered it a novel, but the public again dictated its whim, for they saw the book as a suspense story. Because it was my initial exposure in America, I was labeled a suspense writer and more was expected to follow, particularly since the book was so successful. Therefore, the majority of my books published in America have been in the genre of suspense."

Critical Analysis
Only a few of Martha Albrand's novels are listed above; she wrote many more. Those listed are stories in which espionage plots are involved. As a mystery and suspense writer she covered a range of subjects in her novels; in her wartime novels the Nazis and members of the underground are her main protagonists. After the war her stories were concerned with the threat of Neo-Nazism and Communism.

A Door Fell Shut is the story of the return of Bronsky, a violinist of renown, to his home town, to give a concert in East Berlin. A CIA agent working there is involved in the defection to the West of Cassan, a Russian, and Bronsky is unexpectedly brought into this East–West intrigue and the escape of the Russian over the Berlin Wall.

THEODORE EDWARD LE BOUTHILLIER ALLBEURY
TED ALLBEURY
Pseudonyms: RICHARD BUTLER, PATRICK KELLY
British. Born in Stockport, 24 October 1917.

Titles
A Choice of Enemies. London, Davies, 1973; New York, St. Martin's Press, 1973.
Snowball. London, Davies, 1974; Philadelphia, Lippincott, 1974.
Palomino Blonde. London, Davies, 1975; as *Omega Minus.* New York, Viking Press, 1975.
The Special Collection. London, Davies, 1975.
The Only Good German. London, Davies, 1976.
Moscow Quadrille. London, Davies, 1976.
The Man with the President's Mind. London, Davies, 1977; New York, Simon & Schuster, 1978.
The Lantern Network. London, Davies, 1978.
Consequence of Fear. London, Hart-Davis MacGibbon, 1979.
The Alpha List. London, Hart-Davis MacGibbon, 1979; New York, Methuen, 1980.
The Twentieth Day of January. London, Granada, 1980.
The Secret Whispers. London, Granada, 1981.
The Other Side of Silence. London, Granada, 1981; New York, Scribner, 1981.
Shadow of Shadows. London, Granada, 1982; New York, Scribner, 1982.
All Our Tomorrows. London, Granada, 1982.
The Reaper. London, Granada, 1983.
Pay Any Price. London, Granada, 1983.
The Girl from Addis. London, Granada, 1984.
The Judas Factor. London, New English Library, 1984.
No Place to Hide. London, NEL, 1984.

Children of Tender Years. London, NEL, 1985.
The Choice. London, NEL, 1986.
The Seeds of Treason. London, NEL, 1986.
The Crossing. London, NEL, 1987.
A Wilderness of Mirrors. London, NEL, 1988.
Deep Purple. London, NEL, 1989.

Novels as Richard Butler
Where All the Girls are Sweeter. London, Davies, 1975.
Italian Assets. London, Davies, 1976.

Novels as Patrick Kelly
Codeword Cromwell. London, Granada, 1980.
The Lonely Margins. London, Granada, 1981.

Biography
Ted Allbeury was educated at Slade Primary School, Erdington, Birmingham. He worked as a foundry worker and junior draughtsman before the war. He served in the Army Intelligence Corps (1940–47) and achieved the rank of Lieutenant-Colonel. He worked in sales, advertising and public relations after the war. His first book *A Choice of Enemies* was published in 1973.

He has been writing full-time since the early 1970s.

Critical Analysis
Allbeury took to writing relatively late in life at the age of 54, but since then he has written over twenty books which have made him a best-selling author. His first novel was well received in Britain and America, and it was chosen by the *New York Times* as one of the ten best thrillers of the year.

A Choice of Enemies is partially autobiographical, and is about a man, Ted Bailey, who is blackmailed back into intelligence work 25 years after the Second World War. He comes up against a KGB agent whom he first met in Germany towards the end of the war. Bailey finds that although espionage may have become more technical the game is just as ruthless as it ever was.

Allbeury has achieved his success as a writer with the right mixture of realism and entertainment in his spy novels. As the author himself says: "Reviewers have praised my novels for having authenticity, and I expect that this flows from my having done this kind of work. But I hope that the authenticity has been provided in a fairly subtle way, as I dislike undue dwelling on hardware, organisation, and method."

Although it is not compulsory to have been in Intelligence to be able to write a spy novel, it is still necessary to be a good writer. Allbeury proves that he is a competent writer despite his intelligence experience, in fact sometimes it is a help: "Obviously, the advantage you possess if you have been in the business is that you do not have to work so hard at research! The kind of intelligence that is dealt with nowadays, however, is somewhat different from my time when we needed to know about weapons and plans. Today we are more concerned with the intelligence of intention — what they will do if we do this or that — but the methods and tools of the intelligence officer do not change."

Most of Allbeury's novels are concerned with the theme of betrayal. In *The Judas Factor* we are shown betrayal on both sides. The story re-introduces Tad Anders, a character who first appeared in Allbeury's second novel *Snowball*. Anders does odd jobs for the British Secret Intelligence Service (SIS), usually the dirty jobs. In this story he is sent to East Berlin to kidnap a KGB officer who, by special order, has started a series of assassinations of troublesome exiles. Anders is a maverick agent, useful for doing jobs that nobody else wants: "He had been successful as an SIS officer. Not spectacularly successful, but he had done what was asked of him and had been part of a team."

Anders misses the life, he is a misfit — socially, morally and by birth, the secret life had given him an identity and a security which he now lacks. By returning to this kind of work he thinks that he may recapture a sense of purpose, but events determine his behaviour.

Radio

"Pay any Price" was serialised on BBC radio during the summer of 1983.

ERIC AMBLER

Pseudonym: ELIOT REED (WITH CHARLES RODDA)
British. Born in London, 28 June 1909.

Titles

[Major characters: Charles Latimer; Arthur Abdel Simpson; Valeshoff and Tamara]

The Dark Frontier. London, Hodder & Stoughton, 1936.
Uncommon Danger [Valeshoff and Tamara]. London, Hodder & Stoughton, 1937; as *Background to Danger*. New York, Knopf, 1937.
Epitaph for a Spy. London, Hodder & Stoughton, 1938; New York, Knopf, 1952.
Cause for Alarm [Valeshoff and Tamara]. London, Hodder & Stoughton, 1938; New York, Knopf, 1939.
The Mask of Dimitrios [Latimer]. London, Hodder & Stoughton, 1939; as *A Coffin for Dimitrios*. New York, Knopf, 1939.
Journey into Fear. London, Hodder & Stoughton, 1940; New York, Knopf, 1940.
Judgement on Deltchev. London, Hodder& Stoughton, 1951; New York, Knopf, 1951.
The Schirmer Inheritance. London, Heinemann, 1953; New York, Knopf, 1953.
The Night-Comers. London, Heinemann, 1956; as *State of Siege*. New York, Knopf, 1956.
Passage of Arms. London, Heinemann, 1959; New York, Knopf, 1960.
The Light of Day [Simpson]. London, Heinemann, 1962; as *Topkapi*. New York, Bantam, 1964.
A Kind of Anger. London, Bodley Head, 1964; New York, Atheneum, 1964.
Dirty Story [Simpson]. London, Bodley Head, 1967; New York, Atheneum, 1967.
The Intercom Conspiracy [Latimer]. London, Weidenfeld and Nicolson, 1970; New York, Atheneum, 1969.
The Levanter. London, Weidenfeld and Nicolson, 1972; New York, Atheneum, 1972.
Doctor Frigo. London, Weidenfeld and Nicolson, 1974; New York, Atheneum, 1974.
Send No More Roses. London, Weidenfeld and Nicolson, 1977; as *The Siege of Villa Lipp*. New York, Random House, 1977.

The Care of Time. London,Weidenfeld and Nicolson, 1981; New York, Farrar Straus, 1981.

Novels as Eliot Reed (with Charles Rodda)
Tender to Moonlight. London, Hodder & Stoughton, 1952; as *Tender to Danger*. New York, Doubleday, 1951.

Other Publications
Editor, *To Catch a Spy: An Anthology of Favourite Spy Stories*. London, Bodley Head, 1964; New York, Atheneum, 1965.

Biography
Eric Ambler was educated at Colfe's Grammar School, Lewisham, and London University. He served in the Royal Artillery (1940–46), and was Assistant Director of Army Kinematography (1944–46).

He worked as an engineer's apprentice and an advertising copywriter before he published his first novel, *The Dark Frontier*. He received the Crime Writers Association Award in 1959, 1962, 1967 and 1972; the Mystery Writers of America Edgar Allan Poe Award in 1964; Grand Master Award in 1975; and Svenska Deckarakademins Grand Master in 1975.

Critical Analysis
His first novel, *The Dark Frontier*, was far from being one of his best books, but it marked a revolutionary, disillusioned approach to the spy story, particularly reflected in what one of the characters, Professor Bairstow, had to say: "It looked as if there would always be wars ... What else could you expect from a balance of power adjusted in terms of land, of arms, of man-power and of materials: in terms, in other words, of Money?... Wars were made by those who had the power to upset the balance, to tamper with international money and money's worth."

Ambler sounded the death-knell of the Hannays and the "Bulldog" Drummonds. He had begun to write in a period of intense depression for all thinking people who, in the 1930s, realised the hollowness of the politicians' pretence that the First World War was "the war to end all wars". Aggressive forces were on the march all over Europe and in the Balkans, democracy was being spelt out as a dirty word, and the private manufacture of arms was aiding the enemies of democracy rather more than the countries who actually produced the weapons. Ambler struck a note of neutralism in the spy story, sharply and astringently enlightening the reader that in espionage one side was really as bad as the other and that spies and spy-catchers were not only mainly unheroic, but very often of minor significance and unpleasant mien. In short, the agents and spies were not splendid patriots, but hired killers. Ambler was not a prophet in a didactic sense, but his stories of espionage revealed the truth and obliterated the romance. *The Uncommon Danger* had much the same message as *The Dark Frontier*.

With *Epitaph for a Spy* Ambler came into his own as a highly skilled, thoughtful, realistic and meticulous writer of spy stories. He had done his homework on the spy story and was determined to modernise and improve the genre. Many years later, in his introduction to *To Catch a Spy*, he revealed that his research into the realms of spy fiction went back to Erskine Childers.

More recently, when commenting on a review in the *Times Literary Supplement* which said that all of Ambler's earlier books were influenced by the Ashenden ethos, he replied that they were indeed: "The breakthrough was entirely Mr Maugham's ... there is, after all, a lot of Simenon and a satisfactory quantity of W R Burnett, but only one *Ashenden*."

Perhaps this is one reason why Ambler is a favourite writer of professional Intelligence agents all over the world. While le Carré is the preferred reading of members of the British SIS and Len Deighton has his devotees in America, Ambler undoubtedly wins adherents in the "spook" community all over the world. He has the gift of making a commonplace incident seem dramatic and horrifying. What is even more important, Ambler is the most admirable exponent of the probable and the possible as against the improbable and the miraculous coincidence. It is one of the paradoxes of spy fiction that the "in' writers" — i.e. those who have had inside knowledge of "the game " — tend to write about the improbable rather more than those authors who have never in any way been engaged in Intelligence work. Ambler belongs to the latter category and it is surprisingly but nevertheless recognisably true that he has been far and away the most accurate of all modern spy fiction writers right down to the smallest detail. In all Ambler's books the chain of circumstances is rational and probable, his leading characters are ordinary, cautious people who find themselves caught up in disastrous situations. The detail is faultless, yet Ambler, as far as one knows, was never employed by the Secret Service or any similar organisation.

In *Epitaph for a Spy* Ambler introduced a political element into his work. Even here he was being factual — and singularly prophetic, hinting at the possible emergence of defectors like Philby, someone such as Schimmler who is converted from being a moderate Social Democrat to a Communist. This is echoed again in *Cause for Alarm* and *The Mask of Dimitrios*, in the latter of which there are objective and not unpleasant portraits of a Greek Communist and a Soviet agent. This would have been unheard of in the Buchan–"Sapper"–Le Queux era: had any author then described a Soviet agent as one who could spare the time to do a good turn to someone who had got into trouble through no fault of his own, he would undoubtedly have been dubbed as a fellow-traveller. But such was Ambler's skill and objectivity, his freedom from any hint of propaganda or prejudice and his talent for telling a lively story, that he was never challenged on this account, but only welcomed as a long-needed antidote to the old school of spy thriller writers.

Ambler also chose a different type of capital city for the setting for his books. Whereas hitherto such stories tended to be set in Paris, Berlin, Vienna and Rome, or the smarter hotels of the Riviera, Ambler chose the seedier, but more topical and infinitely more fascinating cities of Istanbul, Belgrade, Sofia. *The Mask of Dimitrios*, which in many respects is Ambler's masterpiece, opens with the discovery in a mortuary of the dead body of Dimitrios. With consummate craftsmanship, the author uses the lecturer and detective-writer, Latimer, to trace the life story of the mysterious Dimitrios. The minor characters are superbly drawn and full of interest in themselves.

After the war when the USSR and the Western Allies turned sour on one another and the Cold War began, Ambler's "neutral" approach to spy fiction became a little dated. Nevertheless, the quality of Ambler's work still compares well with anything that has been written since.

Films

Journey into Fear. RKO, US, 1942. (Remake 1976.)
Background to Danger. Warner, US, 1943.

The Mask of Dimitrios. Warner, US, 1944.
Topkapi. United Artists, US, 1964.

KINGSLEY WILLIAM AMIS
Pseudonym: ROBERT MARKHAM
British. Born in London, 16 April 1922.

Titles
The James Bond Dossier. London, Cape, 1965.

Novels as Robert Markham
Colonel Sun. New York, Harper, 1968.

Biography
Kingsley Amis was educated at the City of London School and St. John's College, Oxford. From 1949 to 1961 he was Lecturer in English at University College, Swansea, and from 1958 to 1959 served as Visiting Fellow in Creative Writing at Princeton University. It was during this period that his novel *Lucky Jim* (1954) became a bestseller and a popular film. Then from 1961 to 1963 Amis was Fellow at Peterhouse, Cambridge and in 1967–68 returned to the States as Visiting Professor of English at Vanderbilt University.

Critical Analysis
While Amis has been at his best as a gentle satirist of the social scene with a nice sense of comedy in his character-drawing, he has shown more than a passing interest in the spy story, notably in his work *Colonel Sun*, written under the pseudonym of Robert Markham. Three years earlier, he produced *The James Bond Dossier*, an amusing analysis of the adventures, the foibles and quirks, the ancestry and credentials of Ian Fleming's larger-than-life hero.

EVELYN ANTHONY
(pseudonym for Evelyn Bridget Ward-Thomas)
British. Born in London, 3 July 1928.

Titles
[Major character: Davina Graham]
The Legend. London, Hutchinson, 1969; New York, Coward McCann, 1969.
The Assassin. London, Hutchinson, 1970; New York, Coward McCann, 1970.
The Tamarind Seed. London, Hutchinson, 1971; New York, Coward McCann, 1971.
The Poellenberg Inheritance. London, Hutchinson, 1972; New York, Coward McCann, 1972.
The Occupying Power. London, Hutchinson, 1973; as *Stranger at the Gates*. New York,

Coward McCann, 1973.

The Grave of Truth. London, Hutchinson, 1979; as *The Janus Imperative*. New York, Coward McCann, 1980.

The Defector [Graham]. London, Hutchinson, 1980; New York, Coward McCann, 1981.

The Avenue of the Dead [Graham]. London, Hutchinson, 1981; New York, Coward McCann, 1982.

Albatross [Graham]. London, Hutchinson, 1982; New York, Putnam, 1983.

The Company of Saints [Graham]. London, Hutchinson, 1983; New York, Putnam, 1984.

Voices on the Wind. London, Hutchinson, 1985.

Biography

Evelyn Anthony was educated privately by a governess, and she attended the Convent of the Sacred Heart, Roehampton, until 1944. She was evacuated to Stansted Hall, Rugby during the war. She gave up going to Oxford to work in the Red Cross at the end of the war.

Her first short story was published in *Everybody's Weekly* in 1949 and her first historical novel, *Imperial Highness*, appeared in 1953: it was a fictional account of the early life of Catherine the Great.

Critical Analysis

Evelyn Anthony has written over twenty books, some of which can be described as spy stories, her other novels are better classed as thrillers. One of the former, *The Tamarind Seed*, was filmed in 1973. *The Occupying Power* won the *Yorkshire Post* Fiction Prize in 1973.

Her novels are set in France, Germany, Russia, Britain, America and Mexico. She says that her favourite theme has been the "mole" and the conflict of loyalty and ideals and patriotic duty. She has never worked in Intelligence, although she "was once asked to do so and refused. I have had friends who worked against the Germans in the war and learnt a lot by listening." Anthony insists on authenticity for the locations of her stories: "The Nazis and the KGB were material for my early plots, but now the settings are more international — oil, terrorism, drugs.... The central character is usually a woman, but with very strong male support."

She says that her early literary influences include Hemingway, and Somerset Maugham. Her favourite spy story writer is John le Carré: "I believe that spy thrillers should stick to the possible and eschew too much fantasy, also brutal and explicit sex. I don't think that is relevant."

Anthony comments: "I'd like more space given by book reviewers to popular entertainment in fiction.... When I started reviews were plentiful and greatly helped me to get established. What in God's name happens to new authors today?"

Film

The Tamarind Seed. Jewel, GB, 1974.

TOM ARDIES
American. Born in Seattle, Washington, 5 August 1931.

Titles
[Major character: Charlie Sparrow]
Their Man in the White House [Sparrow]. New York, Doubleday, 1971; London, Macmillan, 1971.
This Suitcase Is Going To Explode [Sparrow]. New York, Doubleday, 1972; London, Macmillan, 1972.
Pandemic [Sparrow]. New York, Doubleday, 1973; London, Angus & Robertson, 1974.
Kosygin Is Coming. New York, Doubleday, 1974; as *Russian Roulette*. London, Panther, 1975.
Palm Springs. New York, Doubleday, 1978.
In a Lady's Service. New York, Doubleday, 1976; London, Panther, 1978.

Biography
Tom Ardies was educated at Daniel McIntyre Colegiate Institute, Winnipeg, Manitoba. He served in the US Air Force, and worked as a reporter, columnist and editorial writer for the *Vancouver Sun*, Vancouver, British Columbia, 1950–64. He worked as a telegraph editor on the *Honolulu Star Bulletin*, Honolulu, Hawaii, from 1964 to 1965, and was a special assistant to the governor of Guam, 1965-67. Since then he has worked as a full-time writer.

Critical Analysis
Ardies's early novels, *Their Man in the White House*, *This Suitcase Is Going to Explode* and *Pandemic* are superficial tales with implausible plots. The hero of these stories, Charlie Sparrow, lives up to his name by being handsome, cocky, a one with the ladies, and always overcoming his enemies, whether they are his superiors, the CIA or the fiendish enemy he is ordered to battle against. The plots are usually dramatic involving saving the world from one disaster or another.

    Kosygin is Coming and *In a Lady's Service*, the first a spy story, the second a spoof, are his best novels. In the first story Kosygin is due to visit Vancouver, but there is a Latvian fanatic on the loose, and he must be kidnapped before he does any damage. In his spoof Ardies parodies his own plots, with a colourful collection of characters such as Dip Threat.

Film
Russian Roulette. ITC, US, 1975. (based upon *Kosygin is Coming*).

AMOS ARICHA
Israeli.

Titles
Hour of the Clown. New York, Signet, 1981.
Spymaster. London, WH Allen, 1987; as *The Flying Camel*. New York, EP Dutton, 1987.

Novels written with Eli Landau
The Phoenix. New York, Signet, 1979; London, Severn, 1980.

Biography

Amos Aricha is the author of three previous novels and has received two Israeli literary awards. He has also had several one-man shows of his paintings in Israel and the United States. For thirteen years he was chief superintendent of the Israeli Police Force.

Critical Analysis

Aricha's first novel, *The Phoenix*, written with Eli Landau, is about a group of Middle-Eastern power figures, who make a contract with a professional assassin, code-named "the Phoenix", to make a $3 million hit on Moshe Dayan. The assassination is calculated to disrupt and destroy the Egyptian–Israeli Camp David Accords.

His latest novel, *Spymaster*, is the story of Daniel Kottler, who appears to be just another moderately successful Jewish New Yorker with a steady, unexciting job. But in reality his work as a translator for a law firm doing business in the Arab world is just the cover for a far more precarious and deadly trade, that of a CIA assassin.

When Kottler's mother dies, leaving him an assortment of relics from her marriage, he begins to investigate the shadowy career of his father, an Israeli war hero who apparently died during a clandestine operation in 1948 before Daniel was born. But before he can uncover the truth the CIA order him to do one more job — this time to kill a prominent Arab businessman they believe was responsible for planning the massacre of American marines in Beirut. As Kottler gets closer to the target, his earlier investigations of his father become linked with his mission, revealing secrets which have startling consequences for Israel's future.

PHILIP ATLEE

(Pseudonym of James Atlee Phillips)
American. Born in 1915.

Titles

[Major character: Joe Gall]
The Green Wound. New York, Fawcett, 1963; London, Muller, 1964.
The Silken Baroness. New York, Fawcett, 1964; as *The Silken Baroness Contract*. London, Hodder & Stoughton, 1967.
The Death Bird Contract. New York, Fawcett, 1966; London, Hodder & Stoughton, 1968.
The Irish Beauty Contract. New York, Fawcett, 1966; London, Hodder & Stoughton, 1968.
The Paper Pistol Contract. New York, Fawcett, 1966; London, Hodder & Stoughton, 1968.
The Star Ruby Contract. New York, Fawcett, 1967; London, Hodder & Stoughton, 1969.
The Skeleton Coast Contract. New York, Fawcett, 1968.

The Rockabye Contract. New York, Fawcett, 1968.
The Ill Wind Contract. New York, Fawcett, 1969.
The Trembling Earth Contract. New York, Fawcett, 1969; London, Hodder & Stoughton, 1970.
The Fer-de-Lance Contract. New York, Fawcett, 1970.
The Canadian Bomber Contract. New York, Fawcett, 1971.
The White Wolverine Contract. New York, Fawcett, 1971.
The Judah Lion Contract. New York, Fawcett, 1972.
The Kiwi Contract. New York, Fawcett, 1972.
The Shankhill Road Contract. New York, Fawcett, 1973.
The Spice Route Contract. New York, Fawcett, 1974.
The Kowloon Contract. New York, Fawcett, 1974.
The Underground Cities Contract. New York, Fawcett, 1974.
The Black Venus Contract. New York, Fawcett, 1975.
The Makassar Strait Contract. New York, Fawcett, 1976.
The Last Domino Contract. New York, Fawcett, 1976.

Biography

Atlee's brother was David Atlee Phillips, who worked for the CIA for over twenty years and it is possible that his brother may have given him advice.

Critical Analysis

The hero of this series is Joe Gall, who worked as a counter-espionage operative for the "agency", a clandestine intelligence unit sponsored by the State Department. He is forced to become a freelance agent because of his involvement in the Bay of Pigs operation. The early adventures are dominated by gimmicks and larger-than-life villains. In the later stories Gall has matured and the plots are less melo-dramatic.

In *The Kiwi Contract* Gall describes his job: "My work has nothing to do with pilfering papers from wastebaskets or cracking codes. Sneakier and more cerebral types go through those motions. I am usually the last shot in the locker. After sweet reason and diplomatic finesse have failed, they send for the sonsofbitches, and I rank high in that category. So I suppose you could say that I am an environment changer and a time gainer for my country."

Again Gall expresses the same feelings as his contemporary Durell — that he feels superior to the paper-shufflers and analysts — his work is far more important. As a last resort he has the necessary power to remedy an explosive situation.

This series compares well with the Jonas Wilde "Eliminator" stories of Christopher Nicole, and are a step above Joseph Rosenberger's "The Death Merchant" novels, according to Myron J Smith in *Cloak and Dagger Fiction* (1982).

MICHAEL ANGELO AVALLONE, JR.

Pseudonyms: MICHAEL AIDEN, JAMES BLAINE, NICK CARTER, TROY CONWAY, PRISCILLA DALTON, MARK DANE, JEAN-ANNE DE PRE, FRED FRAZER,DORA HIGHLAND, STUART JASON, STEVE MICHAELS, NEMO MORGAN, DOROTHEA NILE, EDWINA NOONE, VANCE STANTON, SIDNEY STUART, MAX WALKER, LEE DAVIS WILLOUGHBY.
American. Born in Manhattan, New York, 27 October 1924.

Titles

[Major character: Ed Noon]
The Tall Dolores. New York, Holt Rinehart, 1953; London, Barker, 1956.
The Spitting Image. New York, Holt Rinehart, 1953; London, Barker, 1957.
Dead Game. New York, Holt Rinehart, 1954; London, WH Allen, 1959.
Violence in Velvet. New York, New American Library, 1956; London, WH Allen, 1958.
The Case of the Bouncing Betty. New York, Ace, 1957; London, WH Allen, 1959.
The Case of the Violent Virgin. New York, Ace, 1957; London, WH Allen, 1960.
The Crazy Mixed-Up Corpse. New York, Fawcett, 1957; London, Fawcett, 1959.
The Voodoo Murders. New York, Fawcett, 1957; London, Fawcett, 1959.
Meanwhile Back at the Morgue. New York, Fawcett, 1960; London, Muller, 1961.
The Alarming Clock. London, WH Allen, 1961; New York, Curtis, 1973.
The Bedroom Bolero. New York, Belmont, 1963; as *The Bolero Murders*. London, Hale, 1972.
The Living Bomb. London, WH Allen, 1963; New York, Curtis, 1972.
There Is Something about a Dame. New York, Belmont, 1963.
Lust Is No Lady. New York, Belmont, 1964; as *The Brutal Knock*. London, WH Allen, 1965.
The Fat Death. London, WH Allen, 1966; New York, Curtis, 1972.
(22 further titles featuring Ed Noon)

Novels as Nick Carter
The China Doll. New York, Award, 1964; London, Digit, 1965.
Run Spy Run. New York, Award, 1964; London, Tandem, 1969.
Saigon. New York, Award, 1964; London, Digit, 1965.

Biography

The son of a stonemason, Michael Avallone was brought up in the Bronx, amongst seventeen brothers and sisters. He was educated at the Theodore Roosevelt High School in the Bronx. After his graduation he enlisted in the US Army, and served as a sergeant in Europe during the Second World War. From 1943 to 1946 he was in Mechanized Cavalry, which was a reconnaissance outfit.

After the war Avallone worked in a stationery store until he started selling his Ed Noon novels in the early 1950s. He worked in a variety of jobs, including editor of pulp magazines, before writing full-time from the early 1960s.

Critical Analysis

Avallone has earned the title in professional writing circles as "The Fastest Typewriter In The East". He has written over 200 books — ranging from private eye mysteries, to Westerns, to all sorts of fiction including Gothic horror, war, science fiction, espionage, books based on movies and television shows, as well as hundreds of short stories, articles, essays and poetry.

Anthony Boucher, one of the major American mystery reviewers said about Avallone in 1958: "For all his faults, he does have narrative impetus; he starts from a stimulatingly fantastic premise, he keeps things moving with lively vigor, and the enterprise, if absurd, is still entertaining. It'd be fine if he'd learn to write — but he needs that knowledge precisely as much as Elvis needs vocal lessons".

It is his series about private eye Ed Noon that has made Avallone internationally famous. He has written more than 36 books featuring this character. The author himself admits that: "Ed Noon is pure Avallone alter ego. He is 100% me. Talks like me, acts like me, loves like me. As with all fantasy wish fulfillments, I just made him a helluva lot handsomer, smarter and purer."

The Noon series can be divided into three periods. First, there is the original hard-boiled period, starting in 1953 when Ed Noon is introduced into the world of the private-eyes. This period extends to about 1967, and the plots are mostly straightforward detective stories.

In the second period from about 1967 until 1972 the Noon novels incline more towards the espionage tale influenced by the tremendous international popularity of James Bond. Noon becomes the personal spy of the President, and is sent on missions of international importance to save the President and the country.

In the current period, which started from 1972, Avallone has not changed his writing style but the content has moved further away from strict categorization. It is not so easy to label the Noon novels as pure detective or spy stories. The recent books are not so much occupied with crime and violence, but rather the consequences of violence and its effect on people.

Avallone admits that in the spy novel it is possible to re-create a picture of the intelligence world, but the author freely admits that he goes "the Ian Fleming route and not the 'Bloody Owl' le Carré one ... spy novels are larks and entertainments ... FIRST ... everything else comes second ... Greene and Ambler said it all *seriously* ... years ago ... today's bluebirds are just repeating them."

DESMOND BAGLEY

British. Born in Kendal, Westmorland, 29 October, 1923. Died 12 April, 1983.

Titles

[Major character: Slade]
The Golden Keel. London, Collins, 1963; New York, Doubleday, 1964.
High Citadel. London, Collins, 1965; New York, Doubleday, 1965.
Wyatt's Hurricane. London, Collins, 1966; New York, Doubleday, 1966.
Landslide. London, Collins, 1967; New York, Doubleday, 1967.
The Vivero Letter. London, Collins, 1968; New York, Doubleday, 1968.
The Spoilers. London, Collins, 1969; New York, Doubleday, 1970.
Running Blind [Slade]. London, Collins, 1970; New York, Doubleday, 1971.
The Freedom Trap [Slade]. London, Collins, 1971; New York, Doubleday, 1972.
The Tightrope Men. London, Collins, 1973; New York, Doubleday, 1973.
The Snow Tiger. London, Collins, 1975; New York, Doubleday, 1975.
The Enemy. London, Collins, 1977; New York, Doubleday, 1978.

Flyaway. London, Collins, 1978; New York, Doubleday, 1979.
Bahama Crisis. London, Collins, 1980; New York, Summit, 1983.
Windfall. London, Collins, 1982; New York, Summit, 1982.
The Legacy. London, Collins, 1982.
Night of Error. London, Collins, 1984.

Biography

Desmond Bagley left school at the age of fourteen. During the Second World War he worked in the aircraft industry. After the war he went to Africa and worked in Uganda in 1947, Kenya in 1948, and Rhodesia in 1949. From 1951 to 1952 he was employed by the South African Broadcasting Corporation at Durban; in 1953 he was the editor of the house magazine for Masonite (Africa) Ltd. He was the film critic of the *Rand Daily Mail*, in Johannesburg from 1958 to 1962, and a writer for Filmlets Ltd., in Johannesburg from 1960 to 1961.

Critical Analysis

Bagley is more of a writer of fast-paced action adventure novels than spy thrillers. The settings are international and range from the Mexican jungle in *The Vivero Letter* to the peaks of the Andes in *High Citadel*.

His first novel, *The Golden Keel*, is an exciting adventure story about the fate of Mussolini's treasure which disappeared towards the end of World War II. A group of men try to get this treasure out of Italy, with everyone from the Italian government to a group of smugglers attempting to steal the gold for themselves. It is a good story and culminates in an exciting sea chase. Bagley's knowledge about military weapons and sailing is shown in this story.

WILLIAM SANBORN BALLINGER
Pseudonyms: FREDERICK FREYER, B X SANBORN
American. Born in Oskaloosa, Iowa, 13 March 1912. Died 23 March 1980.

Titles

[Major character: Joaquin Hawks]
The Chinese Mask. New York, New American Library, 1965.
The Spy in Bangkok. New York, NAL, 1965.
The Spy in the Jungle. New York, NAL, 1965.
The Spy at Ankor Wat. New York, NAL, 1966.
The Spy in the Java Sea. New York, NAL, 1966.

Biography

Bill S Ballinger was educated at the University of Wisconsin, Madison; he graduated with a BSc in 1934. After he left university he worked in advertising, and was a radio and television writer from 1934 to 1977. He was the Executive Vice-President of the Mystery Writers of America in 1957 and an Associate Professor of Writing at California State University, Northridge from 1977 to 1979. He received a Mystery Writers of America Edgar Allen Poe Award for a television play in 1960.

Critical Analysis

Ballinger started writing in the late 1940s, and his first novel, *The Body in the Bed* (1948), was in the tradition of the hard-boiled detective story. This, and his next story, *The Body Beautiful* (1949), featured the private eye Barr Breed. In the early 1950s Ballinger turned away from the conventional detective story and chose to write about many different kinds of crime.

The author is quoted as commenting in 1980 in *Twentieth Century Crime and Mystery Writers* (1985): "I consider myself, primarily, a story-teller. To me the story is the thing. Although I usually try to make a point, as all good stories should, I stay away from moralizing and propaganda. Usually, I also try to include some material — 'information' — which may be of extra interest to my reader.

I have always enjoyed a good plot, the thrill of plotting. Nothing is more pleasant than to receive a letter saying — 'You out-guessed me'. Although I have been writing for 50 years — first as a 'stringer' for newspapers — I intend to keep on with my books."

The hero of Ballinger's spy novels is Joaquin Hawks, who served briefly as an undercover operative for the CIA in Southeast Asia. Hawks is proficient in several languages and a master of disguise. His superior is Horace Berke — Director of Operations in Los Angeles. In the field Hawks's code name is "Swinger".

In *The Chinese Mask* Hawks poses as a Chinese circus performer to rescue three Western scientists imprisoned in Peking. He is disguised as an Arab seaman and a French salesman in *The Spy in the Jungle*, in which he is sent to Laos to prevent a Chi–Com plot to undermine American nuclear missile defence capabilities.

The Joaquin Hawks series was probably the first to survey the explosive political situation in Southeast Asia during the mid-1960s. However, the American public quickly wearied of Vietnam and the Hawks series died a natural death. Ballinger was one of the many authors who created a character in the image of James Bond — capitalizing on the general popularity of the spy hero in the 1960s.

WILLIAM BEECHCROFT

(Pseudonym of William Finn III Hallstead)
American. Born in Scranton, Pennsylvania, 20 April 1924.

Titles

Position of Ultimate Trust. New York, Dodd Mead, 1981.
Image of Evil. New York, Dodd Mead, 1985.
Chain of Vengeance. New York, Dodd Mead, 1986.
The Rebuilt Man. New York, Dodd Mead, 1987.
Secret Kills. New York, Dodd Mead, 1988.

Biography

William Beechcroft was educated in Pottstown, Pennsylvania. He worked as a flight instructor at Scranton Municipal Airport, and has also worked as a draughtsman, a highway designer, and as a director of development and information services at the Maryland Center for Public Broadcasting from 1968 to 1984.

Critical Analysis

Position of Ultimate Trust illustrates one example of American paranoia — that of a conspiracy within the United States to assassinate the President. In this story a prominent senator and an admiral, head of C Section, a dirty tricks department, independent of the CIA and the FBI, plan to assassinate the President. TARDIS, a SALT III plan, is about to be signed, and those hawks who oppose it are driven to action.

The plan to kill the President is compromised because of seven people who witness preparations for this event. To maintain secrecy these seven people have to be killed. However, one of them manages to escape and warn the police of the assassination which is then diverted. Most of the action in this story takes place in Key West, the Everglades and Miami.

FRANCIS BEEDING

(Pseudonym for John Leslie Palmer and Hilary Aidan St. George Saunders. They also wrote as David Pilgrim.) British. **JOHN LESLIE PALMER**: Born in 1885. Died in London, 5 August 1944. **HILARY AIDAN ST. GEORGE SAUNDERS**: Born 14 January 1898. Died 16 December 1951.

Titles

[Major character: Colonel Alastair Granby]

The Six Proud Walkers [Granby]. London, Hodder & Stoughton, 1928; Boston, Little Brown, 1928.

Pretty Sinister [Granby]. London, Hodder & Stoughton, 1929; Boston, Little Brown, 1929.

The Five Flamboys [Granby]. London, Hodder & Stoughton, 1929; Boston, Little Brown, 1929.

The League of Discontent [Granby]. London, Hodder & Stoughton, 1930; Boston, Little Brown, 1930.

The Four Armourers [Granby]. London, Hodder & Stoughton, 1930; Boston, Little Brown, 1930.

The Three Fishers. London, Hodder & Stoughton,1931; Boston, Little Brown, 1931.

Take it Crooked [Granby]. London, Hodder & Stoughton, 1932; Boston, Little Brown, 1932.

The Two Undertakers [Granby]. London, Hodder & Stoughton, 1933; Boston, Little Brown, 1933.

The One Sane Man [Granby]. London, Hodder & Stoughton, 1934; Boston, Little Brown, 1934.

The Eight Crooked Trenches [Granby]. London, Hodder & Stoughton, 1936; as *Coffin for One*. New York, Avon, 1943.

The Nine Waxed Faces [Granby]. London, Hodder & Stoughton, 1936; New York, Harper, 1936.

Hell Let Loose [Granby]. London, Hodder & Stoughton, 1937; New York, Harper, 1937.

The Black Arrows [Granby]. London, Hodder & Stoughton, 1938; New York, Harper, 1938.

The Ten Holy Terrors [Granby]. London, Hodder & Stoughton, 1939; New York, Harper, 1939.

Not A Bad Show [Granby]. London, Hodder & Stoughton, 1940; as *The Secret Weapon*. New York, Harper, 1940.

Eleven Were Brave [Granby]. London, Hodder & Stoughton, 1941; New York, Harper, 1941.

The Twelve Disguises [Granby]. London, Hodder & Stoughton, 1942; New York, Harper, 1942.

There Are Thirteen [Granby]. London, Hodder & Stoughton, 1946; New York, Harper, 1946.

Biography

John Leslie Palmer was educated at Balliol College, Oxford. From 1910 to 1915 he was the Drama Critic and Assistant Editor for the *Saturday Review of Literature*, London; and from 1916 to 1919 he was the Drama Critic for the *Evening Standard*. Palmer was a Member of the British Delegation to the Paris Peace Conference in 1919, and a Staff Member of the Permanent Secretariat of the League of Nations, 1920–39.

Hilary Aidan St. George Saunders was educated at Balliol College, Oxford. He served in the Welsh Guards (1916–19), and worked for the Air Ministry during the Second World War. Saunders was a Staff Member of the Permanent Secretariat of the League of Nations from 1920 to 1937. He worked as Private Secretary to Fridtjof Nansen (1921–23), and was Librarian at the House of Commons from 1946 to 1950.

Critical Analysis

Despite the fact that both Palmer and Saunders were able writers in their own right, they created a partnership which resulted in the works of "Francis Beeding" and wrote about forty novels under that name. Many of the Francis Beeding books were historical novels or of the detective genre, but quite a few were concerned with the Secret Service.

One of the very few spy stories set against the background of the old League of Nations at Geneva came in Beeding's *The Five Flamboys*, doubtless owing much to Saunders's knowledge of both Switzerland and the League HQ. As in so many of the Beeding books, the central figure is the urbane and polite Colonel Granby, who set out to track down the Flamboys.

Many of the Granby Secret Service stories were set in France, including *The League of Discontent*, *The Three Fishers*, *The Four Armourers* and *Take it Crooked*. *The One Sane Man* was one of the best of the Beeding Secret Service stories, which became increasingly topical during the late 1930s. In *The Black Arrows* the authors, taking note of the rising tide of Fascism in Europe, introduced a new hero, John Couper, and a new villain, Jiacomo Berutti. The story is set in Venice and tells of an attempt to sink a major unit of the British Mediterranean Fleet by pirate submarine controlled by the Society of the Black Arrows, an extreme Fascist organisation led by men who are disappointed because Mussolini is not doing enough to advance their cause.

With the advent of the Second World War the Beeding stories became even more topical. *The Secret Weapon* concerns a Secret Service quest for the formula of a top-secret weapon which Hitler is developing. The agent hero goes to Germany, actually meets Hitler and Goering, is involved in the Polish campaign and finally escapes back to England.

Noel Behn

American. Born in Chicago, Illinois, 6 January 1928.

Titles

The Kremlin Letter. New York, Simon & Schuster, 1966; London, WH Allen, 1966.
The Shadowboxer. New York, Simon & Schuster, 1969; London, Hart-Davis, 1970.

Biography

Noel Behn was educated at the University of Wyoming, Laramie, between 1946 and 1947 and Stanford University, California, where he obtained a BA in 1950. He served in the US Army Counter Intelligence from 1952 to 1954. He was a producer at East Chop Playhouse, Martha's Vineyard, Massachusetts in the summer of 1954, and co-manager with the Flint Musical Tent Theatre in Michigan in the summer of 1955. He was the producer and operator of Cherry Lane Theatre, New York, 1956-61, and producer at Edgewater Beach Playhouse in Chicago during the summers of 1957–60.

Critical Analysis

Behn's first espionage story *The Kremlin Letter* has a highly improbable plot involving a group of freelance intelligence operatives sent into Russia under cover to retrieve a letter written to a Russian official by Western politicians.

Nevertheless it is an exciting story, sometimes the violence is rather graphic and the agents show no compunction in their use of blackmail, prostitution and drugs to obtain the information they want. Perhaps the plot is not as fantastic as it seems; since the book was written the public has been subjected to a series of revelations about the methods of the CIA which are as equally brutal as the methods shown in this novel.

The Shadowboxer is set in Germany in 1944. Eric Spangler, the main character, is an agent who has the ability to get into and out of concentration camps at will. He is manipulated by his American superiors to help in the establishment of a provisional German government. In this novel Behn again makes the point that neither side is any better than the other and both will use any method to get what they want.

Film

The Kremlin Letter. TCF, US, 1970.

Kenneth Carter Benton

Pseudonym: **James Kirton**
British. Born in Sutton Coldfield, Warwickshire, 4 March 1909.

Titles

[Major character: Peter Craig]
Sole Agent. London, Collins, 1970; New York, Walker, 1974.
Spy in Chancery. London, Collins, 1972; New York, Walker, 1973.

Craig and the Jaguar. London, Macmillan, 1973; New York, Walker, 1974.
Craig and the Tunisian Jungle. London, Macmillan, 1974; New York, Walker, 1975.
Craig and the Midas Touch. London, Macmillan, 1975; New York, Walker, 1976.
A Single Monstrous Act. London, Macmillan, 1976.

Novels as James Kirton
Greek Fire. London, Hale, 1985.

Biography

Kenneth Benton was educated at Wolverhampton Grammar School and London University, where he obtained a BA Hons in Foreign Languages. He taught for some years in preparatory schools and later lectured in English Language in Florence and Vienna. He joined the Foreign Office in 1937.

He served in Vienna as Assistant Passport Control Officer from 1937 to 1938. After Hitler's invasion he was transferred to Riga, Latvia as Vice Consul. In 1940 the Russians annexed Latvia and in 1941 he was posted to Spain. Further diplomatic posts followed, and he ended his career in Rio de Janeiro as Counsellor of Embassy (1966–68).

Critical Analysis

Benton says that he has always been attracted to spy fiction and he quite likes "being regarded as mainly a spy novelist." He goes on to say, "I have been able to observe the activities of both the British security services to some extent, and this has certainly helped me as a novelist."

His first novel, *Twenty-Fourth Level*, was published in 1969 and introduced his hero Peter Craig. The author describes it as a "non-spy novel, centring on a gold mine in Brazil, in which my hero, Peter Craig, discovered a devious case of fraud and a very attractive Brazilian girl."

Sole Agent, his second novel, and more in line with spy fiction, is set in Lisbon and the surrounding Portuguese countryside. Peter Craig becomes involved when he is asked to find the daughter of the British Ambassador's Defence Attaché. When he starts to make enquiries he discovers that the girl is deeply involved in a plot against the Portuguese government. As the situation is so sensitive Craig is desperate to find her before the secret police do. Once he finds the girl their problems are not over as they are chased by the secret police as well as the KGB.

Craig has no love for spies, as he explains to the girl when she feels sorry for her past lover, who turns out to be a KGB agent: "He's a murderer and a spy. And spies may have their ideals and they may be fine as fathers of families or — as you tell me — in bed, but they're still spies. Termites. If you can't exterminate them you stand the legs of your chair in saucers of water. That's security."

Peter Craig reflects the background of his creator, and the locations of the novels follow the author's diplomatic postings. Craig is a policeman — hence his antipathy towards the spy — he is a Diplomatic Corps Overseas Police Advisor and his behaviour reflects his training as a policeman. He is a professional who understands the necessary manipulations of diplomacy and espionage, but doesn't like it.

In *A Single Monstrous Act*, the story concerns a coven of violent, left-wing anarchists who plan a series of outrages to pave the way for a revolutionary take-over in Britain. Leading them is Professor Thaxton, whose personality seduces impressionable students and whose sexual prowess ensures his placing of informers inside the ranks of government. A review in the *Oxford Times* said: "This political thriller borrows some of the techniques practised so successfully by Frederick Forsyth in *The Day of the Jackal*, with fact and fiction so imperceptibly joined that it takes the reader with a knowledge of home and international affairs rivalling the author's to determine where reality ends and story begins."

GEORGE BERNAU

American. Born in Minneapolis, Minnesota, 14 February 1945.

Titles

Promises to Keep. New York, Warner Books, 1988; London, Macmillan, 1988.

Biography

George Bernau was educated at the University of Southern California where he obtained a BSc in 1966, and at the same university he obtained a Law degree in 1973. From 1973 to 1981 he practised law, and from 1966 to 1970 he worked at the Universal Movie Studios, writing comedy for films.

Critical Analysis

Promises to Keep was released, with a number of other fiction and non-fiction books about President Kennedy and his family, one month before the 25th anniversary of his assassination. In this rather morbid publicity drive, Bernau's book is one of the more recent novels on this event in American history.

In this story Bernau makes out that Kennedy did not die after the shooting in Dallas on 22 November 1963, but recovered. The author says: "This isn't really a conspiracy book. What interests me is how different American politics would have been if Kennedy had lived. We might have been spared the Nixon era. We wouldn't have had Carter, who was a reaction to Watergate. Neither, I think, would America have needed the stabilising effect of Reagan. I'm not sure even now that we've caught up with the effects of assassination on us. It knocked us off our pins for a good 20 years."

In this story Kennedy steps down in 1964 in favour of LB Johnson and his brother Robert Kennedy, and the latter dies in a shot-down helicopter during a tour of Vietnam. Events in the Vietnam war drive Johnson out of office and John F Kennedy returns for a second term. His would-be assassins made him a target out of revenge for the defeat at the Bay of Pigs.

Television

ABC mini-series to be broadcast in the US in the autumn of 1989.

JACK MILES BICKHAM
Pseudonyms: JEFF CLINTON, JOHN MILES, GEORGE SHAW
American. Born in Columbus, Ohio, 2 September 1930.

Titles
The Regensburg Legacy. New York, Doubleday, 1980.
Ariel. London, Severn, 1980.

Biography
Jack Bickham worked as a reporter for the Norman Transcript, Norman, Oklahoma from 1956 to 1960, as assistant Sunday editor on *Daily Oklahoman* newspaper, 1960–66, and as managing editor of the *Oklahoma Courier* newspaper from 1966 to 1969. Then he turned to an academic career and started as an assistant professor, becoming a Professor of Journalism at the University of Oklahoma.

Critical Analysis
In *The Regensburg Legacy* a cache of chemical weapons which had belonged to the Nazis, is discovered at a US Army base in Regensburg, Germany. The weapons are deposited in a remote African country which is suffering from civil strife. The Russians attempt to topple the current president and obtain the weapons.

An ex-CIA man, Joe Dugger, becomes involved when his past agents are killed and attempts are made on his life. He discovers later that he recognises the African president's political opponent as a Russian. Dugger is chased around Europe while he is trying to find out what is happening. He finally ends up in Paris where he manages to avert the assassination of the African president. This story is another example of the veteran CIA agent reactivated in a crisis and operating independently of the agency.

JOHN MICHAEL WARD BINGHAM (LORD CLANMORRIS)
British. Born in York, 3 November 1908. Died in August 1988.

Titles
[Major characters: Brock; Ducane]
Murder Plan Six. London, Gollancz, 1958; New York, Dodd Mead, 1959.
Night's Black Agent. London, Gollancz, 1961; New York, Dodd Mead, 1961.
A Fragment of Fear. London, Gollancz, 1965; New York, Dutton, 1966.
The Double Agent [Ducane]. London, Gollancz, 1966; New York, Dutton, 1967.
Vulture in the Sun [Ducane]. London, Gollancz, 1971.
God's Defector. London, Macmillan, 1976; as *Ministry of Death*. New York, Walker, 1977.
Brock. London, Gollancz, 1981.
Brock and the Defector. London, Gollancz, 1982; New York, Doubleday, 1982.

Biography
Son of the seventh Baron Clanmorris (Ireland), John Bingham succeeded to the title in 1960. After a conventional education at Cheltenham College he spent three years

wandering around Europe and learning to speak German and French. When he returned to Britain in the early 1930s Bingham became a journalist. He first worked for the *Hull Daily Mail* and then came to London and joined the *Sunday Dispatch*, where he later became picture editor. His first book was *My Name is Michael Silby* (1952), a crime novel. His subsequent novels have been published in America, Sweden, Norway, Denmark, France, Holland, Germany, Italy and Japan.

Critical Analysis

John Bingham was a member of the Crime Writers Association and wrote a number of crime novels apart from the spy stories listed above.

He worked for more than a quarter of a century in various branches of the Security Services — mostly in MI5. He was discreet about his intelligence experience, but perhaps some clues can be found in the novels of John le Carré, who worked with Bingham in the early 1960s and became a friend. Lady Clanmorris, who died in early 1988, believed that her husband was the model for George Smiley, the anti-hero of many of le Carré's spy novels.

Bingham's treatment of spy fiction was very different to le Carré's — he was not so cynical as the latter and attributed more honourable motives to his secret agents.

In Bingham's obituary in the *Daily Telegraph* it says that he told friends that he disliked the le Carré approach, and it was this which may have prompted him to write, in the Foreword to *The Double Agent*: "There are two schools of thought about our Intelligence Services. One school is convinced they are staffed by murderous, powerful, double-crossing cynics, the other that the taxpayer is supporting a collection of bumbling, broken-down layabouts. It is possible to think that both extremes of thought are the result of a mixture of unclear reasoning, ignorance and possibly political or temperamental wishful thinking."

JOHN FENWICK BLACKBURN

British. Born in Corbridge-on-Tyne, 26 June 1923.

Titles

[Major character: General Charles Kirk]
A Scent of New Mown Hay [Kirk]. London, Secker & Warburg, 1958; New York, Mill, 1958; as *The Reluctant Spy*. London, Lancer, 1966.
A Sour Apple Tree [Kirk]. London, Secker & Warburg, 1958; New York, Mill, 1959.
Broken Boy [Kirk]. London, Secker & Warburg, 1959; New York, Mill, 1962.
Dead Man Running. London, Secker & Warburg, 1960; New York, Mill, 1961.
The Gaunt Woman [Kirk]. London, Cape, 1962; New York, Mill, 1962.
Colonel Bogus [Kirk]. London, Cape, 1964; as *Packed for Murder*. New York, Mill, 1964.
A Ring of Roses [Kirk]. London, Cape, 1965; as *A Wreath of Roses*. New York, Mill, 1965.

Biography

John Blackburn spent his early life in a country vicarage and was educated at Haileybury College and Durham University. During the Second World War he was in the Merchant Navy and in 1952-53 he served with the Control Commission in Berlin and, so he says, "met several associates of 'the Game' ".

Critical Analysis

Blackburn has published twenty-three novels and some short stories, his first being *A Scent of New Mown Hay*, which was on the not unfamiliar theme of the mad scientist. Most of the locations for Blackburn's books are in Germany, Russia and the United Kingdom. He holds the belief that most professional agents in the spy game are motivated by blackmail, brainwashing or fanaticism rather than finance. "During the war" he says, "I was once approached by an agent in Portuguese East Africa with a view to selling Merchant Navy code books. The offer was most tempting but fear rather than patriotism made me refuse."

Frank Denton, a writer and reviewer, has praised Blackburn's novels: "In style, Blackburn has been compared to John Buchan and Geoffrey Household, in plot to John Creasey. No matter the comparisons, John Blackburn is undoubtedly England's best practising novelist in the tradition of the thriller/fantasy novel."

MELVIN BOLTON

British. Born in Lancashire, 12 November 1938.

Titles

[Major character: Peter Lawson]
The Softener. London, Gollancz, 1984; New York, Franklin Watts, 1986.
The Testing. London, Gollancz, 1987; New York, David & Charles, 1989.
The Offering. London, Gollancz, 1988.

Biography

Melvin Bolton was educated at grammar school. He says that he had a " powerful urge to travel", but " several years after leaving school was forced to recognise the value of formal qualifications", so he returned to England and studied biological sciences and received a BSc Hons and MSc from London University. Bolton has travelled quite extensively and has lived in Africa, Asia and the South Pacific. His early writing was all non-fiction.

Critical Analysis

Bolton's first novel, *The Softener*, is the story of a sophisticated burglar, who, through his house-breaking activities, becomes involved in international intrigue that costs him his wife and makes him a target of a manhunt by the British and Soviet secret services.

The author comments: " My stories so far have combined elements of the spy novel with crime/'thriller' material and I see no reason why spying/intelligence operations should not be a component of escapes, war stories or other genre."

Newgate Callendar of the *New York Times Book Review* wrote of his second novel, *The Testing*: " Mr Bolton has a calm, analytical view about espionage but nevertheless manages to fill the pages with tension. There are no heroics. Here we have skilled professionals, and it is a pleasure to watch them work, these British and South African agents know what they are doing."

Bolton says of his latest book: " *The Offering* is pure fiction as a story but it is set against an authentic background — the Afghan war. Other factual events are incorporated in a deliberate mix of fact and fiction."

Patrick Breslin

American. Born in New York City, 22 March 1940.

Titles

Interventions. New York, Doubleday, 1980.

Biography

Patrick Breslin was educated at a grammar school and Manhattan College in New York City. Later he went to graduate school at New York University where he obtained an MA, and then to the University of California at Los Angeles, where he received a PhD. He has worked as a journalist and in the Peace Corps in Latin America. He has had various writing jobs and participated in political campaigns.

Critical Analysis

Interventions is set in Salvador Allende's Chile in the early 1970s before the election that ousts him from office. Many Chileans believe that the socialist government of Allende means reform, justice and progress. But to the US State Department it represents a defeat and a threat. Operating with reactionary interests the Americans engage in a covert campaign to subvert Allende's democratically elected regime.

Paul Steward, a newly assigned CIA officer, has just arrived in Chile and his assignment is to gather intelligence and spy on Chile's Leftists. He meets up with an old girlfriend who supports the Left. Steward finds his loyalties pulled in different directions as he tries to do his job and save the girl from retribution once Allende's government has fallen.

The author was in Chile at the time of the military coup that overthrew Allende. He is also a specialist in Latin America which gave him a certain insight into the events that happened there. He says: "Spy fiction was the best vehicle to deal with the political and human issues growing out of U.S. intervention in the Chilean political process of the 1970s."

Apart from his own experience Breslin researched this novel with the aid of interviews with intelligence people, memoirs and government investigative reports.

David Brierley

British. Born in Durban, South Africa, 30 July 1936.

Titles

[Major character: Cody]
Cold War. London, Faber, 1979.
Blood Group O. London, Faber, 1980.
Big Bear, Little Bear. London, Faber, 1981.
Shooting Star. London, Collins, 1983.

Czechmate. London, Collins, 1984.
Skorpion's Death. London, Collins, 1985.
Snowline. London, Collins, 1986.
One Lives, One Dies. London, Collins, 1987.

Biography

David Brierley was educated in schools in South Africa, Canada and England. He obtained a BA Hons degree in Philosophy, Politics and Economics at Oxford. He worked as an English assistant at a lycée in Lille, France (1958–59). From 1960 until 1975 he worked as a advertising copywriter in London.

Critical Analysis

Cold War is the first of four books featuring Cody, an ex-spy gone freelance. She is dragged unwittingly into the dirty tricks campaign of a French Presidential election and has to run very fast indeed to stay alive.

Cody realises that she has been made a pawn in this Cold War game, and so has the French scientist Ladoucier — sacrificed so that President Giscard will remain in power and the French communists will be discredited. As a partial explanation of events and Cody's part in them, Crèvecoeur of the Sûreté, says: "The public is gullible, they *want* to believe stories. That is the psychological basis that supports the Cold War."

At one point in this novel Cody reflects upon the work of the CIA: "I don't know what the Agency is meant to be about, and I don't think anyone else does. Destabilizing, infiltrating, disinformation, buying and selling foreign politicians like they were packs of detergents. Is that what fills the agendas at all the sub-committee meetings they have at Langley?"

Cold War is a good, entertaining story. It is refreshing because it is one of the few current spy novels stripped of any sentimentalism. It is not drowned in moral dilemmas — perhaps this is one of the benefits of having a heroine as the protagonist.

In *Blood Group O* Cody again comes across the path of Crèvecoeur, who engineers the situation so that Cody takes on the case of the kidnapped daughter of a wealthy diamond broker. Cody's search to find the girl leads her through the shady, competitive world of French intelligence, the crime mobs of Paris and Blood Group O, an international terrorist group whose aim is to eliminate fascist elements in society. "The reason the human species advanced out of the jungle is not because of physical responses but mental activity," she advises us. "Survivors are the ones whose brains work."

The author says: "I am a novelist. I am not interested in James Bond fantasies of saving the world, nor in 'hardware' — stealing the Russian's secret weapon. My books show the larger world impinging on smaller people. Spy fiction allows a greater degree of 'action' and 'excitement'. But the bloodshed is really no more than a dollop of tomato ketchup on the side of the plate."

Brierley has no experience in intelligence work but he has been approached by people from an intelligence organisation. He says that in El Salvador he was questioned — "informally but determinedly — and later checked on by a member of the CIA."

He identifies favourite themes in his books as: "A political situation, a love confusion, a modicum of espionage are at the heart of my books. Also in most of them, some event in the past exerts a powerful influence, giving people's lives a kick."

JOHN BUCHAN

Scottish. Born in Broughton Green, Peeblesshire, 26 August 1875. Died 11 February 1940.

Titles

[Major character: Richard Hannay]

The Thirty-Nine Steps [Hannay]. Edinburgh, Blackwood, 1915; New York, Doran, 1915.

Greenmantle [Hannay]. London, Hodder & Stoughton, 1916; New York, Doran, 1916.

Mr Standfast [Hannay]. London, Hodder & Stoughton, 1919; New York, Doran, 1919.

The Three Hostages [Hannay]. London, Hodder & Stoughton, 1924; Boston, Houghton Mifflin, 1924.

The Courts of the Morning. London, Hodder & Stoughton, 1929; Boston, Houghton Mifflin, 1929.

A Prince of the Captivity. London, Hodder & Stoughton, 1933; Boston, Houghton Mifflin, 1933.

The Island of Sheep [Hannay]. London, Hodder & Stoughton, 1936; as *The Man from the Norlands*. Boston, Houghton Mifflin, 1936.

Biography

The eldest son of the Revd John Buchan, of Broughton Green, Peeblesshire, John Buchan was educated at Glasgow University and Brasenose College, Oxford. He had an outstanding career at Oxford, winning the Stanhope Essay Prize in 1897 and the Newdigate Prize the following year. He became a barrister of the Middle Temple in 1901 and from later that year until 1903 was private secretary to the High Commissioner for South Africa, Lord Milner. Thus Buchan became a member of that inner circle of bright young men who were close to Milner and whose political advancement dates from this time.

He was attached to the HQ Staff of the British Army in France from 1916 to 1917, being given the rank of temporary Lieutenant-Colonel. When Lloyd George became Prime Minister, Buchan was made Director of Information and this was followed by a spell as Director of Intelligence. From 1927 to 1935 he was Conservative MP for the Scottish Universities (this was before the abolition of the University seats) and during this period he became Lord Commissioner of the Church of Scotland (1933-34). In 1939 he was created the first Baron Tweedsmuir of Elsfield, and in the same year he was appointed Governor-General of Canada.

Critical Analysis

Buchan is an important figure in the development of the spy story. His hero, Richard Hannay, first appeared in *The Thirty-Nine Steps*, which paved the way to Buchan's success as a popular novelist. This story struck exactly the right note and, disregarding its more melodramatic episodes, it had all the right ingredients of the successful spy story — topicality in the midst of war, an exciting chase in which the spy-catcher is pursued by the spy's agents, and a series of cinematic situations amidst splendid background scenery of moor and mountain which made the book a natural for one of Hitchcock's best films (1935). It was remade in 1959 (starring Kenneth More), and again in 1978.

The character of Hannay was too good to waste on a single book and he appears again in *Greenmantle*, which some consider to be the best of all the Hannay stories, of which five were written. As a contrast to *The Thirty-Nine Steps*, in this story Hannay plays the spy instead of the spy-catcher, though Buchan never even applied this term to one who is "on our side", such were the conventions of the day. Here Hannay is out to stop the Germans from using an Islamic prophet for their own ends. *Mr Standfast* was a slight departure from Buchan's normal well-plotted patriotic path in his spy novels in that one of the characters, Lancelot Wake, is a conscientious objector who dies a heroic death while taking a vital message across a river.

Buchan's innate romanticism found its expression in his spy novels in a manner rarely seen in other writers of this genre. *Huntingtower* is perhaps the best example. This was the story of a middle-aged man who set out in search of romance and found it in a whirl of wild adventure, with the aid of a young man, an imprisoned princess, a group of Bolsheviks and some Boy Scouts from the slums. For many this is one of Buchan's best books, though Nicholas Luard, who resembles Buchan in that both men are story-tellers first and foremost, expresses the view that "the first half of *A Prince of the Captivity* remains one of the truest and most spell-binding accounts of an agent working in the field ever written."

This view is important, not merely because it illustrates the story-telling qualities of Buchan, but because it shows how well Buchan's work stands up half a century later. The final comment on his stories may be left to LeRoy L Panek, a critic of spy fiction: "Buchan took the spy novel out of the hands of innocuous romancers like Oppenheim and gave it sinew and meaning. Regardless of chronology or irrelevant 'firsts' Buchan started the modern spy novel, and in its best manifestations the spy novel returns to him."

Films

The Thirty-Nine Steps. Gaumont British, GB, 1935.
The Thirty-Nine Steps. Rank, GB, 1959.
The Thirty-Nine Steps. Rank, GB, 1978.

WILLIAM FRANK BUCKLEY JR.

American. Born in New York City, 24 November 1925.

Titles

[Major character: Blackford Oakes]
Saving the Queen. New York, Doubleday, 1976; London, WH Allen, 1976.
Stained Glass. New York, Doubleday, 1978; London, Penguin, 1979.
Who's On First. New York, Doubleday, 1980; London, Allen Lane, 1980.
Marco Polo, If You Can. New York, Doubleday, 1982; London, Allen Lane, 1982.
The Story of Henri Tod. New York, Doubleday, 1984; London, Allen Lane, 1984.
See You Later Alligator. New York, Doubleday, 1985; London, Arrow, 1985.
High Jinx. New York, Doubleday, 1986.
Mongoose R.I.P. New York, Random House, 1988; London, Hutchinson, 1988.

Biography

William F Buckley Jr. was educated privately at home and in France and England. He graduated from Millbrook School in New York in 1943. He attended the University of Mexico in Mexico City, 1943–44, and graduated with a BA Hons from Yale University in 1950. During the Second World War he served in the US Army and became a 2nd Lieutenant.

Apart from being one of the most vocal intellectual conservatives in America, Buckley has been a CIA operative, a member of the US delegation to the United Nations, a candidate for the mayor of New York, publisher and editor of the *National Review* since 1955, the host of the weekly television show *Firing Line* since 1966 and a prolific columnist and author.

Critical Analysis

William F Buckley Jr. has written eight spy novels to date, beginning with *Saving the Queen* in 1976. All the novels feature CIA operative Blackford Oakes — a graduate of Yale University and a Roman Catholic, like the author.

Buckley was affiliated with the CIA in Mexico for about eight or nine months, where he worked as a deep-cover agent under Howard Hunt. When asked in an interview if his CIA experience had contributed to his spy novels, Buckley replied: "In my first book, *Queen*, the training received by Blackford Oakes is, in exact detail, the training I received. In that sense it's autobiographical."

His experience in the CIA may well have helped Buckley to present espionage operations in his stories, although he claims that this is not one of the reasons behind his writing — he believes that they have an ideological purpose: "To demonstrate that we *are* the good guys and they're the bad guys. I began writing spy novels because I thought the point worth making in a fluid context that would capture a wider audience."

Buckley does not write his novels to inform the reading public about how the CIA works abroad. He sees them partly as a form of entertainment, and also as a way of promoting and supporting the CIA. To him it is an ideal vehicle for expressing his own opinions about espionage, the Cold War and politics.

Most of the Oakes stories are set in the past — in the 1950s and 1960s when the Cold War conflict was at its height — and they illustrate many of the competitive elements that characterised the relationship between the USSR and America during this period. For example, in *Who's On First*, the race is on between the superpowers to put the first satellite into orbit.

Buckley's stories are historical, but they are also allegorical. He believes that the Cold War is the normal state of affairs in the relationship between the USSR and America, and by setting his novels in the past he can express his political views with more conviction. As Robin Winks, a critic of spy and detective fiction, wrote in *The New Republic*: "Buckley intends to carry us, through the eyes of Oakes, from the seemingly clear perceptions of right and wrong of the Cold War years to our own muddy days, unraveling his ever more complex political views as he goes."

These novels are very entertaining and no historical figures are free from Buckley's barbed sense of humour. The plots and the character of Blackford Oakes have matured since the rather preposterous exploits indulged by Oakes with Queen Caroline of England. An indulgence quite justified when seen as Buckley's personal revenge upon the English public school system.

HERBERT BURKHOLZ

Joint Pseudonym: JOHN LUCKLESS
American. Born in New York City, 9 December 1932.

Titles

The Spanish Soldier. New York, Charterhouse, 1973.
Death Freak. New York, Summit Books, 1978.
The Snow Gods. New York, Poseidon Books,1984; London, WH Allen, 1986.
The Sensitives. New York, Atheneum,1987; London, Headline, 1988.
Strange Bedfellows. London, Headline, 1989.

Novels written with Clifford Irving

Spy: History of Modern Espionage (non-fiction). New York, Macmillan, 1969.
The Sleeping Spy. New York, Atheneum, 1983.

Biography

Herbert Burkholz was educated at New York University. He has worked as an insurance broker, editor, ski instructor, bartender and book reviewer. He was a visiting professor and writer-in-residence at the William and Mary College, Williamsburg, Virginia (1975–76).

Critical Analysis

The Sensitives is named after a group of people with the ability to read minds, and there are literally one in a million. Zealously sought and guarded by the world's Intelligence agencies, the sensitives are doomed — not one has ever reached the age of thirty-five.

For most of his life Ben Slade has used his gift on the behalf of the Centre, a section of the CIA and given his loyalty to Pop, who watches protectively over the American sensitives. He is sent to Yugoslavia to win over a Swedish scientist who has spent his life-time developing a new type of microchip, one with great potential. Events on this mission alter his outlook on life and then Ben and his Russian counterpart, Nadia Patrovna, fall in love and decide to risk everything to be together — their decision has terrifying and far-reaching consequences both for themselves and for every other sensitive for whom time is running out.

One reviewer commented on this book: "The author has the sense and discipline to keep his book within the bounds of fictional credibility so that although *The Sensitives* borders on science fiction it is believable science fiction with a good, well developed storyline and interesting, likeable characters — a good mixture of spy thriller and sci-fi."

Strange Bedfellows again features the sensitives who become involved in a complex plot, when a USAF colonel suspected of being a Soviet spy disappears and only the sensitives can prevent the outbreak of nuclear war. A review in *Books* called this story "..... a suspenseful and convincingly imagined exercise in spi-fi."

JON BURMEISTER

South African. Born in Stutterheim, South Africa, 25 May 1933.

Titles

Running Scared. New York, St. Martin's Press, 1973; London, Michael Joseph, 1972.
The Hard Men. New York, St. Martin's Press, 1978; London, Michael Joseph, 1978.

Biography

Jon Burmeister was educated at St. Andrew's College, Grahamstown, South Africa, from which he matriculated and obtained attorney's admission in 1950. He worked as a partner in a law and notary public firm in East London, Republic of South Africa (1960–70). He has been a full-time writer since 1970.

Critical Analysis

Running Scared is the story of Bobo Lunda, the president of an African Republic, who is sent to the Joseph Schwer hospital in Cape Town and installed with full security protection. An ambulance driver at the hospital, Ernie Slade, discovers that he is dying of cancer and he can see no way of leaving his wife with any financial security, until he thinks of a daring plan to kidnap President Lunda and hold him to ransom. The kidnap succeeds and Slade hides him away in a remote hut on the Cape Peninsula, but then the plan begins to go wrong.

The Hard Men is set in Angola, after the Portuguese had left and civil war had broken out between Unita, the FNLA and the MPLA. The CIA were determined that the MPLA — the Marxist-orientated party — should not succeed so they encouraged the South Africans to invade Angola and rid the country of the Cubans who had arrived to help the MPLA. But then the Americans withdrew their support, the South Africans pulled out and Angola became a Communist-governed country, whose troubles were not over.

R WRIGHT CAMPBELL

American. Born in Newark, New Jersey, 9 June 1927.

Titles

The Spy Who Sat and Waited. New York, Pocket Books, 1975.
Circus Couronne. New York, Pocket Books, 1979.

Biography

R Wright Campbell completed a three-year course in illustration at the Pratt Institute in Brooklyn, New York, before serving in the US Army during the Korean War. After basic training he was assigned to the Anti-Aircraft Brigade, Fort Meade, Maryland. He transferred to the 4th echelon repair unit and spent the last year with G2 (General Army Intelligence) at the Pentagon. Campbell decided to take up writing as a career in 1952 when he arrived in Hollywood, selling his first major screenplay two years later.

Critical Analysis

The Spy Who Sat and Waited was his first novel and into this book he grafted some highly original elements. His spy, Wilhelm Oerter, an undistinguished young clerk from a small town in Bavaria, receives orders to change his identity. He becomes Will Hartz, a Swiss, and is consigned on a highly speculative basis to the Orkneys, there to become what is known in the spy trade as "a sleeper".

He waits twenty years. He is reactivated in 1939 and sends back to Germany information concerning the temporary lifting of submarine protection nets in the Flow, thus leading to the sinking of HMS *Royal Oak* by torpedoing by a single U-boat. This is a chilling portrait of one small spy whose whole life is dedicated to his one tiny act of treachery, with appalling results.

"I wanted to write a book that illuminated the existentialist quality of modern life," says Campbell, "showing life as being quite absurd and the things we do or are asked to do being even more absurd. I can think of no character more apt to create hell because it is his duty than a spy or a government assassin. Oerter's finest hour is the moment he refuses to enter into the plot against Hitler."

The novel is based upon an actual event. A Nazi submarine, the U-47 under Lt. Guenther Prien, did in fact sink HMS *Royal Oak* in Scapa on 14 October, 1939. At the time MI5 was blamed for not providing information, but later in 1942 an article was published in the *Saturday Evening Post*, declaring that information was supplied to the Germans by an agent living at Kirkwall. Since then it has been discovered that the story was untrue.

VICTOR CANNING

Pseudonym: **ALAN GOULD**
British. Born in Plymouth, 16 June 1911. Died February 21 1986.

Titles

[Major character: Rex Carver]
Panther's Moon. London, Hodder & Stoughton, 1948; New York, Mill, 1948.
The Golden Salamander. London, Hodder & Stoughton, 1949; New York, Mill, 1949.
A Forest of Eyes. London, Hodder & Stoughton, 1950; New York, Mill, 1950.
Venetian Bird. London, Hodder & Stoughton, 1951; as *Bird of Prey*. New York, Mill, 1951.
Castle Minerva. London, Hodder & Stoughton, 1955; as *A Handful of Silver*. New York, Sloane, 1954.
The Limbo Line. London, Heinemann, 1963; New York, Sloane, 1964.
The Scorpio Letters. London, Heinemann, 1964; New York, Sloane, 1964.
The Whip Hand [Carver]. London, Heinemann, 1965; New York, Sloane, 1965.
Doubled in Diamonds [Carver]. London, Heinemann, 1966; New York, Morrow, 1967.
The Python Project [Carver]. London, Heinemann, 1967; New York, Morrow, 1968.
The Finger of Saturn. London, Heinemann, 1973; New York, Morrow, 1974.
The Mask of Memory. London, Heinemann, 1974; New York, Morrow, 1975.
Birdcage. London, Heinemann, 1978; New York, Morrow, 1979.
The Boy on Platform One. London, Heinemann, 1981; as *Memory Boy*. New York, Morrow, 1981.
Vanishing Point. London, Heinemann, 1982; New York, Morrow, 1983.

Biography

Educated at grammar and technical schools in Plymouth and Oxford, Victor Canning's first book was published in 1934. This was *Mr Finchley Discovers His England* (1934), an unusual and entertaining travelogue. During the Second World War he served in the Royal Artillery, rising to the rank of Major, and it was only after his war experiences that he branched out into what could be called espionage thrillers.

Critical Analysis

Victor Canning has written over 50 novels. His hero, Rex Carver, is a private investigator, but he often becomes involved with the work of British Intelligence; otherwise the heroes of Canning's stories tend to be amateurs who become involved with international intrigue.

Canning insisted that "I do not write spy fiction as such. I just write stories and I hate labelling them". *The Golden Salamander*, which was an outstanding success both as a book and a film (1949), paved the way towards the thriller and mystery novel and this was followed by *Panther's Moon*. It was not, however, until *The Forest of Eyes* that Canning produced a 100 per cent spy story. Robert Hudson, much more like an Ambler hero than a Buchan one, had no hankering for the role of secret agent; he was an engineer and as such went to Yugoslavia. But he soon found himself enmeshed in the Secret Service. In his next book, *Venetian Bird*, Canning combined romantic interest with the story of a down-at-heel English inquiry agent who becomes a hero in spite of himself.

Film

The Golden Salamander. GFD, GB, 1949.

NICK CARTER

Titles

Agent Double-Agent. New York, Award Books, 1973.
Amazon. New York, Award Books, 1969.
Amsterdam. New York, Award Books, 1970.
And Next the King. New York, Ace-Charter, 1980.
The Arab Plague. New York, Award Books, 1970.
The Asian Mantrap. New York, Ace-Charter, 1978.
Assassin: Code Name Vulture. New York, Award Books, 1978.
The Assassination Brigade. New York, Award Books, 1973.
Assault on England. New York, Award Books, 1974.
Assignment: Intercept. New York, Award Books, 1977.
Assignment: Israel. New York, Award Books, 1974.
The Aztec Avenger. New York, Award Books, 1974.
Beirut Incident. New York, Award Books, 1974.
Berlin. New York, Award Books, 1970.
The Black Death. New York, Award Books, 1969.
(At least 128 other titles in paperback in the series)

Critical Analysis

Considered as either a detective or espionage agent, Nick Carter has appeared in more stories and books than any other character in suspense fiction.

Nick Carter — called "N-3" or "Killmaster" in the field — has survived more missions (over 100) than any other secret operative in spy fiction. Carter was, and still is a "house name", that is a hero written about by many authors.

Carter's first adventure was recorded in the 18 September 1886 issue of the *New York Weekly*. The actual creator of Nick Carter was Ormond G Smith (1860–1933). He provided the outline of the first story to John Russell Coryell (1848–1924), who wrote the first story and two sequels, after which a number of writers continued the series.

The most prolific writer was Frederic Van Rensselaer Dey (1869–1929), who wrote more than 1,000 stories, but other authors contributed, including Michael Avallone, W T Ballard, Thomas Chastain, Michael Collins, William Wallace Cook, Frederick W Davis, W Bert Foster, Marilyn Granbeck, Thomas W Hanshew, Thomas C Harbaugh, Ralph E Hayes, George C Jenks, Johnston McCulley, Robert Randisi, Eugene T Sawyer, Martin Cruz Smith, Jeffrey M Wallman, John H Whitson and Lionel White.

There are many more writers who have contributed to this series but who remain anonymous. Carter appeared in dime novels and later pulp magazines for half a century before his adventures were recorded in paperbacks, and during that time Carter has himself been transformed from a young, upright detective to a sophisticated secret agent.

In 1964 book packager Lyle Kenyon Engel transformed Nick Carter into a professional secret agent, no doubt influenced by the popularity of James Bond. Engel employed an army of writers (64) to fill in the plots and characters as directed by him. The first of these books was *Run Spy Run* (1964). Because the Nick Carter novels have been written over such a long period, they are a fascinating record of events in history and contemporary preoccupations. For instance, the plots of the Carter novels dating from the 1960s range from encounters with neo-Nazis, to the machinations of the Mafia, to the prevention of a Communist takeover in Malaysia. (See Joan Rockwell's essay "Normative Attitudes of Spies in Fiction" in Bernard Rosenberg and David M White, eds. *Mass Culture Revisited* [New York, Van Nostrand,1971], p. 339.)

Films

The French were the first to use the Nick Carter stories in films, and he appeared in four serials (1909–12), all starring André Label. The American actor Thomas Carrigan portrayed him in a series of short films in 1920, and Edmund Lowe appeared in a second series in 1922. After a gap of nearly twenty years the dime novel detective was revived and Walter Pidgeon featured in a series of full-length films.

Nick Carter, Master Detective. MGM, 1939.
Phantom Raiders. MGM, 1940.
Sky Murder. MGM, 1940.
Nick Carter va tout casser. 1963.
Nick Carter et le trèfle rouge. 1965.

Radio and Television

In 1943, "Nick Carter, Master Detective" was one of the most durable of all half-hour mystery radio programmes.

In 1972 Robert Conrad played the detective in "The Adventures of Nick Carter", a feature film made for television and set at the turn of the century.

JOHN RUFUS CASSIDY

American. Born in Brookfield, Missouri, 4 August 1922.

Titles

A Station in the Delta. New York, Scribner, 1979.

Biography

John R Cassidy was educated at the University of Missouri. He worked as a teacher at high school in Brookfield, Missouri in 1949. Then he worked as a civilian analyst for the Office of Naval Intelligence, in Washington DC, from 1949 to 1951. He joined the Central Intelligence Agency in 1951 and worked as an operations officer and associate in Latin America, Vietnam and Spain, until he retired in 1973. In 1973 he won the Studies in Intelligence Award from the CIA, for "contribution to the literature of intelligence"; it is not known for which piece of literature this award was given.

Critical Analysis

John R Cassidy is another of these authors who has had experience in intelligence work and has turned to fiction as a literary channel. He obviously draws upon his intelligence experience in his novel.

A Station in the Delta is set in Vietnam in the autumn of 1967. Toby Busch, a field officer in the Clandestine Service of the CIA, arrives in My Tho, a town in the Mekong Delta. His career has been damaged by an incident that occurred in Frankfurt, Germany. He volunteers for service in Vietnam to try to vindicate his past behaviour and to salvage his career.

Busch is unprepared for the situation he meets in war-torn Vietnam. Although married he has an affair with Thérèse, a war widow from Hanoi. Through intelligence contacts he finds evidence of a massive Communist offensive to be launched on Tet, the sacred New Year holiday — during the truce. Busch tries to warn everyone in time so that they can repel attacks. He is unable to convince the Saigon high command until the last moment. His prompt action provides time for some preparation and counter-attack, but nevertheless many innocent victims suffer and die.

In this novel Cassidy shows that he believes in the importance of the individual and his power, with sufficient knowledge, to change the course of events. This is a vivid portrayal of Vietnam, the problems of the environment and the problems of trying to understand the people — not just their language, but their culture as well. The book discusses the difficulties involved in how to accurately portray the war to Americans back home — how the television pictures distort the war and the journalists distort the facts. It is an interesting novel by a man who knows what he is talking about.

GILBERT KEITH CHESTERTON
British. Born in London, 29 May 1874. Died 14 June 1936.

Titles
The Man Who Was Thursday: A Nightmare. Bristol, Arrowsmith, 1908; New York, Dodd Mead, 1908.

Biography
From 1887 to1892 Chesterton was educated at St. Paul's School, London, where at the age of sixteen he showed his talents as a writer by starting a magazine called *The Debater*. Also revealing promise as an artist, young Chesterton went on to the Slade School of Art, at the same time studying English Literature at London University.
During the Boer War he took a pro-Boer standpoint on the platform and in his writing. Between 1900 and 1910 he turned out numerous essays touching on political, philosophical, literary and other topics, and revelling in fierce but friendly debate. His study of Charles Dickens (1906) won wide approval from the critics.

Critical Analysis
One of the greatest masters of prose of his generation, Chesterton, the superb essayist, turned his attention to novel writing and especially to the detective story. His famous creation of Father Brown, the priest-detective, was based on his great friend Father John O'Connor, parish priest of a church in Bradford, who in 1922 received Chesterton into the Roman Catholic Church.

There was a romanticism about Chesterton's approach not only to the detective story, but to the spy story as well, a lifting of the genre to a level of what can perhaps be called an esoteric fantasy, which is one of the features of *The Man Who Was Thursday*, described by "some of the old pros", says Miles Copeland, as "the best spy book ever written."

It is interesting to note Chesterton's attitude to this type of story in contrast to those of, say, Oppenheim or Buchan. Chesterton preferred "the romance of man"to the patriotism of empire. He put it most neatly when he wrote, "Every fantastic skyline of chimney-pots seems wildly and derisively signalling the meaning of mystery ... It is the agent of social justice who is the original and poetic figure, while the burglars and footpads are merely placid old cosmic conservatives, happy in the immemorial respectability of apes and wolves. The romance of the police force is the whole romance of man."

The Man Who Was Thursday: A Nightmare was unique. When the poet, Syme, is shown into the steel chamber of the Underground Movement, Chesterton makes no pretence at the erudition in weaponry in which modern spy novelists love to show off. He simply writes that "there were no rifles or pistols in this apartment, but round the walls of it were hung more dubious and dreadful shapes, things that looked like the bulbs of iron plants, or the eggs of iron birds. They were bombs, and the very room itself seemed like the inside of a bomb." It is all written with a very adroit tongue in the cheek.

It is true that this book is something of a send-up of the spy story, a much more elegant send-up than those of the late 1960s, but so much of it can be related to real-life situations that one can well understand the professional agent laughing his head off when reading it.

Chesterton, in an age when the double-agent was regarded as a joke in fiction and almost unheard of in fact, except in Czarist Russia, summed up perfectly the kind of modern situation we know so well when two rival agents who have exchanged confidences confront one another. Gregory, having been told by Syme that the latter is a police agent, aims a revolver at him. " 'Don't be such a silly man,' he said, with the effeminate dignity of a curate. 'Don't you see it's not necessary? Don't you see that we're both in the same boat ...We've checkmated each other. I can't tell the police you are an anarchist. You can't tell the anarchists I'm a policeman. I can only watch you, knowing what you are; you can only watch me, knowing what I am. In short, it's a lonely, intellectual duel, my head against yours. I'm a policeman deprived of the help of the police. You, my poor fellow, are an anarchist deprived of the help of that law and organisation which is so essential to anarchy.' "

The Man Who Was Thursday anticipates almost every spy story that was ever written. It should still be a model for aspiring writers of espionage fiction, a textbook to prevent them from keeling over too far in the direction of fantasy.

REGINALD SOUTHOUSE CHEYNEY
Pseudonyms: PETER CHEYNEY, HAROLD BRUST
British. Born in London in 1896. Died 26 June 1951.

Titles
[Major characters: Everard Peter Quayle, Johnny Vallon]
Dark Duet. London, Collins, 1942; New York, Dodd Mead, 1943; as *The Counter Spy Murders*. New York, Avon, 1944.
The Stars Are Dark [Quayle]. London, Collins, 1943; New York, Dodd Mead, 1943; as *The London Spy Murders*. New York, Avon, 1944.
The Dark Street [Quayle]. London, Collins, 1944; New York, Dodd Mead, 1944; as *The Dark Street Murders*. New York, Avon, 1946.
The Adventures of Julia. Brighton, Poynings Press, 1945; as *The Adventures of Julia and Two Other Spy Stories*. London, Todd, 1954; as *The Killing Game*. New York, Belmont, 1975.
Dark Hero. London, Collins, 1946; New York, Dodd Mead, 1946.
Dark Interlude [Quayle]. London, Collins, 1947; New York, Dodd Mead, 1947; as *The Terrible Night*. New York, Avon, 1959.
Dark Wanton [Quayle]. London, Collins, 1948; New York, Dodd Mead, 1949.
Dark Bahama [Vallon]. London, Collins, 1950; New York, Dodd Mead, 1951; as *I'll Bring Her Back*. New York, Eton, 1952.

Biography
Peter Cheyney had an undistinguished career in his early life, finding little success as a songwriter, bookmaker, journalist or budding politician. Success came to him suddenly when, aged forty, he created the character Lemmy Caution in *This Man is Dangerous* (1936). Caution was a "private eye"; with him Cheyney got right away from the genteel world of country-houseparty detective stories into the sleazier but more natural environment of crime. During the war years Cheyney became compulsive reading for millions and by the end of the war he was topping one and a half million sales a year, with editions of his books regularly published in America and France.

Critical Analysis

Cheyney's work was mainly in the field of detective stories and thrillers, but he made some incursions into spy fiction, notably *Adventures of Julia and Two Other Spy Stories*, and the Dark series. They were exciting, imaginative stories and, if not of a high literary standard, at least struck out in a new direction. Cheyney may have been a poseur, but he breathed new life into the thriller and rescued dialogue from its hackneyed, cliché-ridden pedestrianism of the 1930s.

Stephen Mertz, a writer and critic, comments on Cheyney's spy fiction: "Cheyney's most original, and most critically acclaimed, work was his so-called 'Dark' series of espionage novels, all of which feature 'dark' in the title, concerning a top secret British counter-intelligence unit operating against Nazi agents in wartime England and abroad. Cheyney's cross-doublecross plotting technique reached its zenith in these uncompromising studies of the cold-blooded world of spies and double agents. With their vivid characterizations, effective low-key writing style, and well-maintained building of suspense, the first two books of this series, *Dark Duet* and *The Stars Are Dark*, represent Peter Cheyney at the very top of his form."

ROBERT ERSKINE CHILDERS

British. Born in London, 25 June 1870. Died in Dublin, 24 November 1922.

Titles

The Riddle of the Sands: A Record of Secret Service Recently Achieved. London, Smith Elder, 1903; New York, Dodd Mead, 1915.

Biography

Childers was educated at Haileybury and Trinity College, Cambridge. From 1895 to 1910 he was a clerk in the House of Commons, though this was temporarily interrupted when in 1900 he was one of the first volunteers accepted for service in the Boer War. He joined the Honourable Artillery Company (HAC) and afterwards was part-author of *The HAC in South Africa*.

Childers joined the Royal Navy in the First World War, taking part in the Cuxhaven Raid in November 1914. For the rest of the war he was Training Officer in the RNAS. He was promoted to Lieutenant-Commander, mentioned several times in dispatches and awarded the DSC.

In 1919 he settled in Dublin and was the principal secretary to the delegation which negotiated an Irish Treaty with the British Government. On the establishment of the Irish Free State Government he joined the Republican Army which set itself the task of opposing the new Free State Government, and so became a participant in the civil war between the pro-Treaty and anti-Treaty forces. Unfortunately, he found himself regarded as a traitor both by the British Government and the Irish Free State Government. On 10 November 1922 he was arrested by Free State soldiers and court-martialled in Dublin. He was tried, condemned to death, and executed two weeks after his arrest.

Critical Analysis

Childers is remembered as a pioneer in spy fiction for his book *The Riddle of the Sands* which was published in 1903. This was a brilliant and lively story of yachting and espionage off the northwest coast of Germany, perhaps the first work of spy fiction other than Fenimore Cooper's to have any pretensions to being literature.

This was fiction based on fact, fiction with a set purpose, that of arousing public opinion behind the clamour for building a stronger navy, and motivated by Childers' curious dual patriotism — an intense love of England and Ireland, which he later found incompatible. Its factual basis was the result of Childers' own yachting experiences in the *Vixen* off the coasts of Germany, Holland and elsewhere.

Paul Johnson, author and former editor of the *New Statesman*, has said of it: "What strikes me about this book are both the resemblances and the huge differences, when it is compared to modern spy fiction. The resemblances are in the stress on technical details: Childers describes the philosophy, theory and practice of inshore sailing with loving care ... the areas he describes, the Baltic coast of Denmark and Schleswig-Holstein, and the low-lying sandy coast between the Elbe and the Ems, he knew intimately. In fact, the geographical structure around which the novel is built is not invented at all; the course taken by the two English heroes could be followed by any skilled yachtsman, and Childers even included maps to help the reader, together with timetables of tides. Writers of modern spy fiction follow this pattern of providing expert technical background, though rarely with the degree of knowledge and skill Childers commanded. Where they differ is in their handling of sex and violence. There is, in fact, a love story in *The Riddle*, but it is presented with such delicacy and reticence that one is scarcely aware of it, and it is never for one moment allowed to interfere with the relentless unfolding of the nautical plot."

The story concerns two young Englishmen who make a trip to the Frisian Islands and discover the Germans rehearsing plans for an invasion of Britain. Carruthers, a Foreign Office man with foppish mannerisms, is in the best tradition of the English amateur confronted with a difficult and dangerous situation, and his friend, Davies, is the perfect foil. The villain is an Englishman who is working for the Germans, a former British naval lieutenant turned traitor. He calls himself Dollman — "the vilest creature on God's earth" is Carruthers' denunciation of him in the conventional attitude to all who forsook their native country in that day and age. Childers plays on fear throughout this book, fear of the sea, of the fog, of the Germans and of the unknown: in this sense he creates the propaganda of fear.

The Riddle of the Sands deservedly became famous because, apart from being a remarkably exciting story, it drew attention to German militarism at a time when nobody else had taken up the theme. It was undoubtedly a patriotic gesture on the part of Childers, for his whole career suggests that he was as devoted to protecting England as he was to the cause of Irish nationalism. The book also alerted a somewhat dilatory British Naval Intelligence Division to shortcomings in naval charts. When two officers made a tour of the area covered in the novel they found that the Admiralty charts were hopelessly out of date. It was shortly after this that the NID was given a drastic overhaul. This book is a remarkable example of the power of propaganda in fictional form — not only did the novel provide entertainment, but it also made members of the public and the British Government aware of a problem which was rectified as a result.

Film

The Riddle of the Sands. Rank, GB, 1978.

THOMAS L CLANCY JR.

American. Born in Baltimore, Maryland, 12 April 1947.

Titles

[Major character: John Patrick ("Jack") Ryan]
The Hunt for Red October [Ryan]. New York, Putnam's, 1984; London, Collins, 1985.
Red Storm Rising. New York, Putnam's, 1986; London, Collins, 1987.
Patriot Games. New York, Putnam's, 1986; London, Collins, 1987.
The Cardinal of the Kremlin [Ryan]. New York, Putnam's, 1988; London, Collins, 1988.

Biography

Tom Clancy was educated at Roman Catholic schools: St. Matthew School, Loyola High School and Loyola College for his bachelor's degree in English Literature. He graduated from college in 1969 and then went to work for the Hartford Fire Insurance Company (The Hartford Group). He left The Hartford in 1971, when he got his agent's licence, and then joined El-Mar Associates, an independent insurance agency in suburban Baltimore. In 1973 he joined the OF Bowen Insurance Agency, which he and his wife purchased in 1980.

Critical Analysis

The author says: "I do not think of myself as a writer trapped or limited to a specific genre. The element of espionage and/or intelligence operations enters into all my books to one extent or another. Probably my most recent, *The Cardinal of the Kremlin*, comes closest to a true spy thriller."

The Hunt for Red October is a highly popular naval thriller that was well received by the critics. The book describes a Soviet captain's attempt to defect to the United States with a thirty-thousand ton Russian submarine, the *Red October*. The US Navy are keen to inspect the submarine, but first they must locate the vessel and escort the captain to freedom while avoiding the Soviet search. In this book there are intricate descriptions of military operations and technical expertise, and the story has been praised for these qualities, as well as Clancy's ability to hold suspense.

Caspar Weinberger, in a review of this novel in the *Times Literary Supplement* wrote: "The technical detail is vast and accurate, remarkably so for an author who originally had no background or experience. Critics who take themselves seriously will no doubt fault the characterization as weak and unrealized, but none except the most jaded will be anything but enthralled by the swift and expertly built crescendo of narrative excitement, the intricacy of the plot, and the chilling but wholly believable series of tightly-knit episodes that build, through many subclimaxes, to a most exciting and satisfying conclusion.

There are many lessons here for those who want to keep the peace. This is emphatically not a work of propaganda. It is rather a splendid and riveting story that demands to be finished in one sitting."

The Hunt for Red October is currently being made into a movie.

Clancy's second novel, *Red Storm Rising*, is about a future world war fought between the United States and the Soviet Union with conventional weapons. When a group of Muslim fundamentalists destroys a Siberian oil operation, thereby triggering a Russian energy crisis, the Soviets arrange a terrorist incident intended to neutralise NATO and invade Western Europe in order to obtain Middle Eastern oil.

Mark Zieman in *The Wall Street Journal* wrote of this novel: "Mr Clancy's new-found status as the Pentagon's pet is both a blessing and a curse to *Red Storm Rising*. Like the earlier *Red October*, this thriller hinges on an almost disquieting aura of authenticity, which the author achieved through hard study. To research the novel, he drove and fired an M-1 tank, shipped aboard a Navy frigate and talked to well-placed sources including a Soviet defector. *Red Storm* sweeps the reader into the heart of the battle, from a nightmare raid over Germany in the controversial Stealth fighter to a desperate submarine battle in the North Atlantic. No detail is spared. As Mr Clancy puts it: 'There's no such thing as a minor fact.' "

Clancy's latest book, *The Cardinal of the Kremlin*, is the story of the competition between America and the Soviet Union to build the first Star Wars missile defence system. Two men are set the task of assessing the Soviets' capabilities — Colonel Mikhail Filitov of the Soviet Union, an old-line warrior distrusted by the army's new inner-circle of technocrats, and CIA analyst Jack Ryan, hero of *The Hunt for Red October*. Filitov comes to his conclusions before Ryan, and this is when trouble starts as the former is America's highest agent in the Kremlin, code-named "Cardinal", and he is about to be betrayed to the KGB. Ryan has to rescue the Russian as well as keep himself alive — and meanwhile the fate of the world is hanging in the balance.

One review described this novel as "a heavyweight and sophisticated spy thriller, drawing without apparent fatigue upon the intricacies of disarmament programmes and laser beams, to spin a compelling yarn that scarcely falters over the 600 plus pages."

Clancy says: "Only after my most recent book have I developed 'serious' contact with the intelligence agencies, and even that degree of contact is exclusively social in nature. Having met people who work in that business is very helpful, however, because one writes about people in a profession rather than the profession itself. You can learn a great deal about anyone from a casual conversation."

ERIC CLARK

British. Born in Birmingham, 29 July 1937.

Titles

Black Gambit. London, Hodder & Stoughton, 1978; New York, Morrow, 1979.
The Sleeper. London, Hodder & Stoughton, 1980; New York, Atheneum, 1980.
Send in the Lions. London, Hodder & Stoughton, 1982; New York, Atheneum, 1980.
Chinese Burn. London, Hodder & Stoughton, 1984; as *China Run*. Boston, Little Brown, 1984.

Biography

Eric Clark was educated at Handsworth Grammar School in Birmingham. He left at the age of sixteen to pursue a career in journalism on a local paper. He worked on various weekly newspapers, and then became a reporter/writer on the staff of the *Daily Mail*, *The Guardian* and *The Observer*, before leaving to write books full-time. Eric Clark was the head of the news investigation department at *The Observer*, and his disclosures on the Mafia involvement in London gambling led the then

Home Secretary, Roy Jenkins, to change Britain's gambling laws (according to him).

Critical Analysis

Black Gambit is the story of an American "unofficial" plan to exchange a well-known Russian dissident with an American — in this case a man serving life for murder. It is an exciting story and shows the intricate planning involved in such an operation, particularly when "official" resources are not available. Unfortunately politics rears its ugly head which has drastic effects upon the outcome of the operation.

Jack Higgins, the pseudonym of Henry Patterson, a spy fiction writer in his own right, wrote: "In *Black Gambit* Eric Clark has succeeded in creating the cold and vicious world of espionage to a frightening degree. Can only be compared to *The Spy Who Came in from the Cold.*"

Clark's latest novel, *Chinese Burn*, has been described as a "modern-day *Thirty-Nine Steps*" because of the Buchan-style chase it describes. The story is about David Piper, a railway engineer, who is forced to run when a defecting Russian is found dead on the doorstep of his Peking hotel. The story follows his efforts to hide, accompanied by his beautiful companion, Chu Ming; they are pursued by the Chinese and the Russians across mainland China. Christopher Pym of *Punch* described this novel as "Well written; Chinese background and way of life studies on the spot, and convincingly conveyed. Full marks for suspense story firmly backed by brilliant descriptive reporting."

This novel was well received in America, where its title was changed to *China Run*. One critic in the *Los Angeles Times Book Review* wrote: "It's a thriller, an escape, and adventure, but best of all, it stirs the blood of us armchair daredevils, and, to boot, you get a fascinating yarn of what it may be like in China nowadays."

When asked why Clark had chosen the form of the spy novel to write fiction, he replied: "Originally because of material I'd collected as a journalist about spies and spying which I couldn't use except as fiction. I worked on many espionage stories. It has many advantages as a form — it is very elastic, and situations can be presented as a microcosm of the wider world. They also enable the author to place characters under maximum stress, a recreating process. Most recently my books have been moving more to 'spy' in smaller letters, 'thriller' in larger. Americans call them 'political thrillers' which is not a bad description."

Asked if he had any favourite themes in his spy fiction he said: "Layers within layers. The impossibility of knowing what is 'true'. The awfulness of man as a bureaucracy. The fact that some things happen not because someone orders them but because someone down in a chain thinks someone above wants it. The individual — in a host of facets. Versus the system, responsibility of, difficulty of survival of ..."

Brian Brendan Talbot Cleeve

Irish. Born in Thorpe Bay, Essex, 22 November 1921.

Titles

[Major character: Sean Ryan]
Assignment to Vengeance. London, Hammond, 1961.

Vote X for Treason [Ryan]. London, Collins, 1964; New York, Random House, 1965.
Dark Blood, Dark Terror [Ryan]. New York, Random House, 1965; London, Hammond, 1966.
The Judas Goat [Ryan]. London, Hammond, 1966; as *Vice Isn't Private*. New York, Random House, 1966.
Violent Death of a Bitter Englishman [Ryan]. New York, Random House, 1967; London, Corgi, 1969.
You Must Never Go Back. New York, Random House, 1968.
Exit from Prague. London, Corgi, 1970; as *Escape from Prague*. New York, Pinnacle, 1973.

Biography

Brian Cleeve was educated at Selwyn House, Broadstairs, Kent, and St. Edward's School in Oxford. He attended the University of South Africa, Johannesburg, from where he graduated with a BA in 1953. Cleeve studied for a PhD at the University of Ireland, Dublin from 1954 to 1956. During the Second World War he served in the Merchant Navy, and he says he had some experience in counter-intelligence. After the war he worked as a freelance journalist in South Africa from 1948 to 1954, then he returned to Ireland and worked as a journalist and broadcaster.

Critical Analysis

The author says that his experience in counter-intelligence during the war prompted him to write spy fiction, and the knowledge he acquired obviously helped him in his writing. Cleeve's series of spy novels, of which there are only four, follow the chequered career of Sean Ryan, an impetuous ex-Irish revolutionary turned cynic. He was recruited from prison by Major Courtney of British Intelligence to infiltrate and investigate groups whose plans may disrupt British security.

The plots in his novels are usually large-scale operations involving the seizure or keeping of power. For instance, in *Vote X for Treason*, a reactionary group of Lords and MPs use commandos and teddy boys trained in health clubs, and a secret oil agreement with Iraq, to engineer a change in government. *Violent Death of a Bitter Englishman* follows the same theme, with a Fascist organisation that plots to seize power on a racist wave to eliminate blacks in England on funds extorted from them by protection rackets.

The author commented recently in *Twentieth Century Crime and Mystery Writers* (1985): "Crime and thriller stories have always appealed to me for the same reason that fairy stories do, and folk tales and myths. They deal directly with the conflict between good and evil, and for that reason touch the most fundamental levels of human experience. In my own crime and thriller novels I *tried* — I only wish I had succeeded — to deal with this theme as seriously as it should be dealt with. I wish that publishers and novel readers were willing to accept serious work in these categories — and I wish too that the whole concept of categories for fiction could be thrown away."

MANNING COLES

(Pseudonym for Cyril Henry Coles and Adelaide Frances Oke Manning)
Other pseudonyms: Francis Gaite
CYRIL HENRY COLES: British. Born in London, 11 June 1899. Died 9 October 1965.
ADELAIDE FRANCES OKE MANNING: British. Born in London, 1891. Died 25 September 1959.

Titles

[Major character: Tommy Hambledon]
Drink to Yesterday. London, Hodder & Stoughton, 1940; New York, Knopf, 1941.
Pray Silence. London, Hodder & Stoughton, 1940; as *A Toast for Tomorrow*. New York, Doubleday, 1941.
They Tell No Tales. London, Hodder & Stoughton, 1941; New York, Doubleday, 1942.
Without Lawful Authority. London, Hodder & Stoughton, 1943; New York, Doubleday, 1943.
Green Hazard. London, Hodder & Stoughton, 1945; New York, Doubleday, 1945.
The Fifth Man. London, Hodder & Stoughton, 1946; New York, Doubleday, 1946.
Let the Tiger Die. New York, Doubleday, 1947; London, Hodder & Stoughton, 1948.
A Brother for Hugh. London, Hodder & Stoughton, 1947; as *With Intent to Deceive*. New York, Doubleday, 1947.
Among Those Absent. London, Hodder & Stoughton, 1948; New York, Doubleday, 1948.
Diamonds to Amsterdam. New York, Doubleday, 1949; London, Hodder & Stoughton, 1950.
Not Negotiable. London, Hodder & Stoughton, 1949; New York, Doubleday, 1949.
Dangerous by Nature. London, Hodder & Stoughton, 1950; New York, Doubleday, 1950.
Now or Never. London, Hodder & Stoughton, 1951; New York, Doubleday, 1951.
Alias Uncle Hugo. New York, Doubleday, 1952; London, Hodder & Stoughton, 1953.
Night Train to Paris. London, Hodder & Stoughton, 1952; New York, Doubleday, 1952.
A Knife for the Juggler. London, Hodder & Stoughton, 1953; New York, Doubleday, 1964.
Not for Export. London, Hodder & Stoughton, 1954; as *All That Glitters*. New York, Doubleday, 1954.
The Man in the Green Hat. London, Hodder & Stoughton, 1955; New York, Doubleday, 1955.
Basle Express. London, Hodder & Stoughton, 1956; New York, Doubleday, 1956.
Birdwatcher's Quarry. New York, Doubleday, 1956; as *The Three Beans*. London, Hodder & Stoughton, 1957.
Death of an Ambassador. London, Hodder & Stoughton, 1957; New York, Doubleday, 1957.
No Entry. London, Hodder & Stoughton, 1958; New York, Doubleday, 1958.
Crime in Concrete. London, Hodder & Stoughton, 1960; as *Concrete Crime*. New York, Doubleday, 1960.
Search for a Sultan (with Tom Hammerton). London, Hodder & Stoughton, 1961; New York, Doubleday, 1961.
The House at Pluck's Gutter (with Tom Hammerton). London, Hodder & Stoughton, 1963; New York, Pyramid, 1968.

Biography

Cyril Coles was educated at a school in Petersfield, Hampshire. He served in the Hampshire Regiment and later with British Intelligence during the First and the Second World Wars. He was an apprentice at John I Thornycroft, the shipbuilders at Southampton, after the First World War. In the 1920s he worked in Australia as a railwayman, garage manager and a columnist on a Melbourne newspaper. He returned to England in 1928.

Adelaide Manning was educated at the High School for Girls in Tunbridge Wells, Kent. She worked in a munitions factory and at the War Office in London during the First World War.

Critical Analysis

Just before the outbreak of the Second World War the ex-Major of British Army Intelligence would natter and reminisce with his neighbour, Adelaide Manning, who was herself an author and was fascinated with his adventures behind German lines in the First World War. And out of these talks, or so the story goes, their famous collaboration was formed under the pseudonym Manning Coles and together they wrote a large number of adventure/spy novels.

From 1940 until the death of Manning in 1959, they wrote 25 stories featuring Tommy Hambledon. The adventures of Thomas Elphinstone Hambledon of the British Intelligence Service were based on Cyril Cole's own experiences of the two wars. During the 1940s the stories were confined to the nasty doings of the Nazis but after the war this theme lost its appeal, so in the 1950s the scene of these books became more international.

Allen Dulles in his *Great Spy Stories From Fiction* (1969), described Hambledon's escapades as a "game of imaginary hare-and-hounds against a changing German background of the last forty years or so: the Kaiser's empire of World War I (*Drink to Yesterday*), the rise of Hitler's Reich (*Toast to Tomorrow*), right up to the divided Germany of the Iron Curtain epoch (*No Entry*)."

JAMES COLTRANE

(Pseudonym for James Paul Wohl)
American. Born in New York City, 3 October 1937.

Titles

The Nirvana Contracts. New York, Bobbs Merrill, 1977.
Talon. New York, Bobbs Merrill, 1978; London, New English Library, 1978.
The Blind Trust Kills. New York, Bobbs Merrill, 1978.

Biography

James Coltrane was educated at Princeton University, New York University and Stanford, where he graduated with a Law degree. He has worked as an attorney in Hilo, Hawaii and New York.

Critical Analysis

Joe Talon is a computer analyst with SANROC, one of the most advanced satellite surveillance systems in the world. Over a large area including India and Red China, Talon observes and monitors the movements of oil and whales, troops and planes, crop failures and floods — anything that could provide vital intelligence information about the earth's surface. When a satellite over Nepal picks up a random error — an unnatural-looking cloud formation obscuring everything below — Talon decides to do some investigating on his own, which makes him a target for murder.

This novel, *Talon*, is excruciatingly written, but worth reading only because it is one of those rare spy novels that has an analyst as the hero. It is written more in the style of a hard-boiled detective story, but unfortunately does not have the necessary bite to carry it off. The hero is an anti-hero, unconventional, as a professional who gets involved in a conspiracy more out of curiosity than anything else.

Despite Talon's talent for analysis (and we get a lot of technical information about his work), he daydreams that he is a spy and yearns for some excitement. But when it comes he doesn't find it quite as rewarding as he imagined. He finds that fighting to stay alive concentrates the mind wonderfully.

RICHARD THOMAS CONDON

American. Born in New York City, 18 March 1915.

Titles

The Manchurian Candidate. New York, McGraw Hill, 1959; London, Joseph, 1960.
Winter Kills. New York, Dial Press, 1964; London, Weidenfeld, 1964.
The Whisper of the Axe. New York, Dial Press, 1976; London, Weidenfeld, 1976.

Biography

Richard Condon was educated at various schools in New York, and has worked as an advertising copy-writer, a motion picture press agent and other jobs on Broadway before launching out as a novelist at the age of forty-two. Since then he has written novels, plays, essays, criticism and various non-fiction books, and has been published in twenty languages.

Critical Analysis

His first spy novel, which can also be described as a conspiracy story, was the sensational *The Manchurian Candidate*. It was made into a highly successful film and said by many to have provided the inspiration for the assassination of President Kennedy in 1963. This focused public attention on the techniques of brain-washing and its potential power as a political weapon. Condon said: "I wrote the novel back from the last scene to the beginning to make sure I included all conveyances to get the book where it should be going". It is a fascinating and exciting story.

Winter Kills is another controversial novel which closely parallels the lives of members of the Kennedy family. The main character, Nick Thirkield, is the half brother of a young, Liberal Irish president assassinated by a lone maniac. The assassin is caught and charged with the murder, but when Thirkield learns that another man may be involved, he re-opens the case.

The film of this book played for three weeks, and instead of going on into the circuit, it disappeared. Condon said in 1986: "The reason it disappeared was that the Kennedy family didn't want it played. I thought hard about what I would do in the same situation. The company that distributed the film did 890 million dollars a year with the defense department in arms procurement. All you have to do is have the senator's third assistant call and say that the senator is very unhappy about this film. It just vanished."

In *The Whisper of the Axe* Condon presents a complex plot involving a scheme to trigger off "the Final American Revolution" of the nation. It introduces as characters a black woman terrorist and an incestuous brother and sister working for the CIA, secret training camps in China, heroin-running and brain-washing once more. Condon has commented: "Every book I've ever written has been about abuse of power. I feel very strongly about that. I'd like people to know how deeply their politicians are wronging them."

Films

The Manchurian Candidate. United Artists, US, 1962.
Winter Kills. Avco Embassy Pictures, US, 1979.

Teodor Jósef Konrad Korzeniowski
Joseph Conrad

British. Born near Mohilow, Poland, 3 December 1857. Died in Bishopsbourne, Kent, 3 August 1924.

Titles

The Secret Agent. London, Harper, 1907; New York, Harper, 1907.
Under Western Eyes. London, Harper, 1911; New York, Harper, 1911.

Biography

Conrad was of Polish parentage. His father was an ardent Polish patriot who became involved in the rising against the Russian authorities in 1862. As a result of this the family were exiled to Vologda. The family spent a few years travelling across Russia, before settling in Austrian Galicia. Conrad studied in Cracow before deciding in 1872 that he wanted a career at sea. He went to Marseilles, became a registered seaman with the French Merchant Navy and after eleven years' service held the rank of first mate. In 1886 he became a naturalised British subject, taking the name of Joseph Conrad.

He began his first story in 1889, but it was not until 1895 that *Almayer's Folly* was published, and this was followed by other works based on his sea experiences — *An Outcast of the Islands* (1896), *The Nigger of the 'Narcissus'* (1897). Success and acknowledgement of his undoubted genius came with *Lord Jim* (1900).

In the First World War Conrad raised funds for refugees from his native Poland and, coincidentally, was one of the few, if not the only author who went to sea in the Royal Navy's "spy ships". These were Q-ships, disguised merchantmen with hidden guns, intended to lure submarines to the surface and their destruction.

Critical Analysis

Conrad turned from tales of the sea to his experiences as a boy in Russia for his two ventures into what might fairly be described as spy stories — *The Secret Agent* and *Under Western Eyes*. Though the background of each owes much to his early years of banishment to Russia and some knowledge of the revolutionary movement in that country, then almost entirely underground, Conrad seems to have acquired a good deal of first-hand information about Russian revolutionaries and anarchists in exile while a seaman.

Many of the anarchists maintained links with the Polish community in clubs around London's dockland and between 1900 and the Siege of Sidney Street in 1910 there was considerable activity among the Russian revolutionaries and anarchists in this area. From this point *The Secret Agent* was topical; indeed, it anticipated the Siege of Sidney Street. Conrad told of an attempted anarchist plot set in the unfashionable environment of Greenwich Park, the details of which closely resemble similar plots and counter-plots between revolutionaries in the East End of London in that period. This book was dramatised in 1922.

In *Under Western Eyes* Conrad becomes the first serious writer to deal effectively with the double-agent. But it could be said that Conrad was writing with burning sincerity and seriousness rather than to entertain; his spies were not characters intended to amuse, but were symbols of what Conrad regarded as the essential evil of revolution. Some critics, notably Julian Symons, feel that Conrad's two novels should not be described as spy novels. Nevertheless, Conrad should be included as an effective contributor to this genre, because of the accuracy of his background (an unusual characteristic in the days of Oppenheim and Le Queux), and because for the first time the double-agent emerges clearly.

BOB COOK

British. Born in Rome, Italy, 22 November 1961.

Titles

[Major character: Michael Wyman]
Disorderly Elements. London, Gollancz, 1985; New York, St. Martin's Press, 1987.
Questions of Identity. London, Gollancz, 1987.
Faceless Mortals. London, Gollancz, 1988.
Paper Chase. London, Gollancz, 1989.

Biography

Bob Cook has travelled widely and was educated in Italy, Australia and England. He read Classics at Cambridge University, where he developed an interest in ancient and modern philosophy. After university he took a variety of jobs, including barman, waiter, insurance clerk, warehouse manager in a clothing company and general factotum in a London despatch company. He now writes full time.

Critical Analysis

In *Disorderly Elements* Michael Wyman, 56 years old, is a fellow of an Oxbridge College and an operative with MI6. After swingeing government cuts in public spending, Wyman is deprived of his fellowship and made redundant by MI6. Neither employer will give him a pension. At the same time his girlfriend discovers that she is expecting his child. Things seem unable to get any worse, but they do: Wyman discovers that there is an infiltrator in MI6. Despite his employers' scepticism, Wyman is determined to expose the leak — but time is running very short ...

This is a very funny novel and is delightful in the way it attacks politics, espionage, university bureaucracy and the English in general — nobody and nothing is sacred. Even the KGB major encountered has a sense of humour, albeit a limited one! This novel was well received in Britain and America; one critic in the *Glasgow Herald* described it as "witty, offtaking and echoing the restless native's scepticism about international espionage."

Another critic, Newgate Callendar of the *New York Times Book Review* wrote: "The writing is unusually alert, and it is hard to believe that *Disorderly Elements* is a first novel. Mr Cook's 56-year-old Michael Wyman is one of the more unusual heroes in espionage fiction, and he is skilfully and sympathetically drawn. Equally realistic are the Russian and American agents. Most of the other people in the book are deliberate caricatures ..."

Disorderly Elements is due to be filmed for television.

In Cook's second novel, *Questions of Identity*, we follow Michael Wyman to Rome where he is a Professor of Philosophy at the university. Once more he becomes involved in the slings and arrows of espionage when a bacteriologist is kidnapped by Red Brigade terrorists who threaten to arrange a mass poisoning of the population.

The author himself says: "I write spy novels because I'm no good at anything else." He sees spy fiction as "a means of arousing other people's interest in the things which interest me, but this goes beyond the business of espionage and politics."

In reply to a question about favourite themes in his books he said: "I am interested in ideas, and how abstruse theories and dogmas (e.g. revolutionary Marxism or radical Monetarism) are translated into concrete actions which affect people's lives. I also have a deep-seated distrust and dislike of people who wield authority, and this attitude permeates just about everything I write."

JAMES FENIMORE COOPER

American. Born in Burlington, New Jersey, 15 September 1789. Died in Cooperstown, New York, 14 September 1851.

Titles

The Spy: A Tale of the Neutral Ground. Philadelphia, Carey, Lea & Carey, 1821.

Biography

James Fenimore Cooper was the son of William Cooper, a prosperous Quaker businessman and the founder of the settlement known as Cooperstown in central New York State. He was educated at a school in Albany, New York, and later at Yale University, from which he was expelled for a youthful escapade.

For three years Cooper was a midshipman in the US Navy, mainly serving in patrol vessels on the Great Lakes. It is possible that he may have become interested or even involved in espionage at this time, as a primitive form of intelligence-gathering was carried out along the Great Lakes and there is an historical note of spy work prior to the Battle of Lake Erie in 1812.

In 1811 Cooper resigned his commission and started writing. In 1826 he went to live in Paris, continuing to write, but later becoming US Consul in Lyon. He was an early advocate of the establishment of a Department of Naval Intelligence in the US Navy, the history of which he wrote. But the American Office of Naval Intelligence was not established until 1882. Cooper's latter years were disturbed by fierce controversies over his outspoken criticisms of American government, and he was involved in various lawsuits in which he was the victor.

Critical Analysis

Cooper's first real writing success came with the publication of *The Spy* in 1821, which Julian Symons has described as "the first spy novel known to me". This was a book that combined adventure, espionage and romance. It was far from being the best of Cooper's works, but its setting of the War of Independence made it highly popular. The spy in this instance was, of course, totally different from the fictional spies who followed at the end of the century. Cooper dealt with espionage in strictly military terms, thus camouflaging the moral dilemmas of spying; nevertheless, he gave the spy hero, Harvey Birch, sympathetic handling.

David John Moore Cornwell
Pseudonym: John le Carré
British. Born in Poole, Dorset, 19 October 1931.

Titles
[Major character: George Smiley]
Call for the Dead [Smiley]. London, Gollancz, 1961; New York, Walker, 1962.
A Murder of Quality [Smiley]. London, Gollancz, 1962; New York, Walker, 1963.
The Spy Who Came in from the Cold [Smiley]. London, Gollancz, 1963; New York, Coward McCann, 1964.
The Looking-Glass War. London, Heinemann, 1965; New York, Coward McCann, 1965.
A Small Town in Germany. London, Heinemann, 1968; New York, Coward McCann, 1968.
Tinker, Tailor, Soldier, Spy [Smiley]. London, Hodder & Stoughton, 1974; New York, Knopf, 1974.
The Honourable Schoolboy [Smiley]. London, Hodder & Stoughton, 1977; New York, Knopf, 1977.
Smiley's People [Smiley]. London, Hodder & Stoughton, 1980; New York, Knopf, 1980.
The Little Drummer Girl. London, Hodder & Stoughton, 1983; New York, Knopf, 1983.
A Perfect Spy. London, Hodder & Stoughton, 1986; New York, Knopf, 1986.
The Russia House. London, Hodder & Stoughton, 1989; New York, Knopf, 1989.

Biography

After attending Sherborne School, Berne University and Lincoln College, Oxford, he started his career as a tutor at Eton in 1956, teaching French and German. He then joined the Foreign Office which we now know covered his intelligence activities. For five years, 1959 to 1964, le Carré was directly involved in secret intelligence work. From 1960 to 1963 this was under the guise of second secretary at the British Embassy in Bonn, and in 1964 as British consul in Hamburg.

Critical Analysis

John le Carré began his writing career while he was still working at the British Embassy in Bonn, West Germany. His first two novels, *Call for the Dead* and *A Murder of Quality*, were more or less straightforward detective stories, but they did serve to introduce his famous character, George Smiley, who acted more like a detective than a secret agent. His third novel, *The Spy Who Came in from the Cold*, became a best-seller and made him famous as one of the main practitioners of spy fiction, a position he still holds today. *The Spy* brought a new vitality and literary style to the spy novel. Graham Greene described it as "the best spy story I have ever read," while J B Priestley paid the tribute that the story was "superbly constructed with an atmosphere of chilly hell."

The Spy won le Carré the Crime Writers Association Gold Dagger Award in 1963, the Somerset Maugham Award in 1964, and an Edgar from the Mystery Writers of America in 1965. The popularity of this novel can be partly attributed to the fact that it was so very different, in style and content, from the escapades of James Bond. But its success was also due to the new realism le Carré brought to the spy novel. In *The Spy* and his subsequent stories the Cold War is presented in a grey, menacing light; espionage is depicted as a sordid occupation, and the people involved are of questionable morals.

One critic, George Grella, stated in the *New Republic*: "More than any other writer, le Carré has established the spy as an appropriate figure and espionage as an appropriate activity for our time, providing both symbol and metaphor to explain contemporary history."

The Spy is centred around the character, Alec Leamas, a fifty-year-old British intelligence agent, who wishes to retire from active duties. But he is persuaded to take one last assignment before leaving. He pretends to defect to the East and gives false information to the East Germans in order to implicate one of their high-ranking intelligence officials. Leamas soon realises that the information he has supplied has framed one official while protecting the identity of the real British spy.

Many critics have seen the work of John le Carré as an obvious reaction to the cult of James Bond, but the author himself denies this. It was not so much that he despised Bond, but that Fleming's stories left a "black hole", or a vacuum, that his novels were able to fill.

One critic, Julian Symons, wrote that "Fleming represented a mood rather than *the* mood of the period in Britain ... *The Spy Who Came in from the Cold* (1963) found a response almost equal to that roused by the Bond books, although of a different kind. The Bond stories were enjoyed as pipedreams, le Carré's for their approach to reality."

Le Carré belongs to the second tradition of spy fiction — the realistic approach, first adopted by Erskine Childers, and continuing with the novels of Maugham, Ambler and Greene. Although le Carré's style and treatment are similar to his predecessors, his material, Symons says, is "firmly rooted in the revelations about

Soviet agents that shook Britain in the fifties." A factor which is most obvious in the novels he wrote in the mid-1970s.

Another similarity that le Carré shared with some of his literary predecessors, and which brings further authenticity to his novels, is that now he admits to have worked for the British Secret Service. Far from hindering his writing this experience has further enhanced his reputation as one of the best authors of this kind of literature.

Trevor Royle recently commented in an essay in *The Quest for le Carré* (1988), that this author "has been drawn to the idea of espionage and in so doing has helped his readership to a better understanding of its many complexities. He may have played at being a spy through his fiction, but like all the best writers that fascination has only fuelled his literary output."

The Looking-Glass War also explores the intrigues of Intelligence Services. It begins with the death of a courier who had been sent to Finland to collect films taken by a commercial pilot who had, ostensibly, flown off course while over East Germany. Orders are given for planting an agent in this territory where, it is suspected, a new type of rocket site is being set up. Le Carré is at his best describing the plans for this operation, the recruitment of the agent, his training and briefing and the cynical, inhuman professionalism of the executive planners. Here is espionage in a team which lacks all *esprit de corps*, but which can cold-bloodedly plan the disavowal of an agent once it becomes clear that his slow transmission on single frequencies on an obsolete radio make his capture inevitable.

A Small Town in Germany is set in the British Embassy in Bonn. In this story a British diplomat, Leo Harting, disappears with very sensitive documents which may damage Britain's chances of joining the Common Market. Alan Turner is ordered to investigate his disappearance and discovers that Harting was amassing evidence that could damage and destroy the political structure of West Germany.

In *Tinker, Tailor, Soldier, Spy*, le Carré begins a loosely connected trilogy, in which George Smiley is pitted against the Russian master spy Karla. This story concerns finding the mole, deciding which of four men is the double-agent at the centre of British Intelligence. In order to do this Smiley goes back through the records of intelligence operations to try to detect a pattern of failures that could be attributed to the machinations of a particular agent.

Smiley's battle against the Russian Karla continue in *The Honourable Schoolboy*, which is set in Hong Kong, where British Intelligence is investigating a prosperous businessman who seems to be working for the Soviets. The central character is Jerry Westerby (although his actions are directed by Smiley), who wants to identify one of Karla's moles, who is working inside Communist China, and capture him for the West.

The trilogy ends with *Smiley's People* — the last confrontation between Smiley and Karla. Smiley decides to force his enemy out into the open so that his only choice is to defect to the West. This operation is conducted unofficially because the British Secret Service, due to political pressure, cannot be involved in an offensive intelligence operation. It becomes instead a personal mission for Smiley and his friends and espionage contacts that he has accumulated over the years. In a review of *Smiley's People* in *The Observer*, A Alvarez remarks: "A genre is as good and deep and flexible as the author who uses it, and le Carré is a very gifted author indeed. So maybe for once literary chic will not prevail; *Smiley's People* will not be condescended to because it gives pleasure and will not let the reader go."

The three novels which make up the Karla trilogy are very much dominated by le Carré's fascination with the history of British Intelligence in the 1950s, and in particular, the treachery of Kim Philby, which is reflected in his fiction. In each novel Smiley sets out to discover information that will entrap the Soviet masterspy, Karla. But somehow this quest appears irrelevant compared to the information that Smiley discovers on the way; in particular, the uncovering of the mole in the British Secret Service. Every action and thought before and after this discovery, called "the Fall" in the novels, seems to permeate the fictional world presented to us.

Le Carré's fascination with the real-life spies within the British Secret Service reaches beyond his fiction — many of his views and opinions can be found in his introduction to *The Philby Conspiracy* (1968) by Bruce Page, David Leitch and Philip Knightley.

Miles Copeland, a shrewd commentator on the world of intelligence (in which, on the American side, he has served), says that le Carré is the favourite writer of British "spooks": "They like the way he captures the mood of their world, its internal rivalries and the personal problems that get tangled up with their professional lives." However, le Carré does not have the same attraction for a number of American intelligence professionals. For instance, Richard Helms, declared in his biography by Thomas Powers, that the novel, *The Spy*, was " a bitter and cynical story of violence, betrayal, and spiritual exhaustion. It was not just the violence Helms minded, but the betrayal, the mood of defeat, the meanness, the numb loneliness of a man for whom loyalty had become a joke."

In *The Little Drummer Girl* le Carré turns to the Middle East as the setting for his novel. There is a great deal more action in the story than is usual in a le Carré novel, and there is also a female protagonist, who is recruited by the Israelis to infiltrate a Palestinian terrorist group and set up its leader for assassination. One critic has written that "Without condoning terrorism, the book makes the reasons for it understandable — perhaps the first popular novel to do so."

Le Carré's recent novel *The Perfect Spy* describes the life of a British Intelligence officer and how he became a double-agent. This book contains a great deal of biographical material from the author's life, in particular his relationship with his father. As a result, it is highly introspective, and does not contain much activity. What action there is is described in a sequence of flashbacks in the life of Magnus Pym.

Le Carré's latest book, *The Russia House*, concerns a derelict English publisher who becomes the unlikely recipient of some of the hottest defence secrets to come out of the Soviet Union for years.

Films

The Spy Who Came in from the Cold. Paramount, GB, 1966.
The Looking-Glass War. Columbia, GB, 1969.
The Little Drummer Girl. Warner, US, 1984.

Television

"Tinker, Tailor, Soldier, Spy" and "Smiley's People" produced as a series by the BBC in Britain in 1980, and broadcast by PBS in America in 1981.
" The Perfect Spy" was serialised in Britain in 1987.

STEPHEN COULTER

Pseudonym: JAMES MAYO
British. Born in 1914.

Titles

The Loved Enemy. London, Deutsch, 1962.
Threshold. London, Heinemann, 1964; New York, Morrow, 1964.
Offshore! London, Heinemann, 1965; New York, Morrow, 1966.
A Stranger Called the Blues. London, Heinemann, 1968; as *Players in a Dark Game*. New York, Morrow, 1968.
Embassy. London, Heinemann, 1969; New York, Coward McCann, 1969.
An Account to Render. London, Heinemann, 1970.
The Soyuz Affair. London, Hart-Davis, 1977.

Novels as James Mayo
[Major character: Charles Hood]
Hammerhead. London, Heinemann, 1964; New York, Morrow, 1964.
Let Sleeping Girls Lie. London, Heinemann, 1965; New York, Morrow, 1966.
Shamelady. London, Heinemann, 1966; New York, Morrow, 1966.
Once in a Lifetime. London, Heinemann, 1968; as *Sergeant Death*. New York, Morrow, 1968.
The Man above Suspicion. London, Heinemann, 1969.
Asking for It. London, Heinemann, 1971.

Biography

Stephen Coulter was educated in Britain and France, and studied in Paris in the early 1930s. He began his career as a newspaperman in the British home counties where, he says, "I was expected to do everything from reporting to making up and sometimes had to drive the delivery vans." He has travelled widely and in 1937 joined Reuters News Agency as one of their Parliamentary staff correspondents.

During the war he served in the Royal Navy and was appointed one of General Eisenhower's staff officers at Supreme Headquarters, assigned to special intelligence work in France and Scandinavia. His work carried him to Paris just after the Liberation and for more than twenty years after the war he was staff correspondent for Kemsley Newspapers, including the *Sunday Times*, in Paris.

One of the interesting sidelines of Coulter's career is that, but for his expertise and research, Ian Fleming might never have been able to write the casino scenes in *Casino Royale*. It was Coulter who provided the background to casino know-how and so saved Fleming from possibly dropping the whole idea. From then on Coulter saw the light and started to write seriously and furiously on his own account.

Critical Analysis

Apart from an admirable study in fiction of the passionate life of Guy de Maupassant, *Damned Shall Be Desire* (1958), Coulter also produced spy fiction under his own name and his pseudonym of James Mayo.

A Stranger Called the Blues was the story of tough American Ed Murray, who is unwillingly sent to Calcutta, smuggles in Nepal, and has a confrontation with the Chinese on the Nepalese border, during all of which he is haunted by an English nanny. One critic said about this book that the "background is so good, it gives you prickly heat."

Embassy contains a more complicated plot in which a French national is murdered in the United States' Paris Embassy and the Embassy officials try to slip the killer away; handing him over to the French authorities would risk the exposure of a far more important second man, a high-ranking Russian under guard in one of the Embassy rooms.

Under the name of James Mayo, Coulter wrote a series of novels featuring the character Charles Hood, who is tall, handsome and cosmopolitan. On the surface Hood appears to be a wealthy dealer in objets d'art, but on occasion he works on British government missions for Special Intelligence. Hood, introduced in *Hammerhead*, is based upon James Bond, but these books are more violent.

The American critic, Anthony Boucher, in discussing the second novel of this series wrote: "*Let Sleeping Girls Lie* has loads of sex, sadism and snobbery, and no sense at all of plot or structure; and Charles Hood's performance as a secret agent makes James Bond look realistic and intelligent."

JOHN CREASEY

Pseudonyms: GORDON ASHE, M E COOKE, MARGARET COOKE, HENRY ST JOHN COOPER, NORMAN DEANE, ELISE FECAMPS, ROBERT CAINE FRAZER, PATRICK GILL, MICHAEL HALLIDAY, CHARLES HOGARTH, BRIAN HOPE, COLIN HUGHES, KYLE HUNT, ABEL MANN, PETER MANTON, J J MARIC, JAMES MARSDEN, RICHARD MARTIN, RODNEY MATTHESON, ANTHONY MORTON, KEN RANGER, WILLIAM K REILLY, TEX RILEY, JEREMY YORK.

British. Born in London, 17 September 1908. Died in Wiltshire, 9 June 1973.

Titles

[Major character: Department Z]
Redhead. London, Hurst & Blackett, 1933.
The Death Miser. London, Melrose, 1933.
First Came A Murder. London, Melrose, 1934.
Death Round the Corner. London, Melrose, 1935.
The Mark of the Crescent. London, Melrose, 1935.
Thunder in Europe. London, Melrose, 1936.
The Terror Trap. London, Melrose, 1936.
Carriers of Death. London, Melrose, 1937.
Days of Danger. London, Melrose, 1937.
Death Stands By. London, Long, 1938.
(18 more titles featuring Department Z)

[Major character: Dr Palfrey]
Traitors' Doom. London, Long, 1942; New York, Walker, 1970.
The Legion of the Lost. London, Long, 1943; New York, Daye, 1944.
The Valley of Fear. London, Long, 1943.
Death in the Rising Sun. London, Long, 1945.
The Hounds of Vengeance. London, Long, 1945.
Shadow of Doom. London, Long, 1946.

The House of the Bears. London, Long, 1946.
Dark Harvest. London, Long, 1947.
The Wings of Peace. London, Long, 1948.
Sons of Satan. London, Long, 1948.
(21 more titles featuring Dr Palfrey)

Novels as Norman Deané
[Major character: Bruce Murdoch]
Secret Errand. London, Hurst & Blackett, 1939; New York, McKay, 1974.
Dangerous Journey. London, Hurst & Blackett, 1939; New York, McKay, 1974.
Unknown Mission. London, Hurst & Blackett, 1940.
The Withered Man. London, Hurst & Blackett, 1940; New York, McKay, 1974.
I Am the Withered Man? London, Hurst & Blackett, 1941.
Where is the Withered Man? London, Hurst & Blackett, 1941.

Novels as Gordon Ashe
[Major character: Patrick Dawlish]
Death on Demand. London, Long, 1939.
The Speaker. London, Long, 1939; as *The Croaker*. New York, Holt Rinehart, 1972.
Who Was the Jester? London, Newnes, 1940.
Terror By Day. London, Long, 1940.
Secret Murder. London, Long, 1940.
'Ware Danger. London, Long, 1941.
Murder Most Foul. London, Long, 1942.
There Goes Death. London, Long, 1942.
Death in High Places. London, Long, 1942.
Death in Flames. London, Long, 1943.
(43 more titles featuring Patrick Dawlish)

Biography
One of the ablest writers of crime fiction, John Creasey was educated at Fulham Elementary School and Sloane School, Chelsea. After taking various clerical posts, he began writing in 1925. His first book, *Seven Times Seven* (1932), was a racy and amusing story of a gang of crooks. When he died he had written 562 books with worldwide sales of more than 80 million copies in 28 different languages. This phenomenal literary feat was achieved by using 24 pseudonyms.

In 1950 Creasey stood as a Liberal Party candidate at Bournemouth and then in 1967 he founded the All Party Alliance in England, a political movement advocating government by the best men from all the parties working together. He fought four by-elections in 1967-68 for APA, once getting 14% of the votes cast. Creasey's astonishing output was fully maintained until his death.

Critical Analysis
With the approach of the Second World War Creasey devoted more attention to developing the spy novel rather than his straightforward crime and police stories. His Department Z stories had espionage in Britain as a common theme. The Department leader, Gordon Craigie, used a surprising variety of patriotic and intrepid agents whose sole purpose was to guard the nation's interests. Creasey's earlier works in this genre had dealt with the pre-war scene and some of them,

notably *The Mark of the Crescent* (1935), proved remarkably prophetic.

Under the pseudonym of Norman Deane, Creasey wrote powerful wartime spy stories in the 1940s, one of which, *Withered Man*, was told through the eyes of a Nazi Secret Service agent, with astonishing realism. In 1938 Creasey created his character Patrick Dawlish (who was somewhat in the Bulldog Drummond tradition), written under the name of Gordon Ashe. When war came Creasey made Dawlish a powerful figure in MI5, but really he should more appropriately have been either MI6 or the SOE, as time and again Dawlish was dropped into occupied Europe, organising resistance against the Nazis.

Another spy fiction character of Creasey's was his highly successful Dr Palfrey, the leader of an Allied Secret Service whose members owed loyalty to the corporate body of Western Allies, not to any individual nation.

Norman James Crisp

British. Born in Southampton, 1923.

Titles

The Gotland Deal. Viking, 1976; London, Futura, 1977.
The London Deal. New York, St. Martin's Press, 1979.
The Odd Job Man. London, Macdonald & Jane's, 1977; New York, St. Martin's Press, 1979.
A Family Affair. London, Macdonald & Jane's, 1979.
In the Long Run. London, Piatkus, 1988.
Ninth Circle. London, Piatkus, 1988.

Biography

N J Crisp attended grammar school in Southampton. He served in the Royal Air Force as a pilot during the Second World War until 1947. After this he had various jobs in administration and sales. Since 1959 he has been a full-time writer.

Critical Analysis

The author has stated: "I write fiction, and I dislike the present day urge to imply that there is always some real life event or experience behind a story. Whatever happened to the art of imaginative writing, of invention, of fictional truth?"

His novel, *The Odd Job Man*, is the story of George Griffin, an encyclopaedia salesman, who does "odd jobs" for whoever has the money to keep him in the style to which he has become accustomed. These extra jobs keep him in gin and money for entertaining his girlfriends. When we encounter Griffin he is in the middle of a job that turns rather sour — under the misapprehension that he is working for the CIA he is told to pick up and deliver a potential defector. When Griffin eventually finds out that his boss is not with the CIA he tries to get out of trouble by doing an exchange with British Intelligence, but his moves are anticipated and Griffin finds himself in very hot water.

Clive Eric Cussler

American. Born in Aurora, Illinois, 15 July 1931.

Titles

[Major character: Dirk Pitt]
The Mediterranean Caper. New York, Pyramid, 1973.
Iceberg. New York, Dodd Mead, 1975; London, Severn, 1986.
Raise the Titanic. New York, Viking, 1976.
Vixen 03. New York, Viking, 1978; London, Sphere, 1979.
Night Probe. New York, Bantam, 1981; London, Sphere, 1982.
Pacific Vortex! New York, Bantam, 1983; London, Piatkus, 1983.
Deep Six. New York, Simon & Schuster, 1984; London, Hamish Hamilton, 1984.
Mayday! London, Severn, 1985.
Cyclops. New York, Simon & Schuster, 1986; London, Sphere, 1987.
Treasure. London, Grafton, 1988.

Biography

Clive Cussler was educated at the Pasadena City College, 1949-51, the Orange Coast College and California State University, Los Angeles. From 1961 to 1975 he has worked in his own and for other advertising agencies. In 1978 he founded the National Underwater and Marine Agency in Washington DC, and is currently the chairman.

Critical Analysis

Cussler has written ten novels to date, which include the bestsellers *Raise the Titanic*, *Night Probe* and *Deep Six*. Although at times the characters appear to be one-dimensional, his stories of espionage and political intrigue are exciting, and the descriptions of deep-sea exploration are imaginative and full of suspense. His novels have been translated into seventeen foreign languages.

All these novels feature Dirk Pitt, who works as a marine expert for NUMA, the National Underwater and Marine Agency, which in reality the author founded. Cussler uses the royalty payments from his books to fund his expeditions.

One of his later novels, *Deep Six*, is about a deadly poison discovered off the coast of Alaska. With the aid of Dirk Pitt the poison is contained, but some of his friends have been killed by the poison. Pitt swears his revenge. At the same time the Presidential yacht has disappeared with the President, Vice-President and two influential congressman on board — and the government is desperate to find them. Pitt's search for those responsible for the poison leads him to a huge South Korean shipping company whose owners are also holding the President captive and subjecting him to mind control, so that ultimately the Russians can direct American policy. Chris Wall, writing in the *Los Angeles Times Book Review*, comments that the author "knows commercial values when he writes them, and, like his *Raise the Titanic*, *Deep Six* manages to keep the pages turning."

Cussler said in a recent interview in the *Chicago Tribune*: "I look upon myself not so much as a writer as I do an entertainer ... It's my job to entertain the reader in such a way that he or she feels that they got their money's worth when they finish the book."

Film
Raise the Titanic. AFD, US, 1980.

LEONARD CYRIL DEIGHTON
British. Born in London, 18 February 1929.

Titles
The Ipcress File. London, Hodder & Stoughton, 1962; New York, Simon & Schuster, 1963.
Horse Under Water. London, Cape, 1963; New York, Putnam, 1968.
Funeral in Berlin. London, Cape, 1964; New York, Putnam, 1965.
The Billion Dollar Brain. London, Cape, 1966; New York, Putnam, 1966.
An Expensive Place to Die. London, Cape, 1967; New York, Putnam, 1967.
Spy Story. London, Cape, 1974; New York, Harcourt Brace, 1974.
Yesterday's Spy. London, Cape, 1975; New York, Harcourt Brace, 1975.
Twinkle, Twinkle, Little Spy. London, Cape, 1976; as *Catch a Falling Spy*. New York, Harcourt Brace, 1976.
XPD. London, Hutchinson, 1981; New York, Knopf, 1981.
Berlin Game. London, Hutchinson, 1983; New York, Knopf, 1984.
Mexico Set. London, Hutchinson, 1984; New York, Knopf, 1985.
London Match. London, Hutchinson, 1985; New York, Knopf, 1986.
Spy Hook. London, Hutchinson, 1988.

Biography
Len Deighton was educated at Marylebone Grammar School, St. Martin's School of Art and the Royal College of Art in London. When he left school he began work as a railway clerk before doing his National Service in the RAF. While he was an art student Deighton worked as a waiter in London and it was probably at this time that he developed an interest in cookery, on which he has written many books. For a while he also worked as an illustrator in New York and as art director of an advertising agency in London. Then, deciding it was time to settle down, Deighton plunged into writing, going to the Dordogne where he started *The Ipcress File*.

Critical Analysis
Deighton has established himself as one of the major practitioners of spy fiction along with Graham Greene, John le Carré and Ian Fleming. His novels are praised for their sense of realism and their portrayal of espionage, and the author's ability to describe different locations, qualities partly achieved by Deighton's extensive research.

Since the publication of The *Ipcress File* he has written twenty-five books of fiction and non-fiction — including the spy novels listed above, as well as highly researched war novels and histories, all of which have appeared to international acclaim.

The hero of *The Ipcress File* plays a part in the rescue of a biochemist who has been abducted to the Lebanon en route to the Soviet Union. There is a fascinating account of affairs in the Soho offices of WOOC(P), a small but important Intelligence Unit, and Deighton gave a new twist to the spy story when, at the end of the book, the chief enemy agent is paid £160,000 to change sides and start up a new little Intelligence Unit.

The Ipcress File was an instant success. "Better than Fleming", said some critics, though it must be admitted this was more due to their dislike of Fleming than their love for Deighton. The book was serialised in the *London Evening Standard* and the film rights were sold soon afterwards. This book introduced a character who was nameless, but he also had a social anonymity — that of a working-class boy from Burnley suddenly precipitated into a strange new world of intrigue among people out of his class whom he did not trust. This background gave Deighton's hero an unusual appeal as well as an added feeling of identification.

T J Binyon wrote in the *Times Literary Supplement* that "The creation of this slightly anarchic, wise-cracking, working-class hero, ... was Deighton's most original contribution to the spy thriller. And this, taken together with his characteristic highly elliptical expositional manner, with his fascination with the technical nuts and bolts of espionage, and with a gift for vivid, startling description, make the first seven [of Deighton's spy] stories classics of the genre."

Deighton's reputation as a spy fiction writer was enhanced by *Funeral in Berlin*, which is about an attempt to smuggle a defecting East German biologist out of Berlin. With the help of a high-ranking Russian agent, former Nazi intelligence officers and a freelance agent of doubtful allegiance, Deighton's hero arranges the details of the defection. The plot has many twists which while entertaining many readers with its intrigues, also annoyed many critics, for as one of them put it "Deighton's prose is elliptical. It needs to be sipped slowly to be appreciated, rather like Yellow Chartreuse." This story also enabled the author to indulge in his love of gimmickry, in entertaining his readers with odd items of erudition of a technical kind, such as how to tap a telephone and what RI and D of C codes were, in providing footnotes and appendices such as the spy novel had never had before. Like le Carré, who started writing at the same time, they were both responsible for educating the public about the realities of espionage, in a far more entertaining and subtle way than had been done before or since.

In later novels Deighton seems to have matured and his approach has become more sophisticated, relying less upon the gimmickry of espionage. In 1983 he started a trilogy which began with the publication of *Berlin Game*, and was followed by *Mexico Set* and *London Match*. These books introduced Bernard Samson, a man in the same mould as Deighton's earlier hero. Although older and more cynical, he shares a healthy disrespect for his superiors and his colleagues who dare to have ambitions.

The first novel of this trilogy begins with two agents waiting near the Berlin wall for a defector to cross over from East Berlin. "Brahms Four", the best source the Department ever had, is the last surviving agent of the Brahms spy network. He wants to get out but he is afraid that he will be betrayed by a high-ranking mole in the Department. He will trust only one man — Samson — to come and get him out. So after five years behind a desk in London, Samson is returned to the field — to Berlin, the city where he grew up and the only place where he feels at home.

Anthony Olcott in the *Washington Post Book World* judges *Berlin Game* to be "among Deighton's best books" because "his Berlin, his characters, the smallest details of his narrative are so sharp." Olcott concludes that it is "a book to strip away the age-withered, custom-staled betrayals of all that quarter century of novels, perhaps even of history, and once again make painful, real, alive, the meaning of treason."

In the second book, *Mexico Set*, the story continues and although Samson has uncovered the spy in British Intelligence — his own wife — he allows her to escape, and because of the proximity of the betrayal he is naturally suspected by his superiors. To test his loyalty he is sent to Mexico where he tries to persuade a Russian KGB agent, Erich Stinnes, to defect. Attempts to "enrol" Stinnes takes Samson from London to Mexico, Paris and Berlin. The book ends with an exciting climax in which the amateurs and the desk men try to take an active part in Stinnes' defection and it erupts into a violent confrontation. Ironically Stinnes is not involved physically in this scene, but he is the catalyst that brings them together. When Samson finally catches up with the Russian he asks Samson:

" 'What happened?'

'Nothing much,' I said. 'Moskvin's a desk man, is he?'

'Yes,' said Stinnes. 'And I hate desk men.'

'So do I,' I said feelingly. 'They're bloody dangerous.' "

In the final novel, *London Match*, the Russian has defected to the British. However, the debriefing is not going well and Stinnes insists on talking to Samson, who has to decide whether he is telling the truth when he says that there is another highly placed Russian spy in the Department, or whether Stinnes is a plant sent over to discredit him further.

Although Julius Lester wrote in the *New York Times Book Review* that *London Match* "is the most complex novel of the trilogy," he praises Deighton's descriptive powers and in his view "the best character" in the book is "the city of Berlin. It is a living presence, and in some of the descriptions one can almost hear the stones breathing."

Deighton's trilogy is an excellent example of the current obsession with moles, and the themes of treachery and betrayal in British and American spy fiction, but more so in British spy fiction, perhaps because we have more real-life examples to draw upon. Apart from Deighton's ability to surprise the reader, which is always refreshing, the characters in this trilogy are excellently portrayed from Samson to his childhood friend Werner Volkmann to the rather effete Dicky Cruyer.

Although we are shown the bureaucratic in-fighting in the Department, it is not a laboured ingredient to these stories. All the action is necessary to the plot; also underlying the novels there is always Deighton's humour and sarcasm which is provided by his character Samson. A sense of humour is always important, particularly in spy fiction, which has a tendency either to take itself too seriously or parody itself. Deighton manages to strike the right balance in his fiction, an ability that many of his fellow writers are unable to achieve.

Deighton has recently begun a new trilogy which again has Bernie Samson as the central character. The first of these is called *Spy Hook* and is to be followed by *Line and Sinker*. The story begins three years after the *London Match* has finished and Samson is still obsessed with his wife's betrayal.

James Adams in a review of *Spy Hook* in the *Sunday Times* wrote: "As always Deighton's laconic style captivates, while his impossibly complex plot leaves the reader baffled but intrigued. Like so many of Deighton's novels, there is the recurring theme of betrayal and failure which stops just short of the depressing."

Films

The Ipcress File. Rank, GB, 1965.
Funeral in Berlin. Paramount, GB, 1967.

Billion-Dollar Brain. United Artists, US, 1967.
Deighton's nameless British spy hero was given the name Harry Palmer in the film adaptations of his adventures.

Television
"Game, Set and Match" was made into a 13-part series by Granada Television and broadcast in 1988.

MICHAEL JOHN DELAHAYE
British. Born in Romsey, Hampshire, 6 April 1946.

Titles
The Sale of Lot 236. London, Constable, 1981.
The Third Day. London, Constable, 1984; as *On The Third Day*. New York, Macmillan, 1984.
Stalking-Horse. London, Constable, 1987; New York, Scribner's, 1988.

Biography
Michael Delahaye was educated at Barton Peveril Grammar School and Durham University. He worked as a teacher of English at the British Institute of Florence, Italy from 1968 to 1969. He joined the BBC in 1969 as a Graduate News Trainee and worked as the BBC Northern Industrialist Correspondent for radio and television from 1972 to 1975. He was a reporter for the BBC's "Tonight" programme, covering subjects such as elections, earthquakes, coup d'états and cover-ups, 1975–79. In 1979 he resigned from the BBC and decided to go freelance and write.

Since 1980 he has been a regular contributor to *The Listener* magazine, and a freelance broadcaster for such programmes as " Panorama", "Timewatch", "Bookmark", and "Friday Report". He is also a guest lecturer on broadcasting for the Institute of European Studies, London.

Critical Analysis
The author uses his experience as a reporter to research his books, and this is apparent in the information they contain. Delahaye's first novel, *The Sale of Lot 236*, can be described as more of a mystery than a spy story. It is about an English fresco expert working in Florence who is blackmailed by a gang of Italian crooks into helping them find an unknown crucifixion by Cimabue. T J Binyon in the *Times Literary Supplement* wrote: "The plot is as thick as a minestrone and as tangled as a plateful of spaghetti; narration is accomplished neatly and deftly; the whole spiced with some delightfully fascinating information on medieval Italian art, and on how best to remove a fresco from the wall of your local church." Christopher Wordsworth in *The Observer* described it as "A fine al dente debut."

The Third Day is set in 1989 and the new American president has threatened to withdraw all military and economic aid from Israel if the lands taken from the Arabs in 1967 are not returned. But the Israelis have a secret weapon, with which they can blackmail the Vatican who can in turn put pressure on the USA — they have found the skeleton of a man crucified in the first century AD. T J Binyon described it as a "more than competent thriller with a good, well-executed plot", while Christopher Lehmann-Haupt of the *New York Times* called it "compelling".

Delahaye's latest novel, *Stalking-Horse*, is about two separate stories that eventually link up to reveal a horrifying situation in which the United States and the Soviet Union are found collaborating on a grand scale. Adrian Medcalfe, an English deskman stationed at NATO headquarters in Brussels, is given a sensitive intelligence assignment in Bulgaria. Meanwhile, in Washington DC, Matthew Di Coiano, a specialist with the National Transportation and Safety Board (NTSB), is sent to investigate the crash of an airline jet with 254 passengers and crew aboard which crashed in the sea near Cape Cod.

Like his other books, this story has been well received in Britain and America. One reviewer in *Publisher's Weekly* wrote: "Remarkably, Delahaye has researched two different organizations — NATO and NTSB — in order to write this novel, yet written about both as if he were an insider. He shows a great gift for the most difficult tasks, gently yielding secrets as the plot unfolds and sustaining suspense throughout a tautly paced narrative." One reviewer in *Bloodhound* magazine described *Stalking-Horse* as such: "This is the conspiracy thriller at its best, a double-narrative game of nations with none of the usual sturm und drang of the paranoid potboiler. Instead, Michael Delahaye gives us tight plotting, credible characters, first-rate suspense and an impressive display of political and technical expertise."

ADAM DIMENT

Titles
[Major character: Philip McAlpine]
The Dolly Dolly Spy. London, Michael Joseph, 1967; New York, EP Dutton, 1967.
The Bang Bang Birds. London, Michael Joseph, 1968; New York, EP Dutton, 1968.
The Great Spy Race. London, Michael Joseph, 1968; New York, EP Dutton, 1968.
Think Inc. London, Michael Joseph, 1971.

Critical Analysis
As can be seen from the titles, these books were very much products of the 1960s — capitalizing upon the popularity of the spy in this period. Instead of copying James Bond, his hero Philip McAlpine appears more like his younger, hippy brother — he is a typical anti-establishment figure of the trendy sixties: long-haired, pot-smoking and only at home in a frilled shirt and white Levis.

He is blackmailed into working for Rupert "The Swine" Quine and his spy department. The kind of adventures McAlpine gets involved in are reminiscent of Bond. For instance in *The Bang Bang Birds* he is ordered to help his American colleagues check up on the Aviary Club in Sweden, which is virtually an advanced Playboy Club for spies. The series was not a great success and in the last novel, *Think Inc.*, we find McAlpine working as an international crook, running away from Quine, and trying to find his own feet.

GREGORY S DINALLO
American. Born in Brooklyn, New York, 22 March 1941.

Titles
Rockets Red Glare. New York, St. Martin's Press, 1988; London, WH Allen, 1988.

Biography
Greg Dinallo had a Roman Catholic grade school education, and obtained an undergraduate degree in Industrial Design at the Pratt Institute in New York in 1962. He worked as an exhibit and architectural designer on the 1964, 1967 and 1970 World Fairs. He designed many corporate and museum exhibits which led to an interest in film-making. He wrote, produced and directed exhibit and corporate films and began to write television dramas in 1975, of which he has written over 50 episodic television scripts and half a dozen movies for television.

Critical Analysis
Rockets Red Glare is the story of Andrew Churcher, the son of a missing Houston industrialist, who discovers a Soviet link to his father and becomes embroiled in a spy world gambit that could sabotage or guarantee Soviet missile supremacy. The plot is rooted in the Cuban missile crisis of 1962, although it is set in the present time. One critic described it as "A very fast paced novel of intrigue and super power brinkmanship. A real insight into the Soviet-American nuclear manoeuverings. Dinallo sets his characters racing through this jet-powered story." It is described as a techno-thriller by the publishers which seems to be a new sub-genre that is becoming more popular.

When asked if any of his fictional characters were based on real people, Dinallo replied "Not specifically, though a few might resemble real people. For example in *Rockets*, industrialist Theodore Churcher could be seen as a cross between Averil Harriman, Armand Hammer and Donald Trump — more like their evil twins."

Dinallo has had no experience in intelligence but he says "the vast amount of source material in this area is certainly helpful in producing realistic works."

KEVIN DOHERTY
British. Born in Ballymoney, Northern Ireland, 1949.

Titles
A Long Day's Dying. London, Sidgwick & Jackson, 1988.

Biography
Kevin Doherty was born and brought up in Ballymoney, a small town fifty miles north of Belfast. His mother was Protestant and his father Roman Catholic. At the age of eleven he was sent to a Roman Catholic boarding school in Belfast, and later went to Belfast University, before moving to England to begin a career in advertising and marketing.

He has worked for and been a director of a number of major British and international companies, including British American Tobacco, Grand Metropolitan and Coca Cola. He now works for Bulmer's in Herefordshire, after taking a year off to write *A Long Day's Dying*.

Critical Analysis

A Long Day's Dying is Doherty's first novel and is the story about what could happen as the exposure of corruption in Moscow bites deeper, and sends high-ranking officials running for cover. One of these is Nikolai Serov, head of the KGB's First Chief Directorate. Not only is he one of Moscow's leading black marketeers and drug kings, he also possesses information so secret that if it were exposed, world peace would be threatened. As Serov acts to avoid his fate, a complex chain of murder and betrayal is triggered that will change lives forever on both sides of the Iron Curtain.

To research this book Doherty went to Moscow several times, and although he speaks some Russian they were difficult months — "I chose Moscow as the centre of the novel because Gorbachov and the wind of change in Russia affect us all." He goes on to say: "But I kept a low profile over there and was careful. I missed the routine of business life in England."

Terry Moorhead, in a review of this novel, wrote: "It is remarkably rare for a cloak and dagger spy thriller to be bang up to date, but Kevin Doherty has achieved that with his novel *A Long Day's Dying*."

In a recent article in *Campaign* Doherty made the point that he took great effort in this book to avoid the worst stereotypes of spy fiction: "I've tried to take Soviet society as it really is, rather than the clichéd view."

Half-way through the novel Doherty set about marketing his book and found "to my absolute shock" that no less than six publishers were interested. "The British seem to have an almost insatiable appetite for this kind of book," he said. And this suggests that the spy novel is still popular literature, and good business as far as the publishers are concerned.

SIR ARTHUR CONAN DOYLE

British. Born in Edinburgh, 22 May 1859. Died 7 July 1930.

Titles

[Major characters: Sherlock Holmes and Dr Watson]
"The Bruce-Partington Plans". In Allen Dulles, ed., *Great Spy Stories from Fiction* (New York, Harper & Row, 1969, pp. 119-44). A short story originally published in 1908.
"The Naval Treaty". In *The Adventures of the Speckled Band and Other Stories of Sherlock Holmes*. With an introduction and notes by William S Baring-Gould (New York, Signet, 1965, pp. 116-46). A short story originally published in 1894.
"A Scandal in Bohemia". In *The Adventure of the Speckled Band and Other Stories of Sherlock Holmes*. With an introduction and notes by William S Baring-Gould (New York, Signet, 1965, pp. 39-59). First published in 1894.

Biography

Arthur Conan Doyle was educated at Stonyhurst Academy and Edinburgh University, where he studied medicine and qualified as a doctor in 1881. Opening a practice at Southsea, Hampshire, England, Doyle soon found that he needed to supplement his income owing to a lack of patients. This was when he created Sherlock Holmes and Dr John H Watson. These two characters appeared for the first time in Doyle's *A Study in Scarlet*, which was published in *Beeton's Christmas Annual* in December 1887.

Critical Analysis

Doyle's main work was associated with the detective story, but some of his Sherlock Holmes stories can be called spy tales. In "The Bruce-Partington Plans", Holmes is brought in to solve a problem which a baffled Secret Service could not cope with. This was the age of rapid technological growth which led to a great deal of industrial espionage; it was from such cases that Doyle and others drew their inspiration for stories about stolen plans, but for commercial spies they substituted the more glamorous "foreign agent".

His other stories have at least a close affinity with spy fiction: in "A Scandal in Bohemia" Holmes plays the role of a King's agent rather than a detective in dealing with Irene Adler.

Films

The character of Sherlock Holmes has inspired a number of films, some of which are listed below. For those interested in pursuing all these adaptations it is recommended that they consult *Halliwell's Filmgoer's Companion*.

Sherlock Holmes. TCF, US, 1932.
The Hound of the Baskervilles. TCF, US, 1939.
The Adventures of Sherlock Holmes. TCF, US, 1939 (British title: *Sherlock Holmes*).
Sherlock Holmes and the Voice of Terror. Universal, US, 1942.
Sherlock Holmes and the Secret Weapon. Universal, US, 1942.
Sherlock Holmes in Washington. Universal, US, 1943.
Sherlock Holmes Faces Death. Universal, US, 1943.
Sherlock Holmes and the Spider Woman. Universal, US, 1944.
The Scarlet Claw. Universal, US, 1944.
The Pearl of Death. Universal, US, 1944.
The House of Fear. Universal, US, 1945.
The Woman in Green. Universal, US, 1945.
Pursuit to Algiers. Universal, US, 1945.
Terror by Night. Universal, US, 1946.
Dressed to Kill. Universal, US, 1946 (British title: *Sherlock Holmes and the Secret Code*).

PETER JOHN DRISCOLL

British. Born in London, 4 February 1942.

Titles

The White Lie Assignment. London, Macdonald, 1971; New York, Lippincott, 1975.

The Wilby Conspiracy. New York, Lippincott, 1972; London, Macdonald, 1973.
In Connection with Kilshaw. London, Macdonald, 1974; New York, Lippincott, 1974.
The Barboza Credentials. London, Macdonald, 1976; New York, Lippincott, 1976.
Pangolin. London, Macdonald, 1979; New York, Lippincott, 1979.
Spearhead. London, Bantam,1988; Boston, Little Brown, 1989.

Biography
Although Peter Driscoll was born in England, he grew up and was educated in South Africa. First he went to St. David's Marist College in Johannesburg, and matriculated in 1958; then he attended the University of the Witwatersrand in Johannesburg, from where he graduated with a BA in 1967. He joined the *Rand Daily Mail* in Johannesburg on leaving school, and has been intermittently involved in journalism ever since, including three and a half years on the staff of ITN, London.

Critical Analysis
Peter Driscoll has written six novels to date and although they do not fall into the category of the classical espionage story, they are worth including because many of them deal with international intrigue and the internal security of the countries in which they are set.

   The author comments: "I feel something of an imposter at being included in a compilation of spy fiction writers. Although all my novels have involved intelligence agents of one sort or another, and to some extent the machinations of intelligence agencies, I do not consider that they belong (with the possible exception of *The White Lie Assignment*) to the classical spy genre. They are more in the nature of adventure thrillers."

   Driscoll's first novel called *The White Lie Assignment* begins in London the day after the Russian invasion of Czechoslovakia. Michael Mannis, a Greek-born, freelance photographer, has just returned from Prague when he is contacted by Joe Goodwin, senior functionary of an elite Whitehall intelligence agency called 3 Committee. Reluctant, inexperienced and suspicious, Mannis agrees to got to Albania to "visit relatives" and take a few photographs. Almost immediately he finds himself in a bewildering game of shadowing and snatch photography in the streets of London.

   The scene moves to the Mediterranean, where, as a member of a small task force on the island of Corfu, Mannis learns that their objective is a new missile site being constructed with the help of the Chinese Communists. All the major cities of Europe are within range of these missiles and the only clue to their location is the confused story of a half-mad shepherd. As their plans begin to go dangerously astray, Mannis becomes aware that a pattern of personal double-crosses is threatening the mission and his life. Pursued by forces of two nations, Mannis and Goodwin are thrown into a conflict that culminates on a lonely road in the Kabylie mountains of Algeria.

   This book was well received in Britain and America. The *London Evening News* called it "tense and ingeniously constructed." The *Oxford Mail* wrote "plenty of good action writing ... an effective debut."

   Peter Driscoll's latest novel, *Spearhead*, is set mostly in Ireland and South Africa. It is the story of Lincoln Kumalo, the most revered of all black nationalist leaders, who has been imprisoned by the South Africans for the last twenty-five years. It is discovered that he has cancer and must have an operation; unwilling to release him and faced with dire consequences if Kumalo dies in their custody, the security forces devise a cunning plot which will rid them of this embarrassment once and for all.

The plot is overheard by one of the prisoners and he manages to smuggle out a message, risking his life, to Kumalo's daughter. Once the message is understood, certain members of the People's Congress take it upon themselves to take action and make arrangements for rescuing Kumalo. To achieve this they enlist the help of Major Patrick Marriner, a former paratrooper, who assembles a disparate group of black nationalists and dissident white veteran soldiers to execute the plan.

This is a very good novel — entertaining and exciting while being informative. The characters are well portrayed and we certainly get a feel for South Africa, the country, the people and the racial tensions which are always under the surface.

The author says about this book: "the background and personality of one character in my latest novel, *Spearhead*, are inescapably based on those of the ANC leader Nelson Mandela. However, the character ... Lincoln Kumalo ... is meant to personify Mandela only in a symbolic sense. Characters should have their own reality, and live subjects rarely make completely satisfactory models."

Some of the themes that he explores in his fiction are: "Underground politics, resistance, guerrilla war and terrorism have been recurring themes. This means that most of my books have an underlying political flavour, but not a political message (at least, not consciously)."

One reviewer verifies this quality in Driscoll's books, and said of *Spearhead*: "Everything here is perfectly judged: the characters have just as much depth and individuality as the plot requires, and Driscoll — without ever moralizing — offers political observations that keep the audience's hearts in the right place. Readers looking for a rousing South African melodrama could hardly do better."

Another review in the *Dublin Sunday Tribune* wrote: "As a thriller, *Spearhead* is riveting stuff and first-rate escapism. But what elevates the novel beyond the mere genre in which it is rooted is Driscoll's equally riveting portrait of the stratified world of South Africa today. Indeed, this is one of those novels in which the very atmosphere of the territory under description seems brilliantly realised, and where you come away from the book believing that you have been in the company of a writer who absolutely knows the complex and malevolent workings of the most despised nation on earth."

Film

The Wilby Conspiracy. United Artists, US, 1975.

Margaret Ann Duffy

British. Born in Woodford Green, Essex, 3 March 1942.

Titles

[Major characters: Ingrid Langley and Patrick Gillard]

A Murder of Crows. London, Piatkus, 1987; New York, St. Martin's Press, 1988.
Death of a Raven. London, Piatkus, 1988; New York, St. Martin's Press, 1989.
Brass Eagle. London, Piatkus, 1988; New York, St. Martin's Press, 1989.

Biography

Margaret Duffy attended Worthing Technical High School until the age of sixteen and then entered the Civil Service. She worked for Inland Revenue at Durington, Sussex and later for Navy Contracts at the Ministry of Defence in Bath.

Critical Analysis

Margaret Duffy started writing spy fiction in 1987, but she writes science fiction as well. The author says: "I was hooked on my hero who for several reasons I had created as an army officer. Spy fiction seemed to be a fitting background for him." Patrick Gillard is the hero of these novels which are set mostly in Britain with the exception of *Death of a Raven* which was partly set in Canada.

In her first novel, *A Murder of Crows*, we are introduced to Ingrid Langley, a successful romantic novelist. Her second husband, Peter Clyde, has been murdered and her first husband, Major Patrick Gillard, having just returned from the Falklands war, works as an agent for the Intelligence outfit D12 and is currently investigating Peter's murder and asks for Ingrid's help. In a review in the *Irish Times*, Edna White wrote: "this first crime novel from Margaret Duffy merits attention, even though the reader may well get bogged down in the intricacies of the plot and in the welter of irrelevant detail. True-romance and spy-fiction are uneasy partners — but a welcome nonetheless for this interesting, diffuse and well-written book."

Death of a Raven is another adventure in the life of best-selling author Ingrid Langley and Patrick Gillard. The Ministry of Defence is worried about a small British firm, DARE, which is doing work for the Canadian Navy at the same time as it is working on British defence missiles. Colonel Daws, Patrick and Ingrid's boss at D12, is concerned about the possibility that the KGB may have infiltrated the company's ranks, and gained access to DARE's secret blueprints. When Andrew Quade, one of DARE's engineers is killed, and the managing director receives personal threats, D12 decide to send Ingrid and Patrick on a secret mission to Canada to find out what is really going on. A review in *Publisher's Weekly* comments: "Although the cliff-hanging episodes suggest comic-strip heroics, it's fun to suspend disbelief and revel in the extravagant adventure."

ALLEN WELSH DULLES

American. Born 7 April 1893. Died 29 January 1969.

Titles

Great Spy Stories From Fiction (ed.). New York, Harper & Row, 1969.

Biography

Allen Dulles graduated from Princeton University in 1914, and after travelling in the Far East, taught English for a year in India. He returned to Princeton and obtained an MA in 1916. He joined the Diplomatic Corps and in 1916 was appointed third secretary in the American Embassy in Vienna. Dulles pursued a career in diplomacy until 1926 when he studied Law at George Washington University and received an LL B. After this he practised law with a New York firm.

Dulles became involved in intelligence when in early 1942 he joined the Office of the Coordinator of Information, the predecessor to the Office of the Strategic Services (OSS). In November 1942 he went to Bern, Switzerland to set up an OSS station there. He remained in Switzerland throughout the war — running agents into Germany and Nazi-occupied Europe. Dulles was instrumental in the creation of the CIA after the war and joined that organisation in 1951, rising to become the Director of the agency in 1953. He remained the DCI until 1961, when he was forced to resign due to the disastrous failure of the Bay of Pigs invasion.

Allen Dulles is included because he wrote two books about his experiences in intelligence — *The Secret Surrender*, and *The Craft of Intelligence* (1963). He also introduced and assembled two anthologies of spy stories, one of fact and the other of fiction. It is the latter which is of interest to the student of spy fiction, his introduction provides some insight into his opinions of the spy story and the evident use he found in this literature.

For instance, Dulles was a great fan of Ian Fleming and claimed that he had read these novels before President Kennedy declared his interest in Bond in 1961. He was fascinated with Fleming's gadgetry. There was one device, a homing radio outfit which Bond planted on Goldfinger's car, which allowed him to follow the villain across France and Switzerland. Dulles said that he was so impressed with this device that: "I put my people in the CIA to work on this as a serious project but they came up with the answer that it had too many bugs in it. The device did not really work very well when the enemy got into a crowded city. The same may be true of many of Bond's gadgets, but they did get one to thinking and exploring, and that was worth while because sometimes you came up with other ideas that did work." This may have been a stunt on Dulles' behalf, but on the other hand it could have been a genuine admission.

In his anthology of spy fiction, Dulles gives a general introduction to the topic and then brief forewords to the individual spy stories, which are also interesting to read.

ROBERT LIPSCOMB DUNCAN
PSEUDONYM: JAMES HALL ROBERTS
American. Born in Oklahoma City, 9 September 1927.

Titles
[All written under the pseudonym of James Hall Roberts]
The Q Document. New York, Morrow, 1964; London, Cape, 1965.
The February Plan. New York, Morrow, 1967; London, Deutsch, 1967.
The Day the Sun Fell. New York, Morrow, 1970; London, Sphere, 1981.
Dragons at the Gate. New York, Morrow, 1975; London, Joseph, 1976.
Brimstone. New York, Morrow, 1980; London, Joseph, 1980.

Biography
Robert L Duncan was educated at the University of Oklahoma, Norman, from where he graduated with a BA in 1950, and an MA in 1972. He worked as a lecturer in television writing at the University of California, Irvine, 1967–68. He was the coordinator of Business Aspects of the Arts Seminar, 1969–70, and he was also the

writer-in-residence at Chapman College, in Orange, California, at the same time. He was an associate professor of journalism at the University of Oklahoma School of Professional Writing, Norman, from 1972 to 1980.

Critical Analysis

This author uses his real name and his pseudonym of James Hall Roberts to write different kinds of books. George Grella, a critic of spy fiction, remarks: "As Roberts he demonstrates the generally neglected potentiality of the thriller to offer both factual and spiritual instruction ... His works as Robert L Duncan, though not without merit, lack the individuality and power of the Roberts books; they generally tend to be founded upon an interesting and unusual idea and then flounder upon the sorts of artificial tensions usually associated with run-of-the-mill suspense novels."

   Dragons at the Gate is a clear example of a spy hero of the maverick variety which has tended to appear in recent spy fiction. In this story a CIA agent stationed in Japan finds out that he is to be the victim of his own agency. As a result he cannot turn to his colleagues or anyone connected with the organisation, so he has to rely upon the loyalty of his own close friends, including a former girlfriend, as well as his own resourcefulness. But as usual in these cases, the superior individual conquers the evil bureaucracy. The hero turns the situation around and humiliates those responsible for betraying him by forcing them to cancel an operation he opposes, removing his former boss from his cushy job, and securing a CIA pension to maintain his silence.

DANIEL EASTERMAN

(Pseudonym for Denis MacEoin)
British. Born in Belfast, Northern Ireland, 26 January 1949.

Titles

The Last Assassin. London, Hodder & Stoughton, 1984; New York, Doubleday, 1984.
The Seventh Sanctuary. London, Grafton, 1987; New York, Doubleday, 1987.
The Ninth Buddha. London, Grafton, 1988; New York, Doubleday, 1989.
The Brotherhood of the Tomb. London, Grafton, 1989; New York, Doubleday, 1990.

Biography

Daniel Easterman was educated at the Royal Belfast Academical Institution. He then attended Trinity College, Dublin (1967-71) where he obtained an MA in English Literature. From there he went to the University of Edinburgh (1971-75), where he graduated with an MA in Persian and Arabic. He then went to King's College, Cambridge (1975-79) to study for a PhD in Persian Studies. From 1979 to 1980 he taught at the University of Fez in Morocco; between 1981 and 1986 he lectured on Islamic Studies at the University of Newcastle.

Critical Analysis

This author writes fiction under the name of Daniel Easterman and uses his real name, Denis MacEoin, for academic works. His first book *The Last Assassin* was based on an extremist Shi'ite sect and their plot to assassinate world leaders, including President Carter, Brezhnev and Anwar al-Sadat. Peter Randall, a CIA field agent, tries to stop this group from achieving their aims. The action takes place in Iran, before and after the revolution, and America. A reviewer of this novel remarked: "Daniel Easterman brings a note of authenticity to this latest apocalyptic novel that raises it above the imagined accounts of armageddon and nuclear confrontation that seem to fascinate the publishing world."

In *The Ninth Buddha* the son of a former British secret agent is kidnapped and taken to Tibet where he is welcomed as a reincarnation of Buddha. The father goes in search of his son, amidst Russian communist agents, White Russian exiles and lamas. One reviewer wrote about Easterman: "In *The Ninth Buddha*, he has established his reputation as a writer of talent, ingenuity and skill and a fine sequel to *The Seventh Sanctuary.*"

Easterman says that he writes spy novels because: "...it was an easy and logical transition from academic writing, requiring a strong factual basis (itself needing research)." He goes on to say: "Moving from writing straight academic material, mainly historical, to fiction, I have been startled to find that the closer one sticks to reality in plot or character, the harder it is to swallow. Events that would shock or interest in a piece of serious non-fiction could seem absurd or impossible if inserted into a work of fiction. Understanding this one fact has taught me more than anything else about the nature of our perception of reality and the role of fiction in shaping it."

Some of the recurrent themes in his books include: "Religious extremism interweaving with politics and intelligence operations. Exotic locations. Bizarre events side by side with hard realism."

MAURICE EDELMAN

British. Born 2 March 1911. Died 14 December 1975.

Titles

A Dream of Treason. Philadelphia, Lippincott, 1955.
A Call on Krupin. Philadelphia, Lippincott, 1960.
The Fratricides. New York, Random House, 1963.

Biography

Maurice Edelman was educated at Cardiff High School and Trinity College, Cambridge. From 1932 to 1941 he was engaged in industry and research in the application of plastic materials to aircraft construction. During the Second World War, largely on the strength of his fluency in various languages (he was an expert both in Russian and French), he was a war correspondent for *Picture Post* in North Africa and France. By 1945 he had become one of the many young intellectuals who had sworn allegiance to the cause of Labour. He was elected M.P. for Coventry West, a seat he held until 1950, then stood for Coventry North, which he represented until 1974, when the constituency became Coventry North-West and he was again re-elected.

He was delegate to the Consultative Assembly of the Council of Europe from 1949 to 1951 and from 1965 to 1970. He did more to improve Anglo-French relations than probably any other British MP and was Vice-President of the Anglo-French Parliamentary Relations Committee and President of the Alliance Française. In recognition of all this he was made an Officer of the Legion of Honour in 1960 and received the Médaille de Paris in 1972.

Critical Analysis

Edelman's first book, *France: the birth of the Fourth Republic*, was published in 1945 and after that he wrote a number of novels which combined politics and the technique of suspense in a manner which had not been tackled since Trollope. This led quite naturally to the espionage story.

A Dream of Treason was a Balchin-like entertainment about a Foreign Office man who, for a devious purpose, is encouraged by higher powers to allow the leakage of certain information only to find that he is to be held personally responsible for his action. Edelman called this "a diplomatic thriller"', adding that he hoped "it may emerge as a moral thriller as well".

Five years later he produced *A Call on Kuprin*; its storyline, about a scientist who is lured from Cambridge University to Russia, bore a marked resemblance to the defection of Peter Kapitza, the Russian scientist who had been the assistant to Lord Rutherford when the latter split the atom at the Cavendish Laboratory in Cambridge. In Edelman's story a British MP is sent to Russia to try to persuade Kuprin to return. He is compromised in a hotel bedroom controlled by the Soviet Intelligence and in which there is a concealed camera. Only a few years later this exact technique was employed by the KGB against Commander Courtney, MP, with disastrous results for the latter's political career.

The Fratricides told of the last days of the OAS campaign for Algérie Française and of an undercover man who infiltrated the OAS for de Gaulle.

CLIVE FREDERICK WILLIAM EGLETON
Pseudonyms: JOHN TARRANT, PATRICK BLAKE
British. Born in South Harrow, Middlesex, 25 November 1927.

Titles

[Major character: David Garnett]
A Piece of Resistance [Garnett]. London, Hodder and Stoughton, 1970; New York, Coward McCann, 1970.
Last Post for a Partisan [Garnett]. London, Hodder & Stoughton, 1971; New York, Coward McCann, 1971.
The Judas Mandate [Garnett]. London, Hodder & Stoughton, 1972; New York, Coward McCann, 1972.
Seven Days to a Killing. London, Hodder & Stoughton, 1973; New York, Coward McCann, 1973.
The October Plot. London, Hodder & Stoughton, 1974; as *The Bormann Brief*. New York, Coward McCann, 1974.
Skirmish. London, Hodder & Stoughton, 1975; New York, Coward McCann, 1975.
State Visit. London, Hodder & Stoughton, 1976.
The Mills Bomb. London, Hodder & Stoughton, 1978; New York, Atheneum, 1978.
Backfire. London, Hodder & Stoughton, 1979; New York, Atheneum, 1979.

The Winter Touch. London, Hodder & Stoughton, 1981; as *The Eisenhower Deception*. New York, Atheneum, 1981.
A Falcon for the Hawks. London, Hodder & Stoughton, 1982; New York, Walker, 1984.
The Russian Enigma. New York, Atheneum, 1982; London, Hodder & Stoughton, 1983.
A Conflict of Interests. New York, Atheneum, 1983; London, Hodder & Stoughton, 1984.
Troika. London, Hodder & Stoughton, 1985.
A Different Drummer. London, Hodder & Stoughton, 1986.
Picture of the Year. London, Hodder & Stoughton, 1987.
Gone Missing. London, Hodder & Stoughton, 1988; as *Missing from the Record*. New York, St. Martin's Press, 1988.
Death of a Sahib. London, Hodder & Stoughton, 1989.

Novels as John Tarrant
The Rommel Plot. London, Macdonald and Jane's, 1977; Philadelphia, Lippincott, 1977.
The Clauberg Trigger. London, Macdonald and Jane's, 1978; New York, Atheneum, 1979.
China Gold. London, Macdonald and Jane's, 1982.

Novels as Patrick Blake
Escape to Athena. London, Fontana, 1979; New York, Berkley, 1979.
Double Griffin. New York, Jove, 1981; London, Macdonald, 1982.

Biography
Clive Egleton was educated at Haberdashers' Aske's Hampstead School from 1938 to 1944. In 1944 he joined the Army under age, enlisting in the Royal Armoured Corps, and was subsequently commissioned into the South Staffordshire Regiment (later the Staffordshire Regiment) in September 1946. He was granted a regular commission and stayed on in the Army until 1975, retiring voluntarily as Lieutenant-Colonel. He became a full-time writer, 1975-81, and then worked as a civil desk officer in the Directorate of Security (Army), 1981-88, during which time he was writing part-time.

Critical Analysis
His first book was *A Piece of Resistance*, a realistic, if frightening look into the future in which Russian forces occupy Britain after destroying Bristol with a nuclear warhead. *Last Post for a Partisan* and *The Judas Mandate* completed the trilogy. In the final book the Soviet occupation force in Britain is being depleted because of the Chinese threat to Siberia, yet the Resistance Movement in Britain, now severely split between those who favour accelerating their campaign and those who would prefer to cooperate with the puppet government, is unable to take advantage of the situation.

Outstanding success came to Egleton when he produced *Seven Days to a Killing*. The story concerned Major John Tarrant, who received a demand for £500,000 in uncut diamonds as ransom for his kidnapped thirteen-year-old son. He had seven days to find these and the life of his son was at stake. But so too was the security of his country and while top intelligence men were prepared to play a dangerous game of bluff, Tarrant was willing to risk everything, including his own life.

The October Plot was a follow-up to the failed plot to kill Hitler in July 1944. It was the fictitious, but not altogether improbable, story of an operation that could have changed the course of the Second World War and brought it to a conclusion almost a full year earlier. Major-General Gerhardt disappears on the day of the abortive plot to kill Hitler and reappears in Britain with a plan to assassinate Martin Bormann, the Nazi's deputy leader. Colonel Michael Ashby, head of MI21, links up with Gerhardt to plan Operation Leopard for 14 October 1944 — nothing less than a daring assassination scheme to be carried out by six carefully chosen men.

Egleton has written over twenty novels and has now established his reputation as a popular writer of spy/adventure stories, which are well received in Britain and America. The author says: "I didn't regard my first book as a spy novel but the critics regarded it as such and as long as my novels are published and read, I don't really mind what they are regarded as."

Clive Egleton is well qualified to write spy fiction as his intelligent stories show. He worked for British Intelligence in the Persian Gulf from 1958 to 1959 and was engaged in counter-insurgency operations in Cyprus (1955–56) and East Africa (1964). Much of his material is drawn from his first-hand knowledge gained while serving in India, Hong Kong, Japan, Egypt, Libya, Cyprus, the Persian Gulf, Kenya, Uganda, France and Germany.

"I was involved in counter-insurgency operations during my army service, and on one occasion was employed as an intelligence staff officer in the Persian Gulf. For the last seven years I have been working in the Army's Directorate of Security. This has of course given me a considerable insight into Whitehall."

But, as the author himself says, often it is not enough just to have experience in intelligence; you must be an able writer as well: "A good spy novel can seem authentic. However, I haven't read one which gives a wholly accurate and realistic picture of the intelligence world. If an author ever really came close to reality, I believe he or she would only succeed in boring the reader to distraction."

Films

The Black Windmill. Universal, GB, 1974 (from the book *Seven Days to a Killing*).
Escape to Athena was originally from a film script filmed in 1979.

JOHN EHRLICHMAN

American. Born in Tacoma, Washington, 20 March 1925.

Titles

The Company. New York, Simon & Schuster, 1976; London, Collins, 1976.
The China Card. New York, Simon & Schuster, 1986; London, Bantam, 1987.
Dorothy Rigby. London, Hodder & Stoughton, 1989.

Biography

John Ehrlichman obtained a BA at UCLA in 1945, and graduated as a Doctor of Jurisprudence from Stanford University in 1951. During the Second World War he served in the 8th Air Force stationed at Bungay, Suffolk. From 1952 to 1969 he worked as a lawyer. He was Counsel to the President in 1969 and Assistant to the

President for Domestic Affairs (1969-73). As one of Nixon's closest advisers, he was forced to resign over Watergate and served some time in prison for his role in this affair. He now writes thrillers.

Critical Analysis

Ehrlichman writes other fiction apart from spy novels and he has written extensively about Nixon and his administration. His first novel, *The Company*, is about a CIA Director determined to protect national secrets from an incoming administration. When he discovers that the new President has set up his own intelligence agency within the White House, which is spying on newsmen and the political opposition, the Director successfully blackmails the President.

The most interesting thing about this book is that Ehrlichman wrote it at all, and perhaps why he wrote it. The plot is a very thinly disguised version of the Watergate scandal. All the major characters are there — Nixon, Hunt, and others — except they are given different names. Ehrlichman implies that the CIA knew about the President's private intelligence unit months in advance, and could have used this information against the President. If this is Ehrlichman's version of the events of Watergate, it seriously implicates the CIA and the Director. It also suggests that the Watergate break-in was only one of many misjudgements.

This is a prime example of a work of spy fiction paralleling fact, and by reinterpretation, manipulating events for the author's own purpose.

The Company became "Washington Behind Closed Doors", a 12-hour TV series that was broadcast in America and Britain. The author had no part in the television project.

His second novel, *The China Card*, provides another explanation for the events which led up to Nixon's much publicised China "initiative" in the early 1970s. A politically naive young American, working in President Nixon's law firm, is implicated as a mole by the Chinese communists. He is trying to bring about a reconciliation between the two nations, but he ends up as a target for elimination by both sides. Ehrlichman further indulges his obsession with Nixon, Kissinger and Haig, revealing their motives in a most mercenary and unpleasant light.

GERALD FAIRLIE

British. Born in London 1 November 1899. Died in April 1983.

Titles

[Major character: Bulldog Drummond]
Bulldog Drummond on Dartmoor. London, Hodder & Stoughton, 1938; New York, Curl, 1939.
Bulldog Drummond Attacks. London, Hodder & Stoughton, 1939; New York, Gateway, 1940.
Captain Bulldog Drummond. London, Hodder & Stoughton, 1945.
Bulldog Drummond Stands Fast. London, Hodder & Stoughton, 1947.
Hands Off Bulldog Drummond. London, Hodder & Stoughton, 1949.
Calling Bulldog Drummond. London, Hodder & Stoughton, 1951.
The Return of the Black Gang. London, Hodder & Stoughton, 1954.

Biography

Educated at Downside and the Royal Military Academy, Sandhurst, Gerald Fairlie served in the Scots Guards from 1917 to 1924. He was not only very much in the "Bulldog Drummond" mould, but was actually the model for Sapper's character.

When Fairlie left the army he set out to write novels, but also became a journalist and a screen writer and was successful in both fields. In six years he had sixteen novels published. During the Second World War Fairlie was the head of a Commando Training School. Though not mentioned in the records of SOE, he saw something of the world of the Secret Service with the Maquis inside France.

Critical Analysis

Although Fairlie had a wide circle of friends, he was closest to Sapper (Lieutenant-Colonel McNeile). When McNeile was dying, he and Fairlie discussed the last Bulldog Drummond story plotted by Sapper and finally Fairlie agreed to write the book — *Bulldog Drummond on Dartmoor*. This was the first of a new series of Drummond books, of which six more followed. Fairlie's versions of the Sapper stories were more in the nature of thrillers than spy novels, and his talent as a scriptwriter enabled him to give a zest to Drummond which McNeile never quite contrived. The truth was that Drummond on screen was usually much better than Drummond in prose.

Films

Bulldog Drummond. Silent, GB, 1925.
The Third Round. Silent, GB, 1925.
Bulldog Drummond. US, 1929.
Temple Tower. US, 1930.
The Return of Bulldog Drummond. GB, 1934.
Bulldog Jack. GB, 1934 (American title: *Alias Bulldog Drummond*).
Bulldog Drummond Strikes Back. US, 1934.
Bulldog Drummond at Bay. GB, 1937.
Bulldog Drummond Escapes. US, 1937.
Bulldog Drummond Comes Back. US, 1937.
Bulldog Drummond's Revenge. US,1938.
Bulldog Drummond's Peril. US, 1938.
Bulldog Drummond in Africa. US, 1938.
Arrest Bulldog Drummond. US, 1938.
Bulldog Drummond's Secret Police. US, 1939.
Bulldog Drummond's Bride. US, 1939.
Bulldog Sees It Through. GB, 1939.
The Challenge. US, 1948.
Thirteen Lead Soldiers. US, 1948.
Calling Bulldog Drummond. GB, 1951.
Deadlier Than The Male. GB, 1967.
Some Girls Do. GB, 1971.

FINIS KING FARR

American. Born in Lebanon, Tennessee, 31 December 1904.

Titles

The Elephant Valley. New York, Arlington House, 1966.

Biography

Finis Farr was educated at Princeton University, from where he graduated in 1926. During the war he served in the US Army Infantry, he served in the China–Burma–India theatre and reached the rank of Major.

Critical Analysis

Farr is another author who had experience in intelligence and then turned to fiction. His one novel, *The Elephant Valley*, is about a top CIA agent who is assigned to find out who has blown up an atomic plant in New York and may want to start World War III.

FREDERICK SHILLER FAUST

Pseudonyms: FRANK AUSTIN, GEORGE OWEN BAXTER, LEE BOLT, MAX BRAND, WALTER C BUTLER, GEORGE CHALLIS, EVIN EVAN, EVAN EVANS, JOHN FREDERICK, FREDERICK FROST, DENNIS LAWTON, DAVID MANNING, PETER HENRY MORLAND, HUGH OWEN, NICHOLAS SILVER, HENRY URIEL, PETER WARD.
American. Born in Seattle, Washington, 29 May 1892. Died 12 May 1944.

Titles

Novels as Frederick Frost
Secret Agent Number One. Philadelphia, Macrae Smith, 1936; London, Harrap, 1937.
The Bamboo Whistle. Philadelphia, Macrae Smith, 1937.
Spy Meets Spy. Philadelphia, Macrae Smith, 1937; as *Phantom Spy.* London, Harrap, 1937.

Biography

Frederick Faust was educated in schools in Modesto, California, and the University of California, Berkeley. He worked as a freelance writer from 1917, and he lived in Italy from 1926 to 1936. He was killed during the Second World War while working as a war correspondent for *Harper's*.

Faust was best known as Max Brand, author of fast-paced, romantic western novels, including *Destry Rides Again* (1930), *Singing Guns* (1938) and *Danger Trail* (1940). He wrote spy novels as Frederick Frost and crime novels as Walter C Butler. Faust also wrote *Calling Dr Kildare* (1940) and its sequels, and he worked on films that were made from those books. He was a prolific pulp writer, who wrote more than one hundred novels.

Critical Analysis

The action in *The Phantom Spy* takes place in Europe, although our hero, Willie Gloster, is an American. In 1937 Faust foresaw the Second World War and this is the background of the story. The Germans have stolen the plans of the Maginot line and the British Secret Service tries to get them back.

At one point Gloster gives his reasons why he should not become involved: "I'm an American. What do I care about European entanglements? Not a damned thing ..." Like a true patriot expressing the isolationist feelings of most Americans at the time, however, he does get involved, in a disguised role, and saves the day.

This book is barely readable and full of high melodrama, but a period piece, and an interesting adaptation of the American spy hero of the time. The book was re-published in 1975 by White Lion Publishers, London.

Ian Lancaster Fleming

British. Born in London, 28 May 1908. Died in Kent, 12 August 1964.

Titles

[Major character: James Bond]
Casino Royale. London, Cape,1954; New York, Macmillan, 1954.
Live and Let Die. London, Cape, 1954; New York, Macmillan, 1955.
Moonraker. London, Cape, 1955; New York, Macmillan, 1955.
Diamonds Are Forever. London, Cape, 1956; New York, Macmillan, 1956.
From Russia, With Love. London, Cape, 1957; New York, Macmillan, 1957.
Doctor No. London, Cape, 1958; New York, Macmillan, 1958.
Goldfinger. London, Cape, 1959; New York, Macmillan, 1959.
Thunderball. London, Cape, 1961; New York, Viking Press, 1961.
The Spy Who Loved Me. London, Cape, 1962; New York, Viking Press, 1962.
On Her Majesty's Secret Service. London, Cape, 1963; New York, New American Library, 1963.
You Only Live Twice. London, Cape, 1964; New York, New American Library, 1964.
The Man With the Golden Gun. London, Cape, 1965; New York, New American Library, 1965.

Biography

Ian Fleming was educated at Eton, Sandhurst and in Europe. He first narrowly failed an examination for the Diplomatic Service and then joined Reuters News Agency. In 1933 he was in Moscow to cover the trial of the six British engineers of the Metropolitan Vickers Electrical Company who had been arrested by the OGPU on charges of spying. Soon afterwards he resigned from Reuters to take a job in merchant banking in the City. Within two years he had moved to the stockbroking firm of Rowe and Pitman where he became a junior partner.

In the spring of 1939 he returned to Moscow officially as a correspondent of the *Times*, but unofficially on a brief trip to make a report for the Foreign Office. Then in the early summer of that year, on the advice of Montagu Norman, Governor of the Bank of England, Fleming was chosen to be Personal Assistant to Admiral John Godfrey, the new Director of Naval Intelligence, with the rank of Lieutenant, RNVR.

Fleming organised the No. 30 Assault Unit, which was modelled on the kind of Intelligence assault unit the Germans had used in Crete in 1941. This became known as Fleming's Private Navy, and in beach reconnaissance, in secretly probing enemy territory and bringing back information, it was a great success. Though he supplied many bright ideas for operations during his NID stint and was highly regarded in US Naval circles as well as at the British Admiralty, Fleming received no decorations for his war work.

At the end of 1945 he became foreign manager of Kemsley Newspapers, personally selecting a team of foreign correspondents to cover the globe. He held this post until the newspaper group became Thomson Newspapers in 1959. It was then that Fleming wrote his first book, not a spy novel, but a foreign correspondent's guidebook which was issued for the education of his staff. It was a masterly and concise guide, quite unrivalled in its field, and today is a collector's rarity. In 1946 he built a house on some land that he owned in Jamaica at Oracabessa. It was here that most of the Bond books were written. Fleming was a man who worked hard and played hard, despite doctors' warnings; he continued to live the life he wanted. His last fatal heart attack occurred on the Royal St. George's Sandwich golf course in Kent.

Critical Analysis

George Grella, a critic of spy and detective fiction, wrote of Fleming in *Twentieth Century Crime and Mystery Writers* (1985): "Whatever his present standing among readers and critics, Ian Fleming accomplished an extraordinary amount in the history of the thriller. Almost singlehandedly, he revived popular interest in the spy novel, spawning legions of imitations, parodies, and critical and fictional reactions, thus indirectly creating an audience for a number of novelists who followed him in the form. Through the immense success of the filmed versions of his books, his character James Bond became the best known fictional personality of his time and Fleming the most famous writer of thrillers since Sir Arthur Conan Doyle."

The character of Bond, the highly sophisticated Secret Service operator, was a combination of a number of people, including Dusko Popov (the British agent codenamed Tricycle), Sidney Reilly and Fleming himself. In a recent article in *The Times*, a Vienna psychiatrist, Dr Joshua Bierer said that: "James Bond was initially written at his instigation so that Ian Fleming could contain his fantasies between the covers of a fictional book, rather than act them out in the reality of pre-war Vienna."

Fleming's creation of Bond compensated a man frustrated by his wartime career, and frustrated in the literary career he wished to have. John Pearson, his biographer, explained that although Fleming pretended to despise intellectuals, he longed to have a great intellectual success. But in his relentless pursuit to become a best-selling author, he sacrificed this ambition and settled for the vicarious life of James Bond.

From 1953 until Fleming's death the Bond books were produced annually. There seemed to be an increasing preoccupation with violence in the novels, for which he was attacked by some critics. More and more they were touched by sadism, and the deaths of some of his characters were bizarre to say the least: in *Doctor No* Bond disposes of the Communist doctor by smothering him in bird droppings. Anthony Curtis wrote that "Fleming's famous accuracy of detail was a brilliant journalistic illusion. The loving care for the minutiae with which he described a game of golf, or a meal of soft-shell crabs enabled him to get away with murder in climatic scenes of wild penny-dreadful improbability."

Live and Let Die, his second book, introduced a new member of SMERSH, the enemy agency Bond so often found himself working against. Mr Big was the villain and Bond's sufferings were alleviated by the attentions of a girl named Solitaire. Bond's women were seductive, desirable and efficient: they were also the type of women Fleming preferred — "well-scrubbed, ... clinical, clean and firm".

The novels all made the most of the Cold War period, with Bond operating against the agents of unfriendly powers (invariably the USSR) — men such as Goldfinger and Scaramanga. Fleming went to immense trouble to research the background and details for his books, using some of his foreign correspondents as advisers and making a trip to Japan before writing *You Only Live Twice*.

George Grella has called Fleming "one of the most appropriate writers of his time", which is an apt description of a novelist who created a spy fiction hero who is as popular today as when he first appeared.

Films

Doctor No. United Artists, GB, 1962.
From Russia, With Love. United Artists, GB, 1963.
Goldfinger. United Artists, GB, 1964.
Thunderball. United Artists, GB, 1965.
You Only Live Twice. United Artists, GB, 1967.
Diamonds Are Forever. United Artists, GB, 1971.
Live and Let Die. United Artists, GB, 1973.
The Man with the Golden Gun. United Artists, GB, 1974.
The Spy Who Loved Me. United Artists, GB, 1977.
Moonraker. United Artists, GB, 1979.
For Your Eyes Only. United Artists, GB, 1981.
Never Say Never Again. Warner, GB, 1983.
Octopussy. Eon, GB, 1983.
A View to a Kill. MGM, GB, 1985.
The Living Daylights. GB, 1987.

JAMES FOLLETT

British. Born in Tolworth, Surrey, 27 July 1939.

Titles

Churchill's Gold. London, Weidenfeld, 1980.
The Tiptoe Boys. London, Transworld, 1982.
Dominator. London, Methuen, 1985.
Swift. London, Methuen, 1986.
Mirage. London, Methuen, 1988.
The Beam. London, Methuen, 1989.

Biography

James Follett was blinded in an accident as a child but his sight was later restored in his early teens. Although trained to be a marine engineer, he spent a period of time filming sharks and hunting for underwater treasure. Before becoming a full-time writer in 1976, he worked for the Ministry of Defence as a technical author.

Since then he has written 12 novels, over fifty radio scripts, and a number of TV scripts, including episodes of "Blake's Seven".

Critical Analysis

Follett has had intelligence experience, presumably in his work with the Ministry of Defence, and he says that "it helped tremendously".

In *Churchill's Gold* the story is set in the past before America joined in the war. Before the Lend-Lease Bill went through Congress in 1941 Britain was virtually on her knees through bankruptcy. In December 1940 top German economists discovered that Britain's last remaining gold reserves were in South Africa: if they could prevent this gold reaching London, the British would be forced to sue for peace.

Captain Robert Gerrard, well known throughout the world's whaling ports for his uncanny ability to hunt the blue whale, and a hand-picked crew are instructed by the Foreign Office official in Cape Town to carry the South African gold to England in conditions of the utmost secrecy. Gerrard's whaling factory ship, the *Tulsar*, is hurriedly converted and armed to carry the disguised bullion and, masquerading as a passenger vessel bound for America, steams out of Durban. That same day a "ghost" U-boat, hurriedly prepared with the newest devices and a crack crew, slips her mooring in the Baltic with instructions to capture the *Tulsar*. U-330's commander is Kurt Milland, Gerrard's first officer on the *Tulsar* before the war; in 1933 Gerrard saved Milland's life during a whaling accident and the two men are old friends. Milland was picked by German Naval High Command as the one man who could predict every move Gerrard would make — and outwit him.

On their common hunting ground, it is inevitable that Milland will track down Gerrard and that, unknown to all but a handful of people, a duel to the death will be fought in the lonely wastes of the Atlantic.

Swift is the story about a satellite which deals daily with interbank transactions between London and New York. This computer is controlled by SWIFT, which guards the system upon which depends the delicate stability of the world's currencies. Charles Rose, a rich, successful gangster, teams up with a Soviet *Tass* correspondent and a brilliant but psychotic computer programmer, and together they plan to destroy the system and use it for their own gains.

Television

The Tiptoe Boys filmed as "Who Dares Wins".

KENNETH MARTIN FOLLETT

British. Born in Cardiff, Wales, 5 June 1949.

Titles

Eye of the Needle. London, Macdonald, 1978; as *Storm Island*. New York, Arbor House, 1978.

Triple. London, Macdonald, 1979; New York, Arbor House, 1979.

The Key to Rebecca. London, Hamish Hamilton, 1980; New York, Morrow, 1980.

The Man from St. Petersburg. London, Hamish Hamilton, 1982; New York, Morrow, 1982.

Lie Down with Lions. London, Hamish Hamilton, 1986; New York, Morrow, 1986.
[Major character: Piers Roper]
The Shakeout. London, Harwood Smart, 1975.
The Bear Raid. London, Harwood Smart, 1976.

Biography

Ken Follett was educated at state schools and University College, London, where he obtained a BA Hons in Philosophy. After graduating he became a newspaper reporter, first with the *South Wales Echo* and then with the London *Evening News*. While at the *News*, in 1973, he wrote *The Big Needle*, a racy mystery which was published as a paperback original in 1974. He then went to work for a small London publishing house, Everest Books, eventually becoming Deputy Managing Director. He continued to write novels in his spare time.

Critical Analysis

Follett's reputation as a popular spy novelist rests primarily upon his four novels, each of which set out to recreate modern history, which might have altered the outcome of a particular event.

Follett's first spy novel, *The Eye of the Needle*, is set in Britain in early 1944 when the Allies devised a deception plan to make the Germans believe that the invasion would be at Calais, and not Normandy. To this end they created a huge army base in Norfolk, complete with plywood planes, huts and tanks to deceive the enemy. History proved that they were taken in by this ploy, but this story is based upon Follett's idea that a German spy penetrated the deception and tried to get the information and proof back to Germany, which could have altered the outcome of the war. Follett's spy is Heinrich Rudolph Hans von Müller-Guder, code-named Die Nadel. He is cold-blooded and efficient and proves that he is capable of killing anyone who gets in his way. However, his murders alert British counter-intelligence and they do everything in their power to stop him from carrying out his mission successfully.

This novel won the author an Edgar from the Mystery Writers of America in 1979. It is an exciting story and compulsive reading. Michael Wood in *Saturday Review* wrote: "There is a nicely rendered sense of England during the war (blackouts, bombing raids, petrol rationing, cups of tea, jolly whimsical humour), a careful dosage of explicit sexual activity, and plenty of cold-blooded violence."

Follett voices his views about spy fiction and says: "Thrillers are fantasies. Such authenticity as they may have is designed to distract the reader's attention from the implausibility of the story." He goes on to say that although he has never had any experience in intelligence his encounters with people involved in the game have bolstered his opinions: "The very occasional meetings I have had with people in intelligence work have confirmed my belief that it is a muddled, inefficient and extremely right-wing milieu that has little in common with the world of bravery and idealism we depict."

His latest novel *Lie Down with the Lions*, is set in Paris and Afghanistan and follows the paths of Ellis, an American CIA agent sent to the country to try to organise the Afghan guerrillas under the leadership of Masud and to repel the invading Russians; Anatoly, a tough KGB adversary to Ellis, determined to kill Masud and crush the resistance; an Englishwoman, Jane, who used to be the lover of Ellis and is now married to a French doctor, Jean-Pierre, who is in fact an agent for the Soviets. One reviewer in the *Washington Post* wrote "Follett has woven a highly readable story, rich in detail and full of surprises, an engaging mix of intrigue tinged with the unexpected."

Follett's first two novels, *The Shakeout* and *The Bear Raid*, although not great commercial successes, were unusual in that they dealt with the neglected topic of industrial espionage.

Film
Eye of the Needle. United Artists, GB, 1981.

Television
The Key to Rebecca was made into a television mini-series.

ROBERT HENRY FOOTMAN
American. Born in Oakland, California, 26 April 1916.

Titles
Once A Spy. New York, Dodd Mead, 1980; London, Severn, 1988.
Always A Spy. New York, Dodd Mead, 1986.
Child Spy. New York, Dodd Mead, 1987.

Biography
Robert Footman was educated at a grammar school in California, and then High School in Kansas City, Missouri. He went to Yale University, from where he graduated with a BA in 1937. After university he taught English at Middlebury College in Vermont. During the war he served as a merchant marine. Then he worked at an advertising agency until 1978, and has been writing full-time since then.

Critical Analysis
In *Once A Spy* the plot was lifted from a *Time* magazine story of the rescue from a Philippine prison of Aurelio Lopez and Sergio Osmend by a San Franciscan, Steve Psinakis. A Filipino friend offered to have the author meet Lopez and Osmend, but he refused. "It was their history, but my story."

The novel is about Harry Ryder, a California management consultant, who retired from the espionage game five years before. The agency want Ryder to go back to work and commit a daring jail-break. Attempts are made on his life before he takes the job, his contact is a rival from the past and his partner is a beautiful woman. *Once A Spy* is described by his publishers as "an exciting thriller/ adventure story set in the Far East, [it] is the first in a new series of spy novels by Robert Footman".

FREDERICK FORSYTH

British. Born in Ashford, Kent 1938.

Titles

The Day of the Jackal. London, Hutchinson, 1971; New York, Viking Press, 1971.
The Odessa File. London, Hutchinson, 1972; New York, Viking Press, 1972.
The Dogs of War. London Hutchinson, 1974; New York, Viking Press, 1974.
The Devil's Alternative. London, Hutchinson, 1979; New York, Viking Press, 1980.
No Comebacks. London, Hutchinson, 1982.
The Fourth Protocol. London, Hutchinson, 1984.
The Negotiator. London, Bantam, 1989.

Biography

Frederick Forsyth was educated at Tonbridge School. He did his National Service in the RAF, becoming a pilot, and then in 1958 entered journalism via the *Eastern Daily Press* first in Norwich and later in King's Lynn. In December 1961 he was offered a job at Reuters in London; the following May he was sent off to Paris and from there to East Berlin. Forsyth returned to London in 1965 when he joined the BBC as a radio reporter. He transferred to television and in February 1967 was appointed assistant diplomatic correspondent.

He left the BBC and went off to Biafra as a freelance. During his coverage of the war he wrote a Penguin Special,*The Biafra Story*, which sold 30,000 copies. He left there in December 1969, shortly before the war ended. This marked a low period in Forsyth's life; he was waiting for a new job to turn up and he filled in the time by writing *The Day of the Jackal* in 35 days. This novel was rejected by a few publishers before Hutchinson bought it and, of course, as the typescript had been read and approved by André Malraux, the former Minister of Culture to President de Gaulle, it helped a great deal.

Critical Analysis

Forsyth's novel, *The Day of the Jackal*, was an instantaneous success and marked a new development in the spy story. Technically, it really comes into the thriller class, but the background is that of espionage, counter-espionage and political assassination. It described how the OAS (Organisation de l'Armée Secrète) decided to hire a professional assassin to kill de Gaulle.

This is a documentary spy thriller, based to a very large extent on fact. All but a few characters were real, although some had their names changed and their descriptions altered to mask the dangers of libel. "I do not have the kind of imagination to spin a character out of the air," Forsyth admitted. "I met the Jackal; although he did not have the smoothness and style of my Jackal. He was simply a professional killer." Forsyth also had the advantage of knowing the lower ranks of the OAS in France as well as the biographical details of some of their leaders. If ever there was a spy novel based on journalistic experience, this was it. The book was translated into eleven languages and published in twenty-six editions, with estimated sales of one million.

There is still fierce controversy as to how factual this novel actually is. Forsyth himself has declined to say whether the assassination plot he described was real and whether the leak of information through the leadership of the Secret Service he described also true. But there were a number of attempts to kill de Gaulle during 1963, the year in which *The Day of the Jackal* is set.

With his next book, *The Odessa File*, Forsyth gave yet another twist to the spy story. This time he made his spy a reporter. It was based on Forsyth's own journalistic experiences, when he spent a year working in East Berlin, covering East Germany, Hungary and Czechoslovakia. The story concerns Arab plots against Israel, in which the Arabs are assisted by ex-SS men who have banded together in a self-help organisation, Odessa. The whole business is investigated by a young West German freelance reporter, Peter Miller, who is on the trail of a former concentration camp commandant who has gone to live in South America. Miller sets out to penetrate the Odessa organisation, whose ramifications extend deep into German political life as well as to the supply of bubonic warheads to Egypt. For background material of the book Forsyth was allowed to draw on the Roschman files of the Jewish Agency which has specialised in hunting Nazi war criminals.

The Dogs of War appeared in 1974. This again was based on Forsyth's African experience: it was also the one subject on which Forsyth felt most strongly. In this story of a small African dictatorship called Zangaro, Forsyth allows some of his bitterness to penetrate his description of violence and bloodshed, of mercenaries and gun-running from Europe.

Forsyth's latest novel, *The Negotiator*, is set in the near future, when it is discovered that in twenty years time the world's oil reserves will be exhausted and there will be no more oil. In the Kremlin, the generals fear for the future of their beloved Red Army and the resulting deployment of resources. In Houston, Cyrus V Miller fears for the future of the military–industrial complex, of which he and his friends are the major prime-movers. Both groups come to the same conclusion — that Saudi Arabia must come under their control. Meanwhile, the new American President goes public with an appeal to the world for a peace treaty between America and the Soviet Union. Then the President's only son is kidnapped and the Russians are suspected — the Negotiator is brought in to find the kidnappers and save the Nantucket Treaty from collapse.

Films

The Day of the Jackal. Universal, GB, 1973.
The Odessa File. Columbia, GB, 1974.
The Dogs of War. United Artists, GB, 1980.
The Fourth Protocol. 1987.

BRIAN HARRY FREEMANTLE

Pseudonyms: JONATHAN EVANS, JOHN MAXWELL, JACK WINCHESTER
British. Born in Southampton, 10 June 1936.

Titles

[Major character: Charlie Muffin]
Goodbye to an Old Friend. London, Cape, 1973; New York, Putnam, 1973.
Face Me When You Walk Away. London, Cape, 1974; New York, Putnam, 1975.
The Man Who Wanted Tomorrow. London, Cape, 1975; New York, Stein & Day, 1975.
Charlie Muffin. London, Cape, 1977; as *Charlie M*. New York, Doubleday, 1977.
Clap Hands, Here Comes Charlie. London, Cape, 1978; as *Here Comes Charlie M*. New York, Doubleday, 1978.
The Inscrutable Charlie Muffin. London, Cape, 1979; New York, Doubleday, 1979.

Charlie Muffin's Uncle Sam. London, Cape, 1980; as *Charlie Muffin USA*. New York, Doubleday, 1980.
Charlie Muffin and Russian Rose. London, Century Hutchinson, 1985.
See Charlie Run. London, Century Hutchinson, 1986.
The Kremlin Kiss. London, Century Hutchinson, 1986.
The Bearpit. London, Century Hutchinson, 1987.
Charlie Muffin San. London, Century Hutchinson, 1987.

Non-Fiction

KGB. London, Joseph,1982; New York, Holt Rinehart, 1982.
CIA. London, Joseph, 1983; New York, Stein & Day, 1983.

Biography

Brian Freemantle was educated at Bitterne Park Secondary Modern School in Southampton. He has worked as a reporter for several newspapers including the *New Milton Advertiser*, the *Evening News*, and *Daily Express*. He became a foreign reporter for the *Daily Express* and Foreign Editor of the *Daily Sketch* and *Daily Mail*.

Critical Analysis

This author undoubtedly comes into the category of spy story writers whose work is well researched. Because of this, he has a big following among the professional intelligence men in America. Miles Copeland, who was first with the OSS and then the CIA, has paid him the tribute that two of Freemantle's books are "virtual case histories of the East–West war of dirty tricks".

Goodbye to An Old Friend was hailed by *Publishers' Weekly* as "a very fine book, meticulously structured, intelligently written and excellent in characterisation". It is a post-Cold War thriller built around an unprepossessing British Foreign Office man, Adrian Dodds, whose speciality is debriefing VIP defectors from the East. The query posed is why Viktor Pavel, Russia's renowned space scientist, should suddenly defect to the West? Honoured in his own country, adored by his family, why should he throw up all this just to seek asylum in England? The governments of America and Britain are eager to accept Pavel and they press Dodds to clear the scientist. But Dodds continues to question Pavel, testing and probing in a tense verbal duel, for he suspects something is not quite right. Finally the Prime Minister himself threatens to destroy Dodd's career unless he follows his superiors' advice. Bowing to pressure, Dodds clears Pavel and triggers a climax that is as fascinating in its complexity as it is shattering in its implications.

Face Me When You Walk Away is a story set in the upper echelons of the Soviet bureaucracy, right up to the Presidium itself. Freemantle makes very clear what is undoubtedly a fact — and probably one of the major factors in the continuing repression in the USSR — that on those levels there is an eternal power struggle with ideological and personal roots that go back to Stalin's day. It is an unusual novel, one of intrigue rather than a thriller. The Swedes are blackmailed into giving the Nobel Prize in literature to a young, emotionally unbalanced Russian. Unlike Solzhenitsyn, he is allowed to leave the country, make his acceptance speech and tour the West. Behind the scenes in Russia there is all manner of manoeuvring around the uses to which this writer is put.

"How accurate is all this?" asked one American critic reviewing the book. "Nobody can tell, though of course in recent years there have been tantalising bits of information about the dirty work of certain Kremlin operators. What Freemantle writes does not seem exaggerated ... in any case this is a grim picture of Soviet life today and in the main one that will be endorsed by most impartial observers who have been there."

One of the most important of Freemantle's books is *The Man Who Wanted Tomorrow*. Deep in the heart of the USSR lives Dr Heinrich Kollman, an ex-Nazi vivisectionist "worse than Mengele". Kollman is wanted by the Israelis as an arch war criminal and by his ex-comrades as the embezzler of a fortune in concentration camp loot. If the truth were known, he would also be wanted by the Russians, but, as the novel opens, he is camouflaged by plastic surgery and two layers of false identities. Dr Vladimir Kusnov, for that is his new name, is finally run to ground in Berlin after a series of intricate manoeuvres that the author narrates with verve and pace.

This book attracted considerable attention in the ranks both of the State Department and the CIA, the latter being convinced that the story was based on one of their own cases. For the novel was in effect an extremely accurate and revealing account of the real-life conflict between Israeli intelligence agencies and the highly secret neo-Nazi movements. In the end the CIA had to admit that this was merely another case of fiction mirroring the truth simply because it was so very well researched.

Freemantle started his series about Charlie Muffin in 1977, since then eight stories have followed. Muffin himself is rather scruffy and in each of the stories he tries to get revenge upon his snobbish superiors in British Intelligence, the CIA, the FBI and the Chinese, all of whom try to kill him. Despite his adventures he manages to survive.

Brian Freemantle has also written two non-fiction books about the KGB and the CIA, which may be of interest to the student of spy fiction.

Film
Charlie Muffin. 1980.

ALAN FURST
American. Born in New York City, 20 February 1941.

Titles
Shadow Trade. New York, Delacorte Press, 1983; London, Quartet Books, 1984.
Night Soldiers. London, Bodley Head, 1988; Boston, Houghton Mifflin, 1988.

Biography
Alan Furst began his writing career in 1976, after a Fulbright Teaching Fellowship in southern France. He has published five novels to date, including a trilogy of murder mysteries about the end of the 1960s, the first of which was nominated for an Edgar award.

Critical Analysis
Alan Furst has written two novels, which the author himself describes as "historical novels about intelligence services", rather than straight spy novels.

His first story *Shadow Trade* is set in contemporary New York: the hero Guyer, is fired from the CIA in June 1977. He is ostensibly dismissed because of the introduction of new technology, but Guyer knows better — that he has made an enemy with influence on the personnel board. Guyer, not knowing any other trade, sets up his own business of clandestine operations with a former colleague. His work is on the borderline of legality and it is in this grey area that he finds himself in trouble.

Night Soldiers has a European setting and the action moves from Bulgaria, to the USSR, Spain, France, Czechoslovakia, Hungary, Yugoslavia, Romania, and New York City. Throughout, the author shows a great sense of place and loyalty to historical detail. We follow the fortunes of a young, intelligent, but uneducated, Bulgarian — Khristo Stoianev — who is recruited into the NKVD and brought to Moscow in 1934 to be trained in the arts of espionage. There he befriends a group of disparate recruits, from all over Europe and they form a secret brotherhood which binds them closer than their loyalty to Russia. His first assignment is in Spain during the Civil War where he sees the "ideals" of Russian communism put into practice.

During the Second World War Khristo suffers various fates but ends up in Switzerland and is set to work on propaganda measures against the Germans. Khristo reflects on the Russian method of gathering intelligence:

"All worthwhile intelligence, *razvedka*, had to come from secret channels, undercover agents, and suborned informants. The rest — the use of open sources — was deemed mere research, women's work, not befitting the heroic Soviet intelligence *apparat*. The dictum, as put by Western intelligence services, ran, *we only believe what we steal*."

His experience showed him that although the Russians were too ruthless the Americans could be too soft:

"They were brave, the Americans, and ingenious to a fault, but they neither liked nor understood security. That took an iron fist, and they and their forefathers had fled the iron fists of the world since the beginning of their country."

These two novels are very evocative in their portrayal of different aspects of espionage. The author is critical of the Russians as well as the Americans, and both the heroes are victims of their own intelligence services.

The author has had no association with intelligence work, but believes that "perhaps it might hinder more than help, since what one could say would be necessarily circumscribed." Furst describes how in the overall themes of his novels he tends "to be occupied with people trying to do a difficult job under very difficult circumstances while subject to political and bureaucratic and technical stresses of all sorts." This is certainly true of *Night Soldiers*, where the hero is pulled emotionally in various directions — by his family, and his friends and lovers, and torn politically between his own country and the domineering force of Russia.

Reginald Bernard John Gadney

Pseudonyms: James Clifford, Paul Bullogh, Adam White
British. Born in Cross Hills, Yorkshire, 20 January 1941.

Titles

Drawn Blanc. London, Heinemann, 1969; New York, Coward McCann, 1972.

Somewhere in England. London, Heinemann, 1970; New York, St. Martin's Press, 1972.
Seduction of a Tall Man. London, Heinemann, 1971.
Something Worth Fighting For. London, Heinemann, 1973.
The Last Hours Before Dawn. London, Heinemann, 1974; as *Victoria*. New York, Coward McCann, 1975.
The Champagne Marxist. London, Hutchinson, 1976; as *The Cage*. New York, Coward McCann, 1977.
Nightshade. London, Heinemann, 1986.

Biography

Reg Gadney was educated at Dragon School, Oxford, Stowe, and St. Catherine's College, Cambridge. He also attended the Massachusetts Institute of Technology. From 1959 to 1962 he served in the Coldstream Guards in Britain, Norway, Libya, France, which included being a NATO winter warfare instructor. He has been a Pro-Rector and Senior Fellow at the Royal College of Art from 1968 to 1984.

Critical Analysis

Reg Gadney does not regard himself as a spy novelist: "It just happens that all the plots of my novels touch upon degrees of espionage and thus also upon loyalty, betrayal and the clandestine."

His first novel, *Drawn Blanc*, is the story of a Czech dissident who is recruited by the British Secret Service. His latest novel, *Nightshade*, concerns an important secret dating back to the Second World War, which if ever discovered will threaten the whole relationship between Britain and America. When SIS officer John Mahon becomes involved in an unofficial investigation into his father's death, the trail leads him unwittingly towards the secret itself. The repercussions are devastating, leaving a trail of murder and destruction which shocks the CIA and nearly destroys the British Secret Service.

When asked if any of his fictional characters were based on real people, Gadney replied: "Increasingly, I confess, I find imaginary people more congenial than people who claim to be real in the proper sense of the word. Therefore, I hope profoundly that none of my characters are based on real people. On the other hand, I know that a number of 'real' people have based themselves on my imaginary ones. I have a sort of pride about that which is sometimes touched by regret and at others gives rise to complete panic."

SARAH GAINHAM

(Pseudonym for Rachel Ames)
British. Born 1 October 1922.

Titles

Time Right Deadly. London, Barker, 1956; New York, Walker, 1961.
The Cold Dark Night. London, Barker, 1957; New York, Barker, 1961.
The Mythmaker. London, Barker, 1957; as *Appointment in Vienna*. New York, Dutton, 1958.
The Stone Roses. London, Eyre & Spottiswoode, 1959; New York, Dutton, 1959.

The Silent Hostage. London, Eyre & Spottiswoode, 1960; New York, Dutton, 1960.
Night Falls on the City. London, Collins, 1967; New York, Holt Rinehart, 1967.

Biography

The daughter of Tom Stainer, she took the pen-name of Sarah Gainham from her maternal great-grandmother. Educated at Newbury High School for Girls, Berkshire, she married Anthony Terry, who had served with British Army Intelligence in the Second World War and was then correspondent of Kemsley Newspapers in Vienna. She went out to Vienna in June 1947 and experienced the gradual build-up to the Cold War during the four-power occupation of that city. "When I arrived in Vienna I was, like nearly all English people at that time, pronouncedly pro-Russian, as well as being young, ignorant and self-opinionated. It was the Russians who cured me in about six weeks."

Sarah Gainham, who also experienced at first hand the Soviet coup in Hungary in 1956 and was for ten years the Central European correspondent for *The Spectator*, has had an exceptional insight into Central Europe generally since the war and, wisely, she has written about the countries that she knows so well.

She was married a second time in 1964 to Kenneth Ames, another Central European newspaper correspondent, who died in 1975.

Critical Analysis

Sarah Gainham started writing in the mid-1950s: her first book, *Time Right Deadly*, was followed by four spy stories: *Cold Dark Night* was about life in Berlin in 1954; *Mythmaker* was set in Vienna in 1947, conjuring up the author's own realisation of what the Cold War was all about; *The Stone Roses* was set in Prague during the grim days of 1948; and *The Silent Hostage* centred on the Adriatic coast of Yugoslavia.

Her best book, and one which became a bestseller (being Book of the Month choice both in Britain and America), was *Night Falls on the City*. She writes with authenticity of detail and background, as one who knows all about the machinations of the Intelligence Services of several countries and has seen the results of some of their mistakes as well as their successes. She admits that her swift change from pro-Russian to anti-Russian views plays a part in her books: "I had a special feeling for using the thriller as a vehicle for ideas, or rather propaganda. I always used them as anti-Russian propaganda. All the best spy thrillers whose origins are known seem to be based on reality. Certainly my own stories were: they are not really fiction at all, only written as fiction."

JOHN EDMUND GARDNER

British. Born in Seaton Delaval, Northumberland, 20 November 1926.

Titles

[Major character: Boysie Oakes]
The Liquidator. London, Muller, 1964; New York, Viking, 1964.
Understrike. London, Muller, 1965; New York, Viking, 1965.
Amber Nine. London, Muller, 1966; New York, Viking, 1966.
Madrigal. London, Muller, 1967; New York, Viking, 1968.

Founder Member. London, Muller, 1969.
Traitor's Exit. London, Muller, 1970.
The Airline Pirates. London, Hodder & Stoughton, 1970; as *Air Apparent*. New York, Putnam, 1971.
A Killer For A Song. London, Hodder & Stoughton, 1975.

[Major character: James Bond]
Licensed Renewed. London, Cape, 1981; New York, Marek, 1981.
For Special Services. London, Cape, 1982; New York, Coward McCann, 1982.
Icebreaker. London, Cape-Hodder, 1983.
Role of Honour. London, Cape-Hodder, 1984; New York, Putnam, 1984.
Nobody Lives Forever. London, Cape-Hodder, 1986; New York, Putnam, 1986.
No Deals, Mr Bond. London, Cape-Hodder, 1987; New York, Putnam, 1987.
Scorpius. London, Cape-Hodder, 1988; New York, Putnam, 1988.
Licence Revoked. London, Cape-Hodder, 1989; New York, Putnam, 1989.
Win, Lose or Die. London, Cape-Hodder, 1989; New York, Putnam, 1989.

[Major character: Herbie Kruger]
The Nostradamus Traitor. London, Hodder & Stoughton, 1979; New York, Doubleday, 1979.
The Garden of Weapons. London, Hodder & Stoughton, 1980; New York, McGraw Hill, 1981.
The Quiet Dogs. London, Hodder & Stoughton, 1982.

Other Novels
To Run A Little Faster. London, Michael Joseph, 1976.
The Werewolf Trace. London, Hodder & Stoughton, 1977; New York, Doubleday, 1977.
The Dancing Dodo. London, Hodder & Stoughton, 1978; New York, Doubleday, 1978.
Golgotha. London, WH Allen, 1980; as *The Last Trump*. New York, McGraw Hill, 1980.

The Generations Trilogy
The Secret Generations. London, Heinemann, 1985; New York, Putnam, 1985.
The Secret Houses. London, Bantam, 1988; New York, Putnam, 1988.
The Secret Families. London, Bantam, 1989; New York, Putnam, 1989.

Short Stories
Hideaway. London, Corgi, 1968.
The Assassination File. London, Corgi, 1974.

Biography

John Gardner was educated at King Alfred's School, Wantage, Berkshire. He joined the Royal Navy in 1944 and transferred to the Royal Marines. He was commissioned and served with 42 Commando Royal Marines in the Far and Middle East. On his return he continued his education at St. John's College, Cambridge (MA Cantab.) and postgraduate work at St. Stephen's House, Oxford.

In 1958 he became the Theatre and Arts Critic of the *Stratford-upon-Avon Herald*. From 1963 he has been a full-time writer. The author says: "I was lucky in that, while at school during the war, my English master was the well-known translator and poetry editor J M Cohen. He alone aroused my interest in writing, though he could never teach me to spell !!!"

Critical Analysis

John Gardner is one of only three espionage writers (along with Deighton and le Carré), who made their débuts in the early 1960s, to have emerged over a quarter of a century as a driving force behind Britain's pre-eminence in the genre.

As Gardner admits his style of writing and the content of his spy novels have varied greatly in this time: "My first book was the autobiographical *Spin the Bottle*. First fiction, however, was *The Liquidator*, a book which eventually became a whole series of books featuring the cowardly, bungling agent Boysie Oakes. It was written as a kind of placebo against the excesses of those who tried to hang onto the coat tails of Ian Fleming. Oakes, a cowardly, inept and lecherous idiot is recruited to Intelligence by mistake, and appointed hired killer — a job he is forced to sub-contract, sometimes with disastrous results.

There is some irony in the fact that, later, having moved on from the comedy of B Oakes to serious espionage fiction, I became the one chosen — in 1979 — to continue the work of Ian Fleming, which I combine with more serious novels of espionage."

In *The Liquidator*, which the *Daily Telegraph* called the "cleverest thriller mutation of the year", Gardner first introduced his secret agent Boysie Oakes, an anti-hero conceived as a swipe at the superhuman infallibility of James Bond. "The book was written as a joke," said Gardner, little suspecting that sixteen years later he would be commissioned to update 007, "but behind it were some of the things I had always wanted to say about this kind of life."

Luxury-loving and lecherous, terrified of flying and physical violence, Boysie was a comic swarm of human weaknesses, a character with whom readers could identify, and in this was just as "realistic" as his more "serious" contemporaries. It was impossible not to identify with, and feel sorry for, the all too human Boysie who, wrongly tagged during World War Two as possessing the killer instinct, was later coerced by Mostyn, the oily Intelligence chief, into the job of unofficial government hit-man, and bravely did his best to enjoy Her Majesty's perks (smart London address, E-type Jaguar and tax-free salary) while secretly sub-contracting the dirty work to a Soho contract killer, Charlie Griffin.

The hapless Boysie Oakes, blighted by malodorous initials, occasional sexual scruples and an uncertain trigger finger, stumbled through eight adventures, and if Gardner had any messages for the world he subordinated them in favour of a high level of comic thrills. This, however, did not stop the *Morning Star* mistakenly perceiving Leftist tendencies in his writing when, in *Amber Nine*, Boysie prevaricated at liquidating Penton, a Labour MP, prior to destroying a neo-Nazi spy school run by the anagrammatic Klara Thirel. Jokes were the order of the day, especially in *Madrigal*, notable for Rosie Puberty, a reverse striptease artist, a brainwashing sequence which spoofed Deighton, and an enigmatic ending. Was it Boysie or Charlie Griffin who had pulled the trigger, finally silencing the sinister Professor Madrigal in mid-speech? Rex Upsdale, the burned-out spy-writing narrator of *Traitor's Exit* switched the jokes into over-drive, encountering Boysie and Mostyn during a madcap plan to get a thinly disguised Kim Philby out of Russia. "But Boysie is a fictional character," objects Upsdale. "Careful, laddie," comes Control's stern rebuke. "Some people have said that about the Prime Minister." In this book featuring a tragi-comedy getaway chase in a disintegrating, daffodil-sprouting circus Austin 7, Gardner reached a comic high which later Oakes books never quite equalled, though *The Airline Pirates* contained deliciously surreal moments. Boysie finally bowed out in *Killer for a Song*, a book prefaced by one of Gardner's many cod quotations.

Boysie's demise was due in part to a waning spy-boom; also to Gardner broadening his writing horizons, producing in 1970 *The Censor*, a story of pornography and hypocrisy, and in 1971 *Every Night's a Bullfight* (later republished in a bowdlerised edition as *The Director*), about a Shakespearian Festival, the background for which he drew from his seven years' experience as theatre critic for the *Stratford-on-Avon Herald*.

In this early 1970s period Gardner's output was disparate and not overtly concerned with espionage, but all these non-genre novels continued a theme begun with Boysie Oakes: a central character who is not quite all that others perceive him to be. This theme — essential to the espionage novel — is very personal to Gardner, who for many years had led his own secret life. In his 1964 autobiography, *Spin the Bottle*, he tells of his early years in the priesthood, the painful and confusing realisation that he was an agnostic and his subsequent recovery from alcoholism.

Gardner went right to the heart of the secret world in *The Werewolf Trace*, a chilling tale of covert surveillance mixed with the supernatural. The book started life as a criminal intelligence operation against the Mafia, with the possibility of a third appearance by Derek Torry, but Gardner changed his mind and forged his continuing theme of past (mostly wartime) events impinging on the present. *Golgotha*, a tale of Britain under Soviet domination written in a whirlwind fourteen days, was followed by *The Dancing Dodo*, a tale of labyrinthine deception following the present-day discovery on Romney Marsh of a World War Two bomber.

The success of these books encouraged Gardner to write a series of pure espionage novels featuring the huge, Mahler-loving spymaster Big Herbie Kruger: *The Nostradamus Traitor*, *The Garden of Weapons* and *The Quiet Dogs*. But by this time Gardner must have found himself in something of a professional dilemma. Just as critics like HRF Keating were calling his Kruger books "the spy novel *in excelsis*" he signed a contract to write a series of updated James Bond adventures, the very books he had set out to debunk with *The Liquidator*.

In 1981 *Licensed Renewed* was published. Bond purists carped at 007 smoking low-tar cigarettes, cutting down his vodka-martini intake and being put behind the wheel of a Saab Turbo (later a Bentley Mulsanne Turbo), but they need not have taken offence. Gardner knew that Ian Fleming was a hard act to follow (see ROBERT MARKHAM) and wisely chose to accomplish his unenviable task by developing the movie Bond rather than Fleming's original creation.

Bond's adventures continued with *For Special Services*, and the publicity these books now received detracted from Gardner's serious work. He was in imminent danger of surrendering much of his hard-earned gravitas. Indeed, many confused readers were already asking if the *real* John Gardner would please stand up. Gardner heeded the message, and after fulfilling a contractual obligation with the curious *Flamingo* (1983), a Casablanca-esque homage to the cinema of his Wantage youth, he did just that.

In parallel with the annual Bond, he embarked on his most ambitious project, a vast espionage trilogy charting the fortunes of two families — one British, the other American — involved in the secret war from the turn of the century to the present day. It dramatised the development of British Intelligence, with Gardner allowing his fictional intrigues to be influenced by a stream of historical events, and for this he marshalled a huge cast against a complex and accurately researched background (a skill previously deployed in *Every Night's a Bullfight*). The historical family saga wasn't a unique literary concept, but it was certainly new to the espionage novel, and Gardner put it to good use. With fiction bolted firmly to available facts, volume one, *The Secret Generations*, filled a gap between dry-as-dust true-life espionographies and the majority of popular spy novels whose "authenticity" came from their authors' skill at creating believable mythologies rather than any real understanding of the secret world.

Despite this successful bid for the high echelons of serious espionage fiction, Gardner never lost sight of the fact that he was primarily an entertainer, and in volume two, *The Secret Houses*, capitalised on one of his past successes. From his earlier trilogy he introduced the fledgling Herbie Kruger, fleshing out the origins of his spymaster with a measure of customary good humour (a bold move in this notoriously po-faced genre) while grooming him for a major role in the third and final volume, *The Secret Families*. Kruger, avidly read by members of Washington DC's Intelligence circles (Century House offers "no comment" on such matters), also brings his weighty intellect to bear in *Maestro* (1990?).

The last comment is left to the author and his views on spy fiction in general: "I believe some of the best writing of this decade has been, and is being, done by those who write novels of espionage. What does bother me is the fact that most of us are lumped under the dread title of Crime Writers which always gives off an aura of Death in the Refectory. While I do not much care for the Crime Novel as such, I do believe that the true novel of espionage must contain a puzzle, a mystery if you like, which should run through the book — a thread to be followed, leading to a conclusion."

Film

The Liquidator. MGM, GB, 1965.

BRIAN FRANCIS WYNNE GARFIELD

Pseudonyms: BENNET GARLAND, ALEX HAWK, JOHN IVES, DREW MALLORY, FRANK O'BRIAN, JONAS WARD, BRIAN WYNNE, FRANK WYNNE.
American. Born in New York City, 26 January 1939.

Titles

Deep Cover. New York, Delacorte Press, 1971; London, Hodder & Stoughton, 1972.
Line of Succession. New York, Delacorte Press, 1972; London, Hodder & Stoughton, 1974.
Hopscotch. New York, Evans, 1975; London, Macmillan, 1975.
The Paladin. New York, Simon & Schuster, 1980; London, Macmillan, 1980.

Biography

Brian Garfield was educated at the University of Arizona. He served in the US Army and Army Reserve (1957-65). He is a rarity among writers, a devotee of jazz music and a professional musician, and originally started his career as a jazz band member. Since 1963 he has been a self-employed writer.

Critical Analysis

Most of Garfield's novels can be described as thriller-narratives, including *The*

Arizonans (1961), *The Vanquished* (1964), *Sliphammer* (1970) and *Relentless* (1973), but some of his best books have been of spy fiction.

Deep Cover told the story of a take-over of America's most important missile base by 300 Russians. A master of Soviet Intelligence had worked for twenty years on his plan to teach these 300 men and women to think, act and talk like Americans. So deep was their cover that they themselves did not know which of their colleagues were part of the masquerade. Not only did they surreptitiously take over the base, but, without being unmasked, their influence extended deep into Washington political life. To combat this unknown factor, which he senses rather than sees, Senator Alan Forrester risks his own career in trying to probe it.

Line of Succession plunges into the complexities of American politics, with the President-elect being kidnapped and held to ransom by a group of extremists eager to secure the release of important prisoners for which they are prepared to barter the President's life. The book is enlivened by CIA machinations (of which Garfield seems to have made a study), and high-tension thrills.

In *Hopscotch*, Miles Kendig, a CIA veteran is forced to retire, and decides to play his own game and outwit the CIA, KGB and FBI. He threatens to expose the espionage secrets of the major powers and sets himself up as the target of an international manhunt. Kendig outwits them all, and realising that they will not be satisfied until they see he is dead, he engineers his own "death".

Writing of *Hopscotch*, which he described as "one of the most compelling thrillers of this season", ex-agent Miles Copeland said: "This latest book [of Garfield's] features a former CIA official named Miles who is roughly my vintage and physical build, who has lived in Birmingham, Alabama, my home town, who wrote a book that made the CIA's 'questors' unhappy, and who decided to annoy them further by enticing them into a 'game' of a sort that has given me a certain amount of notoriety." Perhaps this novel contains a warning to potential and past CIA whistleblowers!

"The oddest story ever written" is how Garfield described his novel *The Paladin*. The story concerns the alleged recruitment by Winston Churchill during the Second World War of a 15-year-old schoolboy as a spy and assassin. "And the most extraordinary thing about it," Garfield was quoted as saying, "is that I believe that it's all true."

The book was written as a novel to avoid legal complications. The central figure is called Peter Hamilton, but his real name is known to the author, who says that his credentials have been checked and that he seems to be authentic.

Brian Garfield commented recently in *Twentieth Century Crime and Mystery Writers* (1985): "My claim to categorization as a 'mystery writer' is tenuous. Normally my stories do not emphasize the unravelling of mysteries. Stanley Ellin defines the difference between mysteries and thrillers by pointing out that in the mystery a crime takes place at the beginning; in the thriller if there is a crime at all, it is more likely to take place at the end rather than the beginning. By that definition I suppose I'm a thriller writer. But I prefer to be simply a writer."

The author also commented: "The 'thriller', or suspense entertainment, provides unlimited space in which the writer can explore history and character; there are no formulae or conventions. And, ever since I reacted with revulsion to the Hollywood film version of my novel *Death Wish*, I've found great stimulus in the challenge of writing novels like *Hopscotch* [and] *Recoil* ... in each of which there is little or no overt violence. (Suspense is a matter of menace, not violence.) The judges who conferred the 1976 [Mystery Writers of America] Edgar Award on *Hopscotch* as best novel of the year confirmed that they did so partly because the book delivered suspense without brutality."

Film

Hopscotch. 1980.

DOROTHY GILMAN

(Pseudonym of Dorothy Gilman Butters)
American. Born in New Brunswick, New Jersey, 25 June 1923.

Titles

[Major character: Mrs Emily Pollifax]
The Unexpected Mrs Pollifax. New York, Doubleday, 1966; London, Hale, 1967.
Uncertain Voyage. New York, Doubleday, 1967; London, Hale, 1968.
The Amazing Mrs Pollifax. New York, Doubleday, 1970; London, Hale, 1971.
The Elusive Mrs Pollifax. New York, Doubleday, 1971; London, Hale, 1973.
A Palm for Mrs Pollifax. New York, Doubleday, 1973; London, Hale, 1974.
A Nun in the Closet. New York, Doubleday, 1975; as *A Nun in the Cupboard*. London, Hale, 1976.
The Clairvoyant Countess. New York, Doubleday, 1975; London, Prior, 1976.
Mrs Pollifax on Safari. New York, Doubleday, 1977; London, Hale, 1977.
The Tightrope Walker. New York, Doubleday, 1979; London, Hale, 1980.
Mrs Pollifax on the China Station. New York, Doubleday, 1983; London, Hale, 1984.

Biography

Dorothy Gilman attended the Pennsylvania Academy of Fine Arts from 1940 to 1945, the University of Pennsylvania, the Moore Institute of Art, and the Arts Students' League from 1963 to 1964. She worked as an instructor of drawing in adult evening school for two years at the Samuel Fleisher Art Memorial. She has also worked as a switchboard operator for the American Bell Telephone Company, and as an instructor in creative writing at Cherry Lawn School, Darien, Connecticut, from 1969 to 1970.

Critical Analysis

Dorothy Gilman's central character is Mrs Emily Pollifax, described as "a bored and lonely widow in her sixties" who applies to the CIA for a job and is chosen as "the least-suspectable person" they can use for important assignments. Mrs Pollifax's various adventures take place in romantic locales such as Turkey, where she is sent to help a double-agent escape; in another story she is sent on a simple courier assignment, but is then kidnapped to Albania.

Mrs Pollifax is a colourful figure and often acts as a female detective in her assignments for the CIA. However, she is one of the few females in spy fiction. Anthony Boucher of the *New York Times Book Review* commented: "Mrs Gilman steers an adroit course between comedy and melodrama, which should delight you whether you're looking for smiles, or thrills."

Film

The Unexpected Mrs Pollifax. United Artists, US, 1970.

NIK GOWING

British. Born in London, 13 January 1951.

Titles

The Wire. London, Hutchinson, 1988; New York, St. Martin's Press, 1989.

Biography

Nik Gowing was educated at the University of Bristol (1970-73). After he left university he started a career in journalism and worked for the *Newcastle Chronicle*. From 1974 to 1978 he worked for Granada Television in Manchester. Since 1978 he has worked as an ITN correspondent.

He is at present Foreign Affairs correspondent for "Channel Four News". From 1980 to 1983 he was ITN's Eastern European correspondent based in Poland. His smuggled report of the imposition of martial law in December 1981 was an international scoop. He collected the 1982 BAFTA award for "Best Actuality" news coverage.

Critical Analysis

The action in The Wire occurs within a secret power struggle being waged inside the Kremlin between the ailing President Brezhnev and the ambitious head of the KGB, Yuri Andropov, who hatches a plot which will bring down Brezhnev by the assassination of General Jaruzelski, and implicate the CIA in his murder. Most of the action takes place in Warsaw, Washington and Moscow, and the story traces the paths of Bogdan, a dedicated Solidarity activist, and Sulecki, a ruthless KGB "sleeper" who has been planted inside the union to discredit Solidarity and the American government by assassinating the Polish leader.

This novel is a work of fiction based on eye-witness reports and the personal experiences of Solidarity activists. Gowing was the Eastern European correspondent for ITN for three years, in the midst of Solidarity's highest and lowest moments. The story was inspired by a tip-off from an officer of the SB (the Polish secret police, which had been harassing Gowing for a few months), that Soviet hardliners, backed by the KGB, were trying to depose General Jaruzelski. Gowing made further enquiries to try to find out more, but he could not confirm the story. Instead he decided to write a novel based upon this incident and using his knowledge of political events in Poland to make his story authentic.

This is a rather long book: some of the characters are weak, and the dialogue is heavy at times. However, Gowing gives us a vivid picture of Poland and its people, especially on the night that martial law is imposed. The author also conveys the strong feeling of nationalism, so much so that Jaruzelski, although Moscow-trained, tried to remain faithful to the Polish people, even though this attitude made him unpopular with both the Russians and the Poles.

The book is interspersed with insights into the profession of journalism. For instance one of the characters voices this fact: "The rule of thumb for any Westerner in Moscow was that any Russian who talks doesn't know, and any Russian who knows doesn't talk." The author is obviously speaking from experience.

Gowing says that he enjoys spy fiction and "it is a way to portray stories" and also, "I cannot easily report in my job at ITN (where I am a diplomatic correspondent)."

JAMES THOMAS GRADY

American. Born in Shelby, Montana, 30 April 1949.

Titles

Six Days of the Condor. New York, Norton, 1975.
Shadow of the Condor. New York, Putnam, 1976.

Biography

James Grady was educated at the University of Montana, from where he graduated in 1971 with a BA in Journalism, having also studied political science and history. He worked as a research analyst for the Montana Constitutional Convention, Helena, 1971–72, and as an analyst and bureaucrat at the Youth Development Bureau, Helena, 1972–73. He worked as an aide for Senator Lee Metcalf in Washington DC in 1974, and as an investigative reporter for columnist Jack Anderson from 1975 to 1979. He has been a full-time writer since 1979.

Critical Analysis

Six Days of the Condor was published in 1974 and is the story of a CIA researcher (employed by an obscure but real branch of the agency) who returns from lunch to discover that all his colleagues have been murdered in his absence. From that moment on Ronald Malcolm, code-named Condor, is on the run trying to escape the agency and the hired killers determined to find him. His job in the agency is to read and analyse spy and mystery stories as they are published in order to spot anything that comes close to reality, and so detect possible leaks of information.

This novel was followed by *Shadow of the Condor* in which Ronald Malcolm reappears and was hailed by one critic as "the most likeable and unlikely CIA agent on record". In this story the body of an Air Force undercover agent based in Europe mysteriously turns up at a Montana missile site. The CIA's job is to find out what led the agent there and who killed him. To divert attention from the agency Malcolm is sent to Montana in disguise. He discovers that all parties are being double-crossed, even by the unusual standards of the world of international intrigue.

Grady says "I was attracted to the espionage genre primarily because I knew something about it, because those types of stories are entertaining, and, when told properly, contain all the elements of good stories. And, in *Six Days of the Condor*, I knew I had a good story."

"I try to write spy fiction as factually as possible. All my backgrounds are solidly factual. I try to use as much real material as possible, weaving truth through my fiction. I try to paint the world of espionage as it is — largely grey, tinged occasionally with blood, peopled extensively by the type of person most people wouldn't want to invite into their homes. Ronald Malcolm is a very ordinary individual, no superman, who works in the field, propelled by a combination of fascination and revulsion, tinged with a sense of general alienation more than anything else."

Film

Three Days of the Condor. Paramount, US, 1975 (book title: *Six Days of the Condor*).

BILL GRANGER

Pseudonym: BILL GRIFFITH
American.

Titles

[Major character: Devereaux]
The November Man [Devereaux]. New York, Fawcett, 1979; London, New English Library, 1981.
Schism [Devereaux]. New York, Crown, 1981; London, New English Library, 1982.
Queen's Crossing. New York, Fawcett, 1982.
The Shattered Eye [Devereaux]. New York, Crown, 1982.
The British Cross [Devereaux]. New York, Crown, 1983; London, Firecrest, 1986.

Novels as Bill Griffith
Time for Frankie Coolin. New York, Random House, 1982.

Biography

An award-winning novelist and reporter, Bill Granger was raised in a working-class neighbourhood on the South Side of Chicago. He began his career in 1963 when, while still in college, he joined the staff of United Press International. He later worked for the *Chicago Tribune*, writing about crime, the police and politics, and covering such events as the race riots of the late 1960s and the 1968 Democratic Convention.

In 1969 he joined the staff of the *Chicago Sun-Times*, where he won an Associated Press award for his story of a participant in the My Lai massacre. He also wrote a series of stories on Northern Ireland for *Newsday*. By 1978 Granger had contributed articles to *Time*, *The New Republic* and other magazines; and became a daily columnist, television critic and teacher of journalism at Columbia College in Chicago.

Critical Analysis

Granger began his literary career in 1978 with *The November Man*, which introduced the cool American spy who later appeared in a whole series of books. His second novel, *Public Murders* (1980), a Chicago police procedural, won the Edgar Award from the Mystery Writers of America in 1981.

Altogether Granger has published seven "November Man" novels, four "Chicago" police mysteries, two non-fiction books written with his wife, and three novels. His books have been translated into ten languages.

Granger's hero, introduced in *The November Man*, is a middle-aged spy named Devereaux, who works for a shadowy organisation called R Section. This department was formed by John F Kennedy after the events at the Bay of Pigs when he decided that it was time to provide an independent watchdog over intelligence — so R Section was formed, hidden in the Department of Agriculture.

In his first novel, *The November Man*, Devereaux investigates an IRA plot to kill one of England's most powerful men, Lord Slough. The plot is complicated by the involvement of a Russian agent and CIA treachery. This novel gained national publicity when the IRA assassinated Lord Louis Mountbatten by planting a bomb on his boat on 27 August 1979. What horrified everyone was that the fictional plot was so close to predicting the motives and methods the IRA actually used in the assassination of Mountbatten. Even though the book was finished by 1978, it was published two weeks before his murder.

Granger wrote an afterword to this novel in 1986 in which he said: "That event [Mountbatten's assassination] was to make this book an infamous reminder that realistic fiction — if it is to be any good at all — is merely a clear mirror vision of what is really happening in the world described. The things that happen in fiction mirror those things that have happened — or will happen soon — in real life. The parallels between what in fact happened off the Irish coast to a cousin of the Queen and what happened in the pages of *The November Man* to the character of Lord Slough were both derived from the terrorism and sorrow of a radically divided Ireland. In one case, a real life ended; in my book, I wrote from knowledge of my own time spent reporting the story of death and terror in Northern Ireland."

In his fourth adventure, *The British Cross*, the November Man finds himself in frozen Helsinki. He is waiting for a potential Russian defector to deliver information which should justify the risks of his defection. Eventually he gets a name: Tomas Crohan. But nobody knows who he is, or if they do they are keeping it to themselves. When Devereaux passes on this name it sends the CIA, the KGB and the British Secret Service into an international conspiracy of silence. Devereaux receives orders to forget the defection and the name, which only fuels his curiosity. His investigation leads him to team up with Rita Macklin, a journalist, who has appeared in the series before, and the trail leads them from Helsinki, to Washington DC, Ireland, Britain and eventually to a psychiatric hospital in Leningrad.

GRAHAM GREENE

British. Born in Berkhamsted, Hertfordshire, 2 October 1904.

Titles

The Confidential Agent. London, Heinemann, 1939; New York, Viking Press, 1939.
The Ministry of Fear. London, Heinemann, 1943; New York, Viking Press, 1943.
The Third Man. New York, Viking Press, 1950.
The Quiet American. London, Heinemann, 1955; New York, Viking Press, 1956.
Our Man in Havana. London, Heinemann, 1958; New York, Viking Press, 1958.
The Human Factor. London, Bodley Head, 1978; New York, Simon & Schuster, 1978.

Biography

Graham Greene was educated at Berkhamsted School, where from all accounts he was on the point of running away on more than one occasion! He went on to Balliol College, Oxford, before starting a career in journalism in Nottingham. In 1926 he joined *The Times* as a sub-editor and it was during this period that his first book was published, *Babbling Brook* (1925). In 1930 he became literary editor of *The Spectator*. *Stamboul Train* (1932) and *Brighton Rock* (1938) helped to make him a popular as well as one of the most consistent and powerful novelists emerging in England over the past fifty years.

Critical Analysis

It was not until shortly before the war that Greene introduces an element of the spy story into his work, most notably in *The Confidential Agent*, in which he introduced "D", the agent of an imaginary Latin government which bore a distinct resemblance to that of the embattled Spanish Republican Government of that era. Greene is not, of course, to be labelled as a spy novelist, but he has used the often interwoven themes of espionage and corruption as a vehicle of his prose.

Undoubtedly Greene's wartime service in Intelligence provided him with much material for his later spy books, not to mention some of the characters in them. His entry in *Who's Who* states that from 1941 to 1944 he was in a "department of the Foreign Office", which is a well-known euphemism for intelligence work, in Greene's case mainly West Africa. One of his main jobs was to watch the activities of the Vichy French in Freetown. It is noteworthy that the section in which Greene worked was that of the Iberian sub-section of Section V of the SIS, which was controlled by none other than Kim Philby.

In many respects *Our Man in Havana* is the best of all Greene's spy stories, leavened and lightened by its undertones of satire. His inside knowledge of the intelligence game, his keenly observant eye for the characteristics and quirks that lie beneath the surface of human beings, the dormant, inborn depravity and, not least, the wrestling with conscience, enable Greene to lift the spy story to the realms of literature of merit.

Perhaps the most widely known of Greene's books, mainly due to the film version, is *The Third Man*. Though this is not strictly a spy story, its background is almost entirely that of the "spy city" which Vienna had become just after the war when there was a four-power occupation and each power had a separate zone. Here Greene was stepping into a situation and environment with which he was not unfamiliar.

Greene has said that the two authors who most influenced his writing were such disparate figures as John Buchan and François Mauriac. Undoubtedly the Buchan influence is to be seen in *Ministry of Fear*, a melodrama about a Fifth Column in wartime London, and now one of his least remembered works. His travels in Indochina before the French were driven out provided material for many articles and *The Quiet American*. This was a spy story in striking contrast to the comic melodrama of *Our Man in Havana*. Like W J Lederer, Greene is supposed to have modelled his central figure, Alden Pyle, on Colonel Edward Lansdale, USAF, one of the CIA's covert operations agents in Vietnam, though he had had extensive experience in the Philippines in the early 1950s. Whether the description is based on him or not, Greene effectively depicts a certain type of idealistic American who, in certain circumstances, can be more dangerous than a straightforward rogue. It was the portrait of a man whose faith in human nature only led to men getting killed. But *The Quiet American*, while having CIA skullduggery as part of its background, was really a plea for commonsense to be used in the Vietnam impasse before too many lives were lost and too many horrors perpetrated on either side. It was a shrewd ex-intelligence officer's report in the guise of a novel, leaving the reader to draw his own conclusions as to what was likely to happen in Vietnam.

Films

Ministry of Fear. Paramount, US, 1944.
Confidential Agent. Warner, US, 1945.
The Third Man. London Films, GB, 1949.

The Quiet American. United Artists, US, 1957.
Our Man in Havana. Columbia, GB, 1959.
The Human Factor. Rank, GB, 1979.

HARRIS CARL GREENE

American. Born in Waltham, Massachusetts, 22 October 1921.

Titles

The Mozart Leaves at Nine. New York, Doubleday, 1960.
The Flags at Doney. New York, Doubleday, 1964.
The Thieves of Tumbutu. New York, Doubleday, 1968.
Cancelled Accounts. New York, Doubleday, 1973.
Inference of Guilt. London, Hale, 1982.

Biography

Harris Greene was educated at Boston University, from where he graduated in 1943. He went on to graduate study at Lehigh University from 1943 to 1944, and George Washington University from 1950 to 1951. He worked as a researcher and reporter for the *Boston Herald Traveler*, 1942-43. He was then employed by the US State Department in 1950, and served as a vice-consul in Genoa and Rome (1950-51); embassy attaché in Athens (1964-68), and first secretary of embassy in Berne, Switzerland (1969-73).

Critical Analysis

Harris Greene was a professional intelligence officer for thirty-six years, both abroad and in senior positions at CIA headquarters. His intelligence experience is reflected in several of his novels, in particular, *The Mozart Leaves at Nine* and *Inference of Guilt*.

The Mozart Leaves at Nine is the story of the US Army Security Chief in Vienna in 1946, who is concerned with hunting down remaining Nazis and Soviet agents.

Inference of Guilt is about several veteran intelligence men whose past catches up with them when one of them, now the Deputy Director for Operations in the CIA, George Wendell, is brought before a Senate investigation looking into the case of Calinescu, a former Romanian Iron Guard chief, now living as a respectable, wealthy businessman in California. At the centre of the investigation is Steve Browning, an elderly operator who was responsible for taking on Calinescu as an informer, and for allowing his immigration to America. But the task of the committee is not made easier by the fact that Browning himself is considered by some in the agency to be a security risk.

This is a good story and the plot is quite plausible. Also the characters are well drawn. The author gives a vivid portrait of the bureaucratic wranglings at CIA headquarters and the rivalry between the old-timers and the ambitious up-and-coming younger generation. One critic and an ex-CIA employee, Joseph Hosey wrote: "The book will be of special interest to those who share the author's experience of the internal workings of an intelligence organization, but the general reader may be distracted by a slightly excessive use of intra-agency allusions. A glossary of terminology is thoughtfully provided to offset this possibility, however, and since the story is well conceived and well told, such a minor fault should not prevent its general enjoyment."

LEONARD GROSS

American. Born in Chicago, Illinois, 21 April 1928.

Titles
The Dossier (with Pierre Salinger). New York, Doubleday, 1984; London, Deutsch, 1984.

Biography
Leonard Gross was educated at the University of California, Los Angeles, from which he graduated with a BA in 1949. He also attended Columbia University. Gross started his career in journalism as a reporter in the San Francisco bureau of the *Wall Street Journal* in 1952. He continued to work as a writer, columnist, theatre critic and screenwriter in New York, South America and Europe, for various magazines until 1980.

Critical Analysis
The Dossier was written in collaboration with Pierre Salinger, who was John F Kennedy's White House spokesman, and who has since worked as the Paris bureau chief of ABC Television for many years.

The story concerns the suspicion of Shlomo Glaser, an Israeli agent who believes that he has evidence that will prove that a candidate for the French Presidency was a Gestapo informer during the Second World War. The allegation seems all the more preposterous as the man in question, Camille Laurent, is a revered Resistance hero. Most people would not believe it but André Kohl, one of the top reporters, and known for his skills as an intrepid investigative journalist for a large New York TV network, cannot ignore the challenge this allegation offers him.

His search leads him to Bolivia, the stronghold of SS General Kurt Hoepner, Laurent's alleged spymaster, the "Executioner of Clermont-Ferrand". André uses his contacts in the East and the West. While an informant in the USSR is willing to supply him with a document that would incriminate Laurent, the Americans are very reluctant to help him at all, perhaps because the Deputy Director of the CIA, believed that Laurent saved his life during the war.

NICHOLAS M GUILD

American. Born in San Mateo, California, 5 November 1944.

Titles
The Summer Soldier. New York, Simon & Schuster, 1978.
The Favor. New York, St. Martin's Press, 1981.
Chain Reaction. New York, St. Martin's Press, 1983.

Biography

Nicholas Guild was educated at the University of California, Berkeley, from where he graduated with an MA in 1968 and a PhD in 1972. He worked as an assistant professor of English at Clemson University from 1973 to 1975, and also at Ohio State University in the same capacity.

Critical Analysis

In *The Summer Soldier* a retired CIA agent returns home one day to find his wife dead and himself the target of a defected KGB operative, whose own wife the American had accidentally killed many years before.

The Favor is about an East German agent who asks assassin Ray Guiness, who owes the agent a favour, to save his daughter, who has been caught by the Allies as part of a counter-espionage scheme in Amsterdam.

Chain Reaction is another counter-espionage tale, an FBI story which harks back to the Second World War. The story is set in 1944 and in a last desperate move the Germans want to acquire the secret of the atomic bomb to use against the Americans and win the war. They have a man on the inside at Los Alamos and they send a German agent to go and get him.

The German agent, Baron von Niehauser, leaves a trail of murders which is picked up by George Havens, an FBI agent working in counter-intelligence. The German agent is found and the plot is foiled, naturally.

WILLIAM HAGGARD

(Pseudonym of Richard Henry Michael Clayton)
British. Born in Croydon, Surrey, 11 August 1907.

Titles

[Major character: Colonel Charles Russell]
Slow Burner. London, Cassell, 1958; Boston, Little Brown, 1958.
Venetian Blind. London, Cassell, 1959; New York, Washburn, 1959.
The Arena. London, Cassell, 1961; New York, Washburn, 1961.
The Unquiet Sleep. London, Cassell, 1962; New York, Washburn, 1962.
The High Wire. London, Cassell, 1963; New York, Washburn, 1963.
The Antagonists. London, Cassell, 1964; New York, Washburn, 1964.
The Powder Barrel. London, Cassell, 1965; New York, Washburn, 1965.
The Hard Sell. London, Cassell, 1965; New York, Washburn, 1966.
The Power House. London, Cassell, 1966; New York, Washburn, 1967.
The Conspirators. London, Cassell, 1967; New York, Walker, 1968.
A Cool Day For Killing. London, Cassell, 1968; New York, Walker, 1968.
The Doubtful Disciple. London, Cassell, 1969.
The Hardliners. London, Cassell, 1970; New York, Walker, 1970.
The Bitter Harvest. London, Cassell, 1971; as *Too Many Enemies*. New York, Walker, 1972.
The Old Masters. London, Cassell, 1973; as *The Notch on the Knife*. New York, Walker, 1973.
The Scorpion's Tail. London, Cassell, 1975; New York, Walker, 1975.
Yesterday's Enemy. London, Cassell, 1976; New York, Walker, 1976.

The Poison People. London, Cassell, 1978; New York, Walker, 1979.
Visa to Limbo. London, Cassell, 1978; New York, Walker, 1979.
The Median Line. London, Cassell, 1979; New York, Walker, 1981.

Biography

William Haggard was educated at Lancing College and Christ Church, Oxford. He entered the Indian Civil Service and eventually became a judge, and during the Second World War he served in the Indian Army, undergoing a course at the Staff College, Quetta. Later he joined the British Civil Service, and for a time was Controller of Enemy Property. Associated with intelligence work during his career, he retired in 1969.

Critical Analysis

Haggard could best be described as a writer of suspense novels with political backgrounds or, as he himself modestly refers to his books, "basically political novels with more action than in the straight novel". At the same time he has ventured into the fringes of the spy novel in a somewhat romantic, Buchanesque style, with echoes of the 1930s in his preoccupation with notions of propriety and correct and civilised behaviour in his intelligence operators.

His first spy novel was *Slow Burner*, in which for the first time appeared Haggard's own special creation, Colonel Russell of the Security Executive, the very quintessence of that *rara avis* of the Intelligence world, the *pukka sahib*. Perhaps Colonel Russell was too pukka for the tastes of the decade, but Buchan would have approved of him. This, however, is not a criticism of Haggard's work, for he created an interesting character who bridged the gap between the 1930s and the 1960s, at least to the extent of having a British Intelligence executive who got along reasonably well with his opposite number in the KGB. There are twenty books in the series which feature Colonel Russell as the main protagonist.

JOHN HALKIN

British. Born in Liverpool, 1927.

Titles

Fatal Odds. London, Hale, 1981; New York, Leisure Books, 1981.
Hantu. London, Bodley Head, 1988.

Biography

John Halkin read modern languages at Cambridge University. After he left university he lived in Singapore for some years, then moved to Nigeria. On returning to Britain he worked as a BBC producer for many years and travelled widely, particularly in Africa.

Critical Analysis

Halkin's first book, *Slither* (1980) was a horror book about a plague of worm-like reptiles infesting Britain's rivers and sewers. He has also written an historical saga set in Kenya from 1896 to1914, as well as two spy novels to date.

His latest book, *Hantu*, is set in South Korea in 1950 during the Korean War in which Peter Ross, an agent of British Intelligence is sent on an undercover assignment in Communist China, where he comes across violence and conspiracy which leads him from the tropical heat of Singapore to the Arctic freeze of Manchuria. This novel was well received in Britain and America and one reviewer in *Publisher's Weekly* described it as "Tightly written and suspenseful from the first, British writer Halkin's espionage thriller ... is a standard in the genre."

Some of the recurrent themes that the author feels may feature in future books are: "The 'Section', a British espionage-cum-sabotage organisation answerable to the prime minister. More importantly, informative handling of foreign settings forms a regular characteristic."

The author comments: "Spying in the strict sense means gathering information and to be successful a spy must remain unnoticed. Trails of corpses are not conducive to good intelligence work. Fiction requires more excitement than a genuine spy would find good for his health."

WILLIAM HENRY HALLAHAN

American. Born in Brooklyn, New York.

Titles

The Dead of Winter. Indianapolis, Bobbs Merrill, 1972; London, Sphere, 1979.
The Ross Forgery. Indianapolis, Bobbs Merrill, 1973; London, Gollancz, 1977.
Catch Me, Kill Me. Indianapolis, Bobbs Merrill, 1977; London, Gollancz, 1979.
The Trade. New York, Morrow, 1981; London, Gollancz, 1981.

Biography

William H Hallahan was educated at Temple University, Philadelphia, and has degrees in both Journalism and English.

Critical Analysis

Hallahan's first publication was *The Dead of Winter* in 1972, which is more of a thriller than a spy novel. His first spy novel was *The Ross Forgery*, followed by *Catch Me, Kill Me*, which won him an Edgar from the Mystery Writers of America in 1977. The story is about a Russian Jew called Boris Kotlikoff, a minor poet who defected to America two years before, who is kidnapped, for no known reason, by Russian diplomats attached to the UN. Kotlikoff left Russia with no state secrets and is no threat to the Soviet Union, so why was he kidnapped?

Three men are involved in the search for Kotlikoff, who is held hostage somewhere in New York City. The three men battle with each other and various other obstacles to find the Russian and find out why he was taken. *Time* magazine called this novel a "masterpiece of bamboozlement, a kind of *Catch-22* between rival and riven US agencies, written in a style that ranges from hardest-boiled egg to soufflé, with nothing poached."

One critic, Don Cole, in *Twentieth Century Crime and Mystery Writers* (1985), described him as follows: "William H Hallahan is a very complex author and his works will be remembered, though not always admired. He may not be our top mystery writer of the day, but part of that could be that perhaps he doesn't *want* to be. But he is certainly one of the most interesting and enticing writers today, and one wonders where his career will lead him next."

DONALD HAMILTON

American. Born in Uppsala, Sweden, 24 March 1916.

Titles

Date with Darkness. New York, Rinehart, 1947; London, Wingate, 1951.
The Steel Mirror. New York, Rinehart, 1948; London, Wingate, 1950.
Night Walker. New York, Dell, 1954; as *Rough Company*. London, Wingate, 1954.
Assignment: Murder. New York, Dell, 1956; as *Assassins Have Starry Eyes*. New York, Fawcett, 1966.

[Major character: Matt Helm]
Death of a Citizen. New York, Fawcett,1960; London, Muller,1960.
The Wrecking Crew. New York, Fawcett, 1960; London, Muller, 1961.
The Removers. New York, Fawcett, 1961; London, Muller, 1962.
The Silencers. New York, Fawcett, 1962; London, Hodder & Stoughton, 1966.
Murderers' Row. New York, Fawcett, 1962; London, Muller, 1963.
The Ambushers. New York, Fawcett, 1963; London, Hodder & Stoughton, 1967.
The Ravagers. New York, Fawcett, 1964.
The Devastators. New York, Fawcett, 1965; London, Hodder & Stoughton, 1967.
The Betrayers. New York, Fawcett, 1966; London, Hodder & Stoughton, 1968.
The Menacers. New York, Fawcett, 1968; London, Hodder & Stoughton, 1968.
The Interlopers. New York, Fawcett, 1969; London, Hodder & Stoughton, 1969.
The Poisoners. New York, Fawcett, 1971; London, Hodder & Stoughton, 1971.
The Intriguers. New York, Fawcett, 1973; London, Hodder & Stoughton, 1973.
The Intimidators. New York, Fawcett, 1974; London, Hodder & Stoughton, 1974.
(10 more titles featuring Matt Helm)

Biography

Donald Hamilton emigrated to America in 1924. He was educated at the University of Chicago, from which he graduated with a BSc degree in Chemistry in 1938. During the Second World War he served in the US Naval Reserve and left as a Lieutenant.

Straight after the war he sold an article to *Yachting Magazine*, a short story to *Collier's*, and a novel to Rinehart Publishers, New York. He has been a self-employed writer since 1946.

Critical Analysis

The hero of Hamilton's novels is Matt Helm, who is often described as the American equivalent of James Bond. During the Second World War he worked for a secret military organisation and learned the arts of spying and assassination. His code name was Eric. Helm resumed his peacetime occupations until the early 1960s when his former chief "Mac", asked him to serve his country and undertake a special mission, recorded in *The Ambushers*, in which he pursues an ex-Nazi fanatic who is attempting to smuggle a Russian missile from Cuba to northern Mexico. Since 1960 Helm has undertaken over 20 missions.

There are many similarities between Bond and Helm — they both work for a large intelligence organisation as assassins, and are mostly involved in counter-espionage. They are single, physically attractive and have many other characteristics in common. These facts have tended to add to the belief that Helm is a copy of Bond, but this is not so. Helm appeared on the scene before Bond existed, and by the time Bond hit the American reading public Helm was firmly established with several adventures in print. No doubt the Bond industry helped to increase Helm sales, but also the series was very much an American product with Helm being closely related to his hard-boiled predecessors — a characteristic that Fleming tried to emulate in his books to appeal to American readers.

Anthony Boucher, the American mystery reviewer, noticed a characteristic of the series which indicates that Helm has a particularly American heritage: "Donald Hamilton has brought to the spy novel the authentic hard realism of [Dashiell] Hammett; and his stories are as compelling, and probably as close to the sordid truth of espionage, as any now being told."

The Helm series is still readable today, and Hamilton's hard, crisp style is reminiscent of the quick wit and repartee of Bogey in the movies. At one point in *The Shadowers* Helm reflects: "I'd had one once, I remembered — a conscience, I mean — but I'd managed to lose it somewhere. At least I'd done my best to. In this business a conscience buys you nothing but trouble."

Hamilton's own comments on the spy novel are: "Entertainment is what it's all about. Messages go by Western Union".

Films

Dean Martin played Matt Helm in four movies which were poor adaptations of Hamilton's books.
The Silencers. Columbia, US, 1966.
Murderers' Row. Columbia, US, 1966.
The Ambushers. Columbia, US, 1967.
The Wrecking Crew. Columbia, US, 1968.

Television

"Matt Helm". 1975. The pilot for a short-lived television series.

SAMUEL J HAMRICK
Pseudonym: **W T TYLER**.
American. Born in Texas, 19 October 1929.

Titles

The Man Who Lost the War. New York, Dial Press, 1980.
Rogue's March. New York, Harper & Row, 1982.

Biography

Samuel J Hamrick, whose novels are published under the pseudonym of W T Tyler, is a twenty-year veteran of the US Foreign Service. After retiring from the State Department in 1980, Hamrick has devoted himself to writing. The Tyler pseudonym, he said, was taken from Wat Tyler, the leader of a fourteenth-century peasant revolt in England. His four critically and commercially successful novels of international intrigue are closely related to the author's diplomatic experience and his knowledge of such countries as Lebanon, Ethiopia, Zaire and Somalia, as well as the political world of Washington DC.

Critical Analysis

Samuel J Hamrick belongs to the new generation of American spy novelists, such as David Ignatius and Alan Furst, who give a more serious and accurate account of espionage, but still manage to tell an entertaining story.

Hamrick has written four novels, but only the two above can be called spy novels. Although he has never worked for an intelligence agency he has some knowledge of the CIA and its officers: "I wasn't an intelligence officer but a foreign service officer (although I served in the army counter-intelligence corps before my diplomatic career began). As a diplomat serving abroad, I knew and worked with intelligence officers. That experience helped to the extent that I knew something about the clandestine services."

Hamrick worked for the State Department for nearly twenty years, and he spent seven of them in central and east Africa. Two of his novels are set in Africa, one of these, *Rogue's March*, is about a coup d'etat in a recently independent nation in central Africa, possibly Zaire, and how the people involved in its disorders — the Africans, the diplomats and the intelligence officers — try to understand and control events.

The principal character is Andy Reddish, a veteran American intelligence officer under diplomatic cover, who is just completing a long tour of duty. Reddish knows some of the country's political leaders, and he is aware of the problems facing a newly independent nation. However, his familiarity with the country and its people does not aid him in his efforts to try to define the political implications of the coup for the benefit of his superiors in Washington DC, especially when they conflict with the official desire to show the event as a counter-Communist seizure.

Dr Joseph Hosey, an ex-employee of the CIA, and a reviewer of spy fiction, commented upon the high level of authenticity in this novel: "Apart from a few necessary safe houses, encrypted cables, ambiguous phone calls, and casual sexual relationships, the day-to-day machinery of the usual fictional intelligence operation is not to be found here. But the atmosphere of doubt, anxiety, caution, and unexpected conflict in which real intelligence operations are in fact conducted has seldom been so well portrayed."

The Man Who Lost the War is about the assassination of a low-level British traitor which leads to a confrontation between two veteran agents — Andrei Strekov of the KGB and David Plummer of the CIA.

The author commented in 1984: "I think of the spy novel as a vehicle of entertainment rather than a forum for public education or getting my own views across (although the one doesn't exclude the other). To the extent that everything is sacrificed to entertainment as in most spy novels on the best seller list, few can be taken seriously. The characters are generally stereotypes, the action absurdly melodramatic, and the writing usually bad."

PALMA HARCOURT

(Pseudonym of Palma Trotman)
British. Born in Jersey, Channel Islands.

Titles

Climate for Conspiracy. London, Collins, 1974; New York, Macmillan, 1986.
A Fair Exchange. London, Collins, 1975; New York, Mackay, 1976.
Dance for Diplomats. London, Collins, 1976; New York, Walker, 1978.
At High Risk. London, Collins, 1977; New York, Walker, 1978.
Agents of Influence. London, Collins, 1978; New York, Walker, 1978.
A Sleep of Spies. London, Collins, 1979; New York, Jove, 1986.
Tomorrow's Treason. London, Collins, 1980; New York, Jove, 1987.
A Turn of Traitors. London, Collins, 1981; New York, Scribner's, 1981.
The Twisted Tree. London, Collins, 1982; New York, Jove, 1987.
Shadows of Doubt. London, Collins, 1983; New York, Beaufort, 1983.
The Distant Stranger. London, Collins, 1984; New York, Beaufort, 1986.
A Cloud of Doves. London, Collins, 1985; New York, Jove, 1987.
A Matter of Conscience. London, Collins, 1986; New York, Beaufort, 1987.
Limited Options. London, Collins, 1987; New York, Beaufort, 1987.
Clash of Loyalties. London, Collins, 1988.
Cover for a Traitor. London, Collins, 1989.

Short Stories

"The Final Score", in *Winter's Crime 14*. London, Macmillan, 1982.
"A Box of Books", in John Creasey's *Mystery Collection*. London, Gollancz, 1984.

Biography

Palma Harcourt was educated at Jersey Ladies' College and St. Anne's College, Oxford, where she obtained an MA. She has worked as a civil servant, a university teacher and a magazine editor.

Critical Analysis

Palma Harcourt is a prolific author. As well as her spy/adventure stories, or diplomatic thrillers, as they are often described, she and her husband write straight crime novels under the name of John Penn, published by Collins Crime Club and Scribner's in America. Her books have been translated into Icelandic, Italian, German, Danish, Dutch, Norwegian, Swedish, Finnish and Japanese. Three have been recorded as audio books.

One of her latest novels, *Clash of Loyalties*, is set in London after the war. The widowed Pandora White remarries and thinks that her secret is safe. Only three close friends know that Alexis Dolkov, an escaped Russian prisoner whom she nursed in Jersey during the German occupation, is the father of her son Bird.

But Alexis's brother Vladimir, an officer in the KGB, discovers the boy's existence and targets him as a potential agent. He waits until the boy is old enough to be recruited. Bird's identity is still unknown when we later meet two brilliant young men at Oxford. Richard Kent and David Windfield are friends and rivals and destined for careers in the Foreign Office. But something happens to upset their plans and which sets them off on different paths. Palma Harcourt keeps us guessing to the end: which of the two, Richard or David, is Bird, and who is working for which side in the intelligence game?

Radio
"Shadows of Doubt". BBC, 1985.

GARY WARREN HART
American. Born in Ottawa, Kansas, 28 November 1936.

Titles
The Double Man. New York, Macmillan, 1985; London, Sphere, 1985.
The Strategies of Zeus. New York, Morrow, 1986.

Biography
Gary Hart's original surname was Hartpence, but it was legally changed in 1961. He was educated at Bethany Nazarene College, where he received a BA in 1958; he also attended Yale University where he took a law degree in 1964. He worked as an appellate attorney and then became a special assistant to Secretary Stewart Udall of the US Department of the Interior, at the US Department of Justice from 1964 to 1966. He went on to practise law privately but eventually rose up the political ladder to become the candidate for the Democratic party's presidential nomination in the 1984 and 1988 elections. Due to a sexual indiscretion and constant media attention and exposures, Hart was forced him to withdraw from the 1988 Presidential campaign.

Critical Analysis
In the mid-1980s Hart published two political thrillers, *The Double Man* and *The Strategies of Zeus*. Both the books concern dashing, dedicated political officials and they both feature pointed comparisons between American and Soviet attitudes. *The Double Man*, which Hart wrote with William S Cohen, when they were both senators, is about a rather naive senator who discovers that a Soviet agent is manipulating terrorists to thwart key capitalists. Margaret Cannon, who reviewed *The Double Man* for the *Toronto Globe and Mail*, declared that Hart and Cohen "know their politics and philosophy, and readers won't be bored."

Hart wrote *The Strategies of Zeus* on his own, and like his first novel it is also concerned with political intrigue — the plot centres on weapons negotiations, and the difficulties involved in balancing patriotism and honour against pleasure and profit. Hart intended the book to be instructive as well as entertaining, and he revealed that he had even considered complementing the story with essays on arms control and nuclear weapons.

He told the *Washington Post* that the book, in addition to its purposes as an "acid test" for his viability as a writer and an educational adventure, would function as a vehicle for creating greater rapport with the American public, which is an interesting dimension to the question of why people write spy fiction. The *Post*'s Paul Taylor reported that Hart intended "to use the novel's publication as an excuse to start talking more about himself."

MICHAEL HARTLAND
British. Born in Cornwall, 7 February 1941.

Titles
[Major characters: David Nairn, Sarah Cable]
Down Among the Dead Men [Nairn].London, Hodder & Stoughton, 1983; New York, Macmillan, 1983.
Seven Steps To Treason [Cable]. London, Hodder & Stoughton, 1985; New York, Macmillan, 1985.
The Third Betrayal [Nairn]. London, Hodder & Stoughton, 1986; New York, Macmillan, 1986.
Frontier Of Fear [Cable]. London, Hodder & Stoughton, 1988; New York, Macmillan, 1988.

Biography
Michael Hartland was educated at Latymer Upper School, Hammersmith, London, and Christ's College, Cambridge (1960-63). Initially recruited to GCHQ from Cambridge, he followed a career in government service for twenty years. He worked for the Department of Education and Science, and he was involved in counter-terrorism. From 1978 to 1983 he worked as a Director of the International Atomic Energy Agency, a United Nations agency based in Vienna but with responsibilities all over the world.

Hartland has been a full-time writer since the publication of his first book in 1983, but he is still consulted on international relations and intelligence by European Commission and British government departments.

Critical Analysis
Michael Hartland's novels are closer to the adventure-thriller mould of fiction, although most of them contain elements of espionage and counter-espionage. All his books have been translated into at least twelve languages.

His first novel, *Down Among the Dead Men*, introduces David Nairn of the Secret Intelligence Service (MI6). High in the Himalayas a Chinese agent is brutally murdered while trying to reach the British Embassy in Kathmandu. China expert Nairn mounts an investigation to uncover a trail of deception and violence snaking back fifty years and forward to the most terrifying clash yet between China and the enemies that surround her. This novel is set mainly in Hong Kong.

Seven Steps to Treason introduces Sarah Cable, the daughter of diplomat Bill Cable, stationed in Vienna. She is kidnapped and her father is blackmailed with information from past deeds to co-operate with the Russians and supply them with secret information. The action of this story occurs against the background of strife-torn Poland where violence has erupted and Moscow is forced to retaliate in kind. This novel won a South West Arts Literary Award in 1984.

While he was working in counter-terrorism Hartland says that the work did "involve close contact with the Secret Intelligence Service (MI6), the Security Service (MI5), GCHQ and the SAS. This experience of intelligence, security and military work helps to keep the background and atmosphere of the books authentic. But perhaps the most useful experience was working for the United Nations in Vienna, spy capital of the world, for five years, with the opportunity to observe the intelligence services of many countries — KGB, GRU, CIA, Mossad etc — at work. I am often asked whether I had any intelligence connection myself in Vienna ...."

Hartland comments: "Espionage is an intriguing business to write or read about. This is a bonus to the fact that the tensions, loves and hostilities between individuals can be explored as effectively in this as in other forms of fiction. I am glad to share all this with my readers, whom I regard as friends with similar interests."

SIMON HARVESTER
(Pseudonym for Henry St. John Clair Rumbold-Gibbs)
British. Born in 1910. Died in April 1975.

Titles
[Major characters: Dorian Silk, Roger Fleming]
A Lantern for Diogenes. London, Rich & Cowan, 1946.
Sheep May Safely Graze [Fleming]. London, Rich & Cowan, 1950.
Obols for Charon [Fleming]. London, Jarrolds, 1951.
Vessels May Carry Explosives [Fleming]. London, Jarrolds, 1951.
Cat's Cradle. London, Jarrolds, 1952.
Arrival in Suspicion. London, Jarrolds, 1953.
Spider's Web. London, Jarrolds, 1953.
Delay in Danger. London, Jarrolds, 1954.
Dragon Road [Silk]. London, Jarrold, 1956; New York, Walker, 1969.
Yesterday Walker. London, Jarrolds, 1958.
Unsung Road [Silk]. London, Jarrolds, 1960; New York, Walker, 1961.
Silk Road [Silk]. London, Jarrolds, 1962; New York, Walker, 1963.
Red Road [Silk]. London, Jarrolds, 1963; New York, Walker, 1964.
Assassins Road [Silk]. London, Jarrolds, 1965; New York, Walker, 1965.
Treacherous Road [Silk]. London, Jarrolds, 1966; New York, Walker, 1967.
Battle Road [Silk]. London, Jarrolds, 1967; New York, Walker, 1967.
Zion Road [Silk]. London, Jarrolds, 1968; New York, Walker, 1968.
Nameless Road [Silk]. London, Jarrolds, 1969; New York, Walker, 1970.
Moscow Road [Silk]. London, Jarrolds, 1970; New York, Walker, 1971.
Sahara Road [Silk]. London, Jarrolds, 1972; New York, Walker, 1972.
Forgotten Road [Silk]. London, Hutchinson, 1974; New York, Walker, 1974.
Siberian Road [Silk]. London, Hutchinson, 1976; New York, Walker, 1976.

Biography
Simon Harvester was educated at Marlborough College, Wiltshire, and he went on to study painting in London, Paris and Venice. During the Second World War he served in the Royal Signals Corps. He worked as a journalist, a publisher's reader and a farmer.

Critical Analysis
Harvester was widely known as a writer of espionage stories on both sides of the Atlantic, having in a remarkable way managed to give his books a global appeal. He had considerable insight into world politics and anticipated the development of the post-Second World War battle for power in Africa and Asia.

Harvester's most widely known spy novels were his series with Dorian Silk . One of Britain's First World War intelligence experts paid Harvester the tribute of calling his character "the truest portrait of a secret service agent". His last book in this series, *Siberian Road*, was published posthumously. This peered deeply into the future, posing such questions as what was the Russian plan for Siberia in the next world war, and how were its vast resources being used, as well as taking a look at "the Chinese Dimension". The authenticity of his settings and the topicality of his themes were the chief feature of Harvester's work.

MICHAEL HASTINGS

(Pseudonym for Dr Michael Bar-Zohar)
Other pseudonyms: MICHAEL BARAK
Israeli. Born in Sofia, Bulgaria, 30 January 1938.

Titles
Novels as Michael Bar-Zohar
The Spy Who Died Twice. Boston, Houghton Mifflin, 1975; London, Weidenfeld, 1976.
The Deadly Document. New York, Delacorte, 1980; London, Weidenfeld, 1980.

Novels as Michael Barak
The Secret List of Heinrich Roehm. New York, Morrow, 1976; London, Weidenfeld, 1977.
Enigma. New York, Morrow, 1978; London, Weidenfeld, 1979.
The Phantom Conspiracy. New York, Morrow, 1980; London, Weidenfeld, 1980.
Double Cross. New York, NAL, 1981.

Novels as Michael Hastings
A Spy in Winter. New York, Macmillan, 1984.
The Unknown Soldier. New York, Macmillan, 1986.
The Devil's Spy. New York, Scribner's, 1988.

Biography
Michael Bar-Zohar emigrated to Israel in 1948 and grew up in a poor immigrant neighbourhood in Jaffa. He was educated at the Hebrew University in Jerusalem where he received a BA in Political Science, and he then attended the University of Paris, France where he obtained an MA and a PhD From 1959 to 1964 he was a correspondent in Paris for several Israeli newspapers and "Galei Zahal" radio station.

In 1964 he published his first book *Suez-Ultra Secret*, a best-selling account of the Sinai campaign in 1956, for which he was awarded the Sokolov Prize (the Israeli Pulitzer Prize) and the Maréchal Foch award of the Académie Française. He started a writing career and wrote several non-fiction books which were published in a dozen languages including *Spies in the Promised Land* (1970) and *Ben-Gurion* (1980), a political biography.

His military service was served in Air Force Intelligence and Paratroopers, participating in the Sinai campaign and in the Six-Day War in 1967. From 1970 to

1973 he was a lecturer in Political Science at Haifa University. He is a member of the Bureau and the Central Committee of the Israeli Labour Party and is very active in Israel's political life. He lectures on various subjects including the Israeli secret services which he has described in several of his non-fiction books.

Critical Analysis

This author has published several novels, some under the pseudonym of Michael Barak and lately under the name of Michael Hastings. He has had experience in intelligence and he says that this has helped him as a writer of spy fiction.

In *The Secret List of Heinrich Roehm*, which is set in the Middle East, his patriotic hero, Lieutenant Colonel Joe Gonen, of Air Force Intelligence, suffers terrible physical torture and risks losing the woman he loves, in order to discover the Arab plot which results in the Yom Kippur war. Fortunately, due to the hero's dedication to duty he is able to save Israel from this disaster.

His newest novel, *The Devil's Spy*, is based on an extraordinary true story of espionage and intrigue that took place in Palestine during the First World War.

Film

Enigma. 1982.

TIMOTHY VILLIERS HEALD

PSEUDONYM: DAVID LANCASTER
British. Born in Dorchester, Dorset, 28 January 1944.

Titles

[Major character: Simon Bognor]
Unbecoming Habits. London, Hutchinson, 1973; New York, Stein & Day, 1973.
Blue Blood Will Out. London, Hutchinson, 1974; New York, Stein & Day, 1974.
Deadline. London, Hutchinson, 1975; New York, Stein & Day, 1975.
Let Sleeping Dogs Lie. London, Hutchinson, 1976; New York, Stein & Day, 1976.
Just Desserts. London, Hutchinson, 1977; New York, Scribner's, 1979.
Murder at Moose Jaw. London, Hutchinson, 1981; New York, Doubleday, 1981.
Masterstroke. London, Hutchinson, 1982; as *A Small Masterpiece*. New York, Doubleday, 1982.
Class Distinctions. London, Hutchinson, 1984.
Red Herrings. London, Macmillan, 1985.
Brought to Book. London, Macmillan, 1988.

Novels as David Lancaster
Caroline R. New York, Arbor House, 1980; London, Hutchinson, 1981.

Biography

Tim Heald was educated at Sherborne School, Dorset. He went to Balliol College, Oxford and obtained a BA Hons in Modern History. When he left university he entered journalism, first as an "Atticus" columnist on the *Sunday Times* from 1965 to 1967 and then as feature editor of *Town* magazine in 1967. He was a feature writer of the *Daily Express*, 1967-72, and associate editor of *Weekend* magazine in Toronto, Canada, 1977-78.

He was Foreign Correspondent (North America) for the *Daily Telegraph* , 1982-83. He has been a freelance journalist since 1983, including working as a contract writer for the *Sunday Telegraph* magazine from 1972 to 1986; a thriller reviewer for the Times from 1983 and contributor to the *Daily Telegraph, Spectator, Punch* and other publications.

Critical Analysis

His first novel, *Unbecoming Habits,* is set in an Anglican friary in Oxfordshire where the Friars are questioned by Simon Bognor, an investigator of the Board of Trade (BOT), who discovers that a couple of them have been smuggling secrets out to Eastern Europe in jars of honey.

Since then nine books have followed, all featuring Simon Bognor, a hero the author himself derides: "Bognor is not very competent and is constantly turning up in unlikely places — stately homes, newspaper diaries, kennels — which I know first-hand and find easy and enjoyable to write about."

In *Red Herrings* Bognor investigates the murder of a VAT inspector found dead in a ditch in a small country village. In his latest adventure, *Brought to Book*, Bognor investigates the murder of a prominent figure in the publishing industry.

Heald's books are closer to detective fiction than spy stories as the author himself explains:" 'Spy novel' isn't actually how I would describe my books though they often seem to have spies of one sort or another in them ... My books are primarily entertainments though I don't believe anything, however trivial, can ever be 'just' entertainment. There is always some information or view being conveyed, however slight. I take the view that in most respects the world is a perfectly ridiculous place — none more so than the world as seen by those involved in 'intelligence'. "

Of his contact with the intelligence world, he recalls, "At Oxford I approached the Foreign Office about work and had a strange interview with a man who talked archly about 'another branch of the Foreign Office'. I consulted my tutor about this and he said he had been similarly approached and had spent a melodramatic few days meeting people in pubs and country houses, but never discovering their names. I did nothing about it. But I have met people who probably are spies or who would like to think they are!"

Paul Henri Henissart

American. Born in New York City, 23 August 1923.

Titles

Narrow Exit. New York, Simon & Schuster, 1973.
The Winter Spy. New York, Simon & Schuster, 1976.
Margin of Error. New York, Simon & Schuster, 1980.

Biography

Paul Henissart was educated at Kenyon College, Ohio, and the Sorbonne in Paris. He worked for *Time* magazine for a period and then became a radio and television correspondent, covering the Algerian War and the Sinai campaign. He worked as a writer for the National Broadcasting Co. in New York, 1959–60, and he was the bureau chief of Radio Free Europe in New York from 1960 to 1963. He worked for the American Broadcasting Co. as a writer, 1964-65, and as a correspondent for the Mutual Broadcasting System from 1966.

His career as an author first attracted attention with his non-fiction title *Wolves in the City* (1971), an account of the OAS underground war and the end of French rule in Algeria.

Critical Analysis

Henissart's first novel, *Narrow Exit*, involves the kidnapping of the leader of the Arab terrorist movement against Israel, by three men hired by the Ha Mossad, the Israeli counter-intelligence agency in Tunis. The plan goes wrong and it is a race for the kidnappers to escape before their hiding place is discovered. The plot is realistic and the tone of the novel is cynical. This is a book not confined to the literary limitations of the spy novel — it deals with many problems attached to espionage, both personal aspects and professional ones.

In *Winter Spy* Colonel Edouard Rappaport is sent by the head of the Hungarian Intelligence Service to kill Robert Winter, an adviser to the American President, who is in fact a double-agent. The assassination is meant to trigger off a sabotage to the peace conference between the superpowers. Rappaport finds himself a victim of the plot and is chased by his own colleagues as well as by the West German police and the CIA.

Margin of Error is the story about a plot to assassinate the Egyptian President Anwar el Sadat, during a visit to a clinic in Switzerland. The CIA is on the trail of a known terrorist but they are unsure of his target until the very last moment.

At one point in the story CIA agent Guthrie remarks upon the nature of espionage: "Intelligence work was an eternal, demeaning, nerve-racking balancing act between long-range benefits to the Service and short-term losses for individuals." A sentiment often voiced by the fictional spy hero lamenting an age-old problem.

In a recent article in *The Writer*, Henissart wrote about his views of spy fiction and the problems attached to writing this kind of fiction: "In the case of spy stories, a writer recreates a clandestine world with whose day-to-day workings most readers are unfamiliar but about which they assume a great deal. It's a world where impossible missions and dirty tricks are expected to proliferate. On this superficial level, spy fiction is escapist reading with its feet on the ground or, if one prefers, in the mud.

But to succeed on another, more serious level — to be more than a comic strip posing as a novel — a spy story should preferably introduce us to human beings who are spies or intelligence officers but who, if things had worked out differently and destiny had operated with less or more inspiration, would be insurance salesmen or conglomerate buccaneers."

Henissart is a good writer and his spy novels are certainly more realistic than some of their more flamboyant companions on the bookshelves. Most of his stories are about terrorism, but he deals equally fairly between the counter-intelligence personnel trying to prevent violence, and the views and motivations of the terrorists themselves. We are shown both sides of the story, but one cannot escape the fact that it is usually innocent victims who suffer.

Shaun Herron

Canadian. Born in Carrickfergus, Northern Ireland, 23 November 1912.

Titles

[Major character: Miro]

Miro. New York, Random House, 1969; London, Hale, 1971.
The Hound and the Fox and the Harper. New York, Random House, 1970; as *The Miro Papers*. London, Hale, 1972.
Through the Dark and Hairy Wood. New York, Random House, 1972; London, Cape, 1973.
The Whore-Mother. New York, Evans, 1973; London, Cape, 1973.
The Bird in Last Year's Nest. New York, Evans, 1974; London, Cape, 1974.

Biography

Shaun Herron was educated at Queen's University of Belfast, Edinburgh University and Princeton University. During the Second World War he served in the British Army. He was the editor of *British Weekly*, London from 1950 to 1957, and then worked as senior editorial writer and columnist for the *Winnipeg Free Press*, Manitoba. Since 1976 he has been a columnist for the Montreal *Star*. He is a writer of radio and television scripts for the BBC and the Canadian Broadcasting Commission. He contributes articles and essays to periodicals and newspapers.

Critical Analysis

Not all Shaun Herron's books are spy novels, but they all deal with themes of treachery and betrayal, and show the author's deep mistrust of large organisations and their destructive effect upon individuals. For instance, *The Bird in Last Year's Nest*, is concerned with a Spanish family torn apart by the revolutionary actions of youth, and the relentless pursuit of this family by the Spanish Civil Guard.

Similarly, *The Whore-Mother* is the story about a young Roman Catholic who gets involved with the Provisional IRA before he understands what kind of people they are.

Herron's claim for being regarded as a spy novelist rests on his series of books featuring Miro. Miro himself is a middle-aged spy and assassin, who when young turned to the American "Firm" (a CIA-type intelligence service) to prove himself and escape from domestic problems (a frigid wife). When we encounter him he has worked for the Firm for twenty-five years and is thoroughly disillusioned with himself and life, and feels like a prisoner. In his first adventure he is given the impossible task of exposing a network of terrorist bombers on his own. His investigations lead him to blow the whistle on the Firm.

In *The Hound and the Fox and the Harper*, as the result of Miro's exposé, he and his wife are chased around Ireland on the run from the Firm and the Russians. In the last book of this series, *Through the Dark and Hairy Wood*, Miro has settled in Ireland as a landowner, but soon becomes involved in the political and social problems of Ireland. Throughout his books Herron displays a deep feeling for his Irish roots and concern for the conflicts which affect the country.

EDWARD DENTINGER HOCH

Pseudonyms: IRWIN BOOTH, ANTHONY CIRCUS, STEPHEN DENTINGER, PAT
MCMAHON, ELLERY QUEEN, R L STEVENS, MR X, R E PORTER
American. Born in Rochester, New York, 22 February 1930.

Titles
[Major characters: Carl Crader and Earl Jazine, Jeffrey Rand]
Sixty short stories about Jeffrey Rand, retired head of British Intelligence's Department of Concealed Communications. All published in *Ellery Queen's Mystery Magazine* (EQMM) from 1965 to 1989, including some of the following:
"The Spy Who Walked Through Walls" in *EQMM*, New York, November 1966.
"The Spy Who Came Out At Night" in *EQMM*, New York, April 1967.
"The Spy Who Worked For Peace" in *EQMM*, New York, August 1967.
"The Spy Who Didn't Exist" in *EQMM*, New York, December 1967.
"The Spy Who Clutched A Playing Card" in *EQMM*, New York, February 1968.
"The Oblong Room" in *Best Detective Stories of the Year* edited by Anthony Boucher. New York, Dutton, 1968.
The Spy and the Thief. New York, Davis Publications, 1971 [a collection of seven stories].
Tales of Espionage. New York, Castle Books, 1989 [a collection of eight stories].

Biography
Edward D Hoch studied at the University of Rochester and served in the US Army from 1950 to 1952. He was employed by Pocket Books, New York, and later worked for the Hutchins Advertising Company of Rochester before becoming a full-time writer in 1968.

Critical Analysis
Since 1965 he has published sixty short stories about Rand, a cipher expert in a mythical British Intelligence branch, entitled the Department of Concealed Communications. All have appeared in *Ellery Queen's Mystery Magazine* and seven of them appeared in a collection, *The Spy and the Thief*. Hoch received the Mystery Writers of America Edgar Allan Poe Award for the best mystery short story, "The Oblong Room", in 1968. He has also written fourteen short stories about Interpol, many of them espionage tales, published in *EQMM*, 1973-84. The Rand stories are set mainly in and around London, though Rand has ventured to Paris, Rome, Moscow, America, Egypt and Australia on various occasions. The Interpol stories have European locations. Most of his works are thrillers and detective mysteries rather than spy fiction.

A number of his short stories have been adapted for television, including "The Man Without A Face" ("McMillan & Wife", NBC-TV, 1974) which was based upon Hoch's novelette "The People of the Peacock" (*Saint* magazine, 1965).

CHARLES H HOMEWOOD
Pseudonym: HARRY HOMEWOOD
American. Born in 1914. Died 18 May 1984.

Titles
A Matter of Priority. New York, O'Hara, 1976.

Biography
Harry Homewood worked as a journalist from 1957 to1973; he served as Mid-west bureau chief for *Newsweek* and as an editorial writer for the *Chicago Sun-Times*. For twelve years he moderated a discussion programme on WTTW-TV, "Fact of the Matter" which was syndicated to thirty-two Public Broadcasting Service stations. He also worked for a while as news director and commentator for WAIT radio.

Critical Analysis
Homewood retired from journalism in 1973 and wrote seven novels including four drawn from his experiences in the Second World War, about life on submarines: *O God of Battles, Final Harbour, Torpedo* and *Silent Sea*.
His one venture into the spy story in *A Matter of Priority* is about a retired CIA agent called back into service to stop a KGB plot to kill the President of the United States.

JOSEPH HONE
Irish. Born in London, 25 February 1937.

Titles
[Major character: Peter Marlow]
The Private Sector. London, Hamish Hamilton, 1971; New York, Dutton, 1972.
The Sixth Directorate. London, Secker & Warburg, 1975; New York, Dutton, 1975.
The Paris Trap. London, Secker & Warburg, 1977.
The Flowers of the Forest. London, Secker & Warburg, 1980; as *The Oxford Gambit*. New York, Random House, 1981.
The Valley of the Fox. London, Secker & Warburg, 1982; New York, St. Martin's Press, 1983.

Biography
Joseph Hone was educated at Kilkenny College, Kilkenny, Stanford Park and St. Columba's College, both in Dublin. He has had a varied career including working as an assistant in a second-hand bookshop in London, as a teacher at Drogheda Grammar School in Ireland, and with the Egyptian Ministry of Education in Cairo, Heliopolis and Suez, as well as jobs in a publishing firm, radio and television.
In 1960 he became co-founder with John Ryan of Envoy Productions, Dublin, and has co-produced a number of plays and musicals at the Theatre Royal, Stratford, East London. His wide experience in radio and television resulted in an appointment as Radio and Television Officer with the United Nations Secretariat in New York in 1968, and for the next two years he travelled extensively, making documentary programmes based on trips to Ethiopia, Kenya, Uganda, Tanzania, Malawi,

India, Pakistan and the Far East. Out of these experiences came *The Dancing Waiters* (1971). Apart from his novels Hone has written several travel books. Since 1969 he has worked as a freelance writer and broadcaster.

Critical Analysis

His first book was *The Private Sector*, which was the first of a series of books about Marlow, a teacher in Cairo who finds himself becoming an agent for the British and a spy for the Egyptians. This work was partly a result of Hone's experiences during 1957-58 when he was a teacher in Europe. He states that he has not been associated with intelligence work, but he has "worked with and met such people, especially while I was a teacher in Egypt and in New York with the UN." The story is set in Cairo in the days after Suez and later, a month before the Six Day War of 1967.

L J Davis in a review in the *Washington Post Book World* said of this author: "His tone is nearly perfect — quiet, morbidly ironic, beautifully controlled and sustained, moodily introspective, occasionally humorous and more often bitter, with a persistent undertone of unspeakable sadness and irrecoverable loss."

Hone's world of Intelligence is a boring place and as Marlow says himself it is not the stuff that spy novels are made of: "Except that our section and the people who worked there, even Williams, were so quite unlike any spy novel. The work — the people — were all too dull, too really dull, to last a paragraph. Not the shabby, down-at-heel, hopeless dullness that is made romantic in some accounts — ours was the quite well-off sort of drabness, the sort which makes for the worst copy and the worst lives. With us, life never imitated art."

Apart from his tone, this critic also praised the author's sense of place and his talent for evoking the atmosphere of Egypt: "Hone, like Greene, has the gift of making exotic locale both commonplace and heartbreakingly lovely, while observing it from a point of view uniquely British and not at all quaint."

The Sixth Directorate continues Marlow's story after he has been in jail for four years, due to a frame-up by his own Department. But now they want him to do a job — to impersonate a KGB agent who is to make an important contact at the UN in New York. The plot is complicated by a woman who used to be the agent's lover, and also by the fact that the agent and his contact belong to the "sixth directorate", a group of dissidents within the KGB that their Soviet bosses are trying to locate and destroy.

The author says "I've now stopped writing 'spy' novels — considering that I've said everything to be said on the subject, especially in my last proper 'spy' novel *The Flowers of the Forest*. I wrote 'spy' novels because I thought I could do it better than others at the time." He goes on to say that his most recurrent subject in his books is: "The theme of the double agent who in the end doesn't himself know whose side he is on."

WILLIAM JOSEPH HOOD

American. Born in Waterville, Maine, 19 April 1920.

Titles

Mole. New York, WW Norton, 1982.
Spy Wednesday. New York, WW Norton, 1986.

Biography

William Hood was educated at the University of Southern Maine and George Washington University. He worked as a reporter for the *Portland Press Herald* from 1939 to 1940. During the Second World War he served in the US Army in Armoured Force and with the Office of Strategic Services (OSS) as a special agent working in their London branch, and later in Switzerland under Allen W Dulles. After the war he joined the Central Intelligence Agency and he worked as a senior official in operations stationed in Austria, Germany, Switzerland, France and England. He retired in 1975 after thirty years in the intelligence business and started writing.

Critical Analysis

Hood's first book, *Mole*, won the National Intelligence Study Center award for the best non-fiction book on intelligence. This work should not, strictly speaking, be included above except that it is an interesting example of a factual book enhanced by the author's experience and imagination. It follows the story of Pyotr Popov, a Soviet intelligence officer who approached the CIA in Vienna in 1952, giving them authentic material to lend credence to his action. Popov acted as a defector-in-place for the Americans for seven years until he was discovered by the KGB and put to death.

At the time of Popov's "defection" Hood was operations chief of the agency station in Vienna and he helped establish the agent in the American intelligence network. In *Mole*, with approved publication from the agency, Hood described the agent's detailed relationship with his CIA contacts and speculates as to how he was discovered. Pseudonyms are used throughout the book to protect the author and other CIA officers involved in the case.

One critic, Hans Moses, has described the book as "informative, interpretative, and entertaining." It is this interpretative aspect that strengthens the link between fact and fiction in this book. The critic goes on to explain: "Although Hood does not claim to have first-hand knowledge of all phases of the operation, he obviously had a major part in it, knows the players as well as the atmosphere, and has an ear for the nuances of intelligence work in post-World War II Europe."

Hood himself explains in the introduction to the book that "it is a memoir, the recollection of an intelligence operation based on the memories of the people who were involved in it." He has also written: "There has been so much outright nonsense written about espionage that I thought it past time for someone to give a more realistic picture of what is involved in handling an important spy. The Popov story is an interesting one — he had been given the best the USSR had to offer, but rejected the system and, on his own, decided to fight against it. Along with telling a true spy story, I hoped to give Popov a small footnote in history."

It is an interesting combination of fact and fiction and may perhaps open the way to more such works by intelligence personnel with an inclination towards writing about espionage history.

Spy Wednesday is a true spy novel and the detail to tradecraft and the "high" and "low" dramas described testify to this authenticity. The story focuses on Alan Trosper, who has resigned from the "Firm", a unit separated from the CIA after "the trouble" — the Congressional and media exposés of CIA actions in the 1970s.

The story is about defectors — one valid and one fake; it is up to our hero to discover who is telling the truth, and in the process he finds out what happened to one of his old agents who was uncovered and killed by the KGB.

Trosper feels compelled to return to the secret world: "What he missed had nothing to do with ideology; it was the pressure, the occasional excitement, and even the companionship spawned by the bruising, secret war." As one critic, Jack Sullivan of the *New York Times Book Review* put it: "The reactivated spy who can't quite give up the business is a stock device of espionage fiction ..."

This may well be so but it does not deflect from the genuine picture of espionage presented to us in this novel. Like every form of literature the spy novel has to follow its literary conventions.

ROBERT SYDNEY HOPKINS
Pseudonym: ROBERT ROSTAND
American. Born in Los Angeles, California.

Titles
The Killer Elite. New York, Delacorte, 1973.
The Raid on Villa Joyosa. New York, Putnam, 1973.
Viper's Game. New York, Delacorte, 1974.
The D'Artagnan Signature. New York, Putnam, 1976.
The Killing in Rome. New York, Delacorte, 1977.

Biography
Robert Hopkins was educated in Los Angeles, and has worked as a lecturer in geography at an American university, managed the Latin-American organisation of a large international company and served briefly with an arm of the US State Department in Washington DC, the Caribbean and the Pacific Islands.

Critical Analysis
Hopkins' first book *The Killer Elite* was the subject of a major United Artists film directed by Sam Peckinpah and starring James Caan, and it aroused special political curiosity by its theme. Since Hopkins had worked in the State Department, some astute readers wondered whether that august establishment really had a special security section named SYOPS (as in his book) and if they did occasionally indulge in tactics which were more similar in style to that of the CIA. Hopkins told how Locken, a SYOPS agent, was deliberately and viciously maimed by one of the world's top three professional assassins. Then the American-in-London chief of SYOPS, a cynical manipulator, asks Locken to do a job for him — to get an African statesman safely out of London with three top agents trying to kill him.

The D'Artagnan Signature shows a remarkable insight into the Franco–Algerian conflict in a battle of one relentless set of killers against another. When France withdrew from Algeria, the men of the OAS, the secret army of the diehard white settlers, were killed or driven into exile. But the millions of pounds extorted by the OAS to finance its campaign of terror remained untouched in a Swiss bank. This was why Alexandre Morin needed the D'Artagnan signature, for the key to the fortune amassed by the underground army was a power of attorney vested in a murdered man, Edgar Duret, OAS treasurer, code-name D'Artagnan. With ruthless single-mindedness, Morin, former head of the OAS's notorious Delta murder organisation, had tracked down everyone — old comrades and enemies alike —

who might provide a clue to the location of the crucial document. Hopkins cleverly welded fact and fiction in this convincingly authentic thriller.

Another book introducing the character Locken of the State Department is *Viper's Game*, which is set on a large Portuguese-administered island in the Pacific, involving Locken in a battle of wits against not only a band of guerrilla fighters, but the Sembi, a savage mountain tribe.

Film

The Killer Elite. United Artists, US, 1975.

SYDNEY HORLER

Pseudonyms: PETER CAVENDISH, MARTIN HERITAGE
British. Born in Leytonstone, Essex, 18 July 1888. Died 27 October 1954.

Titles

[Major characters: Brett Carstairs, Baron Serge Veseloffsky, Sir Brian Fordinghame, Gerald Lissendale]
False-Face [Veseloffsky; Fordinghame]. London, Hodder & Stoughton, 1926; New York, Doran, 1926.
The Curse of Doone. London, Hodder & Stoughton, 1928; New York, Mystery League, 1930.
Miss Mystery [Veseloffsky]. London, Hodder & Stoughton, 1928; Boston, Little Brown, 1935.
The Secret Service [Lissendale]. London, Hodder & Stoughton,1929; New York, Knopf, 1930.
The Man Who Walked with Death [Carstairs]. New York, Knopf, 1931; London, Hodder & Stoughton, 1942.
The Spy [Carstairs]. London, Hodder & Stoughton, 1931.
The Traitor. London, Collins, 1936; Boston, Little Brown, 1936.
Terror on Tip-Toe. London, Hodder & Stoughton, 1939.
The High Game. London, Redman, 1950.
These Men and Women. London, Museum Press, 1951.

Biography

Sydney Horler was educated at Redcliffe and Colston Schools, Bristol. He began his professional life in Fleet Street, first on the *London Daily Citizen* and then on the *Daily Mail*. During the last years of the First World War he worked in the propaganda section of Air Intelligence. After the war he joined the editorial staff of George Newnes and was appointed a sub-editor on *John O'London's Weekly*.

Critical Analysis

Horler resigned from his job to write fiction, and altogether he produced more than 150 novels, only a sample of which are listed above. Not all of his novels were espionage tales but more in the nature of adventure yarns or thrillers. Most of his Secret Service stories, set in Cannes, on the Riviera, Paris and London, were in a similar vein and modelled on Oppenheim; exciting as stories, but highly coloured and artificial. They enjoyed wide popularity in the 1930s.

HARRY HOSSENT

British. Born in London, 12 November 1916.

Titles

[Major character: Max Heald]
Spies Die at Dawn. London, Long, 1958.
No End to Fear. London, Long, 1959.
Memory of Treason. London, Long, 1961.
Spies Have No Friends. London, Long, 1963.
The Spy Who Got Off at Las Vegas. London, Long, 1969.
The Great Spectators. London, Long, 1975.
Gangster Movies. London, Long, 1976.

Biography

Harry Hossent believes that he was first influenced to write thrillers by his English teacher at Glendale County School, who was Christopher Bush, a well-known detective story writer in his day. After a spell in the film business Hossent joined the AP of America and stayed with that agency until he joined the RAF in the Second World War. After the war he had a job with UP, then went into an advertising agency and later became London manager of the Irish News Agency.

Critical Analysis

"I can't remember the title of my first book," he says. "It was a 50,000 word paperback. It was October, I needed some money for Christmas and I saw an advertisement asking for 50,000 word thrillers. So I locked myself in the kitchen and I typed the words 'The blonde was very dead'. After that it all seemed to work."

Since then he has enjoyed writing spy stories "about the seedier parts of Europe". Hossent writes competent, unpretentious spy fiction. The chief character he has developed in his books is the somewhat cynical Max Heald, a Second World War Squadron-Leader seconded to an unnamed department of the SIS (a kind of division of "dirty tricks").

GEOFFREY EDWARD WEST HOUSEHOLD

British. Born in Bristol, 30 November 1900. Died October 1988.

Titles

[Major character: Roger Taine]
Rogue Male. London, Chatto & Windus, 1939; Boston, Little Brown, 1939.

Arabesque. London, Chatto & Windus, 1948; Boston, Little Brown, 1948.
High Place. London, Joseph, 1950; Boston, Little Brown, 1950.
A Rough Shoot [Taine]. London, Joseph, 1951; Boston, Little Brown, 1951.
A Time to Kill [Taine]. Boston, Little Brown, 1951; London, Joseph, 1952.
Fellow Passenger. London, Joseph, 1955; Boston, Little Brown, 1955.
Watcher in the Shadows. London, Joseph, 1960; Boston, Little Brown, 1960.
Olura. London, Joseph, 1965; Boston, Little Brown, 1965.
Doom's Caravan. London, Joseph, 1971; Boston, Little Brown, 1971.
Red Anger. London, Joseph, 1975; Boston, Little Brown, 1975.
Hostage-London: The Diary of Julian Despard. London, Joseph, 1977; Boston, Little Brown, 1977.
The Last Two Weeks of Georges Rivac. London, Joseph, 1978; Boston, Little Brown, 1978.

Biography

Geoffrey Household was educated at Clifton School, Bristol and Magdalen College, Oxford. He, together with Eric Ambler, were both skilled and highly competent writers who, shortly before the Second World War, sought the format of the spy story as a medium of their ideas. After leaving Oxford, Household lived in various parts of the world, undertaking a variety of jobs.

In Bucharest, where he spent eight years, he was confidential secretary to the Bank of Romania, after which he worked in Spain for some time in the banana trade and as the foreign representative of a firm of printing-ink manufacturers. Arriving in America in the depths of the depression in the 1930s, he made a living by writing playlets for broadcasting. He finally settled in England to become a professional writer, but it was not until he wrote *Rogue Male* that success really came to him.

Critical Analysis

Rogue Male became one of the classical thrillers of all time. It was made into a film called *Man Hunt*, and was broadcast as a television film in 1976, which showed that the story had lost none of its appeal or effectiveness over all those years.

The story was about an Englishman, Sir Robert Hunter, who decided to undertake a one-man spy mission to track down and kill a dictator. It was fairly clear that the dictator in question was Adolf Hitler. The tale starts with Hunter being trapped by the secret police while watching the terrace of the dictator's hunting lodge through the telescopic sights of his rifle. Captured, tortured and given up for dead by his inquisitors, Hunter escapes back to England after hair-raising adventures that make *Rogue Male* as good an escape story as Buchan's *Thirty-Nine Steps*. But in England, where officialdom and government circles want to have nothing to do with a man who has tried to kill a foreign head of state and failed, he finds himself in equal danger, shunned by some of his own countrymen and still hunted down by agents of his enemies overseas. The scenes in Dorset where Hunter goes to ground in a fox-hole and lives perilously while being sought by the enemy are especially thrilling. It is a novel of ideas as well as a superb thriller and the suspense is maintained right up to the end. The outstanding success of *Rogue Male* was never repeated by Household.

Film

Man Hunt. TCF, US, 1941 (book title: *Rogue Male*).

JOHN REGINALD HOWLETT
British. Born in Leeds, 4 March 1940.

Titles
[Major character: Railway Joe Morgan]
The Christmas Spy. New York, Harcourt, 1975.

Biography
John Howlett was educated at Tonbridge School and Jesus College, Oxford. He is perhaps best known as the co-author of the film, *If*.

Critical Analysis
In *The Christmas Spy* he introduced a new style of spy, Railway Joe, an agent in his mid-forties employed by an unnamed security organisation under its Parisian controller. Howlett himself sums his character up as "the sad man of post-war Europe, regressed from the ideals of anti-Nazi resistance to the cynical chessboard manoeuvres of the eternal power game. Wrong man, wrong side, wrong war." It is what he calls "the loneliness and the sense of alienation" of the spy game that marks Howlett's approach to the genre.

His spy had been left out in the cold since, as a seventeen-year-old boy of Italian parentage fresh from his English public school, he was seconded to the Italian underground apparently to fight the Fascists in Italy. Rootless, tortured, devoid of any lasting personal attachment, except to his gentle, homosexual brother, Railway Joe had been given a new name by the British, who patched up his war-shattered personality without leaving him any real identity.

The Christmas Spy is a chilling story which focuses on an assignment begun on a bitterly cold Christmas Eve in a little Swiss village, and carried through right across Europe. In it, the author has added a new quality and dimension to the modern spy novel. Howlett's other work includes film and radio scripts and biographies associated with the cinema.

RICHARD HOYT
American. Born in Hermiston, Oregon, 28 January 1941.

Titles
[Major character: John Denson]
Decoys [Denson]. New York, Evans, 1980; London, Hale, 1982.
30 for a Harry [Denson]. New York, Evans, 1981; London, Hale, 1982.
The Manna Enzyme. New York, Morrow, 1982.
Trotsky's Run. New York, Morrow, 1982; London, Severn, 1987.
The Siskiyou Two-Step [Denson]. New York, Morrow, 1983; London, Hale, 1984.
Cool Runnings. New York, Viking, 1984.
Fish Story [Denson]. New York, Viking, 1985; London, Hale, 1987.

Head of State. London, Severn, 1987.
The Dragon Portfolio. New York, TOR Books, 1986; London, Grafton, 1988.

Biography

Richard Hoyt was educated at Columbia Basin College, Pasco, Washington, and the University of Oregon, Eugene, from where he received a BS and MS in Journalism. He attended the Washington Journalism Center in Washington DC, and the University of Hawaii, Honolulu, where he received a PhD in American Studies in 1972. He served in the US Army from 1963 to 1966 as a Special Agent in Army Intelligence.

He was a reporter for the Honolulu *Star-Bulletin* , 1968–69, and a reporter and later Assistant City Editor for the Honolulu *Advertiser*, 1969–72; at the same time he worked as a correspondent for *Newsweek* magazine. He was Assistant Professor of Journalism at the University of Maryland, 1972–76, and Assistant Professor of Communications at the Lewis and Clark College, Portland, Oregon from 1976 to 1983. Since 1983 he has been a full-time writer.

Critical Analysis

Over the last few years Hoyt has written a number of suspense and mystery novels. One critic particularly recommends *Trotsky's Run* and described it as "a political espionage thriller which is reminiscent — but not derivative — of Richard Condon's *The Manchurian Candidate*." The story is about a Soviet mole who becomes the leading candidate for the presidency of the United States, the plot being complicated by the candidate's belief that he is the avenging reincarnation of Leon Trotsky. The Russians try to solve the crisis by removing him.

Hoyt's novels featuring John Denson are detective mysteries rather than spy stories, but the hero is different from the usual protagonists — one reviewer has described him as "soft-boiled", as opposed to the harder versions.

Hoyt writes with a lot of humour, and in one of his more recent books, *The Dragon Portfolio*, the author vents this humour upon various monoliths of American society such as universities, the American President and, of course, espionage. The story is a complicated one, involving a variety of colourful characters, including two Texan entrepreneur brothers looking for more money to add to their fortune; Lucien Salvant, a bored American professor who wants to escape the petty infighting of his academic colleagues: Gene Holt, an international gangster looking for a refuge; the beautiful Ella Nidech, the CIA's "man" in Hong Kong, and last, but not least, James Burlane, the "delicate man", who deals with "sensitive" jobs given him by his bosses in the CIA, and usually involving someone's death.

At one point in this story, James Burlane expresses his feelings when he is threatened with an investigation by a senator: " 'Jesus Christ, Ara, can you imagine what will happen if Rollo Hinkley gets even a hint of my delicate work? You've chosen me to do everything you don't want discussed in Congress or leaked to the newspapers. I do what we all know has to be done, fuck the rules. I'm the public's private hit man, Ara.' "

So much for Congressional oversight of the CIA!

Hoyt displays a healthy flippant attitude towards authority which is revealed in the unorthodox behaviour of his characters. His humour is refreshing and his plots are entertaining, let's hope that he continues to write more books in this vein.

EVERETTE HOWARD HUNT
Pseudonyms: JOHN BAXTER, GORDON DAVIS, ROBERT DIETRICH, DAVID ST. JOHN
American. Born in Hamburg, New York, 9 October 1918.

Titles
[Major character: Peter Ward]

Novels as David St. John
On Hazardous Duty. New York, New American Library, 1965; as *Hazardous Duty*. London, Muller, 1966.
Return from Vorkuta. New York, New American Library, 1965; London, Muller, 1967.
The Towers of Silence. New York, New American Library, 1966.
Festival for Spies. New York, New American Library, 1966.
The Venus Probe. New York, New American Library, 1966.
One of Our Agents is Missing. New York, New American Library, 1967.
The Mongol Mask. New York, Weybright & Talley, 1968; London, Hale, 1969.
The Sorcerers. New York, Weybright & Talley, 1969.
Diabolus. New York, Weybright & Talley, 1971.
The Coven. New York, Weybright & Talley, 1972.

Novels as Howard Hunt
The Berlin Ending. New York, Putnam, 1973.
The Hargrave Deception. New York, Stein & Day, 1980.
The Gaza Intercept. New York, Stein & Day, 1981
Cozumel. New York, Stein & Day, 1985.
The Kremlin Conspiracy. New York, Stein & Day, 1985.

Biography
Howard Hunt was educated at Brown University, Providence, Rhode Island. He joined the OSS in 1943 and worked as an operative in the Chinese theatre. He joined the CIA in the late 1940s, and in the twenty-two years he spent with the agency he worked in Paris, Tokyo, Montevideo, Madrid and Mexico City. He worked on the successful coup in Guatemala in 1954, and for a while he was involved in the plan to oust Castro from Cuba, which resulted in failure at the Bay of Pigs. Hunt's personal memoirs of this operation were detailed in *Give Us This Day* (1973).

In 1970 Hunt retired from the CIA and became Vice-President and Creative Director at Robert R Mullen, a public relations firm, where he worked for two years. During this time he was a consultant to President Richard Nixon. After the public exposure of his role in the Watergate scandal he served two terms in federal prison. Since his release in 1977 he has spent his time writing and lecturing.

Critical Analysis
Howard Hunt has written over forty books, many of them spy novels, under a variety of pseudonyms. His most popular series was the one concerning CIA agent Peter Ward, written under the name of David St. John. There are ten titles in this series.

All the time that Hunt was working for the CIA he was employed as a clandestine political operator, he was not an agent like his fictional character Peter Ward, although they shared many similarities. For instance, they both graduated from Brown University and were active in Washington society. Because of Hunt's association with the agency he is constantly praising that organisation. One of the advantages of this association with intelligence is the author's use of realistic terminology and accurate tradecraft, as well as his authentic portrayal of his locations. Many of the stories were set in the countries where Hunt had been stationed. Nevertheless Hunt does not give away any secrets despite his long experience in the intelligence business. One of the main reasons for this is that all his novels and non-fiction books that he writes are liable to censorship by the CIA.

Instead of using his knowledge of espionage to create realistic spy novels Hunt chose the sensational approach in his stories, perhaps because he thought that the two were incompatible in a best-seller. The Ward series was partly used as a propaganda weapon which he explains in his autobiography, *Undercover — Memoirs of An American Secret Agent* (1974). When a publisher suggested that he write an American equivalent of the James Bond books, Hunt says: "I submitted the idea to Dick Helms, who agreed that certain public-relations advantages would accrue to CIA if such a series were well received."

These novels were also a platform for the author's social and political views, which were far more liberally scattered than any secrets he had to give away. As Earle Davis, a literary critic pointed out: "In his novels he attacks the Kennedys, Jack Anderson, Mrs Graham of the *Washington Post*, the State Department, big city crime, and various liberal Congressmen or bureaucrats associated with New Deal tendencies."

In Hunt's later spy novels he pursues different themes, such as terrorism in *The Gaza Intercept*, which centres around the Arab–Israeli conflict. However, the author still holds to his conservative opinions and there are constant references to the view that the CIA has gone soft on Communism. Another theme he develops is that the hero of these later stories is very often a maverick agent. He may have worked for the agency once, but in the tales of *The Hargrave Deception*, *The Berlin Ending* and *The Kremlin Conspiracy*, the protagonist becomes involved in the machinations of the KGB and the CIA, while becoming the enemy of both.

Hunt received a great deal of publicity as a novelist due to the part he played in the Watergate scandal. As a result a number of his books were republished under his own name and he became a celebrated writer, which may not be entirely justified upon literary merits, but has enabled him to earn a living.

DOUGLAS RICHARD HURD

British. Born 8 March 1930.

Titles

Truth Game. London, Collins, 1972.
Vote to Kill. London, Collins, 1975.

Novels written with Andrew Osmond

Send Him Victorious. London, Collins, 1968.

The Smile on the Face of the Tiger. London, Collins, 1969; New York, Macmillan, 1969.
Scotch on the Rocks. London, Collins, 1971.
War Without Frontiers. London, Hodder & Stoughton, 1982.

Novels written with Stephen Lamport
Palace of Enchantments. London, Hodder & Stoughton, 1985.

Biography
The Rt Hon. Douglas Hurd, MP was educated at Eton, where he was the King's Scholar and Newcastle Scholar, and Trinity College, Cambridge. He entered the Diplomatic Service in 1952 and for four years he served in Peking, thus gaining an early introduction to Far Eastern politics and intrigue, which have featured in some of his books.

From 1956 to 1960 he worked in the United Kingdom Mission to the United Nations and after that had a three-year stint at the Foreign Office. He was stationed in Rome, 1963-66, and then joined the Conservative Party Research Department, eventually becoming private secretary to the Conservative leader, Edward Heath. During Heath's term of office Hurd served as his political secretary. Since 1974 Hurd has been MP for mid-Oxfordshire. He was appointed Home Secretary in 1985, and four years later returned to his earlier sphere of activity when made Secretary of State for Foreign Affairs.

Critical Analysis
It was in his post-Foreign Office period that Douglas Hurd branched out as a novelist and in *Who's Who* he describes his principal recreation as "writing thrillers". He first produced *The Arrow War* (1967), which was, in fact, history. This was followed by what Hurd himself calls "political thrillers rather than spy fiction, though I suppose you are right in saying that the two have much in common."

These novels have attracted considerable interest and serious comment among politicians and foreign affairs specialists and, indeed, British spooks in the Far East, who have been shaken out of their complacency by some of Hurd's revelations. But in some respects they are textbooks for indolent and complacent officialdom and the SIS, MI5 and the Foreign Office should make them compulsory reading.

Referring to his collaboration with Andrew Osmond, Douglas Hurd says: "We have tried to start from an ordinary situation with ordinary people, described in detail from past experiences of our own. Then we have added an explosive ingredient which is not absolutely improbable, e.g. a violent outbreak of Scottish nationalism (*Scotch on the Rocks*), a Chinese ultimatum against Hong Kong (*The Smile on the Face of the Tiger*), or, ... a campaign to get British troops out of Ireland (*Vote to Kill*). The mixture of the ordinary and the extraordinary has to be kept in balance all the way through. As a member of the Foreign Service I met a good many people involved in Intelligence, but I cannot say that they influenced me particularly. I know Hong Kong reasonably well, but it is fascinating not because of the spies — a dull lot — but because of the extraordinary notion of a vast capitalist Chinese city kept steady by a British Governor, Ghurkas, etc. I have no desire at all to attack the British institutions which we describe, though it is often right to laugh at the way they work."

ANTHONY HYDE

Canadian. Born in Ottawa, Canada, 1946.

Titles

The Red Fox. New York, Knopf, 1985; London, Hamish Hamilton, 1985.

Biography

Anthony Hyde has written for the National Film Board, the Canadian Broadcasting Corporation and the National Museum. He has also collaborated with Christopher Hyde, his brother and a novelist, under the joint pseudonym of Nicholas Chase. They wrote *Locksley* (1983), a retelling of the Robin Hood legend.

Critical Analysis

The Red Fox is the story of Robert Thorne, a journalist and a "Russian expert" who is asked to help his old girlfriend, May Brightman, to track down her father, a millionaire fur dealer who has disappeared. Thorne's search leads him around America to Paris and then the USSR, and he finds out that Harry Brightman was once a spy for the Russians. This book contains elements of a murder mystery, an adventure story and an historical novel as it weaves its way in and out of the past and moves from place to place.

Anthony Olcott wrote in a review: "*The Red Fox* is something of a patchwork, stitched up of bits that can be marvelously entertaining, but which fail fully to coalesce; curiously, this thriller's lack of focus may well be the fault, not of author Anthony Hyde's inexperience (and certainly not lack of talent), but rather of the genre's limitations, for Hyde attempts to bring to a conventional medium emotions and insights of a complexity uncommon in escapist fiction."

NOEL HYND

American.

Titles

Flowers from Berlin. Star Publishers, 1986.
Revenge. London, WH Allen, 1988.
Sandler Inquiry. London, WH Allen, 1978.

Novels written with Christopher Creighton

The Khrushchev Objective. New York, Doubleday, 1987; London, WH Allen, 1988.

Critical Analysis

Noel Hynd has written a number of spy thrillers on his own, but it is his novel written with Christopher Creighton that concerns us here. *The Khrushchev Objective* was written with Creighton, who co-authored the thriller *Paladin* with Brian Garfield. This story is set in April 1956 when the Soviet high command has agreed to visit a Western democracy. But as Party Chairman Khrushchev and

President Bulganin set sail towards their historic meeting with Prime Minister Anthony Eden, sinister events have been set in motion, which erupt into a dramatic conspiracy, with a mixture of kidnapping, extortion and political assassination which nearly erupts into World War Three.

In this book the authors have combined fact and fiction to explain the "Crabb Affair". This incident occurred in Portsmouth when a frogman was observed examining a Russian battle cruiser and destroyer, which were part of the entourage which brought the Russian party to Britain. The Russians accused the British of spying on them, the frogman turned out to be retired Commander Lionel Crabb, who had examined the ships without the knowledge or authority of the Admiralty. Fourteen months later a body identified as Crabb's was washed ashore at Chichester harbour.

The events of this incident have never been explained satisfactorily. In 1970, Admiral of the Fleet, the Earl Mountbatten of Burma, allowed Christopher Creighton to write a book explaining what exactly had happened. Both men were involved in the affair, and Creighton suggested that the story might be best told as a novel, which would allow him flexibility with certain details that could never be revealed. It was also a way to disguise certain individuals as well as places, so that they could not be identified.

This book is a prime example of a story that has used the form of the spy novel to describe real events which otherwise could not be told.

DAVID REYNOLDS IGNATIUS

American. Born in Cambridge, Massachusetts, 26 May 1950.

Titles

Agents of Innocence. New York, WW Norton, 1987; London, WH Allen, 1988.

Biography

David Ignatius was educated at St. Albans School, Washington DC. He graduated *magna cum laude* from Harvard College in 1973 in Social Studies. He attended King's College, Cambridge (1974-75) and received a Diploma in Economics.

Ignatius is a journalist and he worked for 10 years as a reporter for *The Wall Street Journal*, covering the steel industry, the CIA, the US Senate, the State Department and the Middle East. Since 1986 he has been an editor at *The Washington Post*.

Critical Analysis

Agents of Innocence is the first novel by David Ignatius and is a fascinating account of the relationship between the CIA and the PLO in the political turmoil of the Middle East. The author says that his novel "parallels the real history of the Middle East during the 1970s, and the CIA–PLO relationship is similar to one that really existed. But the characters are imaginary." From 1980 to 1983 Ignatius covered the Middle East for *The Wall Street Journal* and it is this experience which gives such authenticity to his novel.

"As a writer and a reporter I try to penetrate to the heart of the way the world works and to describe what I see in the simplest and most direct way. That is what spies are supposed to do, so there's a neat fit." Ignatius sees the world of espionage as "a world painted in shades of gray, rather than black and white, and spy fiction is the fiction of grays."

The novel begins in Beirut in 1969 with the arrival of Tom Rogers, the new intelligence officer attached to the embassy. He is ordered by the station chief to penetrate the Palestinian intelligence outfit, specifically Fatah — the largest Palestinian guerrilla group, which he succeeds in doing with the aid of Fuad, an Arab who is pro-American. The story follows the relationship between Rogers and his "agent" in the PLO and the difficulties in maintaining this relationship with pressures imposed from above, and on both sides.

Hoffman, Rogers's station chief, resigns from the CIA, and years later meets up with Rogers and gives his opinion of the organisation: " '... the agency today is a collection of lawyers, accountants, lobbyists, and bureaucrats, with a bunch of fancy hardware up in the sky. But when it comes to making things happen on the ground, there's nothing left. It's amateur hour.' "

The Palestinians have the last word in the opinion of Fuad, the Arab who acted as go-between for the CIA and the PLO, and who voices his criticism of American efforts in the Middle East: " 'Americans are not hard men. Even the CIA has a soft heart. You want so much to achieve good and make the world better, but you do not have the stomach for it. And you do not know your limitations. You are innocence itself. You are the agents of innocence.' "

This is a very realistic novel, giving us an insight into American foreign policy and the place of an intelligence organisation in its implementation. We are shown the difficulties a case officer faces in an operation and the bureaucratic pressures imposed upon his methods. Hopefully we will see more novels of such quality by this author.

JAMES O JACKSON

American.

Titles

Dzerzhinsky Square. London, Severn, 1986.

Biography

James O Jackson has been a Moscow correspondent for the *Chicago Tribune* and United Press International, and he has witnessed the Soviet invasion of Czechoslovakia while he was working as UPI's Prague correspondent. He is now *Time* magazine's Moscow bureau chief, and was the first journalist to obtain an interview with Soviet premier Mikhail Gorbachev.

Critical Analysis

Dzerzhinsky Square is concerned with the story of Grigory Nikolayevich Malmudov, a brave soldier of the Red Army during the Second World War, who is taken prisoner by the Germans. At the end of the war all he wishes to do is return to his country, but then he discovers that many prisoners of war are being executed by the Russians for collaboration with the enemy. Desperate to return home he is presented with a solution from the Americans — if he will relay reconnaissance reports from Russia he will be given papers and a new identity and will be smuggled back into his own country. Despite the fact that he cannot return to his wife and family Malmudov accepts the offer and becomes Alexander Nikolayevich Kuznetsov, alone and with a manufactured past, he returns to the Soviet Union as a spy for the Americans.

This is an interesting story and the author conveys a good sense of place. It is not strictly a spy novel in the classic sense, but it is a good psychological study of an agent in place, who does not have the compensation of being used in his capacity as a spy. After his return to Russia he stops sending reports to the Americans after a year, but he lives in terror of being discovered. In the end the pressure proves too much and he confesses his betrayal and is executed. It is a sad story and shows the strong forces imposed on an individual who finds himself a victim of circumstance and history.

ALAN JUDD

British. Born in 1947.

Titles

Tango. London, Century Hutchinson, 1989.

Biography

Alan Judd is recently married and living in London. After leaving secondary modern school he trained to be a teacher, but did not take up teaching as a career. For a while he had various labouring jobs before joining the British Army with whom he served in Northern Ireland, thus providing himself with background for his first novel, *A Breed of Heroes* (1981). After leaving the Army he went as a mature student to Oxford, where he read philosophy and theology. Following this he joined the Foreign Office, serving in South Africa, but is now a full-time writer.

Critical Analysis

His first novel, described as "brilliant and original" by Margaret Forster, won him the Royal Society of Literature award and he was later chosen as one of the twenty best young British novelists.

He has been described as "the Evelyn Waugh of the 1980s", a title which he fully lives up to in his most recent book, *Tango*, which is a hugely amusing story of a bumbling Englishman in a South American country of doubtful stability where he finds himself being asked to help British Intelligence to organise a coup d'état. The undercover organisation involved is called Special Information Services, plc.

William Henry Holmes in a review in the *Sunday Telegraph* wrote of this book: "Alan Judd's *Tango* is a very entertaining novel about an innocent abroad: the ineffectual William Wooding, who is sent to run a bookshop in a dubious South American country. He is disillusioned to find that the bookshop's reputation was dependent entirely on its stock of pornography, and suddenly finds himself at the centre of attention because he knows the country's handsome new President, having been at school with him in England."

The tango is Judd's favourite dance: his interests include ballroom dancing and obsolescent second-hand cars, of which he has forty.

ANDRÉ JUTE

Australian. Born in Oudtshoorn, South Africa, 1945.

Titles

Reverse Negative. New York, WW Norton, 1979; London, Secker & Warburg, 1980.
The Zaharoff Commission. London, Secker & Warburg, 1982; New York, David & Charles, 1983.
Festival. London, Hale, 1986.
Eight Days in Washington. London, Hale, 1986.

Biography

André Jute was educated at the universities of Stellenbosch near Cape Town and Adelaide in Australia. He worked in advertising as a travelling troubleshooter, in commerce and industry as a marketer and management consultant, and in politics as an adviser.

Between what he calls "these more or less respectable jobs" he kept himself by driving racing cars and "playing poker or bridge as the company demanded". An Australian citizen, he divides his time between Adelaide, South Australia and County Cork, Ireland. The eclectic settings of his novels reflect his extensive travels. He has worked as a full-time writer since 1974.

Critical Analysis

Jute's first novel, *Reverse Negative*, tells, in the unique format of the main character's diary interspersed with computer syntheses, of what the other characters have probably done, the story of how Philby's last plot frames an elderly Cambridge don as the Fourth Man. In Britain, France, Israel, Russia, Germany, Switzerland and Italy, the don fights off the British, American, Israeli and Russian intelligence agents who want to kill him before he can talk — or worse, capture him and force him to talk.

The *New York Times* thought it "wild but exciting. It is a grand job with plenty of irony." The *London Evening News* agreed that it "plunges into the black farce of the Cambridge group history with malicious glee" and concluded that the novel was "so bizarre, it's probably all true".

Most reviewers, and all those with a background in intelligence work, were impressed with the compelling aura of realism in the novel. Copies of the manuscript were confiscated by officers of ASIO (Australian Intelligence) and the British Special Branch. Jute cannot account for this stupidity, though he surmises that someone with more power than brains must have thought he was pointing a finger at Blunt. He insists he was not, and that all his facts, however pointed, can be had from the shelves of any really good library. "I knew about poor old Anthony Blunt before I wrote the book, but so did a devil of a lot of other people, and I thought him rather a joke, of interest more for the shelter British libel law afforded him than for his past as a spy. The shocking truth — at least for that peculiarly British insularity which informs discussion of their spies — is that Blunt was beneath notice."

In *The Zaharoff Commission* Jute meticulously reconstructs in a novel the mission the armaments merchant Sir Basil Zaharoff undertook for Lloyd George and Georges Clemenceau, to determine whether Germany could be defeated by armed might before the Bolsheviks subverted her.

One critic, John Webb, writing in the *Adelaide Advertiser* draws the connection between the historical and the fictional: "Jute joins a select few historians of the more serious order in crediting Zaharoff with the diplomatic coup that stopped World War I. The story unfolds and races along into a succession of intriguing and often bizarre events with the speed of any thriller hard to put down. But the element of historical fact claims for it a place among the better works, in all their forms, to which this war gave rise." Here, as in *Reverse Negative*, Jute includes, in addition to a bibliography, a fascinating appendix of ascertainable facts about his real-life characters because, he says, "it is only fair to let readers know how far, if at all of course, I have strayed from biographical truth in the service of narrative. I count those who wish to confuse fiction with fact among the enemies of society."

DEREK KARTUN

British. Born in Kent, 9 August 1919.

Titles

[Major character: Alfred Baum]
Beaver to Fox [Baum]. London, Century, 1983; New York, St. Martin's Press, 1986.
Flittermouse [Baum]. London, Century, 1984.
The Courier. London, Century, 1985; New York, St. Martin's Press, 1985.
Megiddo [Baum]. London, Century, 1987; New York, Walker, 1987.
The Defector. London, Century, 1989.

Biography

Derek Kartun was educated in London and Paris. He has worked as a journalist, advertising copywriter and businessman. His first book was *I, Norman Harris* (1980), a comic novel of angst in the garment industry. He writes adventure novels as well as spy fiction.

Critical Analysis

Kartun's first novel, *Beaver to Fox*, introduces Alfred Baum, number two in French counter-intelligence, who in this story has to put a stop to a group of terrorists exploding bombs around the city of Paris, to achieve maximum havoc. One terrorist, a victim of a hit-and-run driver is found with top secret documents in his possession. This leads Baum in his investigation to suspect that a high government official is shielding the terrorists. A review in *Publishers Weekly* wrote: "Kartun takes a dim view of the vices cabinet members are prey to — ambition, jealousy, sexual hangups and stupidity — and he knows his European politics. More importantly, he understands the psychology of vicious malcontents who want nothing less — or more — than chaos. A literate, stunning and credible execution."

In *Flittermouse* a French politician commits suicide in a London hotel, and the British want to know why. Perhaps he was a spy? But who was he spying for? The French government are reluctant to investigate so the British send one of their agents to France, who finds it very hostile territory when he begins to dig into the past of the politician to discover the identity of his spymasters.

When Kartun was asked whether a spy novel can convey an accurate picture of the intelligence world, he replied: "Can be, no doubt, but hardly ever is. For one thing, it would lack tension and colour. For another, only former intelligence officers could be truly accurate about it. Even the researched books on Philby etc are not accurate. There are many deliberate and unintentional errors in *Spycatcher* too. There isn't much virtue in accuracy in this context anyway."

Harold King

Pseudonyms: William Haroldson, Brian Harris
American. Born in Grand Rapids, Michigan, 27 February 1945.

Titles
Paradigm Red. New York, Bobbs Merrill, 1975.
Four Days. New York, Bobbs Merrill, 1976.
The Taskmaster. New York, Coward McCann, 1977.
Closing Ceremonies. New York, Coward McCann, 1979.

Novels as William Haroldson
The Contenders. New York, Pocket Books, 1979.

Novels written with Lawrence Block
Code of Arms. New York, Coward McCann, 1980.

Novels as Brian Harris
World War III. New York, Pocket Books, 1982.

Biography
Harold King was educated at Pennsylvania State University from 1963 to 1965, and Texas Tech Law School in 1970. He also attended West Texas State University in 1970 and the University of Oklahoma, from where he graduated in 1974 with an MA. King started a career in journalism and worked at various newspapers. For his military service he served in the US Marine Corps from 1965 to 1967, in Vietnam.

Critical Analysis
The Taskmaster is about Alec Gunther, a CIA officer demoted to a desk job after failing in an operation in Germany. He is ordered by his bosses to trace the mysterious "Taskmaster" — an ex-Cuban agent who is killing off all the retired Agency men whom he holds responsible for the failure of the 1961 Bay of Pigs operation.

In *Closing Ceremonies* a team of Nazi-hunters in Paraguay raid an underground memorial and steal the urn which contains Hitler's ashes; this act draws the attention of various groups, including the remaining Nazi leaders, living in exile, who want the urn back.

Code of Arms was written with Lawrence Block and is the story of an American pilot who wants to prevent a Nazi invasion of Britain in 1940. So he gets in touch with sympathetic members of the German leadership led by Rudolf Hess.

There are a number of authors, including King, who use Nazism or neo-Nazism as the main threat to civilisation, and the enemy in their stories.

Television
Paradigm Red was produced as the movie *Red Alert* by Columbia Broadcasting System in 1977.

MICHAEL KURLAND

Pseudonym: JENNIFER PLUM
American. Born in New York City, 1 March 1938.

Titles

Novels written with Chester Anderson
A Plague of Spies. New York, Pyramid, 1969.

Novels written with Bart Whaley
The Last President. New York, Morrow, 1980.

Biography

Michael Kurland was educated at the University of Maryland from 1959 to 1960, studied in Germany 1960–61, and attended Columbia University from 1963 to 1964. His military service was in US Army Intelligence from 1958 to 1962. He worked as a high-school English teacher in Ojai, California in 1968, and was the managing director of the *Crawdaddy Magazine* in 1969. He was also the occasional director of plays for the Squirrel Hill Theatre from 1972.

Critical Analysis

In *The Plague of Spies* Peter Carthage, an agent of the private espionage firm War Inc., is sent to infiltrate and destroy a team of international assassins gathered in a monastery on the island of Elba. This novel won an Edgar from the Mystery Writers of America in 1971.

The Last President is an interesting story — that of a young CIA agent and a retired OSS veteran who risk a coup d'etat against Richard Nixon. He had remained in office after the scandal of Watergate, and gradually blackmailed his opponents into silence, and was trying to take over all the top posts of the government including the military.

DUNCAN KYLE

(Pseudonym for John Franklin Broxholme)
Other pseudonym: JAMES MELDRUM
British. Born in Bradford, Yorkshire, 11 June 1930.

Titles

A Cage of Ice. London, Collins, 1970; New York, St. Martin's Press, 1971.
Flight into Fear. London, Collins, 1972; New York, St. Martin's Press, 1972.
A Raft of Swords. London, Collins, 1974; as *The Suvarov Adventure*. New York, St. Martin's Press, 1974.
Terror's Cradle. New York, St. Martin's Press, 1974; London, Collins, 1975.
In Deep. London, Collins, 1976; as *Whiteout!* New York, St. Martin's Press, 1976.
Black Camelot. London, Collins, 1978; New York, St. Martin's Press, 1978.
Green River High. London, Collins, 1979; New York, St. Martin's Press, 1980.
Stalking Point. London, Collins, 1981; New York, St. Martin's Press, 1982.

The King's Commissar. London, Collins, 1983; New York, St. Martin's Press, 1984.
The Dancing Men. London, Collins, 1985.
The Honey Ant. London, Collins, 1988.

Novels as James Meldrum
The Semenov Impulse. London, Fontana, 1975.

Biography
Duncan Kyle was educated at Bradford Grammar School. He served in the Intelligence Corps of the British Army from 1948 to 1950. He worked as a junior reporter on the Bradford *Telegraph and Argus* from 1946 to 1948, and he has worked at GCHQ. He worked in journalism for twenty-five years and ended up as Editorial Director of Odhams magazines. His first book, *The War Queen*, an historical novel about Boadicea, was published in 1967.

Critical Analysis
Kyle says that among his early literary influences were Kipling, Stevenson, Ballantyne "Plus JB Priestley, whom I used to see in the street quite often." He says that his books are "espionage and adventure stories rather than strictly 'spy' ", which is a more accurate description of his tales.

His first spy/adventure novel, *A Cage of Ice*, is an exciting story about an amateur, Surgeon John Edwards, caught up in world of espionage and battling against the professionals. He receives a letter from Moscow, and addressed to a Professor Edward F.A.G.S. There are three obvious mistakes which do not make any sense to our hero until he is ruthlessly pursued and several attempts are made on his life. Eventually Edwards is brought into the custody of the CIA, and together they try to decipher the message that the letter and the envelope are trying to convey. As a result Edwards becomes part of a professional team to rescue a man imprisoned in the depths of Arctic Russia. This man must be rescued as only he has the knowledge to avert a world catastrophe.

There is a nice reference to John le Carré and the fictional world of the spy, when our hero bears witness to a brain-storming session amongst the intelligence professionals: "The room filled rapidly and I watched, fascinated, as the intelligence elite came into the room. *The Spy Who Came in from the Cold* was described as the most realistic of all spy novels: a tale of a seedy and cynical agent, broke, down on his luck, and working in a world whose cynicism was a thousand times greater than his own. This looked like father's night at the Parent-Teachers' Association, or a gathering of sales managers. These guys went home nights and tinkered with cars or hand-drills, grew roses, held week-end cook-outs in the garden barbecue pit. I doubted if there was a gun in the room and that's more than you can say about your friendly neighbourhood PTA in some towns I can think of."

In his latest novel, *The Honey Ant*, the story concerns John Close, a young Perth solicitor, who is handling the Green Estate, which consists of eighty square miles of priceless land in Western Australia. It has been left to Captain Strutt who lives in England. For John Close it is a routine matter, but for Strutt it is a dream come true.

Life changes for both men when strange and dangerous opponents try to change the terms of the will. They try to solve the mystery which eventually erupts in violence in a remote place called Stringer Station.

Derek William Lambert

Pseudonym: Richard Falkirk
British. Born in London, 10 October 1929.

Titles

Angels in the Snow. London, Michael Joseph, 1969; New York, Coward McCann, 1969.
The Red House. London, Michael Joseph, 1972; New York, Coward McCann, 1972.
The Yermakov Transfer. London, Arlington, 1973; New York, Bantam, 1973.
The St. Peter's Plot. London, Corgi, 1974; New York, Bantam, 1974.
I, Said the Spy. London, Arlington, 1977; New York, Stein & Day, 1977.
The Red Dove. London, Hamish Hamilton, 1980.
The Judas Code. London, Hamish Hamilton, 1982.
The Man Who Was Saturday. London, Hamish Hamilton, 1984.
Triad. London, Hamish Hamilton, 1987.

Biography

Derek Lambert was educated at Epsom College and he studied journalism in the RAF. He has worked for provincial newspapers around Britain, and for the *Daily Mirror* and the *Daily Express* in India and Europe. He was the *Express* staff correspondent in Africa and Russia.

Critical Analysis

Lambert's first novel, *Angels in the Snow*, is a suspense novel based on his experiences in Moscow. Under the pseudonym of Richard Falkirk, Lambert has written a number of books that can be described as "historical" detective fiction, the major character is Edmund Blackstone, and the stories are set in early nineteenth-century London. Lambert's books have been translated into 15 languages.

The author commented in *Twentieth Century Crime and Mystery Writers* (1985): "I have always tried for realism, hoping at the same time to impart literary value to adventure/thriller novels without being self-indulgent. I use backgrounds that I covered as a journalist, in particular Moscow, and I try to equate the merits and deficiencies of both East and West: neither are necessarily the goodies or the baddies ... I cannot resist World War II; nor, mercifully can readers. Why? I think it is because good and evil were then so unequivocally defined and patriotism was clear-cut. If we thriller writers can assert such qualities in novels set in the 1980s then we can develop creatively without swastikas and iron crosses as crutches."

Trevor James, a Senior Lecturer in English Literature at Darwin Community College in Australia, wrote of his books: "Most of Derek Lambert's stories are in the thriller-spy mode with fast-moving narrative, broadly drawn characters, varied international settings, and dramatic, if not always surprising, endings. While the ingredients are familiar the reader's interest does not slacken. Lambert relies upon action rather than depth or subtlety, and embeds his stories in a contemporary background with some proximity to historical and political fact. This context, with its sometimes thinly veiled allusions to political identities, enables Lambert to exploit extreme and unusual situations for the stories without undue strain on a reader's credulity."

Martha Gellhorn, a novelist, wrote in the *Weekend Telegraph*: "Lambert's thrillers are intricately plotted and solid with factual detail. Each one presents entirely different characters and takes place wherever it suits him."

As a final comment the author said "We're all spies — watch the lace curtain moving next door — so the genre will never die."

AARON LATHAM

American. Born in Spur, Texas, 3 October 1943.

Titles

Orchids for Mother. Boston, Little Brown, 1977.

Biography

Aaron Latham was educated at Amherst College, from where he graduated with a BA in 1966; he also attended Princeton University from where he received a PhD in 1970. He worked as a reporter for the *Washington Post*, 1969-71, and was an associate editor for *Esquire* magazine, New York, from 1971 to 1974.

Critical Analysis

Orchids for Mother relates the story of the rivalry between Francis Xavier Kimball, code-named "Mother", director of counter-intelligence and head of the company's Israeli desk, and Ernest O'Hara, chief of covert operations. Mother initiates a plan to bring down the Director of the CIA and the Secretary of State in a spectacular scandal. The White House is paralysed by the Watergate scandal, which is just about to break.

When President Nixon finally chooses O'Hara for the post of DCI, the rivalry accelerates and leads to illegal penetration of domestic government agencies, blackmail, murder, and even suppression of vital foreign intelligence that would have alerted Israel about the impending Yom Kippur attack.

Mother is forced to resign from the Agency and he decides to take his revenge upon O'Hara. He engineers his own murder and pins it on O'Hara, who is forced to resign.

The whole plot is rather contrived and unbelievable — cryptonymic jargon is liberally scattered throughout the book, Langley headquarters is described in detail, but this information does not lend authenticity to this novel, rather it has the opposite effect. Also the behaviour of the main protagonists seems highly unlikely, we hope. Latham makes no effort to disguise characters such as Nixon and Kissinger, and nobody comes out a hero.

Douglas S Blaufarb, a veteran of the CIA and a critic of spy fiction, commented upon the author and his novel: "Latham is a trendy young journalist whose opinions are representative of his type. Judging by his book, he believes that recent administrations have been run by power-mad psychopaths. His book appears to have two purposes: to expose the doings of such types — and particularly the leadership of the CIA — and to combine political topicality, sensationalism and sex into a sure-fire money-maker."

Thomas James Leasor

British. Born in Erith, Kent, 20 December 1923.

Titles

[Major character: Dr Jason Love]
Passport to Oblivion. London, Heinemann, 1964; Philadelphia, Lippincott, 1964.
Passport to Peril. London, Heinemann, 1965; as *Spylight*. Philadelphia, Lippincott, 1966.
Passport in Suspense. London, Heinemann, 1967; as *The Yang Meridian*. New York, Putnam, 1968.
Passport for a Pilgrim. London, Heinemann, 1968; New York, Doublday, 1969.
Host of Extras. London, Heinemann, 1973.

Biography

James Leasor was educated at the City of London School and Oriel College, Oxford. He served in the British Army in Burma, India and Malaya in the Second World War and became a captain in the Royal Berkshire Regiment. At Oxford he edited *The Isis* and then joined the staff of the *Daily Express* in 1948, becoming in turn William Hickey columnist, foreign correspondent and feature writer.

His first novel was *Not Such A Bad Day* (1946), but he has also branched out into non-fiction with such works as *Rudolf Hess: the Uninvited Envoy* (1961) and *Singapore: the Battle that Changed the World* (1968). Leasor has also taken a keen interest in films and has been a director of Pagoda Films since 1959.

Critical Analysis

Leasor's character Dr Jason Love appeared at the same time as James Bond and although he did not become such a popular figure, he had his following and many of the stories were put on film. Love was a different character from Bond — he was a British country doctor enticed into espionage by the appeals of Douglas MacGillivray, an old comrade in Burma during the war, and now a highly placed spymaster in British Intelligence.

Love also shares certain characteristics of his creator such as his love for classic cars, like the Cord roadster.

James Leasor commented in the *Twentieth Century Crime and Mystery Writers* (1985): "I grew up a John Buchan enthusiast, and although I started my writing career with non-fiction books, I always intended to write thrillers. After several false starts and 14 rewrites I sold my first, *Passport to Oblivion*, in 1964 ... All my thrillers are based on fact and before I write them I visit the countries and places where I intend to set the action so that I can research the backgrounds thoroughly. I have long been attracted by the American Cord car and own one of the few open Cords in Britain — so I gave my fictitious character this car to drive. I write these stories because I enjoy writing them."

WILLIAM JULIUS LEDERER

American. Born in New York City, 31 March 1912.

Titles

The Ugly American. New York, Norton, 1958; London, Gollancz, 1959.

Biography

William J Lederer attended the De Witt High School in New York, and went on to the US Naval Academy and Harvard. He served with the US Navy from 1930 to 1958, finishing up with the rank of Captain. From 1958 to 1963 he was Far Eastern reporter for *Reader's Digest*, and since then he has worked as a freelance writer.

Critical Analysis

Apart from various solo works, he is perhaps best known for *The Ugly American*, which he wrote in collaboration with Eugene Burdick. The hero of this work is believed to have been based on that remarkable CIA covert operations agent, Air Force Colonel Edward Lansdale, whose exploits in the Philippines in the 1950s and later in Vietnam, were so publicised that he was made the model for the heroes of at least two books. (See Graham Greene's *The Quiet American* (1955).)

At the front of the book there is A Note From the Authors: "This book is written as fiction; but it is based on fact. The things we write about have, in essence, happened. They have happened not only in Asia, where the story takes place, but throughout the world — in fifty-nine countries where over two million Americans are stationed.

At the end of the book we have added a documentary epilogue which we hope will convince the reader that what we have written is not just an angry dream, but rather the rendering of fact into fiction. The names, the places, the events, are our inventions; our aim is not to embarrass individuals, but to stimulate thought — and, we hope, action."

Film

The Ugly American. U-I, US, 1962 .

WILLIAM TUFNELL LE QUEUX

British. Born in London, 2 July 1864. Died 13 October 1927.

Titles

Guilty Bonds. London, Routledge, 1891; New York, Fenno, 1895.
The Great War in England in 1897. London, Tower, 1894.
Secret Service. London, Tower, 1896.
England's Peril. London, White, 1899.
The Bond of Black. London, White, 1899; New York, Dillingham, 1899.
The Invasion of 1910. London, Nash, 1905.

Behind the Throne. London, Methuen, 1905.
The Mystery of a Motor-Car. London, Hodder & Stoughton, 1906.
The Great Plot. London, Hodder & Stoughton, 1907.
Spies of the Kaiser. London, Hurst & Blackett, 1909.
The Mystery of the Green Ray. London, Hodder & Stoughton, 1915.
No. 70 Berlin. London, Hodder & Stoughton, 1916.
Bolo, The Super-Spy. London, Odhams Press, 1918.
Cipher Six. London, Hodder & Stoughton, 1919.
The Intriguers. London, Hodder & Stoughton, 1920; New York, Macaulay,1921
Hidden Hands. London, Hodder & Stoughton, 1926; as *The Dangerous Game*. New York, Macaulay, 1926.
The Chameleon. London, Hodder & Stoughton, 1927; as *Poison Shadows*. New York, Macaulay, 1927.

Biography

His early life seems to have been spent travelling with his parents, having a somewhat haphazard private education in London, at Pegli, near Genoa and in France. During these travels he accumulated a vast amount of information, especially concerning military history and current affairs.

For a while he studied art in Paris and lived in the Latin Quarter, but wanderlust caused him to abandon a career in painting and sketching and to tour France and Germany on foot. On the strength of his travels he became a journalist and was a roving correspondent until in 1891 he was appointed foreign editor of London's *Globe* newspaper. This post was given to him because of a series of articles he had written for *The Times* about the revolutionary movement in Russia. It was on his trip that he thought up the idea for his first book, *Guilty Bonds*, which was actually banned in Russia. The theme of this book was political intrigue.

In 1893 Le Queux resigned his editorship to spend all his time writing books, of which he produced more than a hundred during his lifetime, only a sample of which are listed above. His writing was intermingled with a good deal of travel and journalism: in the early part of the century he visited Algeria, Morocco and the Sahara desert; in 1907 he travelled in Albania, Macedonia, Montenegro, Serbia and Turkey; the following year he made a trip to the Arctic and in 1909 he was in the Sudan. During the Balkan War he was a correspondent of the *London Daily Mail*.

Critical Analysis

Le Queux's lively imagination as a novelist was somewhat of a handicap to him as a journalist and, when it comes to sober fact, he was not always a reliable witness and was given to extravagant embellishment of a situation — sometimes presenting downright fiction as fact. For this reason it is not easy to assess all that he himself wrote about his activities.

In *Who's Who* he stated that he had "intimate knowledge of the secret service of continental powers" and that he was "consulted by the Government on such matters". Presumably he meant the British Government. Certainly he was involved in Secret Service work both before and during the First World War, but one suspects that Le Queux did the volunteering and the authorities were quite often conned by him.

It is well known that pre-1914 agents of the British Secret Service were badly paid: either they had to be patriotic gentlemen of independent means or crooks who made their own "perks" and financed themselves by means of dubious tricks. Le Queux, who always fantasised himself as a patriotic English gentleman, insisted that his spy stories were written to pay his expenses as a freelance member of the British Secret Service! This is not as improbable as it sounds.

Certainly Le Queux was one of the earliest writers of spy fiction proper and he set the pattern for the genre for the best part of a quarter of a century. Something less than a third of the books he wrote were spy fiction, but they made a greater impact than those of Oppenheim in the latter part of the nineteenth and early part of the twentieth century. Though his warnings of the unpreparedness of Britain to face a continental invasion had none of the literary quality of Erskine Childers, his sheer sensationalism and journalistic sense for the topical made his novels potent propaganda. Le Queux reached a huge readership and his adherents were numerous.

Le Queux's first novel concerning military threats to Britain was *The Great War in England in 1897*, in which he described a Russo-French plot for the invasion of England. *Secret Service* had as its background the anti-Jewish pogroms in Russia; its chief character was a Jewish nihilist. Three years later he produced *England's Peril*. Le Queux, though of French origin, was not then concerned with helping to improve Anglo–French relations: he was fanatically the foreigner who had become more British than the British.

Le Queux's further travels in Europe and North Africa, as well as the Middle East, convinced him that the real threat to Britain's security came from Germany and he then set out to pin-point that country as the potential enemy in his spy novels, using them as a powerful propaganda instrument. *The Invasion of 1910* was the first of his anti-German novels and this was swiftly followed by *The Mystery of a Motor-Car*, in which a country doctor is called upon to attend the victim of a motor-car accident only to find himself involved in a German plot.

When war actually came Le Queux continued the same theme in such books as *No. 70 Berlin*, *The Mystery of the Green Ray*, and many others. He tended to make his plots increasingly preposterous, though some of the background detail was authentic. In a sense he was a war casualty from a literary point of view, for he became so obsessed with the war that this robbed his writing of any objectivity or detachment.

PETER CHAD TIGAR LEVI

British. Born in London, 16 May 1931.

Titles

[Major character: Ben Jonson]
Grave Witness. London, Quartet, 1985.
Knit One, Drop One. London, Quartet, 1987.

Biography

Peter Levi was educated at Beaumont and Oxford University from where he received an MA. He became a priest in 1964 and resigned his priesthood in 1977, to become a Tutor and Lecturer in Classics at Campion Hall, Oxford, 1965-77. He was a student at the British School of Archaeology at Athens, 1965-68. He became a Lecturer in Classics at Christ Church, Oxford from 1979 to 1982 and was the Professor of Poetry at the University of Oxford, a post that he has held since 1984 and has only just given up in October 1989.

Critical Analysis

In a review of his second novel, *Knit One, Drop One*, the reviewer stated that it was "a sequel to the far superior *Grave Witness*. Ben Jonson, Oxford professor of archaeology, is asked to go to Paris to study a new computer that can decode ancient semi-destroyed manuscripts, hieroglyphics and perhaps even inscriptions on buried treasures. When the computer is stolen Peter is pursued by agents for several countries, including his own, because they think he knows something. He doesn't. It all works out but at a leaden pace."

The hero who appears in both books is Ben Jonson "who is often sucked into situations but is not a spy", says the author.

In answer to the question of whether an accurate picture of the intelligence world can be conveyed in fiction he replied: "Yes, but no one would believe how boring and how futile the plain truth would be." He went on to say that "I have known some spies, and it was a great help."

GORDON BATTLE LIDDY

American. Born in Hoboken, New Jersey, 30 November 1930.

Titles

Out of Control. New York, St. Martin's Press, 1979.

Biography

Gordon G Liddy was educated at Fordham University, from where he graduated with a law degree. From 1957 to 1962 he worked for the Federal Bureau of Investigation (FBI) as a field agent in Indianapolis and Gary, Indiana. He also became a supervisor in crime records division in Washington DC. He returned to the practice of law until 1971, when he became an adviser, ostensibly on drug problems, and a member of the special investigations unit (the White House "plumbers") for the White House Domestic Council in Washington DC. From 1971 to 1972 he was a general counsel for the Committee to Re-Elect the President (CREEP).

He was imprisoned for his involvement in the Watergate scandal, and since his release in 1977 he has worked as a lecturer, writer and a security adviser.

Critical Analysis

In *Out of Control* the CIA suspects that Gregory Ballinger, the head of one of America's largest multi-national corporations, is a Soviet agent, and they try to find out Ballinger's real aims. They break into his office but they do not find any incriminating evidence, so they call in Richard Rand — a "rogue", a former agent who left the agency under a cloud, and is now famous for his spectacular financial manipulations.

Rand discovers the aim of the Russian plot (to gain economic control of the free world) and tries to defeat Ballinger financially, but he finds that both Ballinger and the CIA are trying to silence him. With the help of his Mafia friends and those in the Chinese Tongs, he manages to elude the assassins who pursue him across America to Bogotá and back to New York, where he has a final confrontation with Ballinger.

The plot is rather melodramatic and the characters are stereotyped. One critic in *Newsweek* described the book as "a passable thriller", while another from the *Washington Post* commented that the novel "gets caught because it commits the one unforgiveable sin for thrillers: it is boring." Several commentators remarked that some critics had dealt harshly with Liddy's novel because of their biases against the author. Liddy himself agreed, insisting that "most people reviewed me and not the book." It may be a factor difficult to ignore but Gordon Liddy's career is far more colourful than his prose.

THOMAS WILLIAM LILLEY

British. Born in London, 25 September 1924. Died in 1989.

Titles

[Major character: Carter]
The Projects Section. London, Macmillan, 1970.
The K Section. London, Macmillan, 1972.

Biography

Tom Lilley's education was, he says, "interrupted by war and more noticeably by the Battle of Britain. I joined the RAF at the age of eighteen and furthered my education in Bomber Command." In 1948 he joined HM Overseas Civil Service and saw service in Malaya during the Emergency, Singapore, British North Borneo, Hong Kong and Brunei. After twenty years' service he retired as Deputy Head of the Special Branch (Police) in Sabah, most of his service having been spent in this Branch, first-hand knowledge of which provided the background to his first two novels.

Critical Analysis

The first of his novels was *The Projects Section*. Some critics carped that the book was "not very vivid" and that "clichés were plentiful", but Lilley is well worth inclusion among contemporary authors of spy fiction if only because he presents some aspects of the Malayan jungle war between the British and Chinese that history has not recorded.

The story is an account of the extraordinary measures taken by the Special Branch to eliminate the leaders of the Communist insurrection in Malaya. Traps are set, based on research and appraisal of the personal characteristics and behaviour of the individuals concerned. Carter of the Special Branch, hero of the story, gets to know his enemies and exploits their weaknesses. His own weakness, a beautiful Malayan mistress, is almost his undoing.

While the book does not explore the morality of violence in depth, it does demonstrate vividly the effect on personality of continued association with violence. Henry Keating wrote in the London *Times* that "Lilley wanted to show what the Malayan War was really like", and that "this truth was as beastly as it is possible to conceive. The Communists are shown flaying alive British soldiers and snipping to death with scissors suspected traitors. The British are shown doctoring food in discovered enemy dumps and allowing the innocent to be killed to preserve security. Perhaps without proof that is no longer obtainable, the indictment cannot be told as fact. But it cannot either be told as fiction ... But fiction can bring out one answer: a well-conceived novel can tell not how foul certain people were, but how appalling in similar general circumstances man can be to man."

Lilley himself saw his books rather differently: "I seek to show the impossibility of effectively fighting terrorism and remaining within the law." The answer is the same whether in the jungle or Northern Ireland.

His second book was *The K Section*, this time about police activity behind the scenes in a British Southeast Asian colony in danger of being taken over by the Communists. Lilley's hero Carter is now head of K Section and grappling with Russian intrigues and Chinese Tongs with equal adaptability. A desperate Russian reaction to the Special Branch success produces a tremendous catastrophe — a planned explosion on the cathedral steps after a State wedding, wiping out some royal guests and all the leading administrators. "Incidentally," wrote Lilley, "in chapter 20 of *The K Section* I spell out Communist technique on how to start a riot out of a lawful demo in precisely the way the Red Lion Square riot in London took place — over two years later."

ROBERT LITTELL

American. Born in 1935.

Titles

The Defection of AJ Lewinter. Boston, Houghton Mifflin, 1973; London, Hodder & Stoughton, 1973.
The October Circle. Boston, Houghton Mifflin, 1976; London, Hodder & Stoughton, 1976.
Mother Russia. New York, Harcourt Brace, 1978; London, Hutchinson, 1978.
The Debriefing. New York, Harper, 1979; London, Hutchinson, 1979.
The Amateur. New York, Simon & Schuster, 1981; London, Cape, 1981.
The Sisters. New York, Bantam, 1986; London, Cape, 1986.

Biography

Robert Littell served in the US Naval Reserve and reached the rank of Lieutenant. He worked as an editor for *Newsweek* magazine, based in Eastern Europe and the Soviet Union.

Critical Analysis

On the basis of his experience behind the Iron Curtain as general editor for *Newsweek*, Littell wrote his first spy novel, *The Defection of AJ Lewinter*, which is about an American scientist who defects to Russia. Complications arise when the Russians and the Americans try to evaluate what they have got, and what they have lost. The *New York Times* declared that it is "One of the best Cold War thrillers for years". The book won him the Crime Writers Association Gold Dagger award in 1974, and an Edgar from the Mystery Writers of America.

Robert Littell rates the worth of the individual high above that of any organisation, particularly secret ones. This is a constant theme in his stories, but shown most clearly in *The Amateur*. The hero, Charles Heller, a CIA cryptologist, blackmails his bosses into training him as a killer so that he can take revenge upon the professional terrorists who murdered his fiancée. Heller manages to carry out his personal mission without being killed by the terrorists or the CIA. This story is of further interest because the author claims that it is based on a true story, but could not be written as such because of the publication restrictions imposed upon employees of the CIA.

Anatole Broyard of the *New York Times Book Review* wrote that part of *The Amateur 's* appeal is the fact that "its hero is an amateur in a world of professionals, which means that the book really pits us against them, all the professional thems in government everywhere."

The Sisters is another example of one of the novels that offers an explanation for events that led up to the assassination of President Kennedy.

In a recent interview Littell said: "I write spy books to eat. To get readership, you have to deal with what people are familiar with. East–West conflict is the gist of the front page, what consumes the world. A well-written novel in which the characters are well-developed is exciting to read but also offers a supplement to the front pages."

Littell gets his inspiration from the news headlines, memoirs of former CIA and KGB agents supply details and his imagination supplies the rest. Many of his characters, on both sides, are victims of their own intelligence organisations, and the author makes no effort to disguise his opinions, but this does not detract from the story because it is done with subtle wit and irony — the true art of entertaining.

Film

The Amateur. Twentieth Century Fox, US, 1982.

NICHOLAS LAMBERT LUARD

Pseudonym: JAMES MCVEAN
British. Born in London, 26 June 1937.

Titles

The Warm and Golden War. London, Secker & Warburg, 1967; New York, Pantheon, 1968.
The Robespierre Serial. London, Weidenfeld, 1975; New York, Harcourt Brace, 1975.
Travelling Horseman. London, Weidenfeld, 1975.

The Orion Line. London, Secker & Warburg, 1976; as *Double Assignment*. New York, Harcourt Brace, 1977.
The Dirty Area. London, Hamish Hamilton, 1979; as *The Shadow Spy*. New York, Harcourt Brace, 1979.

Biography

Nicholas Luard spent his early childhood in Iran, in both the capital and the Kashgai tribal areas in the northern desert. He was educated privately in Britain at Winchester, the Sorbonne University in Paris, Cambridge University and the University of Pennsylvania. Having enlisted in the Coldstream Guards at the age of eighteen, he was commissioned, detached from royal guard duties and then trained as a NATO long-range patrol commander with a special sabotage and forward intelligence unit. He was assigned to this unit on the strength of his linguistic talents (he is not only fluent in German, French and Spanish, but specialises in local dialects) and his athletic record (member of the Rhine Army athletic championship team and ranked as a welter-weight boxer).

Known at Cambridge as "the King of Satire", Luard was a contemporary of that band of brilliant young men, including Dr Jonathan Miller and Peter Cook, and in the early 1960s was in the vanguard of the satire movement which was sweeping the West End of London, finally reaching the general public through the television programme "TW3". Luard was part-founder and part-owner of *Private Eye* magazine and also launched the highly popular home of satire in Soho, the Establishment Club.

Critical Analysis

Luard's first book was *The Warm and Golden War*, a subtle and sophisticated political novel about a multi-millionaire who hires mercenaries to open up a segment of the Austro-Hungarian frontier to let through 1,000 refugees to the West. The book was based on the author's experiences on the border during the 1956 Hungarian revolution.

The general settings of his books tend to be in areas of "conflict" which Luard knows well. *The Orion Line*'s climax takes place on another troubled border — that between France and Spain where the Catalan and Basque Separatists are operating. *The Dirty Area* is set in the mouth of the Mediterranean where tensions, intrigue and violence have been constant factors for centuries.

In *The Robespierre Serial* Luard told a convincing espionage story about an Arab grandee who, having meddled in too many intrigues, sought refuge in the West when he was in danger of assassination. He settled in Spain where a British agent, unaware that his own Ministry had organised a pretended assassination in order to frighten the CIA, took over the assassin's role in earnest and almost succeeded, despite the efforts of his superiors to stop him.

Travelling Horseman is about the inner core of the PLO's Black September terrorist arm, which, wrote one critic, "Luard appears to have penetrated ... a true documentation". Nevertheless it is fiction, but the CIA — or at least some of its executives — are still convinced that Luard obtained his plot and many of the details from one of their indiscreet operators.

Luard's own comment on the CIA reaction to *The Robespierre Serial* was: "They knew that I had high-grade sources in the Agency and they also knew my prime interest was in writing books about field operations. A popular and widely-held misconception — which the Agency assiduously promotes — is that the CIA is primarily worried about leaks concerning its technological espionage equipment, 'EIInt' in their jargon. In fact leaks about EIInt developments — satellite surveillance to planted bugs — worry them very little. They are well known to the other side and they don't damage the Agency's image. But what does worry the CIA are revelations and stories about field operations. Field operations involve individuals. They're fast, unpredictable, often messy and if exposed potentially explosive in their consequences. *The Robespierre Serial* dealt with a field operation that went wrong. That was why the Agency's response to the book was so extreme. I was delighted! They bought more copies (for study, evaluation and, if necessary, repudiation) than any other single purchaser in America!"

Luard's interest in the espionage game probably dates back to his childhood. He grew up in Teheran in the Second World War when the city was a hive of intrigue. His step-father was a much decorated SOE agent. "If I had to single out one theme that I'm particularly attracted to — and explore in my books — it would be that of the 'man alone'. The agent, the operative, who gets cut off from his superiors and his logistical base, and has to act on his own. This of course means that I'm concerned with field operations rather than analytical-evaluative espionage. I do use the same fictional (i.e. disguised) general organisation in several books and also several of the same 'background' characters. But the central figure, the protagonist, changes from book to book. This reflects real life field operations. A man suited for a certain operation in France won't necessarily be suited for quite a different operation in, say, Tangier."

ROBERT LUDLUM

Pseudonyms: JONATHAN RYDER, MICHAEL SHEPHERD
American. Born in New York City, 25 May 1927.

Titles

The Scarlatti Inheritance. Cleveland, World, 1971; London, Hart-Davis, 1971.
The Osterman Weekend. Cleveland, World, 1972; London, Hart-Davis, 1972.
The Matlock Paper. New York, Dial Press, 1973; London, Hart-Davis MacGibbon, 1973.
The Rhinemann Exchange. New York, Dial Press, 1974; London, Hart-Davis MacGibbon, 1975.
The Gemini Contenders. New York, Dial Press, 1976; London, Hart-Davis MacGibbon, 1976.
The Chancellor Manuscript. New York, Dial Press, 1977; London, Hart-Davis MacGibbon, 1977.
The Holcroft Covenant. New York, Marek, 1978; London, Hart-Davis, 1978.
The Matarese Circle. New York, Marek, 1979; London, Granada, 1979.
The Bourne Identity. New York, Marek, 1980; London, Granada, 1980.
The Parsifal Mosaic. New York, Random House, 1982; London, Granada, 1982.
The Aquitaine Progression. New York, Random House, 1984; London, Granada, 1984.

The Bourne Supremacy. London, Grafton, 1986.
Icarus Agenda. London, Grafton, 1988.
The Bourne Ultimatum. London, Grafton, 1989.

Novels as Jonathan Ryder
Trevayne. New York, Delacorte Press, 1974; London, Weidenfeld & Nicolson, 1974.
The Cry of the Halidon. New York, Delacorte Press, 1974; London, Weidenfeld & Nicolson, 1974.

Novels as Michael Shepherd
The Road to Gandolfo. New York, Dial Press, 1975; London, Hart-Davis MacGibbon, 1976.

Biography
Robert Ludlum was educated at various schools in Connecticut and the Wesleyan University at Middletown, Connecticut, from where he graduated in 1951 with a BA. During the Second World War he served in the US Marine Corps (1945-47). He worked as a stage and television actor from 1952. He was the producer at the North Jersey Playhouse at Fort Lee (1957–60), and Playhouse-on-the-Mall, at Paramus, New Jersey, 1960–69. He has been a freelance writer since 1969.

Critical Analysis
Many of Ludlum's books are concerned with conspiracies on a grand scale. For instance, in *The Chancellor Manuscript*, a writer of a political thriller fights for his right to prove that FBI chief J Edgar Hoover was assassinated. The researcher, Peter Chancellor, is thwarted in his efforts by Inver Brass — a watchdog group consisting of men of high standing in their professions who are using Hoover's papers for their own ends.

Again, *The Osterman Weekend* is about a CIA chief who turns out to be a double-agent but who sows suspicion amongst those around him to try to deflect suspicion from himself.

Myron J Smith, the author of *Cloak and Dagger Fiction* (1982), wrote of him and his books: "An astute student of intelligence matters who never had any formal connection with any government agency, Ludlum frequents the reference room of the New York Public Library to do research before undertaking each new title. In his travels over the years, one of his favorite tricks has been to take hundreds of photographs of the scenery around him — photos which can later provide the intricate place details for story climaxes. Ludlum's tales have become so successful that they are now automatic best sellers — almost before they are published!"

Film
The Osterman Weekend. Warner Brothers, US, 1983.

Gavin Tudor Lyall

British. Born in Birmingham, 9 May 1932.

Titles

[Major character: Harry Maxim]

The Wrong Side of the Sky. London, Hodder & Stoughton, 1961; New York, Scribner's, 1961.

The Most Dangerous Game. New York, Scribner, 1963; London, Hodder & Stoughton, 1964.

Midnight Plus One. London, Hodder & Stoughton, 1965; New York, Scribner's, 1965.

Shooting Script. London, Hodder & Stoughton, 1966; New York, Scribner's, 1966.

Venus with Pistol. London, Hodder & Stoughton, 1969; New York, Scribner's, 1969.

Blame the Dead. London, Hodder & Stoughton, 1972; New York, Viking, 1973.

Judas Country. London, Hodder & Stoughton, 1975; New York, Viking, 1975.

The Secret Servant [Maxim]. London, Hodder & Stoughton, 1980; New York, Viking, 1980.

The Conduct of Major Maxim [Maxim]. London, Hodder & Stoughton, 1982; New York, Viking, 1983.

The Crocus List [Maxim]. London, Hodder & Stoughton, 1985.

Uncle Target [Maxim]. London, Hodder & Stoughton, 1988; New York, Viking, 1988.

Biography

Gavin Lyall was educated at King Edward VI School, Birmingham, and Pembroke College, Oxford, from where he received a BA Hons in English in 1956. He served as a pilot in the RAF, 1951–53, and worked as a reporter for *Picture Post*, London, 1956-57. Then he was a film director at BBC Television from 1958 to 1959. He also worked as a reporter for the *Sunday Graphic* and the *Sunday Times*. He was Chairman of the Crime Writers Association from 1966 to 1967.

Critical Analysis

The author says: "I don't think of myself as a spy novelist particularly. I'm interested in espionage as a thread running through political and military life." And he goes on to say, "I rather wandered into 'spy-writing' because, in trying to do a Whitehall thriller, I found that espionage and security were part of the basic pattern of life there. I'm not very interested in the spy *per se*, nor in his organisations, only how he and it affect the larger world."

His first novel, *The Wrong Side of the Sky*, was published in 1961 and is the story of two disgraced pilots who meet again in Greece and go in search of jewels lost during the independence of India. The author describes this book as a "flying thriller".

Most of his early novels can be classified as adventure stories, influenced by the works of Hammett and Chandler. It was not until the publication of *The Secret Servant* in 1980 that Lyall ventured into the world of espionage. The book introduced the character Major Harry Maxim, a former SAS man, who is assigned to 10 Downing Street as military adviser on security. In this first story Maxim is ordered to watch over a professor who is vital to the British strategic negotiations with the Europeans. The second book, *The Conduct of Major Maxim*, has a more complicated plot involving the East Germans and the internal rivalry between MI5 and MI6.

Julian Symons, a critic of detective fiction, wrote of the early Maxim stories: "The plotting of these two books, especially the latter, is tight and cohesive, the style easy and sometimes humorous or sardonic, without any loss of pace. These adventure thrillers are the best things he has done."

In his latest novel, *Uncle Target*, Maxim comes up against Arab terrorists who kidnap Jordanian Colonel Katbah in London. Maxim dispatches the kidnappers and before he dies the Colonel informs him of the whereabouts of a new super-tank, the MBT90. So Maxim is sent out with a unit to the Jordanian desert to destroy this prototype. The plot is complicated by a revolt by members of the Jordanian army, which breaks out in the spot where the tank is being tested. The revolt, encouraged by the Syrians and backed by the Russians, could lead the tank to fall into Soviet hands. Maxim finds the tank but then it becomes the only form of escape and he and his crew travel miles across the desert trying to evade the rebel army. A review in the *Washington Post Bookworld* declared "With *Uncle Target*, Gavin Lyall has again written a novel of military adventure and political intrigue about as well as it can possibly be done."

Some of the themes that he covers in his books include: "Loyalty and its problems. To one's friends, to one's own concept of the state or to others' concept of the state."

Television

"The Secret Servant". 1985. A 3-part serial in which Gavin Lyall was an unofficial "adviser" to the director. He also had a very slight involvement in the script.

JOHN DANN MacDONALD

American. Born in Sharon, Pennsylvania, 24 July 1916. Died 28 December 1986.

Titles

[Major character: Travis McGee]
The Deep Blue Good-By. New York, Fawcett, 1964; London, Hale, 1965.
Nightmare in Pink. New York, Fawcett, 1964; London, Hale, 1966.
A Purple Place for Dying. New York, Fawcett, 1964; London, Hale, 1966.
A Quick Red Fox. New York, Fawcett, 1964; London, Hale, 1966.
A Deadly Shade of Gold. New York, Fawcett, 1965; London, Hale, 1967.
Bright Orange for the Shroud. New York, Fawcett, 1965; London, Hale, 1967.
Darker than Amber. New York, Fawcett, 1966; London, Hale, 1968.
One Fearful Yellow Eye. New York, Fawcett, 1966; London, Hale, 1966.
Pale Gray for Guilt. New York, Fawcett, 1968; London, Hale, 1969.
The Girl in the Plain Brown Wrapper. New York, Fawcett, 1968; London, Hale, 1969.
Dress Her in Indigo. New York, Fawcett, 1969; London, Hale, 1971.
The Long Lavender Look. New York, Fawcett, 1970; London, Fawcett, 1970.
A Tan and Sandy Silence. New York, Fawcett, 1972; London, Hale, 1973.
The Scarlet Ruse. New York, Fawcett, 1973; London, Hale, 1975.
The Turquoise Lament. Philadelphia, Lippincott, 1973; London, Hale, 1975.
The Dreadful Lemon Sky. Philadelphia, Lippincott, 1975; London, Hale, 1976.
The Empty Copper Sea. Philadelphia, Lippincott, 1978; London, Hale, 1979.
The Green Ripper. Philadelphia, Lippincott, 1979; London, Hale, 1980.

Free Fall in Crimson. New York, Harper, 1981; London, Collins, 1981.
Cinnamon Skin. New York, Harper, 1982; London, Collins, 1982.
The Lonely Silver Rain. New York, Knopf, 1985.

Biography

John Dann MacDonald was educated at the University of Pennsylvania, Syracuse University and Harvard. During the Second World War he served in India and Asia with the Office of Strategic Services, and rose to the rank of Lieutenant-Colonel.

Critical Analysis

MacDonald began his career by writing mysteries for the "pulp" magazines popular in the 1940s and 1950s, but he soon moved on to paperback novels. Altogether he wrote over 35 novels, including "serious" fiction, science fiction and non-fiction, as well as many short stories. He is best known for his Travis McGee stories which began with the publication of *The Deep Blue Good-By* in 1964.

McGee is strong, handsome, a former minor professional football player, six foot four and super-capable. He lives on a houseboat and makes his living by hiring himself out as a private-eye. He also has his share of romances. Although not all of these books are spy stories, McGee is sometimes mixed up in the game. MacDonald himself, in a 1984 television interview, described McGee as a "tattered knight on a spavined steed".

DAVID KENDREW MACE

British. Born in Sheffield, 23 December 1951.

Titles

Demon-4. London, Grafton, 1984; New York, Berkley, 1986.
Fire Lance. London, Grafton, 1986.
The Highest Ground. London, New English Library, 1988.
Frankenstein's Children. London, New English Library, 1989.

Biography

David Mace was educated at a grammar school in Sheffield. He then studied architecture at Sheffield University, but did not graduate. He worked at a variety of jobs and then moved to West Germany in 1979. He obtained an MA in German and English Philosophy at Freiburg University in 1986 and then returned to England.

Critical Analysis

In his first novel *Demon-4* the world has been ruined by a limited nuclear war. Short of manpower and material, the US and the USSR are forced to cooperate to contain the mess. In Antarctic waters a robot weapon is out of control and only scratch forces are available to take it out. One woman must do the job or be a scapegoat.

The author says that he does not "write classic spy fiction in the le Carré or Deighton mold. Instead (after a brief and unhappy flirtation with science fiction) I've moved towards mainstream thrillers which are making steadily more emphatic use of elements traditionally associated with the classic spy novel: surveillance, information gathering, penetration and counter-penetration, covert operations, military intelligence, counter-terrorism, backroom political rows. I'm applying these to much wider areas than the claustrophobic post-war confrontation of East and West, and adding the ingredients of 'conscientious objector' and public whistle-blower. I feel that's the way public interest, and thus the market, is beginning to move. Could be wrong, of course, but if not it gives spy fiction an unexpected but vigorous future."

Mace's latest novel, *The Highest Ground*, is about super-power politics which erupts into violence, extending the conflict into space. The Pentagon wants SDI — the "Star Wars" defence system that is the high ground of the new space age. But Rosemary Maclaughlin and Joseph Hyland, have a different idea — they want to claim the world of space for humankind and peace. The Russians also want to have the strategic advantage of weapons in space. As South Africa flares into violence and becomes the focus of world politics, so astronauts and cosmonauts are drawn towards a horrifying engagement on the highest ground of all — the Moon.

The author comments: "Secrecy and espionage — political or commercial — are free from constraints of publicly acceptable behaviour. Thematically, this opens a window onto attitudes lurking beneath the surface of society. Also, in the covert world, the individual is confronted directly with moral crisis."

Some of the recurrent themes that appear in David Mace's novels are: "Moral crisis of the individual caught between professional requirement and personal conscience. Divisive and destructive nationalism or group interest never quite erasing human trust. The abhorrence of using and abusing people as mere functional components. Human life is more important than anyone's doctrine."

HELEN CLARK MACINNES

American. Born in Glasgow, 7 October 1907. Died 30 September 1985.

Titles

Above Suspicion. Boston, Little Brown, 1941; London, Harrap, 1941.
Assignment in Brittany. Boston, Little Brown, 1942; London, Harrap, 1942.
I and My True Love. New York, Harcourt Brace, 1953; London, Collins, 1953.
Pray for a Brave Heart. New York, Harcourt Brace, 1955; London, Collins, 1955.
North from Rome. New York, Harcourt Brace, 1958; London, Collins, 1958.
Decision at Delphi. New York, Harcourt Brace, 1961; London, Collins, 1961.
The Venetian Affair. New York, Harcourt Brace, 1963; London, Collins, 1964.
The Double Image. New York, Harcourt Brace, 1966; London, Collins, 1966.
The Salzburg Connection. New York, Harcourt Brace, 1968; London, Collins, 1969.
Message from Malaga. New York, Harcourt Brace, 1971; London, Collins, 1971.
Agent in Place. New York, Harcourt Brace, 1976; London, Collins, 1976.
Prelude to Terror. New York, Harcourt Brace, 1978; London, Collins, 1978.

Biography

Helen MacInnes was educated at the Hermitage School, Helensburgh, Glasgow University and University College, London. In 1932 she married Gilbert Highet who, since 1950, had been Professor of Latin at Columbia University, New York. He died in 1978. She started writing books in the early 1940s with such works as *Above Suspicion* and *Assignment in Brittany*, quickly acquiring a reputation for novels of adventure and suspense.

Critical Analysis

MacInnes turned increasingly towards the well-constructed spy story with such later books as *Pray for a Brave Heart*, *Venetian Affair* and *The Double Image*. She has been described as "the Queen of Spy Writers" (*Sunday Express*) and she certainly shows a special talent for what one critic called her "satin-smooth novels of international intrigue". In 1961 three of her earliest books were re-issued under the title *Assignment: Suspense* with an introduction posing three questions which the author said she had often been asked about her novels: what is true? how much is invented? did you yourself experience any of those situations? Her reply was that in her novels "the physical backgrounds are as factual as I can make them" and that "the characters and plots were invented and that it was a misconception that novelists write only from experiences".

Her novels generally covered one of three areas: some deal with the Second World War; others, such as the *Salzburg Connection*, seemed to take a peep back at certain secrets and trends in that war which are still relevant today; and still others embraced the theme of plots from without to weaken and ultimately overthrow the Western world. She travelled widely after the war and used these experiences in settings for her books, notably in *North from Rome*, *Decision at Delphi*, *The Venetian Affair* and *Message from Malaga*.

Helen MacInnes had that penchant of female spy and suspense story writers of using a brilliant and distinguished amateur as her hero and chief agent. And her heroes, while undergoing all manner of trials, invariably emerge unscathed, which in a modern spy story gives a certain unreality to the episodes if repeated too often. At the same time this technique is linked with the interpolation of moral messages into her work. But, these foibles apart, such stories as *I and My True Love*, *The Salzburg Connection* (one of her best books) and *Agent in Place* manage to keep the reader in a state of animated suspense.

Films

Above Suspicion. MGM, US, 1943.
Assignment in Brittany. MGM, US, 1943.
The Venetian Affair. MGM, US, 1966.
The Salzburg Connection. TCF, US, 1972.

EDWARD MONTAGU COMPTON
COMPTON MACKENZIE

British. Born in West Hartlepool, 17 January 1883. Died in 1973.

Titles

Water on the Brain. Garden City, NY, Doubleday, Doran, 1933.
Whisky Galore. London, Cassell, 1947.

Biography

Compton Mackenzie was educated at St. Paul's School and Magdalen College, Oxford. He originally studied law, and even thought of acting as a profession. His first publication was a book of poems (1907) and his first successful novel was *The Passionate Elopement* (1911), followed by such best-sellers as *Carnival* (1912) and *Sinister Street* (1913–14).

Early on in life (1900–1) he was a 2nd Lieutenant in the 1st Herts. Regiment and when the First World War began he joined the Royal Naval Detachment in the Dardanelles Expedition of 1915. Invalided during the same year, he was appointed Military Control Officer in Athens in 1916 and later Director of the Aegean Intelligence Service, Syria. During this period Mackenzie was mixed up in a good many cloak-and-dagger activities of a type which aroused strong criticism among both enemies and neutral parties of the British Secret Service. Mackenzie described something of the Secret Service machinations in Greece in that war in his book *Athenian Memories* (1931).

What brought Mackenzie into deep trouble was his *Greek Memories* (1932; withdrawn and re-issued 1940). In this book he told about a colleague of his in British Intelligence who devised a plan for blowing up a certain bridge near Constantinople. This officer was so tediously attentive to detail that he obtained samples of various types of coal used in that part of Turkey in order to choose a few pieces, to be forwarded to England, to serve as models for the casings of the bombs. Mackenzie was charged under the Official Secrets Act, brought to trial at the Old Bailey in 1933 and fined £100. It was a ridiculous sentence in the land which had a reputation for justice.

In the Second World War Mackenzie was a Captain in the Home Guard and he was also invited by the Indian Government to visit all the battlefields of the Indian Army during that war. From 1931 to 1934 he was Rector of Glasgow University and in 1952 he was knighted.

Critical Analysis

Mackenzie got his revenge on both MI5 and MI6 when he wrote his spoof novel on the British Secret Service, *Water on the Brain*. This could not be banned because it was fictional! There was also a certain amount of satire directed against MI5 in his wartime humorous novel, *Whisky Galore*.

The hero of *Water on the Brain* was a hen-pecked, retired Army major named Arthur Blenkinsop, recruited into the Secret Service under the cover of a banana importer. In the preface to a new edition of the book, published two decades later, Mackenzie wrote that at the time of publication his novel must have seemed "a fantastic Marx Brothers affair", but that during the Second World War "many more people discovered that those responsible for Secret Intelligence do, in very fact as often as not, behave like characters created by the Marx Brothers." It is a tribute to Mackenzie's sense of realism and his satire that, halfway through the war, when the Americans were building their own Intelligence Services, they used *Water on the Brain* as a text-book for their trainees.

COLIN MACKINNON

American.

Titles

Finding Hoseyn. London, Century Hutchinson, 1987.

Biography

Colin Mackinnon is a Washington journalist who writes about the Middle East. He lived in Iran for six years, first working for the Peace Corps, and then as a director of the Teheran office of the American Institute of Iranian Studies. He has a PhD in Near Eastern languages and is the editor of *Middle East Executive Reports*.

Critical Analysis

In *Finding Hoseyn* we follow the story of a veteran journalist, Jim Morgan. The story is set in Teheran in 1977, during the last days of the Shah's reign. An Israeli engineer is gunned down in the street; at first Morgan believes that it is just another random terrorist killing, but then the story is squashed and strange things start to happen. Morgan's instincts are instantly alerted and he begins to think that there is a major story behind the murder.

Morgan uses his large network of contacts to investigate the story and ferret out the mysterious assassin, Hoseyn. The trail leads him from Paris, to Munich and then Beirut. The more he finds out the more dangerous he becomes to those who do not wish him to discover the truth.

The author presents us with a colourful portrayal of the Middle East, but the plot is virtually unintelligible. The novel uses the device of a parallel plot in which the Mossad are trying to check events, only to discover that they have been double-crossed.

ALISTAIR STUART MACLEAN

Pseudonym: IAN STUART
British. Born in Glasgow, 1923. Died in February 1987.

Titles

[Major character: Captain Mallory]
The Guns of Navarone [Mallory]. London, Collins, 1957; New York, Doubleday, 1957.
The Last Frontier. London, Collins, 1959; as *The Secret Ways*. New York, Doubleday, 1959.
Ice Station Zebra. London, Collins, 1963; New York, Doubleday, 1963.
When Eight Bells Toll. London, Collins, 1966; New York, Doubleday, 1966.
Where Eagles Dare. London, Collins, 1967; New York, Doubleday, 1967.
Circus. London, Collins, 1975; New York, Doubleday, 1975.

The Golden Gate. London, Collins, 1976; New York, Doubleday, 1976.
River of Death. London, Collins, 1981; New York, Doubleday, 1982.
Partisans. London, Collins, 1982; New York, Doubleday, 1983.
Santorini. London, Collins, 1986.

Novels as Ian Stuart

The Dark Crusader. London, Collins, 1961; as *The Black Strike.* New York, Scribner's, 1961.

Biography

In 1914, at the age of 18, Alistair Maclean joined the Royal Navy and began five years service as a torpedo-man in the East Coast Convoy Escorts. It was from these experiences that he drew heavily for his novels about the sea. After the war Maclean went to Glasgow University and then became a teacher at a junior secondary school in Rutherglen, Glasgow. In 1955 he had an instant success with his first book, *HMS Ulysses*, which made him a fortune, followed by the equally successful *Guns of Navarone*.

Critical Analysis

Some have assessed Maclean's earnings as around £250,000 a year from his books, film scripts and other activities. But success did not make this author big-headed: "I'm not a born writer," he insisted, "and I don't enjoy writing. I wrote each book in thirty-five days flat — just to get the darned thing finished." It was first as a writer on the sea and naval life and then as a thriller writer that Maclean made his name. He saw almost every book as a film before he started to write it and his real talent was that he told a story with speed, economy and attention to detail. He allowed nothing to hold up the action: one reason why there is no sex in Maclean's novels was, he said, because it slowed down the narrative and hindered the action.

He did venture into spy fiction; his first of this genre was *The Last Frontier*. Maclean has also written under the pseudonym Ian Stuart, notably *The Dark Crusader*, in which a tough but none too bright secret agent is sent on a mission which lands him on a Polynesian island where a new rocket is waiting to be tested. Rather more complicated in plot was *Ice Station Zebra*, in which a British Secret Service team sets off in an American submarine ostensibly to rescue the survivors of a British meteorological post in the Arctic which has been gutted by fire. In fact their quest is to recover a capsule from outer space containing a long-range, top-secret reconnaissance camera and its films — before the Russians get there. This is good, strong melodramatic stuff for the screen, but makes improbable reading. Indeed, most of Maclean's books read like film scenarios, which is undoubtedly his intention.

Films

The Guns of Navarone. Columbia, GB, 1961.
The Secret Ways. U-I, US, 1961.
Ice Station Zebra. MGM, US, 1968.
Where Eagles Dare. MGM, GB, 1969.

Joe Maggio

American. Born in Atlantic City, New Jersey, 19 March 1938.

Titles

Company Man. New York, Putnam, 1972.
Scam. New York, Viking, 1980.
Days of Glory and Grieving. New York, Viking, 1981.

Biography

Joe Maggio worked for the CIA as an agent in Cuba, Laos and Vietnam from 1965 to 1966. He has also worked as a columnist for the *Mainland Journal* in Pleasantville, New Jersey, and as a staff writer for the *Miami Beach Sun* in Miami Beach. Maggio is a keen sailor and has been the master of several schooners sailing all over the world. He has worked as a freelance writer since 1971.

Critical Analysis

The author has commented: "I'm a writer. I have had no choice in that decision. It's simple: I write. Motivation came in the form of war. Vietnam. Early Vietnam before the escalation while I was under contract to the government running gunboats on the Mekong Delta. Those were the years that pushed through my first novel, a cleansing sort of work ... My work for the government was dirty and left its mark."

Company Man was written as an exposé of the inner workings of the CIA. It was meant to be a work of fiction, but is really a thinly disguised description of the author's covert action adventures in the CIA, from the Bay of Pigs to the Congo and Laos.

Victor Marchetti

American.

Titles

The Rope Dancer. New York, Grosset & Dunlap, 1971.

Biography

Marchetti's introduction to the world of intelligence came in 1952 when he was serving in the US Army in Germany. He was sent to the European Command's "special school" at Oberammergau to study Russian and the techniques of espionage. For a while he was on special duties on the East German borders; then he returned to America to attend college, specialising in Soviet studies and history and eventually joined the CIA in 1955. He became a Soviet specialist, mostly on military affairs, and from 1966 to 1969 was a staff officer in the Office of the Director of the CIA. His highest position in the Agency was as executive assistant to Admiral Rufus Taylor, who was Deputy Director of Central Intelligence from 1966 to 1969.

Critical Analysis

Victor Marchetti is best known for his non-fiction work, *The CIA and the Cult of Intelligence* (1974), which was described as "the bombshell bestseller that blows the cover of the CIA", and became the subject of a prolonged legal battle between authors (John D Marks was the co-author), publishers and the CIA. By Federal Court order the authors were required to submit the manuscript of the book to the CIA for review prior to publication. Under the terms of the court ruling, the CIA ordered the deletion of 339 passages of varying length. Later these deletions were reduced to 168 items. Marchetti wrote that the CIA had "secured an unwarranted and outrageous permanent injunction against me, requiring that anything I write or say, factual, fictional or otherwise, on the subject of intelligence must first be censored by the CIA."

The background to this request undoubtedly lies to some extent in the publication of Marchetti's novel, *The Rope Dancer*, of which one critic, writing in 1975, said, "this terrifying piece of fiction has more truth in it than his best-selling non-fiction CIA exposé." And so, apparently, thought the CIA. *The Rope Dancer* did not attract anything remotely like the sales of his later non-fiction books (though it aroused wide interest after the publication of *The Cult*), but it certainly alarmed some members of the CIA.

It was a novel all about the Agency, though Marchetti called it the NIA, and in effect was an exploration of the inner workings of a spy's mind. The plot concerned a highly placed American who suddenly went over to the Russians and revealed a good deal about the administrative workings of the organisation. The CIA executives believed the novel went far too near the truth for comfort and that restraints should be put on Marchetti in future — thus the court ruling three years later over *The CIA and the Cult of Intelligence*.

Marchetti became critical of the CIA while he was still working for the organisation. For example, in an article in *The Nation* entitled "The CIA: The President's Loyal Tool", he wrote: "The CIA is basically concerned with interfering in the affairs of foreign countries", and in a foreword to his book on the CIA he stated: "Disenchanted and disagreeing with many of the Agency's policies and practices, and for that matter, with those of the Intelligence community, and the US Government. I resigned from the CIA late in 1969". He felt unable to speak out publicly: "I therefore sought to put forth my thoughts — perhaps more accurately my feelings — in fictional form. I wrote a novel, *The Rope Dancer*, in which I tried to describe for the reader what life was actually like in a secret agency such as the CIA, and what the differences were between myth and reality in this overly romanticised profession."

GEORGE MARKSTEIN

British. Born in 1929. Died 15 January 1987.

Titles

The Cooler. London, Souvenir, 1974; New York, Doubleday, 1974.
The Man from Yesterday. London, Souvenir, 1976.
Chance Awakening. London, Souvenir, 1977; New York, Ballantine, 1978.

The Goering Testament. London, Bodley Head, 1978; New York, Ballantine, 1979.
Traitor for a Cause. London, Bodley Head, 1979; New York, Ballantine, 1981.
Ultimate Issue. London, NEL, 1981; New York, Ballantine, 1982.
Ferret. New York, Ballantine, 1983.

Biography

George Markstein worked as a US military correspondent and as a feature writer for a London daily newspaper. He later served as story editor and consultant for Thames Television in London.

Apart from writing spy stories he wrote a number of dramas and screenplays such as "The Odessa File" for the screen, and "The Prisoner" and "Special Branch" for television.

Critical analysis

Markstein was a realistic spy novelist who used his fiction to inform the public about certain facts which otherwise would not be known. At some stage in his career he signed the Official Secrets Act, therefore he could not divulge any information gained in the course of his duties. He managed to be informative while entertaining in his stories.

For example, in his first book, *The Cooler*, the name refers to an establishment in Scotland, and was given by British agents and spymasters in the Second World War. "The cooler" was set up to deal with agents who had returned from occupied Europe or elsewhere, who were psychologically unfit or had strong opinions which made them critical of their superiors, or those who knew too much to be allowed to retire from the game. They were isolated in "the cooler" because their knowledge made them dangerous. This place did exist as it was acknowledged after the war by Professor M R D Foot, an official historian, who was allowed in his book to mention four lines about the establishment.

In *Chance Awakening* one man becomes a pawn in a treacherous game of secret warfare and deadly pursuit. From this book the author created the Patrick McGoohan television series "The Prisoner", which became a cult in its own right in the late 1960s and early 1970s.

In *The Goering Testament* a discredited crime reporter Harry Heron becomes involved in a battle between international intelligence agencies to find and recover the Reich Marshal's final written statement.

JOHN PHILLIPS MARQUAND

American. Born in Wilmington, Delaware, 10 November 1893. Died 16 July 1960.

Titles

[Major character: Mr Moto]
No Hero. Boston, Little Brown, 1935; as *Mr Moto Takes a Hand.* London, Hale, 1940.
Thank You, Mr Moto. Boston, Little Brown, 1936; London, Jenkins, 1937.
Think Fast, Mr Moto. Boston, Little Brown, 1937; London, Hale, 1938.
Mr Moto Is So Sorry. Boston, Little Brown, 1938; London, Hale, 1939.

Last Laugh, Mr Moto. Boston, Little Brown, 1942; London, Hale, 1943.
Stopover: Tokyo. Boston, Little Brown, 1957; London, Collins, 1957.

Biography

John P Marquand was educated at Harvard University from where he graduated in 1915 with a BA. During the First World War he served in the US Army, Artillery and rose to the rank of First Lieutenant. He worked as a reporter and magazine writer for the *Boston Transcript* in 1916, then from 1919 to 1920 he was a Sunday magazine feature writer for the *New York Herald Tribune*. After this he worked for a year for the J Walter Thompson advertising agency as a copywriter. From 1921 he was a freelance writer. He wrote short stories for such magazines as *Ladies' Home Journal*, *Collier's* and *Saturday Evening Post*.

Critical Analysis

Marquand achieved recognition as a serious writer with the publication of *The Late George Apley: A Novel in the Form of a Memoir* (1937). This novel was a great success and he received the Pulitzer Prize for it in 1938.

As an author he was less proud of his ventures into spy fiction. In an interview in 1959, he said about his Japanese secret agent: "Mr Moto was my literary disgrace.

him." Despite the author's reservations the series of Mr Moto novels continue to be reprinted. The character was so popular at the time that Twentieth Century Fox released a series of Mr Moto movies between 1938 and 1939, in an effort to capitalize upon his popularity. Mr Moto died as a literary character following events on 7 December 1941, although two other titles were published. It is interesting to note that in the film of *Stopover Tokyo*, made in 1957, the Moto character was eliminated.

Mr Moto is a Japanese aristocrat with many talents and a university education. He speaks a number of languages and his knowledge ranges from navigation to mixing cocktails. Most of the stories have a recognizable formula: they are set in foreign exotic locations and their hero is usually a young, naive American who falls in love with an attractive girl who is involved or becomes involved in some espionage activity. Mr Moto usually aids the American hero to resolve the mystery and get the girl.

Films

Think Fast, Mr Moto. TCF, US, 1937.
Thank You, Mr Moto. TCF, US, 1937.
Mr Moto's Gamble. TCF, US, 1938.
Mr Moto Takes a Chance. TCF, US, 1938.
Mysterious Mr Moto. TCF, US, 1938.
Mr Moto's Last Warning. TCF, US, 1939.
Mr Moto in Danger Island. TCF, US, 1939.
Mr Moto Takes a Vacation. TCF, US, 1939.
Stopover Tokyo. TCF, US, 1957.
The Return of Mr Moto. TCF, US, 1965.

ALFRED EDWARD WOODLEY MASON

British. Born in Camberwell, London, 7 May 1865. Died 22 November 1948.

Titles

The Summons. London, Hodder & Stoughton, 1920; New York, Doran, 1920.
The Winding Stair. London, Hodder & Stoughton, 1923; New York, Doran, 1923.

Biography

A E W Mason attended Dulwich College before going on to Trinity, Oxford, where he won an exhibition in Classics in 1887. Mason had a distinguished career, both academically and socially, being an outstanding speaker at the Oxford Union and a member of the University Dramatic Society. His experience with the latter made him take up acting as a career and for some years he toured the provinces.

Both Oscar Wilde and Sir Arthur Quiller-Couch encouraged him to take up writing rather than continue acting and in 1895 he had his first novel published, *A Romance of Wastdale*. This was followed immediately afterwards by *The Courtship of Morrice Buckler* (1896), of which a contemporary critic said : "This puts Mr Mason in the front rank of cloak and dagger writers." For a while after this he turned his attention to the historical novel and eventually found fame with his still popular romance, *The Four Feathers* (1902).

He was Liberal MP for Coventry from 1906 to 1910. In the First World War he served in the Royal Marines, reaching the rank of Major, but his principal war service was as a highly enterprising secret agent of the NID.

Critical Analysis

As a writer, Mason was more skilled both in narrative and characterisation than Oppenheim or Le Queux and he proved equally successful with his detective stories, of which the Inspector Hanaud series was easily the best. Substantial earnings from his books enabled Mason to satisfy his zest for travel and almost schoolboyish love of adventure.

Mason's biographer, Roger Lancelyn Green, gives a detailed account of some of his activities as a secret agent, but Admiral Sir William James commented that although Mason "used his experiences for several of his novels, the true story of his adventures in Spain, Morocco and Mexico was still unpublished when he died thirty years later. It would have been a prince of thrillers."

Mason, no doubt, performed a number of intelligence missions, but the only ones that have been recorded appear rather trivial and far-fetched. Nevertheless, Mason's influence in the Secret Service remained considerable even after the war. It is said that he was "entirely responsible for winning over as a spy for the British the head of a powerful smuggling ring operating in Southern Spain. This was Juan March, who lived in Majorca and became one of the most influential men in Spain and a millionaire."

Mason was offered a knighthood, but declined the honour, commenting that as he had no family (he never married), there was not much point to it. *The Summons* was a romance with undertones of espionage, involving the exploits of Spanish spies, while something of his Moroccan adventures emerges in *The Winding Stair*. In later years he turned back to his detective stories, for which he is best remembered.

Francis Van Wyck Mason

Pseudonyms: Geoffrey Coffin (with Helen Brawner); Frank W Mason, Ward Weaver

American. Born in Boston, Massachusetts, 11 November 1901. Died 28 August 1978.

Titles

[Major character: Hugh North]

Seeds of Murder. New York, Doubleday, 1930; London, Eldon Press, 1937.
The Vesper Service Murders. New York, Doubleday, 1931; London, Eldon Press, 1935.
The Fort Terror Murders. New York, Doubleday, 1931; London, Eldon Press, 1936.
The Yellow Arrow Murders. New York, Doubleday, 1932; London, Eldon Press, 1935.
The Branded Spy Murders. New York, Doubleday, 1932; London, Eldon Press, 1936.
Spider House. New York, Mystery League, 1932; London, Hale, 1959.
The Shanghai Bund Murders. New York, Doubleday, 1933; London, Eldon Press, 1934.
The Sulu Sea Murders. New York, Doublday, 1933; London, Eldon Press, 1936.
The Budapest Parade Murders. New York, Doubleday, 1935; London, Eldon Press, 1935.
The Washington Legation Murders. New York, Doubleday, 1935; London, Eldon Press, 1937.

(15 more titles featuring Hugh North)

Biography

Educated at Berkshire School, Sheffield, and Harvard, Mason had planned to take up a diplomatic career, but his father's sudden death forced him to abandon these ambitions and go into business. He started his own importing firm, buying rugs, antique books and other items on trips to Europe and North Africa. In the First World War he was a 2nd Lieutenant with the Allied Expeditionary Force in France from 1918 to 1919 and in the Second World War he served as a General Staff Corps Officer and chief historian in the civil and military government section. He was made a Colonel and he numbers among his honours the Croix de Guerre.

Critical analysis

Possessed of a lively and objective mind, with a penchant for diligent research, he drew heavily on his travels for background for his novels, some of which are set in unexpected areas of the world. For his novels of international intrigue and espionage he created the character of Colonel North, a cosmopolitan sleuth.

The North series lasted nearly forty years, covering the changing politics of the post-war period and continuing into the Cold War era. By the end of the Second World War North was permanently attached to the Military Intelligence division of the US Army, or G-2. North's promotion is paralleled in the development of the series — the early stories are more or less straight detective fiction. North becomes involved in the intrigues because he is there, not because he is in Army Intelligence. As the series progresses North finds himself in such areas as Cuba and the Middle East, thus reflecting topical areas of political unrest.

John Cecil Masterman

British. Born 12 January 1891. Died 6 June 1977.

Titles

An Oxford Tragedy. London, Dover, 1986 (first published in 1933).
Fate Cannot Harm Me. London, Gollancz, 1935.
The Case of the Four Friends. London, Hodder & Stoughton, 1956 (republished by Chivers Press, London, 1986).

Biography

J C Masterman was educated at Royal Naval Colleges at Osborne and Dartmouth. He started life as a midshipman, but soon turned to his natural environment, the academic world, when in 1909 he won a scholarship to Worcester College, Oxford. He achieved a lectureship at Christ Church shortly before the First World War, during which he was interned in Germany for four years.

His years between the two wars were mostly taken up by his academic life at Oxford University (he was Censor of Christ Church, 1920–26). It was during this time that he wrote his first two novels. During the Second World War he was concerned with the manipulation of enemy agents, or as Masterman himself expressed it in his official report to the Director-General of the Security Service in 1945, "by means of the double-cross system we actively ran and controlled the German espionage system in this country."

The double-cross system was a remarkable apparatus of deception whereby both those who were pro-Allies and posing as German agents, and real German agents captured in Britain were induced to serve the Allied cause by supplying to Germany information devised and manipulated by British Intelligence. Afterwards Masterman turned this report into a history of the whole affair in *The Double-cross System in the War of 1939-45* (1972).

"As time passed," wrote Masterman, "it occurred to me and to others that there might well be a case for publication ... it was also right to give credit for a successful operation to those who deserved it ... this I took to be important because the general opinion of the Secret Service was low [at that time, 1971] ... Failures are exaggerated, successes never mentioned."

After the war Masterman, who was knighted in 1959, became chairman of various bodies including a Committee on the Political Activities of Civil Servants, the Army Education Advisory Board, and a member of the BBC General Advisory Council, as well as being Vice-Chancellor of Oxford University from 1957 to 1958. Masterman's autobiography, *On the Chariot Wheel*, was published in 1975.

Critical Analysis

Masterman's first spy novel was *An Oxford Tragedy*. Professor Norman Holmes Pearson, of Yale University, who served with the American Office of Strategic Services in London, wrote that this book "may even have played a part in drafting him for the 'XX' Committee whose task it was to pass on and manage the complex manipulation of double agents" in the Second World War. *Fate Cannot Harm Me* was also written in the same period between the wars.

In 1956 he published another novel which told a story very similar to that of the double-cross system and of life in war-time Lisbon — "a kind of international clearing-ground, a busy ant-heap of spies and agents". This was *The Case of the Four Friends*, which in its subtitle Masterman described as "a diversion in prediction". He portrayed a centre where "secrets and information — true and false, but mainly false — were bought and sold".

WILLIAM SOMERSET MAUGHAM

British. Born in Paris, 25 January 1874. Died St.-Jean Cap Ferrat, 16 December 1965.

Titles

Ashenden; or, The British Agent. London, Heinemann, 1928; New York, Doubleday, 1928.

Biography

Maugham was educated at King's School, Canterbury, Kent, and from 1891 to 1892 he studied at the University of Heidelberg. He studied medicine at St. Thomas's Hospital, London and qualified as a surgeon in 1897, but he never practised.

During the First World War Maugham joined a Red Cross unit in France as a dresser, ambulance driver and interpreter. After a short while he was transferred to the Secret Intelligence Service and spent a year in Geneva as a secret agent. Finally, in 1917, he was sent to Russia with the task of supporting the Provisional Government against the Bolsheviks, who planned to make a separate peace with Germany.

In his book *The Summing Up* (1938), Maugham claimed that the Russian revolution might have been prevented if he had arrived six months earlier. There is ample evidence in the Private Papers of Sir William Wiseman in the E M House Collection, Yale University Library, that Maugham played a considerable role in the espionage in Russia in 1917. Wiseman was the head of the British Secret Service organisation in America during the war. His papers contain letters and lengthy reports by Maugham in which he names the chief German agent in Russia, analyses the political situation and makes various suggestions. The outcome of all this experience was what Eric Ambler has described as "the first fictional work on the subject [the life of the secret agent] by a writer of stature with first-hand knowledge of what he is writing about."

Critical Analysis

The title of Maugham's first and only book on espionage was *Ashenden; or, The British Agent* : it was not only based on his personal experience in the world of espionage, but it was the first exposure of what espionage really meant — not romantic melodrama, but long periods of boredom, fear, human weakness, callousness and deceit.

Ashenden was in a way the first of the anti-heroes, though nothing like as unpleasant as the latter-day anti-heroes. The book is really a collection of short stories, beginning in Geneva and ending in Petrograd during the revolution. The agent Ashenden, who is the central linking figure of all the stories, is in some ways a self-portrait of Maugham himself. Ashenden was not a brilliant performer of courageous deeds: he worried about missing trains and had an attack of nerves when a fellow agent was about to murder a Greek spy.

The realism of *Ashenden* contrasted markedly with the heroics and melodrama, the highlife of Oppenheim and Le Queux: "Ashenden's official existence was as orderly and monotonous as a City clerk's. He saw his spies at stated intervals and paid them their wages; when he could get hold of a new one he engaged him, gave him his instructions and sent him off to Germany; he waited for the information that came through and dispatched it; he went into France once a week to confer with his colleague over the frontier and to receive orders from London; he visited the market-place on market-day to get any messages the old butter-woman had brought him from the other side of the lake; he kept his eyes and ears open; and he wrote long reports which he was convinced no one read till having inadvertently slipped a jest into one of them he received a sharp rebuke for his levity." This piece of descriptive fiction is worth comparing with Alexander Foote's experiences as a real-life Soviet agent in Geneva in the Second World War as told in *Handbook for Spies* (1949): the parallel between fiction and fact is almost incredible.

Perhaps after *Ashenden* any other ventures by Maugham into spy fiction would have been an anti-climax. He was a wise enough writer to realise he had laid a new milestone in the history of this genre and that was enough.

Film

Ashenden was filmed as *The Secret Agent* in Britain in 1936 and directed by Alfred Hitchcock.

CHARLES MCCARRY

American. Born in Pittsfield, Massachusetts, 14 June 1930.

Titles

[Major character: Paul Christopher]
The Miernik Dossier. New York, Saturday Review Press, 1973; London, Hutchinson, 1974.
The Tears of Autumn. New York, Saturday Review Press, 1975; London, Hutchinson, 1975.
The Secret Lovers. New York, Dutton, 1977; London, Hutchinson, 1977.
The Better Angels. New York, Dutton, 1979; London, Hutchinson, 1979.
The Last Supper. New York, Dutton, 1983; London, Hutchinson, 1983.

Biography

Charles McCarry began his career as a journalist, then he was a speechwriter for President Eisenhower, before he joined the CIA in 1958. He remained with the agency for nine years, working in Europe, Africa and Vietnam. He retired from the CIA in 1967 to become a freelance writer.

Critical analysis

McCarry has produced five spy novels so far, the first of which was *The Miernik Dossier* in 1973. This novel is constructed in the form of a dossier, with agents' reports, headquarters' communications, intercepted letters and transcriptions of bugged conversations. It is a skilfully made novel and original in its method of involving the reader in the inner workings of intelligence collection.

McCarry's hero Paul Christopher criticises his own intelligence service in this story, because he believes that the Cold War atmosphere has had a bad effect upon the attitudes and priorities of agency personnel. Christopher does not see espionage as a game when people die as a result of their antics. McCarry shows in his novels that one of the tragedies of the Cold War is the highly suspicious atmosphere it generates between the East and West. This puts pressure on the agency to obtain information and then act upon it, but it has also spawned a bitter rivalry between the superpowers involving innocent people in the struggle. In these novels one gets the impression that there can be no ultimate victors in such warfare — only victims.

McCarry's second novel *The Tears of Autumn* is also concerned with the pursuit of truth and the costs of its acquisition. The novel is set in 1963 after the assassination of President Kennedy. Paul Christopher believes that he knows who is responsible, but when he has collected the evidence nobody is interested in hearing his explanation. This book was published in 1974, a time when several CIA apostates, like Victor Marchetti, were voicing their criticisms of the agency. Some CIA officials believed that McCarry had joined their ranks.

In a recent interview in *Publisher's Weekly* in July 1988, McCarry acknowledged that his experience in intelligence has helped him give authenticity to his spy novels: "But beyond that he will not discuss the Agency. 'It seems difficult for some people to understand that the oath of secrecy is not to the Agency as such but to your colleagues.' "

The author is also disturbed that he is described as a spy novelist: " 'I never knew I was writing thrillers until I read it in the papers,' he says, 'I thought I was writing naturalistic novels about people involved in the worlds of intelligence and politics.' He knows too much about intelligence work to find most spy genre novels credible: 'It's like a sex manual written by a Trappist monk; the positions are simply impossible. And though they can be entertaining, these books have nothing to do with the way things really are, which is the province of the writer.' "

McCarry is certainly accurate in his portrayal of the murky world of intelligence. Thomas Powers, who wrote a biography of Richard Helms and the CIA confirms this quality in McCarry's stories: " ... his novels capture a sound feel for intelligence in the field, which involves a good deal of political intrigue, but not much melodrama."

Apart from the hero, Paul Christopher, McCarry introduces a variety of characters who reappear throughout the novels. In *The Last Supper*, the story spans from the 1920s to the present and resurrects these characters in a dramatic finality which tends to suggest that it may be the last story in which we encounter Christopher and his colleagues.

WILSON McCARTHY

American. Born in Washington DC, 1930.

Titles

The Fourth Man. London, Hutchinson, 1972.
The Detail. London, Hutchinson, 1973.

Biography

A man who has had a varied career in different parts of the world, Wilson McCarthy served as an infantryman with the US forces in the Korean War and later worked for Presidents Kennedy and Johnson in various capacities. At one time he directed the Presidential Advance and he has had wide experience of Secret Service operations and techniques, all of which has given him the know-how and background for some exciting and well-constructed spy stories.

After leaving the White House McCarthy joined MGM as their European representative, primarily as a trouble-shooter. He then returned to America as an executive with the company before moving into the production area of the business to make films. Leaving MGM to join Warner Brothers as a producer, he next formed his own company in the animation field before moving to Britain, where he lived for three years prior to going to Ontario in 1974.

Critical Analysis

Outstanding among McCarthy's spy thrillers are *The Fourth Man* and *The Detail*. The former tells how the President of the United States is threatened with assassination. The Mafia rightist organisations and individual psychopaths (a formidable combination!) are conspiring, each for their own motives, to rid American political life of what they see as a radical scourge. The American Secret Service is aware of the threat to its institutions, but seemingly powerless to prevent it.

McCarthy is extraordinarily skilful in dealing with this theme and making it seem plausible and somehow frighteningly natural. His novel plunges the reader into an ambiguous world of double-crossing and deceptions and, behind it all, there is still a nagging doubt: could it really have happened in the Kennedy era?

The Detail is again concerned with the American Secret Service's responsibility for protecting the President, but with emphasis this time on another role — that of safeguarding the American currency. Peter Maas, author of *The Valachi Papers*, wrote of the book that it made *"The French Connection* look like a Sunday School outing."* What is especially interesting about this fictional thriller is the authentic picture it draws of the American Secret Service — how it is much smaller than the FBI, but has powers extending far beyond its size, powers which are not easily understood outside the country. The action shifts from Los Angeles airport to Washington DC, London and Palm Springs, with Scotland Yard and the British Customs involved.

ROBERT MCCRUM

British. Born in Cambridge, 7 July 1953.

Titles

In the Secret State. London, Hamish Hamilton, 1980; New York, Simon & Schuster, 1980.

Biography

Robert McCrum was educated at Sherborne School, Dorset and Corpus Christi College, Cambridge. He has travelled widely in Europe and the Far East and now lives in London, where he works as a publisher.

Critical Analysis

In the Secret State is about the power of secret information and the corrupting influence it has upon those who hold the secrets. Frank Strange is the director of a government agency which is so secret that not even its personnel are aware of its full powers, including Strange. On the day he retires a man is found dead, he worked for the mysterious C Directorate within the agency.

Strange starts his own investigation originally suspecting that the dead man was a spy and that the organisation had been penetrated from the outside. But the more information he obtains the more he is led to the conclusion that there is a conspiracy from within — a corruption from the inside and therefore harder to detect. Strange blames it upon the "absurd mystique of secrecy".

The plot is a bit melodramatic at times and some of the military characters are stereotyped. Frank Strange is an idealised character, like a poor imitation of George Smiley — the father figure everyone depends on. For a while we are in doubt whether to believe Strange or the other executives in the agency, as we are presented with the evidence through the eyes of a relatively new recruit, Quitman, whose loyalties are confused by events. This is an interesting novel with a strong message to our government and secret services.

Television

In the Secret State was broadcast by the BBC in 1985, and was later repeated in 1987.

PHILIP DONALD McCUTCHAN

Pseudonym: DUNCAN MacNEIL
British. Born in Cambridge, 13 October 1920.

Titles

[Major character: Commander Esmonde Shaw]
Gibraltar Road. London, Harrap, 1960; New York, Berkley, 1965.
Redcap. London, Harrap, 1961; New York, Berkley, 1965.
Bluebolt One. London, Harrap, 1962; New York, Berkley, 1965.
The Man from Moscow. London, Harrap, 1963; New York, Day, 1965.
Warmaster. London, Harrap, 1963; New York, Day, 1964.
Moscow Coach. London, Harrap, 1964; New York, Day, 1966.
The Dead Line. London, Harrap, 1966; New York, Berkley, 1966.
Skyprobe. London, Harrap, 1966; New York, Day, 1967.
The Screaming Dead Balloons. London, Harrap, 1968; New York, Day, 1968.
The Bright Red Businessman. London, Harrap, 1969; New York, Day, 1969.
The All-Purpose Bodies. London, Harrap, 1969; New York, Day, 1970.
Hartinger's Mouse. London, Harrap, 1970.
This Drakotny ... London, Harrap, 1971.
Sunstrike. London, Hodder & Stoughton, 1979.
Corpse. London, Hodder & Stoughton, 1980.
Werewolf. London, Hodder & Stoughton, 1982.
The Hoof. London, Hodder & Stoughton, 1983.
Rollerball. London, Hodder & Stoughton, 1984.

Greenfly. London, Hodder & Stoughton, 1987.
The Boy Who Liked Monsters. London, Hodder & Stoughton, 1989.

Biography

Philip McCutchan was educated at St. Helen's College, Southsea, Hampshire, and the Royal Military Academy, Sandhurst. He served in the Royal Navy in the Second World War as a Lieutenant, RNVR. For three years afterwards he sailed with Orient liners on the Australian run and then, for a time, was an assistant headmaster at a preparatory school.

Critical Analysis

He began writing in 1956 and his best-known books are probably those in the popular Commander Shaw series. McCutchan says: "The *Commander Shaw* novels could loosely be described as 'spy' since he was originally Naval Intelligence." There are 19 titles in the series which began in 1960 and continues to the present.

McCutchan also writes detective stories (featuring Detective Chief Superintendent Simon Shard) and sea thrillers. Commander Shaw works for one of the branches of the Ministry of Defence — 6D2. All his missions are politically sensitive and as a result there is a fast pace and the plots are inventive.

In his latest adventure, *The Boy Who Liked Monsters*, Shaw investigates a series of diplomatic disappearances, and then a murder. At stake, he discovers, is nothing short of world peace.

PATRICIA MCGERR

American. Born in Falls City, Nebraska, 26 December 1917. Died in 1985.

Titles

[Major character: Selena Mead]
Is There a Traitor in the House? New York, Doubleday, 1964; London, Collins, 1965.
Legacy of Danger. Washington, Luce, 1970.

Short Stories

"Grand Prize for Selena", in *This Week* (New York), 23 February 1964.
"Holiday for a Lady Spy", in *This Week* (New York), 5 April 1964.
"Fox Hunt for Selena", in *This Week* (New York), 12 December 1964.
"Ballad for a Spy", in *This Week* (New York), 18 April 1965.

Over twenty other short stories featuring Selena Mead, published in *Ellery Queen's Mystery. Magazine*, *This Week* and various editions of *Alfred Hitchcock Presents*, and other magazines.

Biography

Patricia McGerr was educated at Trinity College, Washington DC, and the University of Nebraska, Lincoln, where she received a BA in 1936, and Columbia University, New York, from where she obtained a degree in Journalism. She worked as the Director of Public Relations for the American Road Builders

Association in Washington DC from 1937 to 1943. She was the assistant editor of *Construction Methods* magazine, New York, 1943–48. Since then she has worked as a full-time writer.

Critical Analysis

Patricia McGerr was better known for her detective novels and stories, but she is included in this work because of her character Selena Mead, a glamorous counter-espionage agent employed by a top-secret security branch known as Section Q.

Selena first appeared in *This Week* magazine in October 1963, after Patricia McGerr was asked to write a counter-spy series for the magazine. The author admitted that at the time she knew very little about the espionage world and was not familiar with the writings of either Ian Fleming or John le Carré. She also did not like violence in any form, therefore created her heroine in a particular mould, as the author described her: "A glamorous Washington widow, well-born and gently bred, at home in the upper strata of international society....So Selena came into being — beautiful, charming, cultivated, and very, very rich....She was educated on four continents, graduated from Vassar, is fluent in an unspecified number of languages, has mastered most of the arts and sciences....Her complexion is flawless, her eyes deep-set, her features resemble — at the reader's option — a Greek statue or an Italian cameo....And, lest so much perfection block off sympathy, she is tragically bereaved of the man she loved. Duty may draw her round the party circuit, but her heart remains in mourning."

HERMAN CYRIL MCNEILE

Pseudonym: SAPPER

British. Born in Bodmin, Cornwall, 28 September 1888. Died 14 August 1937.

Titles

[Major character: Captain Hugh "Bulldog" Drummond]
Bull-Dog Drummond: The Adventures of a Demobilized Officer Who Found Peace Dull. London, Hodder & Stoughton, 1920; New York, Doran, 1920.
The Black Gang. London, Hodder & Stoughton, 1922; New York, Doran, 1922.
The Third Round. London, Hodder & Stoughton, 1924; as *Bulldog Drummond's Third Round.* New York, Doran, 1924.
The Final Count. Hodder & Stoughton, 1926; New York, Doran, 1926.
The Female of the Species. London, Hodder & Stoughton, 1928; New York, Doubleday, 1928.
Temple Tower. London, Hodder & Stoughton, 1929; New York, Doubleday, 1929.
The Return of Bulldog Drummond. London, Hodder & Stoughton, 1932; as *Bulldog Drummond Returns.* New York, Doubleday, 1932.
Knock-Out. London, Hodder & Stoughton, 1933; as *Bulldog Drummond Strikes Back.* New York, Doubleday, 1933.
Bulldog Drummond at Bay. London, Hodder & Stoughton, 1935; New York, Doubleday, 1935.
Challenge. London, Hodder & Stoughton, 1937; New York, Doubleday, 1937.

Short Stories

The Dinner Club. London, Hodder & Stoughton, 1923; New York, Doran, 1923.

Biography

Sapper was the pseudonym used by Lieutenant-Colonel Herman Cyril McNeile, who was educated at Cheltenham College, and the Royal Military Academy, Woolwich. He joined the Royal Engineers in 1907, became a Captain in 1914 and retired at the end of the war to start writing books.

Critical Analysis

Crude and totally unsophisticated thrillers, in outlook they were similar to the sturdy patriotism of John Buchan, but in style, dialogue and construction they were not in the same class. Yet Sapper became famous through the creation of his character Bulldog Drummond who, for a period of some fifteen years, was almost a household name.

Drummond, the 1920ish portrait of a "clean-limbed young Englishman", was out for adventure and always ready to check the fiendish plots of Carl Peterson and any other "Hun", "Wog", "Dago" or other foreigner. This was the language of Sapper: his characters spoke in stilted clichés, expressed right-wing views, frequently indulged in anti-semitism and regarded all lovely young Englishwomen as purity personified. Nobody seemed to raise any objection to this nonsense in the 1920s and 1930s and a great deal of Sapper material was filmed, Ronald Colman being an outstanding Bulldog Drummond of the period.

Not all the Bulldog Drummond series were of the spy genre; Drummond often worked with Ronald Standish, a private investigator, as in such novels as *Knock-Out* and *Challenge*. There was much that was unpleasant in the Sapper books, sometimes in the violence, more often in the sentiments. In *Black Gang* Drummond tells two Jews "my friends do not like your trade, you swine" and then beats them up. Sapper introduced many such touches into his stories. The plots of his spy stories were blatantly right-wing, but then perhaps this was just a reflection of public opinion at the time. After McNeile's death Gerald Fairlie took over the character of Bulldog Drummond and continued the series, but modified the excesses of the hero's character.

For the films of Bulldog Drummond see **GERALD FAIRLIE**.

IB JORGEN MELCHIOR

American. Born in Copenhagen, Denmark, 17 September 1917.

Titles

Order of Battle. New York, Harper & Row, 1972; London, Souvenir Press, 1973.
Sleeper Agent. New York, Harper & Row, 1975; London, Souvenir Press, 1976.
The Haigerlock Project. New York, Harper & Row, 1977; London, Souvenir Press, 1977.
The Watchdogs of Abaddon. New York, Harper & Row, 1979; London, Souvenir Press, 1979.
The Marcus Device. New York, Harper & Row, 1980.

The Tombstone Cipher. New York, Bantam, 1983.
Eva. New York, Dodd Mead, 1984; London, Hale, 1988.
V-3. New York, Dodd Mead, 1985; London, Hale, 1988.
Code Name: Grand Guignol. New York, Dodd Mead, 1987; London, Hale, 1988.

Biography

Ib Melchior was educated in Denmark and graduated from the University of Copenhagen. He then joined a British theatrical company, The English Players, based in Paris, as an actor and toured Europe, becoming Stage Manager and Co-Director of the company. Just before the outbreak of the Second World War he came to America with this company to do a Broadway show.

During the war he served with the OSS for a while and was then transferred to the US Military Intelligence Service. He spent two years in the European Theatre of Operations as a Military Intelligence Investigator attached to the Counter Intelligence Corps.

After the war he started his career in television and writing. He has directed over 500 TV shows, both live and filmed. He has also written a number of articles and stories for national American magazines and European periodicals.

Critical Analysis

Many of Melchior's novels are based upon his experience as Military Intelligence Investigator for the Counter Intelligence Corps in the European Theatre of Operations during the Second World War. *Order of Battle*, *Sleeper Agent*, *The Haigerlock Project*, *Eva*, and *V-3* are just a few of the books in which he uses his experience. His novels have been published in 25 countries.

His first novel, *Order of Battle*, is set in the last weeks of the Second World War, and the action takes place in the nineteen days between the death of President Roosevelt and Hitler's suicide, and the story tells of the determination of the Allies to find and destroy the fabled Nazi Werewolf organisation. The Werewolves are a carefully selected and dedicated force who have based themselves in an impregnable Alpine fortress. They are determined to destroy the American Occupation armies and to assassinate General Eisenhower, which will enable them to turn the Nazi defeat into a victory.

One reviewer, Will Wharton, described the novel as follows: " ...With mounting momentum and captivating suspense the account moves on to a conclusion we know as history — though never before narrated with such verve and authenticity. That's understandable. The author ... actually participated in the events related. He was decorated by the United States, Sweden and Denmark for his exploits, while in the US Military Intelligence Service, from whose document, 'Order of Battle of the German Army, 1943', he took his title."

Most of his spy novels return to the setting of the Second World War and the Nazis are usually the enemy, but this is natural considering his experience during the war. His latest novel, *Code Name: Grand Guignol*, is no exception.

In this story British Intelligence had learned on the eve of D-Day that the Nazis were desperately trying to complete some sort of secret weapon that threatened to destroy the whole invasion operation. It is left to a small group of civilians to find this weapon and destroy it. These civilians are members of the Grand Guignol theatre, who during the war helped to transport a number of Allied refugees to freedom, now they are confronted with a desperate challenge, without any help from the military. It is up to them to finally defeat the Nazis and secure an Allied victory.

A reviewer in *Publisher's Weekly* wrote: "This story ranks high in suspense, atmosphere and heartwarming moments as the band proves the value of the old adage: all for one, one for all. Melchior offers fine entertainment ..."

JAMES WILLIAM MITCHELL

Pseudonym: JAMES MUNRO
British. Born in South Shields, County Durham, 12 March 1926.

Titles

[Major character: David Callan]
A Magnum for Schneider. London, Jenkins, 1969; as *A Red File for Callan*. New York, Simon & Schuster, 1971.
Russian Roulette. London, Hamish Hamilton, 1973; New York, Morrow, 1973.
Death and Bright Water. London, Hamish Hamilton, 1974; New York, Morrow, 1974.
Smear Job. London, Hamish Hamilton, 1975; New York, Putnam, 1977.

Novels as James Munro
[Major character: James Craig]
The Man Who Sold Death. London, Hammond, 1964; New York, Knopf, 1965.
Die Rich, Die Happy. London, Hammond, 1965; New York, Knopf, 1966.
The Money That Money Can't Buy. London, Hammond, 1967; New York, Knopf, 1968.
The Innocent Bystanders. London, Jenkins, 1969; New York, Knopf, 1970.

Biography

James Mitchell was educated at St. Edmund Hall, Oxford, where he received a BA and an MA after which he worked as an actor and a travel agent in Britain and Paris, 1948-50. He was a lecturer in English at South Shields Technical College from 1950 to 1959 and then worked as a television writer in London for four years, and as a Lecturer in Liberal Studies at Sunderland College of Art in County Durham, 1963–64.

Critical Analysis

Mitchell has commented: "The writing of thrillers is a craft, and to be acknowledged as a craftsman would for me be more than adequate praise... Thrillers — at least the ones I write — deal with men who live in isolation, and who are subject to the pressures of pursuit, the risks of capture and ultimately death. Certainly the men are remarkable, but then so are the pressures and the risks. They survive because they too are craftsmen, with guns, knives, their bare hands — and with their brains too. They are heroes not because they kill — their opponents do that as well as they — but because, despite the things they must do, they believe in goodness to the point where they will die for it."

Writing under his own name Mitchell created the character David Callan, who is a "moral" killer working for a secret organisation employed by British Intelligence. Callan certainly is a loner, and his constant isolation was conveyed in the long-running television series of that name first broadcast in the 1970s.

Under the name of James Munro he wrote a number of books featuring James Craig, a resourceful but sometimes violent British agent, who works for Department K of British Intelligence. The world Mitchell portrays in all his books is decidedly murky and he leaves it to his heroes to maintain any standard of morality.

MICHAEL JOHN MOLLOY

British. Born in Hertfordshire, 22 December 1940.

Titles

The Black Dwarf. London, Hodder & Stoughton, 1986.
The Kid From Riga. London, Hodder & Stoughton, 1987.
The Harlot of Jericho. London, Macdonald, 1989.

Biography

Michael Molloy attended the Ealing School of Art before starting a career in journalism. He was Art Editor at the *Daily Mirror* in 1964, and then worked as Editor for the *Mirror* magazine, 1969–70 and Editor of the *Mirror* , 1975–85. He is now the Editor-in-Chief of Mirror Group Newspapers.

Critical Analysis

Molloy's second novel, *The Kid from Riga*, concerns Lewis Horne, an intelligence officer and academic writer, who becomes involved in a plot that began forty years ago in the ruins of Berlin. Violent events in Europe and the Middle East point to a mole working very deep in the British Security Services — the mysterious kid from Riga — whom the Russians have trained very carefully, but it is up to Horne to find out exactly who he is and stop him.

CHRISTOPHER JOHN MULLIN

British. Born on 12 December 1947.

Titles

A Very British Coup. London, Hodder & Stoughton, 1982.
The Last Man out of Saigon. London, Gollancz, 1986; New York, Bantam, 1989.

Biography

He was educated at the University of Hull, from where he received an LL B. Since then he has worked as a freelance journalist and has travelled extensively in Indochina and China. He worked as a sub-editor for the BBC World Service from 1974 to 1978, and as an Editor for the *Tribune* from 1982 to 1984. He was an Executive Member of the Campaign for Labour Democracy, 1975–83, and a member of the Labour Co-ordinating Committee, 1978–82. He has been the Labour MP for Sunderland South since 1987.

Critical Analysis

Chris Mullin's first novel, *A Very British Coup*, is the story of an attempt by an intelligence service to overthrow an elected government.

His next spy novel, *The Last Man out of Saigon*, concerns MacShane, a CIA operative, who finds himself in Vietnam three days before the end of the war. He is sent by his boss, Lazarowitz, who runs his own show from an office at CIA headquarters. MacShane's job is to set up a network of agents who will undermine the new communist regime. But his cover is blown and he is arrested, and instead of being killed as a spy, he is sent to be "re-educated" in a remote part of the country where he learns to be a rice farmer. MacShane gradually comes to the realisation that he has been a victim of American propaganda and his experiences in Vietnam change his views.

This is a strange book as nothing really happens: the hero is rather stilted in his behaviour, and the pace is a little slow, but the author's presentation of Vietnam is vivid and fresh, especially as it is not a common setting for a spy novel.

Television

A Very British Coup was serialised in 1988.

David William Alexander Mure

British. Born 25 October 1912. Died 9 September 1986.

Titles

The Last Temptation: A Novel of Treason. London, Buchan & Enright, 1984.

Biography

David Mure was born in Scotland and educated at Wellington College. During the Second World War he served in the 60th Rifles (King's Royal Rifle Corps) and in 1942 was co-opted into the deception organisation, where he became intimately connected with what became known as the Double-Cross System.

He joined "A" Force in the Middle East, serving under Brigadier Dudley Clarke. The purpose of this Force was to play back to the German Abwehr, in Athens and Istanbul, the radio sets of captured spies, without letting the Germans know that the spies had been captured. It was thus substantially possible to deceive the German High Command, and to divert many divisions from the Russian front to guard the Balkans against invasions which never took place.

Mure was chairman of the committee which played a part in keeping 400,000 German troops in south-eastern Europe, away from the Allied invasion of Normandy. He was also case officer for at least five major double-agent networks — a unique experience.

Critical Analysis

As a writer, Mure originally concentrated on non-fiction, and his two books *Practice to Deceive* (1977) and *Master of Deception* (1980) told much about his work during the war. The latter work was a biography of Brigadier Dudley Clarke. It is worth noting that the late Sir Maurice Oldfield, head of MI6, declared that *Practice to Deceive* was among his favourite espionage books. Mure turned to fiction, instead of a factual account, in the last years of his life because of his conviction that this was a better medium for his version of the truth behind certain events. What he did, in effect, was to criticise the so-called "freedom" of modern writers, because due to what he had written in *Master of Deception*, he had been threatened and denounced.

Mure's very last work was *The Last Temptation: A Novel of Treason*. It is a brilliantly perceptive novel which uses fiction as a way of revealing the truth about real people and historical events. In doing this he wrote that: "as Editor, I have taken the liberty of providing a cast of characters that lists the dream characters and (in most cases) the real people who play them; in references to the heads of the Secret Service, of course, the appropriate security precautions have been strictly observed."

In this book Mure disguised the real characters under names taken from *Alice in Wonderland*, sometimes censoring those to whom he was referring, while at others revealing the truth. For example "Red King" was Stalin, "Humpty Dumpty" was Churchill, "Duchess" was Guy Burgess, "Red Queen" was Anthony Blunt and "Red Knight" was Kim Philby.

BERNARD CHARLES NEWMAN
Pseudonym: DON BETTERIDGE
British. Born in Ibstock, Leicestershire, 8 May 1897. Died 19 February 1968.

Titles
[Major characters: Sergeant/Inspector Marshall; Papa Pontivy]
Spy. [Marshall]. London, Gollancz, 1935; New York, Appleton Century, 1935.
German Spy. [Marshall]. London, Gollancz, 1936; New York, Curl, 1936.
Lady Doctor–Woman Spy. London, Hutchinson, 1937.
Death under Gibraltar. London, Gollancz, 1938.
Death to the Spy. [Pontivy]. London, Gollancz, 1939.
Maginot Line Murder. London, Gollancz, 1939; as *Papa Pontivy and the Maginot Murder*. New York, Holt, 1940.
Secret Weapon [Pontivy]. London, Gollancz, 1941.
Death to the Fifth Column. [Pontivy]. London, Gollancz, 1941.
Black Market. [Pontivy]. London, Gollancz, 1942.
Second Front–First Spy. [Pontivy]. London, Gollancz, 1944.
Moscow Murder [Pontivy]. London, Gollancz, 1948.
Operation Barbarossa [Pontivy]. London, Hale, 1956.
The Spy at Number 10 [Pontivy]. London, Hale, 1965.

Novels as Don Betteridge
[Major character: Tiger Lester]
Balkan Spy. London, Jenkins, 1942.
The Escape of General Gerard. London, Jenkins, 1943.
Potsdam Murder Plot. London, Jenkins, 1947.
Spies Left! London, Hale, 1950.
Not Single Spies. London, Hale, 1951.

Spy–Counter Spy. London, Hale, 1953.
Case of the Berlin Spy. London, Hale, 1954.
The Gibraltar Conspiracy. London, Hale, 1955.

Short Stories
Spy Catchers. London, Gollancz, 1945.

Biography
Bernard Newman was educated at Bosworth School. He served with the British Expeditionary Forces in France from 1915 to 1919 and, the story goes, because he was unable to stay on a horse the Army gave him a bicycle. And it was cycling which became Newman's great passion ever afterwards: he made innumerable tours by this means (always on bicycles he called "George"), until after his sixtieth birthday.

He entered the Civil Service in 1920 and at one time he was in danger of being dismissed because the Foreign Office objected to a book of his, *Danger Spots of Europe* (1938).

When war broke out Newman was engaged as a lecturer first with the British Expeditionary Force and then, in 1942, as a staff lecturer with the Ministry of Information. After 1945 Newman cycled behind the Iron Curtain on a number of occasions and travelled as far as India, Pakistan and the United States. He wrote many articles summing up the political situation in countries he had visited. In 1954 he was made a Chevalier of the Légion d'Honneur.

Critical Analysis
Newman started writing what were almost conventional thrillers, like *Death of a Harlot* (1934), while at the same time touching on the theme of military strategy, for example *The Cavalry Went Through* (1930).

The backgrounds to Newman's books, which, after these early ones, were mainly about spies in fact and fiction, were always well researched. He collected the necessary details on his cycling tours around Europe. He made espionage very much his special subject and from 1934 onwards he was in great demand as a lecturer on spies and spying and on European affairs.

It was *Spy* which made Newman's name and brought him into the limelight of controversy. This was a subtle psychological study of Ludendorff's nervous collapse in September 1918, and Sir Basil Liddell Hart wrote after Newman's death "it was based on my account of that episode, along with a maxim of mine that the mind of the enemy commander is the basic target in war, and it purported to relate how a British officer had infiltrated into Ludendorff's staff and played demoralisingly on his mind. As it cited my maxim and conveyed that I had uttered it in the narrator's presence, the publishers submitted the proofs of the book to me ... Many of the reviewers tended to regard the book as factual rather than fictional."

The book was a great success and the press generally thought it was the genuine confession of a secret agent until its author admitted with some glee that he had made it all up. The whole affair was a marvellous leg-pull, but only until one or two inquiring newspapers had discovered that the author's claims could not be entirely substantiated.

Altogether Newman wrote 128 spy novels, and only a sample of these are listed above. He was one of the first to realise the threat from the Nazis and the Fascists, and this theme was explored in his early novels such as *German Spy* and others written in the late 1930s. Generally speaking, Newman concentrated on espionage in Europe, which he knew so intimately. He caught the new mood of authenticity and topicality in spy fiction.

Spy Catchers was a collection of short stories and is still one of the best books written around the subject of counter-espionage. Newman was especially good when dealing with the use of radio for code messages, and the story "Spy by Music", dealt with musical codes. There was a suspicion that the Germans were making use of these in their broadcasts. A team of experts started to study them and discovered that a musical alphabet was being used, with one or more letters allotted to the minim. Nobody was better at producing fascinating stories around codes and ciphers than Newman, who always went to immense trouble and in this instance actually worked out his own musical code and reproduced it in the book.

CHRISTOPHER ROBIN NICOLE

Pseudonyms: ROBIN CADE, PETER GRANGE, CAROLINE GRAY, MARK LOGAN, CHRISTINE NICHOLSON, ALISON YORK, ANDREW YORK.
British. Born in Georgetown, British Guiana, 7 December 1930.

Titles

[Major character: Jonas Wilde]
The Eliminator. London, Hutchinson, 1966; Philadelphia, Lippincott, 1967.
The Co-Ordinator. London, Hutchinson, 1967; Philadelphia, Lippincott, 1967.
The Predator. London, Hutchinson, 1968; Philadelphia, Lippincott, 1968.
Operation Destruct. London, Hutchinson, 1969; New York, Holt Rinehart, 1970.
The Deviator. London, Hutchinson, 1969; Philadelphia, Lippincott, 1969.
The Dominator. London, Hutchinson, 1969.
Operation Manhunt. London, Hutchinson, 1970; New York, Holt Rinehart, 1970.
The Infiltrator. London, Hutchinson, 1971; New York, Doubleday, 1971.
Operation Neptune. New York, Holt Rinehart, 1971; London, Hutchinson, 1972.
The Expurgator. London, Hutchinson, 1972; New York, Doubleday, 1973.
The Captivator. London, Hutchinson, 1973; New York, Doubleday, 1974.
The Fascinator. London, Hutchinson, 1975; New York, Doubleday, 1975.

Biography

Christopher Nicole was educated at Harrison College in Barbados and Queen's College in British Guiana. He left school at the age of sixteen and worked for the Royal Bank of Canada in West Indies branches for ten years. He started writing in the early 1950s, and his first novel, *Off White*, was published in 1959.

Critical Analysis

Nicole says that his main writing is historical fiction, which he writes under his real name. All his spy fiction is written under the pseudonym of Andrew York, and he has made his reputation through his creation of that lone Secret Service hired assassin, Jonas Wilde. The author says that "spy writing has always been a hobby".

Jonas Wilde was launched in 1966 with *The Eliminator*, the first of nine in the series. A review in *The Guardian* described Wilde as having "everything that James Bond had and perhaps more." The book was filmed and the whole series of the Wilde books has been successful in America and in translation into many languages.

The code-name of Jonas Wilde is The Eliminator, and in the last book of the series Nicole tries to arrange his retirement on the island of Ibiza. Wilde enjoys the sunshine and endless bottles of wine, but there are those who believe that Wilde is too valuable to retire. His old employers, his old enemies and others who only know him as the most dangerous man in the world, all want to discover if he can still be useful. So he becomes involved in a bizarre adventure, with the oil-rich prince of Xanda, a man as deadly as Wilde.

Film

The Eliminator was filmed as *Danger Route* by United Artists in 1967.

FREDERICK WILLIAM NOLAN
Pseudonym: DONALD SEVERN
British. Born in Liverpool in 1931.

Titles
Wolf Trap. London, Piatkus, 1983; New York, St. Martin's Press, 1984.
Red Centre. London, Grafton, 1987; New York, St. Martin's Press, 1987.
Sweet Sister Death. (first of six-part series). Random Century, 1989.

Biography
Frederick Nolan attended secondary schools in Wales and Liverpool. He joined Corgi Books as an assistant editor in 1960, and after four or five years he became an editorial reader. After that he worked for other publishing houses such as Penguin, Collins and Granada, as a director of marketing, publicity and advertising. He has worked as a full time-writer since 1972.

Critical Analysis
His first novel was *The Oshawa Project* (1974), which he describes as a "Jackal"-esque novel of a plot to assassinate an American general not unlike George S Patton. He says that it is only lately that he has turned to spy fiction, although many of his novels have had an espionage content. "It is a demanding but fascinating genre — the trick is to try and outguess tomorrow's headlines." The author goes on to say that "The 'real' intelligence world would be a very dull topic for a novel; all of the best practitioners 'enhance' it, not to say *invent* it for the real practitioners to copy."

Nolan not only writes spy fiction, he also writes westerns under the name of Frederick H Christian, and historical romances under the pseudonym Danielle Rockfern. He is currently writing a new series of six books under the name of Donald Severn about counter-terrorism.

A reviewer in *Publisher's Weekly*, wrote of *Wolf Trap*: "This is a World War Two thriller set largely in Germany and Czechoslovakia that dramatizes the furious rivalries within the Third Reich's intelligence system (the SS, Gestapo, Abwehr and Criminal Police). Nolan makes a plausible connection between a British plot to assassinate Hitler (code-named 'Wolf Trap'), Rudolf Hess's flight to Scotland and the assassination of Reinhard Heydrich, the 'Butcher of Prague'."

Red Centre is concerned with a scheme promoted by a Soviet military intelligence officer, Drosdow, of the GRU, to destroy Star Wars and give the Soviets military control of space. To carry out his plan he uses Cuban agents, Florida drug dealers and American and British intelligence agencies. David Caine, working for an illegal British "firm" in America and Frank Forsyth, a CIA maverick stumble upon Drosdow's plot, and by separate paths they both appear at the violent conclusion.

A review by Arnold Beichman in the *Washington Times*, remarked about this novel: "Frederick Nolan knows his way around the corridors of the intelligence world. His book has many pages full of intelligence procedural details and acronyms to attest to his knowledgeability and to add verisimilitude to a fast-moving and expertly plotted spy thriller."

PETER O'DONNELL

British. Born in London, 11 April 1920.

Titles

[Major character: Modesty Blaise]
Modesty Blaise. London, Souvenir, 1965; New York, Doubleday, 1965.
Sabre-Tooth. London, Souvenir, 1966; New York, Doubleday, 1966.
I, Lucifer. London, Souvenir, 1967; New York, Doubleday, 1967.
A Taste For Death. London, Souvenir, 1969; New York, Doubleday, 1969.
The Impossible Virgin. London, Souvenir, 1971; New York, Doubleday, 1971.
The Silver Mistress. London, Souvenir, 1973.
Last Day in Limbo. London, Souvenir, 1976.
Dragon's Claw. London, Souvenir, 1978.
The Xanadu Talisman. London, Souvenir, 1981.
The Night of the Morning Star. London, Souvenir, 1982.
Dead Man's Handle. London, Souvenir, 1985.

Short Stories

Pieces of Modesty. London, Pan Books, 1972.

Biography

Peter O'Donnell was educated at Catford Central School, which he left at the age of seventeen to work for Amalgamated Press, magazine publishers. He left them two years later to serve in the Royal Corps of Signals from 1939 to 1946.

After the war he worked in a small book publishers from 1946 to 1951. Then he went freelance, writing for children's comics, women's magazines and national newspapers, specialising in strip cartoon. He launched Modesty Blaise in cartoon in 1963, and in the form of a novel in 1964. His work includes film, television, novels, strip cartoon and stage plays.

Critical Analysis

The author expressed doubts that he should be included in a collection of spy fiction, "I don't think I fit this category. In all my books there's only one occasion in which a character could be called a spy." Nevertheless, O'Donnell is included because his character Modesty Blaise is one of the few heroines in spy fiction, and the fact that the character was initially developed out of a strip cartoon shows an interesting relationship between the cartoon and the spy novel.

Modesty Blaise started life as a strip cartoon character in the London *Evening Standard*, but this should not detract from her strength as a spy heroine for a novel. The fact that she was developed into a spy fiction heroine proves the successful form of her origins. Modesty is seen as a female equivalent of James Bond because she appeared at the same time. However, she is superior in many ways and for the pace of the action and the economy of words, O'Donnell has no equal.

Modesty usually appears with her faithful companion Willie Garvin. She started in big-time crime and she has now "retired", but because she is bored she is quite willing to do odd jobs for British Intelligence, which involves the two characters in all sorts of adventures. In 1966 *Modesty Blaise* was made into a feature film and the author comments: "I wrote the original screenplay. It was re-written four or five times by different writers. Only one line of the original was left."

Kingsley Amis in a review of *Last Day in Limbo* in the *Evening Standard*, praised these books: "Peter O'Donnell's *Modesty Blaise* thrillers are peppered with ingenious ideas... The other ingredients are a sharply-twisting story line, varied locations, a really formidable criminal project to be foiled, lots of healthy violence, nasty villains, well-sketched minor characters, expert grading of tension, and above all the bond of faith and respect between Modesty and Willie Garvin, her lieutenant. Theirs is one of the great partnerships in crime fiction, bearing comparison with (though necessarily different from) that of Sherlock Holmes and Dr Watson."

Film

Modesty Blaise. Twentieth Century Fox. GB, 1966.

FRANK O'NEILL

American. Born in Charleston, South Carolina.

Titles

[Major character: Giovanni Sidgewick Stears]
Agents of Sympathy. London, Hodder & Stoughton, 1986.
The Secret Country. London, Hodder & Stoughton, 1987.

Biography

Frank O'Neill's father was American and his mother English. Just after the war he returned with his mother to England, and at the age of eight they moved to Geneva,

Switzerland where he attended school. Later he went to an English public school and the University of Oxford where he studied history. He had several jobs in the wine trade and then returned to America and worked on various newspapers in Atlanta, Georgia. He started writing poetry and short stories at an early age, and is now living in Charleston as a full-time writer.

Critical Analysis

The author says: "*Agents of Sympathy* was conceived halfway up a ski-lift in Zermatt, Switzerland, and was written in Charleston." This novel is set in the turbulent Middle East, where a mythical Arab state called Berbia, seems to be the only stable corner of the Arab world. Islamic agents backed by the KGB set out to de-stabilise this peaceful state, but the Americans are determined to stop them.

Mike Duffy, in a review of this book in the *Manchester Evening News*, wrote: "This is a painstakingly researched first timer for an author with a keen eye for detail of whom we are sure to hear again."

In his second novel, *The Secret Country*, a high-level general in the East German KGB sends a messenger to the West to let them know that he wishes to defect, and that he also has a plan which will destroy the Warsaw Pact. It is the job of a CIA London operative, Giovanni Stears, who first appeared in *Agents of Sympathy*, to assess whether the general is a genuine defector or a fake, and so determine whether his plan is feasible or not.

One reviewer of this book commented: "The background of the action — travel, geographical details and the like — has obviously been well researched by the author, and adds much to the story's realism and enjoyment.... The pervading atmosphere of fear and mistrust is convincingly conveyed, and in this the author may have been helped by his own disturbing experience."

GEORGE J A O'TOOLE

American

Titles

An Agent on the Other Side. New York, McKay, 1973; London, Barker, 1974.
The Cosgrave Report. New York, Wade, 1979.
Poor Richard's Game. New York, Delacorte, 1982.

Biography

G J A O'Toole is a former chief of the Problem Analysis Branch of the CIA and now works as a professional writer. He also writes non-fiction books which include *The Spanish War: An American Epic —1898*, and *The Encyclopedia of American Intelligence and Espionage (1988)*.

Critical Analysis

O'Toole served as an intelligence officer for the CIA for three years. He is an expert on the use of computers in intelligence work. His other interests include parapsychology, cryptography and flying light aircraft. "But", he says, "some of my most interesting accomplishments are, unfortunately, classified".

An Agent on the Other Side is a highly improbable tale, which is a little surprising in view of the author's experience in intelligence. However, it is not unique as many authors with the same experience have shown little concern for authenticity.

In the middle of 1968, on the eve of the Soviet invasion of Czechoslovakia, a woman with psychic powers is approached by the CIA. She claims to be in touch with the spirit of Oleg Penkovsky. In her seances she reveals detailed secret Russian invasion plans.

But the CIA learns that another medium in Prague, a film-maker called Chudnik, has been selling identical information to the West German government. It is believed that it comes from the same source, and that it is a deception operation. Nevertheless, to confirm this the CIA involves John Sorel, a young film-maker, and they persuade him to go to Czechoslovakia to bring Chudnik back to America. Sorel gets caught and finds himself embroiled in a complicated plot involving deception, blackmail and double-agents.

In an Author's Note to this novel, O'Toole has written: "*An Agent on the Other Side* is a lie. Lying, however, like most human endeavors, can be done either poorly or well. Inspector Spinka gives us his two criteria for a good lie; it must contain many elements which are true, and it must include something so improbable that it seems it could not have been invented. In that sense, I have tried to make the story a good lie."

ANTHONY OLCOTT

American. Born in Red Lodge, Montana, 10 April 1950.

Titles

Chevengur. New York, Ardis, 1978.
Murder at the Red October. Academy Chicago, 1981.
May Day in Magadan. New York, Bantam, 1984; London, Macmillan, 1984.

Biography

Anthony Olcott was educated at Stanford University from where he obtained a BA in 1971, an MA in 1973, and a PhD in 1976. He worked as an Assistant Professor of Slavic at the University of Virginia, Charlottesville, 1975–76. He worked as a beverage manager at the Chenango Inn, Norwich, New York in 1977 and was the manager of the book department at Colgate University Bookstore in Hamilton, New York from 1978 to 1981.

Critical Analysis

Olcott commented: "Writing has always been a goal, but one assiduously avoided for years while I did other (mostly academic) things. It seems that writing requires a certain stock of experience, maturity, or perhaps simply age. For whatever reasons, skills have converged over the past few years, and now I generate projects faster than I can execute them."

Jean White of the *Washington Post Book World* wrote that Olcott's *Murder at the Red October* "is an exceptional novel, offering penetrating glimpses of life in contemporary Russian society while telling the tense story of a murder investigation within the Soviet bureaucracy."

In *May Day in Magadan* Ivan Duvakin is the hero of the story. He is now exiled to

Siberia because he stumbled on a major party scandal in Moscow and helped a KGB colonel investigate it. In the remote Siberian outpost of Magadan he comes across another crime against the state — this time the stealing of furs, he reports his findings but discovers that the corruption goes far deeper than he at first suspected.

EDWARD PHILLIPS OPPENHEIM

Pseudonym: ANTHONY PARTRIDGE

British. Born in London, 22 October 1926. Died 3 February 1946.

Titles

Expiation. London, Maxwell, 1887.
The Mysterious Mr Sabin. London, Ward Lock, 1898; Boston, Little Brown, 1905.
Mr Grex of Monte Carlo. London, Methuen, 1915; Boston, Little Brown, 1915.
The Double Traitor. Boston, Little Brown, 1915; London, Hodder & Stoughton, 1918.
The Kingdom of the Blind. Boston, Little Brown, 1916; London, Hodder & Stoughton, 1917.
The Pawns Count. London, Hodder & Stoughton, 1918; Boston, Little Brown, 1918.
The Zeppelin's Passenger. Boston, Little Brown, 1918; as *Mr Lessingham Goes Home*. London, Hodder & Stoughton, 1919.
The Strange Case of Mr Jocelyn Thew. London, Hodder & Stoughton, 1919; as *The Box with Broken Seals*. Boston, Little Brown, 1919.
The Great Impersonation. London, Hodder & Stoughton, 1920; Boston, Little Brown, 1920.
The Devil's Paw. Boston, Little Brown, 1920; Hodder & Stoughton, 1921.
The Great Prince Shan. London, Hodder & Stoughton, 1922; Boston, Little Brown, 1922.
The Wrath to Come. Boston, Little Brown, 1924; London, Hodder & Stoughton, 1925.
Matorni's Vineyard. Boston, Little Brown, 1928; London, Hodder & Stoughton, 1929.
The Spy Paramount. London, Hodder & Stoughton, 1935; Boston, Little Brown, 1935.

Biography

Oppenheim was educated at Wyggeston Grammar School, Leicester, where he won the history prize, but had "shocking reports for his maths". He left school at the age of sixteen to help his father who at that time was in financial difficulties. In 1887 his first novel *Expiation* was published. On the strength of this Oppenheim was able to secure a contract to write six serial stories for the *Sheffield Weekly Telegraph*. He had a quick, fertile and imaginative mind and the additional asset of being a voracious reader of newspapers, which he avidly combed for ideas.

Critical Analysis

Oppenheim was fascinated by the world of secret diplomacy and set out not merely to explore it but to use it as a background for his fiction. In 1898 *The Mysterious Mr Sabin* was published. He described this as "the first of my long series of stories dealing with that shadowy and mysterious world of diplomacy.... So long as the world lasts, its secret international history will continue to engage the full activities of the diplomatist."

He was a prolific writer — altogether he turned out 115 novels and 39 books of short stories — but never a polished one. (There is only a selection of his novels listed above.) His stories were the Edwardian version of spy fiction, a mixture of romance, adventure, espionage, secret diplomacy and high life intermingled with criminal activities and gambling in the world's greatest cities, Budapest and Vienna being two of his favourite settings early on. Eventually he gravitated towards the colourful cities and resorts of which he wrote and thus added some first-hand knowledge to his work. Monte Carlo then became a favourite setting for his spy stories, notably *Mr Grex of Monte Carlo*. He loved the good things of life and had a zest for exploring the capitals of Europe.

Like William Le Queux and Erskine Childers, though to a lesser extent, he became one of a small band of writers deeply concerned about what in the early 1900s was known as "the German menace". This was a theme which he introduced into some of his novels, despite the fact that it lost him his popularity as an author in Germany in the years just before 1914.

Oppenheim's heroes and heroines appealed to the snobbery of the average reader of those days: the men were from Eton and the Guards, the women from Embassy parties and elegant country house gatherings. In the First World War he was employed escorting journalists of neutral countries on tour of the battlefront in France, and it was during this period that he wrote the best of his novels of espionage. For example, *The Kingdom of the Blind* was a story full of lively adventures, including submarine attacks and Zeppelin raids and purported to reveal something of the methods of Secret Service operators. He followed this up with *The Pawns Count*, another Germany spy tale which opens, like so many of Oppenheim's narratives, in a fashionable London restaurant where John Lutchester, of the British Secret Service, Oscar Fischer, a German American, and a beautiful New York girl, Pamela Van Teyl, are keenly interested in securing the formula of a new and wonderful explosive.

It was after the First World War that Oppenheim began to earn enormous sums from his books; many of his works were serialised in America in journals like *Colliers* and the *Saturday Evening Post*.

Emma Magdalena Rosalia Maria Josefa Barbara Orczy; Baroness Orczy

British. Born in Tarna-Ors, Hungary, 23 September 1865. Died 12 November 1947.

Titles

[Major character: Sir Percy Blakeney]
The Scarlet Pimpernel [Sir Percy]. London, Greening, 1905; New York, Putnam, 1905.
I Will Repay [Sir Percy]. London, Greening, 1906; Philadelphia, Lippincott, 1906.
Eldorado [Sir Percy]. London, Hodder & Stoughton, 1913; New York, Doran, 1913.
Sir Percy Hits Back [Sir Percy]. London, Hodder & Stoughton, 1927; New York, Doran, 1927.
A Spy of Napoleon. London, Hodder & Stoughton, 1934; New York, Putnam, 1934.

Biography

The family lived in Budapest and Brussels, where Emma was a pupil in a convent school, and then in Paris before settling in London when she was fifteen. Emma studied at the West London School of Art and Heatherleys, and was sufficiently successful as an artist to have three pictures hung at the Academy.

Critical Analysis

Baroness Orczy first concentrated on children's stories, but it was a spy story that brought her greatest fame and recognition. This was *The Scarlet Pimpernel*. The manuscript of this work was rejected by at least twelve publishers but, doggedly determined to succeed, Emma and her husband turned it into a play which was accepted for production and presented in Nottingham in 1903. It was an instant success and the novel was soon published.

The story was not only an exciting romance set during the French Revolution, but introduced as its chief character the seemingly indolent and affected fop, Sir Percy Blakeney, who, beneath his mask of frivolity and idleness, was a brave and efficient secret agent who rescued aristocrats from the guillotine under the noses of the revolutionaries.

So successful was the Scarlet Pimpernel that Baroness Orczy re-introduced him in *I Will Repay*, *Eldorado* and *Sir Percy Hits Back*, all of which were published in an omnibus volume in 1933, together with the original story. There was always a love story worked into all the Baroness Orczy's espionage tales, which may have irritated those who like their spy fiction "straight", but Sir Percy, with his quick-changing, baffling disguises — as pipe-smoking old woman, charcoal-burner, Republican officer, or whatever — remained a firm favourite for many years. Not all the Pimpernel stories should be classified as spy fiction, however, and it was with historical romances that this author was mostly concerned.

Her most positive espionage book — *A Spy of Napoleon* — was a story of the days of the Third Napoleon and told how Gérard, sentenced to death for treason, was spirited away by Papa Toulon of the Secret Service to marry one of his most efficient spies.

Films

The Scarlet Pimpernel. London Films. GB, 1934.
The Elusive Pimpernel. London Films. GB, 1950.

Television

"The Scarlet Pimpernel". 1982.

ANDREW PHILIP KINGSFORD OSMOND

British. Born in Barnoldsby, Lincolnshire, 16 March 1938.

Titles

Saladin. New York, Doubleday, 1975.

Novels written with Douglas Hurd
Send Him Victorious. London, Collins, 1968.
Smile on the Face of the Tiger. London, Collins, 1969; New York, Macmillan, 1969.
Scotch on the Rocks. London, Collins, 1971.

Biography

Andrew Osmond was educated at Harrow and Oxford University. He did his National Service with the Gurkhas Regiment in Malaya. In 1961 he was one of the founding proprietors of *Private Eye*, but after eighteen months he sold out his interest to Nicholas Luard and joined the Foreign Office, "not as a spy, though they did ask me," he says. He served in France, West Africa, London and Rome — "hated it and got out, as did Douglas Hurd with whom I'd written half of *Send Him Victorious*. Collins accepted the day I reached England, broke and jobless." After writing two other political novels with Douglas Hurd, Osmond returned to *Private Eye* for four years as its managing director.

Critical Analysis

Osmond has written one spy novel on his own called *Saladin*. This is a story woven around the murdering of the eleven Israeli athletes by the Black September gang on 5 September 1972, telling how this brutal event marked a turning point in the Arab–Israeli conflict and how escalating violence seemed to make a fourth Middle East War almost inevitable. A small group of Israelis and Palestinians strive against the odds to bring about a settlement, their aim being to create a Palestinian state acceptable to both sides. Their leader is Anis Kubayin, code-name Saladin, and their chief instrument is Stephen Roscoe, an ex-British Army officer, retaining all the lethal skills he learned in his years in the Special Air Service.

The group's objective was to cause a major act of sabotage and so to capture the world headlines and create a political initiative. Fact and fiction are neatly woven together in this book and Osmond uses the framework of the spy novel to deliver a political message — a battle-cry for peace. The book was a considerable success and nine countries bought the rights.

Osmond believes the spy fiction genre both "ought and will grow up a bit." He would rather have his work labelled didactic (my adjective, not his) than be called

Henry Patterson

Pseudonyms: Jack Higgins, Martin Fallon, James Graham, Hugh Marlowe
British/Irish. Born in Newcastle on Tyne, 27 July 1929.

Titles

East of Desolation. London, Hodder & Stoughton, 1968; New York, Doubleday, 1969.
In the Hour Before Midnight. London, Hodder & Stoughton, 1969; as *The Sicilian Heritage*. New York, Lancer, 1970.
Night Judgement at Sinos. London, Hodder & Stoughton, 1970; New York, Doubleday, 1971.

The Last Place God Made. London, Collins, 1971; New York, Holt Rinehart, 1972.
The Savage Day. London, Collins, 1972; New York, Holt Rinehart, 1972.
A Prayer for the Dying. London, Collins, 1973; New York, Holt Rinehart, 1974.
The Eagle Has Landed. London, Collins, 1975; New York, Holt Rinehart, 1975.
Storm Warning. London, Collins, 1976; New York, Holt Rinehart, 1976.
Day of Judgement. London, Collins, 1978; New York, Holt Rinehart, 1979.
The Cretan Lover. London, Collins, 1980; New York, Holt Rinehart, 1980.
Solo. London, Collins, 1980; New York, Stein & Day, 1980.
Luciano's Luck. London, Collins, 1981; New York, Stein & Day, 1981.
Touch the Devil. London, Collins, 1982; New York, Stein & Day, 1982.
Exocet. London, Collins, 1983; New York, Stein & Day, 1983.
Confessional. London, Collins, 1985.
Night of the Fox. London, Collins, 1986.
Brought in Dead. London, Collins, 1988.

Biography

Henry Patterson was educated at Leeds Training College for Teachers, and the University of London, from where he received a BSc in Sociology in 1962. He served in the Royal Horse Guards in the British Army, 1947–49. He worked in commercial and civil service posts from 1950 to 1955. He was a History teacher at a comprehensive school in Leeds from 1958 to 1964, and then a Lecturer in Liberal Studies at Leeds College of Commerce, 1964–68. He was a Senior Lecturer in Education at the James Graham College in Yorkshire, 1968–7, and a Tutor at Leeds University, 1971–73.

Critical Analysis

Although Harry Patterson writes under a number of pseudonyms, he is best known under the name of Jack Higgins. His reputation as a best-selling writer began with the publication of *The Eagle Has Landed* in 1975, which was his most successful book. It is the story of a Nazi plot to kidnap Winston Churchill in 1943. A small group of German paratroopers try to alter the balance of the war by the attempt, and the British and Americans race against time to stop them.

All his books contain action, adventure and suspense, and though many of his books return to the setting of the Second World War, in *Exocet*, the author proved that he was as adept in contemporary dramas as well as those of the past. In this book the Russians help the Argentinians in their efforts to get more Exocet missiles in their conflict with the British over the Falklands. The British Intelligence agency D15 try to prevent the hijack of the French missiles. Patterson's books have been translated into 42 languages, and although he is prolific he manages to maintain a standard of quality which contributes to his steady popularity.

Film

The Eagle Has Landed. ITC, GB, 1976.

JOHN PEARSON

British. Born in Carshalton, Surrey, 1930.

Non-fiction Titles

The Life of Ian Fleming. New York, Bantam, 1967.
James Bond: The Authorized Biography of 007. New York, William Morrow, 1973.

Biography

John Pearson was educated at King's College, Wimbledon, and Peterhouse, Cambridge, where he gained a double first in History. Pearson was working as a television scriptwriter at the BBC when Ian Fleming offered him a job as his assistant in writing the Atticus column of the *Sunday Times*.

At the age of thirty-two he gave up journalism to write books, one of which was *The Life of Ian Fleming*. The character of James Bond fascinated a number of writers after Fleming's death. Kingsley Amis produced *The James Bond Dossier* in 1966, which was an analysis of the character of Bond, his morals and his methods. Pearson went one better than this in 1973 when he published *James Bond: The Authorized Biography of 007*. This was what he himself termed "a fictional biography", though it gallantly tried to maintain the spoof that Bond was a real person.

The book dealt at some length with Bond's childhood, his expulsion from Fettes for hanky-panky with a housekeeper, his enlistment in the Secret Service at the age of seventeen (they must have been hard up for personnel in those pre-war days!), and for good measure gave him as a secretary "the delightful Miss Una Trueblood". Fleming himself is made to pop in and out of the story and at the book's end Bond, who has been recovering from hepatitis in Bermuda, is sent off on yet another mission, this time to Australia, which is something of an anti-climax.

It was perhaps a pity that Pearson did not conduct some research behind the Iron Curtain on the subject of Bond. For Russian Intelligence took the Bond stories seriously, regarding them as deliberate anti-Soviet propaganda, and commissioned a Bulgarian writer, A. Gulyashki, to write a book in which the Communist hero defeated Bond.

JACQUES PENDOWER

Pseudonyms: KATHLEEN CARSTAIRS, TOM CURTIS, PENN DOWER,
T C H JACOBS, MARILYN PENDER, ANNE PENN

British. Born in Plymouth, Devon, 30 December 1899. Died in 1976.

Titles

[Major character: Slade McGinty]
The Dark Avenue. London, Ward Lock, 1955.
Hunted Woman. London, Ward Lock, 1955.
Mission in Tunis. London, Hale, 1958; New York, Paperback Library, 1967.
Double Diamond. London, Hale, 1959.
The Long Shadow. London, Hale, 1959.
Anxious Lady. London, Hale, 1960.

The Widow from Spain. London, Hale, 1961; as *Betrayed*. New York, Paperback Library, 1967.
Death on the Moor. London, Hale, 1962.
The Perfect Wife [McGinty]. London, Hale, 1962.
Operation Carlo. London, Hale, 1963.
Sinister Talent [McGinty]. London, Hale, 1964.
Master Spy [McGinty]. London, Hale, 1964.
Spy Business. London, Hale, 1965.
Out of This World. London, Hale, 1966.
Traitor's Island [McGinty]. London, Hale, 1967.
Try Anything Once. London, Hale, 1967.
A Trap for Fools. London, Hale, 1968.
The Golden Statuette. London, Hale, 1969.
Diamonds for Danger. London, Hale, 1970.
She Came By Night. London, Hale, 1971.
Cause for Alarm. London, Hale, 1971.
Date with Fear. London, Hale, 1974.

Biography

Jacques Pendower was educated at a grammar school in Plymouth. During the First World War he served in the British Army and attained the rank of Second Lieutenant. He worked as a revenue investigating officer before 1950. He was a founding member (and at one point Chairman) of the Crime Writers' Association from 1960 to 1961.

Critical Analysis

Pendower was a prolific writer of detective, adventure and spy novels. He tended to write spy novels under his own name, and detective stories under his more famous pseudonym T C H Jacobs.

His main character in his spy novels was Slade McGinty, although he features in only four of the stories.

RITCHIE JOHN ALLEN PERRY

Pseudonym: JOHN ALLEN
British. Born in King's Lynn, Norfolk, 7 January 1942.

Titles

[Major character: Philis in all books except *MacAllister*]
The Fall Guy. London, Collins, 1972; Boston, Houghton Mifflin, 1972.
Nowhere Man. London, Collins, 1973; as *A Hard Man to Kill*. Boston, Houghton Mifflin, 1973.
Ticket to Ride. London, Collins, 1973; Boston, Houghton Mifflin, 1974.
Holiday with a Vengeance. London, Collins, 1974; Boston, Houghton Mifflin, 1975.
Your Money and Your Wife. London, Collins, 1975; Boston, Houghton Mifflin, 1976.
One Good Death Deserves Another. London, Collins, 1976; Boston, Houghton Mifflin, 1977.
Dead End. London, Collins, 1977.

Dutch Courage. London, Collins, 1978; New York, Ballantine, 1982.
Bishop's Pawn. London, Collins, 1979; New York, Pantheon, 1979.
Grand Slam. London, Collins, 1980; New York, Pantheon, 1980.
Fool's Mate. London, Collins, 1981; New York, Pantheon, 1981.
Foul Up. New York, Doubleday, 1982.
MacAllister. New York, Doubleday, 1984.

Biography

Ritchie Perry was educated at King Edward VII School, King's Lynn and St. John's College, Oxford, where he received a BA Hons in History in 1964. He worked as a trainee manager at the Bank of London and South America, Brazil, 1964–66. Then he worked as a teacher at various schools in Norfolk and Nottingham from 1966 to 1974. Since 1975 he has been a teacher for the Bedfordshire County Council at Luton.

Critical Analysis

Perry's novels are not strictly spy stories but can be better described as adventure thrillers with semi-political backgrounds. The major character in all his novels is Philis, who works for Pawson in SR 2, a rather shadowy government department. Perry is a good storyteller, and although there is some violence in his tales, he has a wry sense of humour; his backgrounds are also well researched.

The missions of Philis vary in purpose and in environment; for instance, in *The Fall Guy* Philis has the job of finding the source of cocaine being smuggled into England from South America. *One Good Death Deserves Another* is about a Greek assassin who is hired to kill the West German chancellor during a visit to Brazil; SR 2 agent Philis has to eliminate this man before he does any harm.

Perry commented: "As with most things in my life, I drifted into writing. The local library could no longer provide me with the dozen or so books I needed each week and it occurred to me that I ought to be able to produce fiction of my own. As such my books are self-indulgences, designed as much to entertain me as any potential readers. A shocking admission, but there it is. If I knew how one of my books was going to finish before I started on it, the book would never be typed out. It would bore me as much as it would to read a work by another author when I knew how the story was going to end. I suspect this may be one of the strengths of my stories — it must be very difficult for a reader to guess how a book will finish when the author isn't sure himself."

WILL PERRY

British.

Titles

The Kremlin Watcher. New York, Dodd Mead, 1978.

Biography

Will Perry is an Englishman who lives in New York. He has been a foreign correspondent and a police reporter in both Britain and America. He is the author of *Murder at the UN* and *Death of an Informer*, which was awarded an Edgar by the Mystery Writers of America.

Critical Analysis

In *The Kremlin Watcher* the story is about a workers' uprising in Poland. People in Washington DC try to find out what will happen— whether or not the Russian army will go in and crush the revolt. For political reasons as well as reasons of state, it is vitally important that the President has the answer as soon as possible. This novel traces the paths of two men who may have the answer, Frank Dober, CIA chief of station in Warsaw, and Leo Farel, a scholarly Kremlinologist in New York.

Dober has two agents whom he relies upon for information, although he knows that they cannot be entirely trusted. He puts his career on the line by believing his agents. Farel has his own techniques for finding out Soviet secrets, methods mistrusted by many in the government because he is an outsider. Despite the urgency to find an answer to the problem, Farel becomes involved in trying to solve a murder case in New York, because he promised his young daughter, a murder that leads back to Poland. The two investigations are not connected, but the murder investigation offers an interesting sub-plot and equates the analyst with the detective.

The race to find out what the Soviets intend to do with regards to Poland turns into a competition between the analyst and the chief of station, the man on the spot. They are both used as pawns in the rivalry between the CIA and the State Department, both organisations competing for the attention of the President.

This is an interesting novel and is one of the few that deals intelligently with the function of the analyst in the processing of intelligence. There is a clear comparison between the analyst and the man in the field, showing the difficulties involved in the interpretation of information.

LUDOVIC PETERS

(Pseudonym for Peter Ludwig Brent)
British. Born in Beuthen, Germany, 26 July 1931. Died in 1984.

Titles

[Major character: Ian Firth]
Cry Vengeance. London, Abelard Schuman, 1961; New York, Abelard Schuman, 1961.
A Snatch of Music [Firth]. London, Abelard Schuman, 1962; New York, Abelard Schuman, 1962.
Tarakian [Firth]. London, Abelard Schuman, 1963; New York, Abelard Schuman, 1963.
Two Sets to Murder [Firth]. London, Hodder & Stoughton, 1963; New York, Coward McCann, 1964.
Out by the River [Firth]. London, Hodder & Stoughton, 1964; New York, Walker, 1965.
Two After Malic [Firth]. London, Hodder & Stoughton, 1965; New York, Walker, 1966.
Riot '71 [Firth]. London, Hodder & Stoughton, 1967; New York, Walker, 1967.

Double-Take. London, Hodder & Stoughton, 1968.
Fall of Terror. London, Hodder & Stoughton, 1968.
The Killing Game. London, Hodder & Stoughton, 1969.

Novel as Peter Brent
No Way Back from Prague. London, Hodder & Stoughton, 1970.

Biography
He was educated at a secondary school in England. He worked as a cleaner, editor, film extra, porter, post office sorter, teacher, doorman and dishwasher.

Critical Analysis
Peters' novels are mostly in the spy/mystery vein, with occasional lapses into the detective story. The theme of Fascism seems to dominate most of his stories.

In his first novel *Cry Vengeance* he introduces the theme of an English agent who is the only man who can control an explosive Balkan situation and saves the world from a terrible war. The hero of this story is Colonel Rhys, a character that was dropped in the next book to be succeeded by Inspector Ian Firth of Scotland Yard's Special Branch.

Peters continues the theme of right-wing extremism up to and including *Riot '71*. His books are essentially thrillers — concerned with action, violence, a little sex and exotic locations. In some cases such as *Tarakian* and *Out by the River*, the country involved is an unnamed Communist state, with fools as leaders. Others like *A Snatch of Music* and *Two Sets to Murder*, use the glamorous international settings of Capri, the south of France and San Francisco. Peters was successful in presenting local colour but not so accurate with his depiction of the major characters, who become familiar by repetition and not because we learn more detail about them.

DAVID ATLEE PHILLIPS
American. Born in Fort Worth, Texas, 31 October 1922. Died 7 July 1988.

Titles
The Carlos Contract. New York, Macmillan, 1978.

Biography
David Atlee Phillips was a struggling actor when the Second World War broke out. He became a nose gunner in a Liberator bomber, but was shot down over Austria and captured. However, he managed to escape to the American lines.

In 1948 he went to Chile where he bought and ran the *South Pacific Mail*. Here he was approached by the local chief of the CIA: "We want you to give Uncle Sam a little help in your spare time." And so began a career in intelligence which included revolutions in Chile, clandestine radio stations in Guatemala, involvement in the Bay of Pigs disaster, and gunboat diplomacy in the Dominican Republic. He became one of the most senior men in the agency as Director of the Western Hemisphere Division.

Phillips resigned from the CIA in 1975, after the Congressional Committees had aired the dirty deeds of the agency. He decided to answer the critics of the CIA as a private citizen by appearing on television, lecturing and writing articles, he also wrote about his experiences in the CIA in *The Night Watch* (1977). He set up the Association of Former Intelligence Officers, an organisation founded by former intelligence officers to defend and promote a strong American intelligence service as vital to national security. He also edited their quarterly paper *Periscope*.

Critical Analysis

In *The Carlos Contract* an ex-CIA man "Mack the Knife" is employed unofficially by the agency to put out a contract on an international terrorist, Carlos, who is systematically assassinating CIA station chiefs.

It is a well-written book and Phillips gives us plenty of authentic detail of how a secret agent goes about his work. There are also plenty of references to the damage caused to the CIA as a result of the exposure of the "family jewels"; not only are the American public alarmed by the revelations of CIA secrets but so are America's allies. There are also digs at ex-CIA whistleblowers, such as Philip Agee and others, who have revealed their own secrets about the agency. Despite the moralizing it is an entertaining story by a man with great experience in the intelligence world.

Henry Chapman Pincher

British. Born in Ambala, India, 29 March 1914.

Titles

The Penthouse Conspirators. London, Michael Joseph, 1970.
The Skeleton at the Villa Wolkonsky. London, Michael Joseph, 1975.
The Eye of the Tornado. London, Michael Joseph, 1976; New York, Stein & Day, 1976.
Dirty Tricks. London, Sidgewick & Jackson, 1980; New York, Stein & Day, 1981.

Biography

Chapman Pincher was educated at Darlington Grammar School and King's College, London. He was a Carter Medallist in 1934 and took a BSc degree with honours in Botany and Zoology. From 1936 to 1940 he served in the Royal Armoured Corps and then became a staff officer in the Rocket Division of the Ministry of Supply, a post he held until 1946.

He is best known as Defence, Science and Medical Editor of the *Daily Express* and in this capacity he has over the past forty years brought off many news scoops, not least in the field of defence and security. His early books touched on these subjects as *A Study of Fishes* (1947) and *Into the Atomic Age* (1947) and his first novel was *Not With a Bang* (1965).

Critical Analysis

He has written four spy novels to date. *The Eye of the Tornado* is an exciting action-packed tale about an IRA plot to hijack Polaris missiles. Having made it clear that the fantasy hijack could become reality, Pincher then reveals that the IRA have merely been used by another power and that the hijack is a step towards a massive coup designed to crush democratic Britain. This calls for a Cabinet Minister who is a traitor and Pincher makes this feasible, too. Probably no other Fleet Street reporter in recent years has had such excellent contacts in the twilight world of defence and intelligence, and none understands better the workings of current security arrangements in Britain and elsewhere.

In 1967 he caused a controversy over the British Government's D notice system of disguised censorship when he disclosed, in the *Daily Express*, that British Security men were scrutinising commercial cables being sent from Britain by private individuals and businessmen. This resulted in Harold Wilson, the Prime Minister, having to admit that the practice of cable-reading had been going on since 1927. A committee was called to investigate Pincher's article but he was finally vindicated from any violation of the D notice.

Early in 1981 Pincher accused the former head of MI5 of being an agent of the KGB, the idea was dismissed in Parliament by the Prime Minister, Margaret Thatcher, but the controversy is still raging.

Edgar Allan Poe

American. Born in Boston, Massachusetts, 1809. Died 7 October 1849.

Titles

[Major character: C Auguste Dupin]
The Purloined Letter. Originally published in 1845.
The Gold Bug. Originally published in 1843.
(Both these stories can be found in Philip V D Stern, ed., *The Portable Poe*, New York, Penguin Books, 1977.)

Biography

He attended the University of Virginia, Charlottesville in 1826, but left in disgrace without finishing his studies. In 1827 his first volume of poetry was published and he served in the US Army for two years. From 1833 he was employed on different magazines at Richmond, New York and Philadelphia. His famous poem "The Raven" was published in 1845 and became very popular. In 1843 he set up his own magazine called *Stylus*.

Critical Analysis

Apart from his genius as a poet of great imagination and sensitivity and a writer of mystery and horror stories, Edgar Allan Poe was at one and the same time the father of the detective story and the spy tale. Purists may repudiate his entitlement to be included in this volume, yet the facts remain that he undoubtedly influenced many subsequent writers of stories of espionage and that his supreme detective, C Auguste Dupin, was in some respects more spy, or unofficial secret agent, than detective. In no work is this shown so clearly as in *The Purloined Letter*, for the tale contains all the ingredients of the classic spy story. A top-secret document is stolen from the royal departments, and the authorities strongly suspect that the culprit is a Minister, too important and influential to be arrested without positive proof. The secret police search the hotel apartment in which the Minister lives but without success. It is then that Dupin is called in to investigate the whole affair and discreetly locate the missing document.

In another direction, and in an oblique way, Poe also gave some impetus to the future shape of some spy stories by his interest in cryptography. In an article in a Philadelphia weekly magazine in 1840 Poe, who had then been studying cryptography for some time, opined that there was no such thing as an unsolvable cipher and offered to solve any such message sent to him. He received about 100 ciphers and solved all but one — and that one he denounced as a fake intended to deceive him. Out of his interest in this subject came *The Gold Bug* which, though not a spy story, is still one of the best stories yet written about ciphers and codes.

Thus, with Poe, real life inspired fiction and some of his fiction inspired real-life developments in Intelligence. For from 1850 onwards the intelligence game became very much the war of the cryptographers, a period when each major military power included courses in cryptography in its training programme.

JOYCE PORTER
British. Born in Marple, Cheshire, 28 March 1924.

Titles
[Major character: Eddie Brown]
Sour Cream with Everything. London, Cape, 1966; New York, Scribner's, 1966.
The Chinks in the Curtain. London, Cape, 1967; New York, Scribner's, 1967.
Neither a Candle nor a Pitchfork. London, Weidenfeld & Nicolson, 1969; New York, McCall, 1970.
Only with a Bargepole. London, Weidenfeld & Nicolson, 1971; New York, McKay, 1974.

Biography
Joyce Porter was educated at the High School for Girls at Macclesfield, Cheshire (1935–42) and at King's College, London, where she obtained a BA Hons in 1945. She served in the Women's Royal Air Force (1949–63) and reached the rank of Flight Officer.

Critical Analysis
The hero of this series is Eddie Brown a secret agent, and on most of his missions he is sent abroad. He is rather inept and gets himself in awkward situations such as in *Neither a Candle nor a Pitchfork* when a lesbian Russian official tries to seduce him while he is in female disguise. These are very light-hearted stories and Joyce Porter's tongue is firmly placed in her cheek.

JOSEPH JOHN POYER

American. Born in Michigan, 30 November 1939.

Titles

Operation Malacca. New York, Doubleday, 1968.
North Cape. New York, Doubleday, 1969.
The Balkan Assignment. New York, Doubleday, 1971.
The Chinese Agenda. New York, Doubleday, 1972.
The Shooting of the Green. New York, Doubleday, 1973.
Day of Reckoning. London, Weidenfeld, 1976.
The Contract. New York, Atheneum, 1978.
Tunnel War. New York, Atheneum, 1979.
Vengeance 10. New York, Atheneum, 1980.
Devoted Friends. New York, Atheneum, 1982.

Biography

Joe Poyer was educated at the Michigan State University, where he obtained a BA degree in Communication Arts. He has come to the fore in spy fiction in the last few years with five spy novels to date.

Critical Analysis

The Chinese Agenda is one of the few modern novels to touch on the subject of espionage in China. Poyer told in this book the story of a secret mission that began in conditions of the utmost danger and ended in wholesale slaughter. The story takes place on the Sino-Soviet border, in the Tien Shan Mountains, a high range of treacherous, snow-capped peaks. Twelve thousand feet high in that range is a pass leading into the interior of the Tien Shan and deep inside that terrain is a secret installation that threatens the peace of the world. To probe this secret a joint American–Soviet intelligence team is sent on what appears to be a suicidal mission. Six men cross the border into China, but only one comes back.

Joe Poyer has been praised by a number of critics for carefully researched spy fiction. He is at present the manager of Project Operations for a pharmaceutical company in California.

ALAN ANTHONY PRICE

British. Born in Rickmansworth, Hertfordshire, 16 August 1928.

Titles

[Major character: Dr David Audley]
The Labyrinth Makers. London, Gollancz, 1970; New York, Doubleday, 1971.
The Alamut Ambush. London, Gollancz, 1971; New York, Doubleday, 1972.
Colonel Butler's Wolf. London, Gollancz, 1972; New York, Doubleday, 1973.
October Men. London, Gollancz, 1973; New York, Doubleday, 1974.
Other Paths to Glory. London, Gollancz, 1974; New York, Doubleday, 1975.
Our Man in Camelot. London, Gollancz, 1975; New York, Doubleday, 1976.

War Game. London, Gollancz, 1976; New York, Doubleday, 1977.
The '44 Vintage. London, Gollancz, 1978; New York, Doubleday, 1978.
Tomorrow's Ghost. London, Gollancz, 1979; New York, Doubleday, 1979.
The Hour of the Donkey. London, Gollancz, 1980.
Soldier No More. London, Gollancz, 1981; New York, Doubleday, 1982.
The Old Vengeful. London, Gollancz, 1982; New York, Doubleday, 1983.
Gunner Kelly. London, Gollancz, 1983; New York, Doubleday, 1984.
Sion Crossing. London, Gollancz, 1984; New York, Mysterious Press, 1985.
Here Be Monsters. London, Gollancz, 1985; New York, Mysterious Press, 1986.
For the Good of the State. London, Gollancz, 1986; New York, Mysterious Press, 1988.
A New Kind of War. London, Gollancz, 1987; New York, Mysterious Press, 1988.
A Prospect of Vengeance. London, Gollancz, 1988.

Biography

Anthony Price was educated at King's School, Canterbury and Merton College, Oxford, where he obtained a BA in History. After being commissioned during his National Service (1947–49) he entered journalism in 1952. He was the editor of the *Oxford Times* from 1972 to 1988. His special interests are archaeology and military history, both of which are reflected in the detailed backgrounds to his novels.

Critical Analysis

He won the Crime Writers' Association Silver Dagger Award for his first novel, *The Labyrinth Makers*, and the Gold Dagger for *Paths to Glory*. His first novel is about the internal rivalry within the Soviet security services in 1970, set against a background of the pre-war Stalin purges and the disappearance of the Schliemann Treasure (from Troy) from Berlin in 1945.

David Audley appears in all these novels but as the author says: "not necessarily as the leading character: his colleagues share that role more or less in turn, or even the CIA can supply the hero." The CIA does indeed supply a hero in *Our Man in Camelot*, when we follow the thoughts of Mosby, a CIA agent sent to rouse the interest of Audley in an ancient historical controversy, while inadvertently eliciting his help in solving a KGB plot.

Anthony Price is very much a thinking man's spy fiction author and many of his books rise well above the average level of this literature because of his sense of humour and wit. At times there is much talk and little action, but this is usually compensated in a dramatic denouement.

The author says: "I enjoyed reading spy stories more than murder stories. Nothing I could imagine would be more outrageous than what actually happens. Ours is the second Great Age of Treason (the first was in the 16th century) ... I think I once wrote 'the past lies in wait to ambush the present', and that I suppose is my favourite theme: the excavation of an event in the fairly recent past to establish the truth about a present mystery or problem, the action often being set against some more distant historical event."

NICHOLAS PROFFITT

American.

Titles

The Embassy House. New York, Bantam, 1986.

Biography

Nicholas Proffitt, a former journalist, made his debut as a novelist with the critically acclaimed *Gardens of Stone* in 1983, of which United Press International said, "[It] may very well be the best novel on the Vietnam War ... It earns Nicholas Proffitt a place alongside James Jones and Norman Mailer."

The son of a military family, Proffitt served as a sergeant in the 1st Battalion, 3rd Infantry of the US Army — The Old Guard — which formed the inspiration for his first novel. He has been a correspondent and later bureau chief for *Newsweek* in Beirut, London, Nairobi and Saigon, and has won two Overseas Press Club Awards for International Reporting for his coverage of the 1973 Arab–Israeli War and the fall of South Vietnam in 1975.

Critical Analysis

Embassy House is unusual in that there are not many spy novels set in Vietnam during the war, perhaps because the scenes conjured up are too close to reality. Despite this handicap, Proffitt has written an exciting and entertaining story, no doubt gained from the author's first-hand experience of living in the country and seeing the evidence of the devastation caused by war.

"Embassy house" was the name given to the CIA headquarters in each of the provincial capitals of Vietnam. In early 1970, to one of these compounds, comes a Special Forces Captain, Jake Gulliver, a veteran of more than seven years "in-country" now reluctantly re-assigned to the CIA in the politically unstable southern Mekong delta. Gulliver is an accomplished soldier, code-named the "Sand-man", because of his expertise as an assassin. He was a proud Green Beret, but is now reduced to following his orders in the implementation of Operation Phoenix. This was the drastic measure adopted by the CIA to purge the Vietcong from local villages and hamlets, carried out by irregular teams of American-advised troops. Many of these Vietnamese soldiers were unreliable and had dubious criminal pasts. It is Gulliver's job to train them as an effective unit against the enemy.

Gulliver's superior in the CIA is Bennet Steelman, an ambitious career man, code-named "Razor" who is determined that the Phoenix Program will continue although he has no wish to dirty his own hands. Gulliver's friend and fellow-soldier is Dang, a Vietnamese soldier who has fought by his side against the Vietcong. He introduces Gulliver to Nhu, a beautiful actress, who becomes his mistress.

The fragile political situation is shattered by the arrest and torture of an innocent man by Lieutenant Swain — a brash, insensitive soldier, who is meant to replace Gulliver. These events result in explosive consequences. Gulliver finds himself in the middle with sympathy for both sides, and emotionally involved with Sally Teacher, an idealistic CIA case officer, also trying to make sense out of the political confusion.

This is a good novel which raises far more issues than the usual spy story, but although its moral messages are heavy, it is an entertaining book, showing us a side of the Vietnam war which is not usually seen or written about. There is a certain amount of gruesome violence, but for once this is necessary to convey the tense atmosphere of the country and the situation which encourages such violence.

A J QUINNELL

(Pseudonym)
British. Born in 1941.

Titles

Man on Fire. New York, William Morrow, 1980; London, Macmillan, 1981.
The Mahdi. London, Macmillan, 1981; New York, William Morrow, 1982.
The Snap. London, Macmillan, 1982; as *Snap Shot*. New York, William Morrow, 1983.
Blood Ties. London, Hodder & Stoughton, 1984.
Siege of Silence. New York, Dutton/NAL, 1986; London, Hodder & Stoughton, 1986.
In the Name of the Father. London, Hodder & Stoughton, 1987; New York, Dutton/NAL, 1987.
Papa's Envoy. London, Hodder & Stoughton, 1988; New York, Dutton/NAL, 1988.

Biography

A J Quinnell is a pseudonym, and the author wishes to remain anonymous. However, there are a few details which the author himself has given away — he is 48 years old, and of British nationality, although he says that he has never spent very much time in Britain.

Critical Analysis

Quinnell has written seven spy novels to date and it appears that he will continue to do so. The author comments: "Due to the recent year of detente between east and west writing spy stories as such is becoming increasingly difficult. We are simply running out of villains!"

Man on Fire is about an ex-Foreign Legionnaire, Creasey, who has fallen on hard times. He takes up a new job as a bodyguard to an eleven-year-old girl of a rich Italian family. Creasey is humanised by this contact and the two develop a close relationship. When the girl is kidnapped Creasey goes on a rather violent and sadistic revenge spree. It is an exciting story and presents vivid scenes of Italy, Malta and Gozo. The book was described by one reviewer in *The Observer* as "Technically convincing; emotionally too, which is considerably rarer." This story was nominated for the 'Best Novel' Edgar in 1981 by the Mystery Writers of America.

In *The Mahdi* the story concerns an American-British plan to create a new prophet to control and contain the zeal of Islam. The plot is highly improbable and demands a high suspension of belief. However, Chapman Pincher, an authority on British espionage wrote that the plot is so ingenious that Quinnell might have done better to sell the idea to the CIA or MI6. This theme was also handled by John Buchan in *Greenmantle*, and inevitably some reviewers have made comparisons between the two — one reviewer in *The Guardian* described the book as "Buchan with laser beams".

In each story Quinnell has dealt with a different theme in all areas of the world and in some cases has incorporated real events, such as the Israeli raid in June 1981 on the Iraqi nuclear installation near Baghdad, which is the subject of his novel *Snap Shot*.

The author comments: "My approach to spy fiction is like any other fiction: in order for it to be believed it must be accurate both in mood and detail. Eighty per cent of producing such novels lies in the research."

Film

Man on Fire was released as a film in September 1987.

PETER RABE

American.

Titles

[Major character: Manny De Witt]
A Shroud for Jesso. New York, Fawcett, 1955; London, Fawcett, 1956.
Blood on the Desert. New York, Fawcett, 1958; London, Muller, 1960.
Girl in a Big Brass Bed [De Witt]. New York, Fawcett, 1965.
The Spy Who Was Three Feet Tall [De Witt]. New York, Fawcett, 1966.
Code Name Gadget [De Witt]. New York, Fawcett, 1967.

Critical Analysis

Peter Rabe was persuaded into writing crime fiction by his publishers, Fawcett Gold Medal, and his first three books appeared in consecutive months in 1955. He went on to write over 20 novels, many in the style of the hard-boiled detective story.

He wrote a few spy novels, starting with *A Shroud for Jesso*, which touched on the espionage theme with a gangster inadvertently becoming involved in spying. His first true venture into international intrigue came with his book *Blood on the Desert*. The story is set in the Middle East and the plot is full of ambiguous loyalties and shifting allegiances.

In the 1960s, like a number of other American authors, Rabe started an espionage series featuring Manny De Witt, a lawyer for the multi-national firm of Lobbe Industriel. His jobs often involve some espionage activity. Although there are only three titles in this series they are written in a different style to his other novels. They are often quite amusing and the plots are usually quite convoluted.

Bill Crider, a critic writing in *Twentieth Century Crime and Mystery Writers* (1985), comments: "Unjustly neglected at present. Peter Rabe's books will amply repay the effort required to locate them. Few writers are Rabe's equal in the field of the hardboiled gangster story, and all his works offer consistent and sometimes thought-provoking entertainment."

Ian James Rankin

British. Born in Cardenden, Fife, 28 April 1960.

Titles

Watchman. London, Bodley Head, 1988.

Biography

Ian Rankin was educated at a state school and then attended the University of Edinburgh (1978–82), from which he graduated with an MAHons in English Language and Literature. He has worked as a swineherd, a taxman and a viniculturist. He now writes for a magazine in London.

Critical Analysis

Rankin started writing short stories from an early age, and says that he was more influenced by television than books. He tends not to read spy fiction "for fear of subconsciously stealing ideas."

He has written two previous books — *The Flood* (1986) and *Knots & Crosses* (1987), which are crime novels. The author says: "Spy novels for me represent the most *pure* literary form — that of detection, of finding things out about the 'world'." He tries to convey in his books a "Notion of 'territory' — be it an individual's right to privacy, respect for national borders, or dabbling in things one shouldn't."

Watchman is Rankin's third novel. The central character is Miles Flint a surveillance officer, an experienced watcher and listener with an odd obsession with beetles which leads him to classify people into different categories of insect. The story begins in Ireland and quickly moves to London, amidst an IRA bombing campaign. When Miles becomes puzzled by inconsistencies in his surveillance operations, he becomes involved in a hunt of his own where everyone becomes suspect. He is sent on a mission to Northern Ireland where he finds himself on the run and depending on an IRA terrorist for survival. Eventually Miles returns to London, where he and a journalist on the same trail, combine forces to expose the conspiracy. It is an exciting novel with a fast pace.

One of the characters voices his disgust with espionage: "Lies, damned lies, deceit and the manipulation of history: that was the role of intelligence".

One critic, Wendy Rowland, in the *Literary Review*, has described this novel as an "intelligent book which succeeds in keeping its eye on the human and moral dilemma of its fallible hero amid an awful world of lies and confusion without ever becoming po-faced".

John Coleman in the *Sunday Times*, commented: "Rankin squares up to a circuitous conspiracy with wit, passion and persuasive know-how."

Charles Robertson

American. Born in Glasgow, Scotland, 5 March 1941.

Titles

The Elijah Conspiracy. New York, Bantam, 1980.
The Omega Deception. New York, Bantam, 1984.

The Red Chameleon. New York, Bantam, 1985.
Directive 16. New York, Pocket Books, 1988; London, Severn, 1989.
Culebra Cut. New York, Pocket Books, 1989.

Biography

Although he was born in Scotland, Charles Robertson emigrated to America in 1954 at the age of thirteen. He was educated at public schools and attended the University of Connecticut where he received a BA; he also went to Fairfield University where he received an MA.

Critical Analysis

When asked why he writes spy fiction he commented: "I find them enjoyable to read and to write. I think of my work as being in the mystery–suspense–thriller category; 4 of my 5 published novels have had elements of espionage in them. The fifth (*The Children*, Bantam,1982) was a suspense novel." The author went on to say, "I believe that, for the most part, the spy novel is generally more exciting than the real world of intelligence. Occasionally the real world of intelligence provides genuine excitement that is sometimes too incredible to be believed if it were reproduced as fiction."

In *The Omega Deception* the story is set in the Second World War, concerning Germany's race to manufacture an A-bomb before they are defeated. The Allies manage to snatch Niels Bohr, the great Danish physicist, from the Germans. But Bohr's notes are left behind and if they fall into the hands of the Nazis they could succeed in their efforts. So the British send in a commando team to try to prevent this from happening.

Directive 16 also looks back to the Second World War; the novel is named after the order given by Hitler to prepare for the invasion of England. The story is set in 1940 during the Blitz on London. In America Roosevelt is seeking a third term as President and the electorate are split between those who want to help Britain and Europe against Hitler and those who want to keep America out of the war at all costs. Joseph Kennedy is the Ambassador in England, and although he takes the credit for helping Roosevelt win the election, he is pro-German and against American involvement. One reviewer commented: "The writing is clean and crisp, the story line interesting, suspenseful, and easy to follow."

The author believes "That there really are good guys and bad guys. I don't subscribe to the currently popular thesis that the US and the Soviet Union operate from the same moral framework."

DEREK ROBINSON

Pseudonym: DIRK ROBSON
British. Born in Bristol, 12 April 1932.

Titles

Rotten With Honour. New York, Viking, 1973.
The Eldorado Network. New York, Norton, 1980.

Biography

Derek Robinson was educated at Downing College, Cambridge from where he graduated with a BA in 1956 and an MA in 1958. He worked as a copywriter for advertising agencies in London and New York from 1956 to 1966. He has worked as a freelance writer since 1966.

Critical Analysis

In *Rotten With Honour* a young British banker who does a bit of moonlighting as a spy, must beat an old Russian master agent to the recovery of a nuclear scientist, who has discovered a new kind of weapon.

The Eldorado Network dates back to the Second World War and the double-cross system employed by the British Secret Service during the war. After initial drawbacks, the Abwehr is surprised by the high quality of intelligence from a young Spaniard inserted in England as a Nazi spy in 1941 — what they do not know is that their agent is a plant cultivated by the famed British XX Committee.

The author has written: "I did not set out to be a 'war' novelist, but somehow the problem of violence, of man's appetite for war, seems to arise again and again. All three novels have been about attitudes to war — the phony glamour of the World War I air war, the confused logic of the Cold War, the ambivalence of an English island occupied by the Nazis. They are all political in the sense that I deliberately set out to make the reader re-assess his opinions. Other than that they are just meant to be good stories, with action, conflict, and humour. Especially humour, which I consider to be the acid test of any novel."

SAX ROHMER

(Pseudonym of Arthur Henry Sarsfield Ward)
Other pseudonym: MICHAEL FUREY
British. Born in Birmingham, 15 February 1883. Died 1 June 1959.

Titles

[Major character: Fu Manchu]
The Mystery of Dr Fu-Manchu. London, Methuen, 1913; as *The Insidious Dr Fu-Manchu*. New York, McBride, 1913.
The Devil Doctor. London, Methuen, 1916; as *The Return of Dr Fu-Manchu*. New York, McBride, 1916.
The Si-Fan Mysteries. London, Methuen, 1917; as *The Hand of Fu-Manchu*. New York, McBride, 1917.
The Golden Scorpion. London, Methuen, 1919; New York, McBride, 1920.
Daughter of Fu Manchu. London, Cassell, 1931; New York, Doubleday, 1931.
The Mask of Fu Manchu. New York, Doubleday, 1932; London, Cassell, 1933.
The Bride of Fu Manchu. London, Cassell, 1933; as *Fu Manchu's Bride*. New York, Doubleday, 1933.
The Trail of Fu Manchu. London, Cassell, 1934; New York, Doubleday, 1934.
President Fu Manchu. London, Cassell, 1936; New York, Doubleday, 1936.

The Drums of Fu Manchu. London, Cassell, 1939; New York, Doubleday, 1939.
The Island of Fu Manchu. London, Cassell, 1941; New York, Doubleday, 1941.
Shadow of Fu Manchu. New York, Doubleday, 1948; London, Jenkins, 1949.
Re-Enter Dr Fu Manchu. London, Jenkins, 1957; as *Re-Enter Fu Manchu*. New York, Fawcett, 1957.
Emperor Fu Manchu. London, Jenkins, 1959; New York, Fawcett, 1959.

Biography

Sax Rohmer worked as a journalist, covering the underworld in London's Limehouse. He also wrote songs and sketches for entertainers. Later on in his life he spent some time in New York.

Critical Analysis

A purist would no doubt object to the inclusion of Sax Rohmer in this book, but one cannot escape the fact that the Dr Fu Manchu stories involved spying (on both sides), and that he marked an era in which all villains tended to be either German or Chinese: it was not until long afterwards that the Russian villain superseded the "heathen Chinée" whom this popular novelist found it so easy to exploit.

Pre-1914, while the Western world looked approvingly on the Japanese desire to modernise, they still regarded China as the "Yellow Peril". Rohmer struck the appropriate note in 1913 when he published the first of his Dr Fu Manchu stories — *Dr Fu-Manchu*. This paved his way out of trouble into fame and wealth: it was, however, all blatantly racist — to use an overworked and often wrongly used epithet. But in this instance the epithet was deserved: much of the admittedly photogenic trash which Rohmer turned out was as damaging in its way as any of the anti-Semitic pamphlets of the Nazis. Anita Page said of Sax Rohmer that he "flashed against exotic backgrounds such diabolically ingenious and irresistible villains as one trusts the world has never seen."

Fu Manchu, the all-powerful oriental potentate, had his own spies and methods of spying, but Nayland Smith, the English hero who battles against him for more than a quarter of a century was an improbable mixture for a spymaster or a counterspy — part amateur detective, part Burmese Commissioner (in the days when Burma was part of the British Empire) and, against all the probabilities of the spy game, a controller of the British Secret Service and the CID, as though these two were combined! Fu Manchu could so easily have been made into one of those fascinating Chinese warlords who had the virtues as well as the vices of his race: instead Rohmer described his "green eyes" as being "an emanation of Hell".

Book sales rocketed throughout Rohmer's life and in 1955 he is said to have sold the film, television and radio rights in his books for more than four million dollars.

Fu Manchu gradually became a symbol, not of success, but of an awful warning to prospective thriller and spy story writers of what to avoid if their works were to have any credibility or quality.

Films

The Mysterious Dr Fu Manchu. Paramount, 1929.
The Return of Dr Fu Manchu. Paramount, 1930.
Daughter of the Dragon. Paramount, 1931.
The Mask of Fu Manchu. MGM, 1932.
Drums of Fu Manchu. MGM, 1939.

The Face of Fu Manchu. Anglo-EMI, GB, 1965.
The Brides of Fu Manchu. Anglo-EMI, GB, 1966.
The Vengeance of Fu Manchu. Anglo-EMI, GB, 1967.
The Blood of Fu Manchu. Anglo-EMI, GB, 1969.
The Castle of Fu Manchu. Anglo-EMI, GB, 1970.

JOSEPH ROSENBERGER

American

Titles

Death Merchant: The Death Merchant. New York, Pinnacle, 1972.
Death Merchant: Operation Overkill. New York, Pinnacle, 1972.
Death Merchant: The Psychotran Plot. New York, Pinnacle, 1972.
Death Merchant: Albanian Connection. New York, Pinnacle, 1973.
Death Merchant: The Chinese Conspiracy. New York, Pinnacle, 1973.
Death Merchant: Satan Strike. New York, Pinnacle, 1973.
Death Merchant: The Castro File. New York, Pinnacle, 1974.
Death Merchant: The Billionaire Mission. New York, Pinnacle, 1974.
Death Merchant: The Laser War. New York, Pinnacle, 1974.
Death Merchant: The Mainline Plot. New York, Pinnacle, 1974.
Murder Master: The Caribbean Caper. New York, Manor, 1974.
Death Merchant: The KGB Frame. New York, Pinnacle, 1975.
Death Merchant: Manhattan Wipeout. New York, Pinnacle, 1975.
Death Merchant: The Mato Grosso Horror. New York, Pinnacle, 1975.
Death Merchant: The Zemlya Expedition. New York, Pinnacle, 1976.
(24 other titles featuring the Death Merchant)

Critical Analysis

Richard Camellion lives up to his name in these adventures — he is a master of disguise, deception and destruction, and is called in whenever the local authorities and the CIA cannot cope. His code name is the "Death Merchant".

Compare with other series, such as the Joe Gall series by James Atlee and the "Eliminator" tales of Christopher Nicole (**ANDREW YORK**, pseud.).

ANGUS ROSS

(Pseudonym for Kenneth Gigga)
Other pseudonyms: **STAN KENNY, HENRY MARLIN, IAN SAVAGE**
British. Born in Gawthorpe, Yorkshire, 19 March 1927.

Titles

[Major character: Marcus Aurelius Farrow]
(All novels feature Farrow, except *A Bad April*)
The Manchester Thing. London, Long, 1970.

The Huddersfield Job. London, Long, 1971.
The London Assignment. London, Long, 1972.
The Dunfermline Affair. London, Long, 1973.
The Bradford Business. London, Long, 1974.
The Amsterdam Diversion. London, Long, 1974.
The Leeds Fiasco. London, Long, 1975.
The Edinburgh Exercise. London, Long, 1975.
The Ampurias Exchange. London, Long, 1976; New York, Walker, 1977.
The Aberdeen Conundrum. London, Long, 1977.
The Burgos Contract. London, Long, 1978.
The Congleton Lark. London, Long, 1979.
The Hamburg Switch. London, Long, 1980; New York, Walker, 1980.
The Menwith Tangle. London, Hale, 1982.
The Darlington Jaunt. London, Hale, 1983.
The Greenham Plot. Milan, Mondadori, 1984.
A Bad April. London, Firecrest, 1984.
The Luxembourg Run. London, Firecrest, 1985.
The Tyneside Ultimatum. London, Firecrest, 1988.
The Leipzig Manuscript. London, Firecrest, 1989.

Biography

Angus Ross claims that "I got my education by courtesy of the Royal Navy in various ports of the world". He served in the Fleet Air Arm from 1944 to 1952, after which he worked in the newspaper and magazine field in the provinces and Fleet Street until 1972.

Critical Analysis

The first in the series of spy novels by Angus Ross was *The Manchester Thing*, in which he introduced his central character, Marcus Aurelius Farrow, a newspaperman drawn by chance and against his will into a murder investigation, which leads him in turn to the twilight world of espionage. This first book ended with Farrow's recruitment into the Secret Service. From this followed a whole series of Farrow books of which there are 19 to date.

Ross's view of espionage is that it "doesn't happen only in Washington, Bonn, Rome and Berlin, but also places like Leeds and Bradford, Dunfermline and Aberdeen." His hero, Farrow, reflects this outlook, being a down-to-earth character, but an inherently decent man with humanist principles, who is always clashing with his partner, Charles McGowan, who is totally dedicated to the Service and devoid of compassion.

Ross says: "My writing is not confined to spy fiction. I also write short stories, essays, other novels, literary criticism and works of non-fiction. But I have written many spy novels because I know a good deal about spies and spying; I regard the mode as an important genre in the field of fiction, and I believe that a great many readers are interested and entertained."

One of his most recent spy novels, *The Greenham Plot*, was based upon real events, but because of what happened there, the book was considered to be "too sensitive" to be published in Britain — however, it was published abroad.

HOLLY ROTH

Pseudonyms: **K G BALLARD, P J MERRILL**
American. Born in Chicago, 1916. Died in 1964.

Titles

[Major character: Lieutenant Kelly]
The Content Assignment [Kelly]. New York, Simon & Schuster, 1954; London, Hamish Hamilton, 1954.
The Mask of Glass. New York, Vanguard Press, 1954; London, Hamish Hamilton, 1955.
The Van Dreisen Affair. New York, Random House, 1960; London, Hamish Hamilton, 1960.
Button, Button [Kelly]. New York, Harcourt Brace, 1966; London, Hamish Hamilton, 1967.

Novels as K G Ballard

Gauge of Deception. New York, Doubleday, 1963; London, Boardman, 1964.

Biography

Holly Roth abandoned a modelling career to become a writer. She worked as a journalist for several newspapers and magazines before becoming a successful author of mystery and espionage novels. In the twelve years of her short career as a mystery writer, she wrote 14 books under the names of K G Ballard and P J Merrill, as well as under her own.

Critical Analysis

Her first novel *The Content Assignment*, was one of her most popular, and was recognized by Barzun and Taylor in *A Catalogue of Crime* as "an excellent spy and counter-spy story". The book is about an English journalist who falls in love with an American female CIA agent, who disappears in Berlin. The journalist picks up the trail and follows her to New York, meanwhile becoming the unwitting tool of the CIA.

   The Mask of Glass was written at the height of McCarthyism and is an interesting example of the paranoia it reflected. It is a story of a plot to take over America by a well-organised and powerful Communist group. This group manage to blackmail prominent politicians and other members of the administration to perform various tasks, then they are replaced by Communist look-alikes. It is up to a young, inexperienced CIA agent to expose the conspiracy.

KENNETH ROYCE

(Pseudonym of Kenneth Royce Gandley)
Other pseudonym: OLIVER JACKS
British. Born in Croydon, Surrey, 11 December 1920.

Titles

[Major character: Spider Scott]
My Turn to Die. London, Barker, 1958.
The Soft Footed Moor. London, Barker, 1959.
The Long Corridor. London, Cassell, 1960.
The Night Seekers. London, Cassell, 1962.
The Angry Island. London, Cassell, 1963.
Day the Wind Dropped. London, Cassell, 1964.
Bones in the Sand. London, Cassell, 1967.
A Peck of Salt. London, Cassell, 1968.
Single to Hong Kong. London, Hodder & Stoughton, 1969.
The XYY Man [Scott]. London, Hodder & Stoughton, 1970; New York, McKay, 1970.
The Concrete Boot [Scott]. London, Hodder & Stoughton, 1971; New York, McKay, 1971.
The Miniatures Frame [Scott]. London, Hodder & Stoughton, 1972; New York, Simon & Schuster, 1972.
Spider Underground. London, Hodder & Stoughton, 1973; as *The Masterpiece Affair*. New York, Simon & Schuster, 1973.
Trapspider. London, Hodder & Stoughton, 1974.
The Woodcutter Operation. London, Hodder & Stoughton, 1975; New York, Simon & Schuster, 1975.
Bustillo. London, Hodder & Stoughton, 1976; New York, Coward McCann, 1976.
The Satan Touch. London, Hodder & Stoughton, 1977.
Third Arm. London, Hodder & Stoughton, 1980; New York, McGraw Hill, 1980.
10,000 Days. London, Hodder & Stoughton, 1981; New York, McGraw Hill, 1981.
Channel Assault. London, Hodder & Stoughton, 1982; New York, McGraw Hill, 1983.
The Stalin Account. London, Hodder & Stoughton, 1983.
The Crypto Man [Scott]. London, Hodder & Stoughton, 1984; New York, Stein and Day, 1984.
The Mosley Receipt. London, Hodder & Stoughton, 1985.
No Way Back. London, Hodder & Stoughton, 1986.
The President is Dead. London, Hodder & Stoughton, 1988; as *Patriots*. New York, Crown, 1988.
Fall-Out. London, Hodder & Stoughton, 1989; New York, Crown, 1989.

Novels as Oliver Jacks

Man on a Short Leash. London, Hodder & Stoughton, 1974; New York, Stein and Day, 1974.
Assassination Day. London, Hodder & Stoughton, 1976; New York, Stein and Day, 1976.

Biography

In the Second World War Ken Royce served in the 1st Northern Rhodesia Regiment and the King's African Rifles, reaching the rank of Captain. From 1948 to 1972 he was managing director of a London travel agency which gave him the opportunity to find new settings for his books.

Critical Analysis

Royce started writing in 1958 with *My Turn to Die*, which is a spy thriller set in France. *The XYY Man* introduced his hero Willie "Spider" Scott, an ex-criminal who steps out of Wormwood Scrubs with the knowledge that next time he will get ten years behind bars. But an offer from a shadowy intelligence executive involves Spider playing hookey with men in the Chinese Legation, not to mention getting beaten up by agents of BOSS and threatened by an African agent of "Free Zimbabwe". Spider re-appears in four other stories. Royce says that Spider is based on an actual cat burglar, or "creeper" who gave him first-hand advice for background to his stories.

Bustillo is set entirely in Japan, and concerns an American who left the CIA after becoming disillusioned with the agency. He runs to Japan to start a new, anonymous life there, but his past catches up with him and he becomes involved in another conspiracy.

Royce did a brief spell in intelligence, and he says that his experience during the war is still useful. About the spy novel he says: "Like all genre, there are good and bad books, but a really good thriller stands up to any modern novel and is often more representative of what goes on in the world. Don't ask my opinion of 'who dunnits'; I turn into a different person."

Television

The XYY Man, *Concrete Boot*, *Miniatures Frame* and *Spider Underground* were all adapted for television in the mid-1970s, and Bulman, a character from the series, was used in three series of "Strangers" and subsequently in a thirteen-hour and a seven-hour series called "Bulman". He is now the longest serving detective on British television, 11 years to date.

Richard Sapir and Warren Murphy

Americans. Richard Sapir: Born in New York City, 27 July 1936. Died 27 January 1987. Warren Murphy: Born in Jersey City, New Jersey, 13 September 1933.

Titles

[Major character: The Destroyer]
The Destroyer: Created, The Destroyer. New York, Pinnacle Books, 1971; London, Corgi, 1973.
The Destroyer: Death Check. New York, Pinnacle Books, 1971; London, Corgi, 1973.
The Destroyer: Chinese Puzzle. New York, Pinnacle Books, 1972; London, Corgi, 1973.
The Destroyer: Mafia Fix. New York, Pinnacle Books, 1972; London, Corgi, 1974.
The Destroyer: Dr Quake. New York, Pinnacle Books, 1972; London, Corgi, 1972.
The Destroyer: Death Therapy. New York, Pinnacle Books, 1972; London, Corgi, 1974.
The Destroyer: Union Bust. New York, Pinnacle Books, 1973; London, Corgi, 1974.
The Destroyer: Summit Chase. New York, Pinnacle Books, 1973; London, Corgi, 1975.
The Destroyer: Murder's Shield. New York, Pinnacle Books, 1973; London, Corgi, 1975.

The Destroyer: Terror Squad. New York, Pinnacle Books, 1973; London, Corgi, 1975.
The Destroyer: Kill or Cure. New York, Pinnacle Books, 1973; London, Corgi, 1975.
The Destroyer: Slave Safari. New York, Pinnacle Books, 1973; London, Corgi, 1976
The Destroyer: Acid Rock. New York, Pinnacle Books, 1973; London, Corgi, 1975.
The Destroyer: Judgement Day. New York, Pinnacle Books, 1974; London, Corgi, 1976.
The Destroyer: Murder Ward. New York, Pinnacle Books, 1974; London, Corgi, 1976.
(41 more titles featuring The Destroyer)

Biographies

Richard Sapir was educated at Columbia University, New York, where he obtained a BSc in 1960. He worked as a newspaper reporter and editor, and in public relations.

Warren Murphy attended St. Peter's College, Jersey City (1968–69). He served in the US Air Force Alaskan Air Command, 1952–56, and achieved the rank of Sergeant. He worked as a reporter and editor, and as a public relations counsellor and speechwriter.

Critical Analysis

The last 21 books in this series were written by Murphy alone, otherwise the rest are written in collaboration. The first two books in the series were treated in a serious way, but by the time that *The Chinese Puzzle* was published in 1972, the authors had decided that topical satire and fantasy would be their trademarks in future adventures.

The Destroyer is the codename of Remo Williams who is employed by CURE—the world's most secret crime and spying organisation. The Destroyer is the ultimate secret weapon — a cold, calculating killing machine. In each episode the Destroyer is sent on a mission which involves saving the world from some terrible disaster. Our hero has to deal with mad scientists as well as nasty, dirty Russian and Chinese communists. These adventures are very Bondian and highly improbable, but they were popular at the time.

DONALD PETER SEAMAN

British. Born in London, 25 May 1922.

Titles

The Bomb That Could Lip Read. New York, Stein & Day, 1974.
The Defector. London, Hamish Hamilton, 1975; as *The Chameleon Course*. New York, Coward McCann, 1976
The Terror Syndicate. New York, Coward McCann, 1976.
The Duel. Garden City, NY, Doubleday, 1979.
Chase Royal. London, Hamish Hamilton, 1980.

Biography

Donald Seaman was educated at Palmers School, Grays, Essex. From 1946 to 1947 he served as an assistant purser with the Merchant Navy, in order to gather background material for a book on Palestine during the mass migrations there in this period.

After a spell in provincial journalism in Shropshire and Northants, he joined the staff of the *Daily Express* in 1948, spending twenty-four years with this paper covering wars and insurrections in Cyprus, Suez, Iraq, Syria and Aden, the Arab–Israeli wars, the Indo–Pakistan wars, Bangladesh, Nigeria and other parts of Africa.

He served with the British Army from 1939 to 1946 in the Middle East, Italy, Holland and Germany. During his journalistic career he twice represented the *Express* in Moscow and later was chief of their New York bureau, leaving voluntarily in 1973 to write books full time.

In 1951 he was assigned to cover the Burgess–Maclean missing diplomats case: "I worked five years on the story under Lord Beaverbrook's direction trying to break through cover of official silence, denials, half-truths and evasion." Finally Seaman, with co-author John S Mather, produced a book on the defection of these men, entitled *The Great Spy Scandal*.

Critical Analysis

It was this early experience of espionage and treachery that led Seaman to write spy fiction: "In those years," he says, "inevitably I met up with secret agents, defectors and traitors — working on both sides of the fence. Whatever their nationality, I admire the first, pity the second and despise the third: and I hope that something of that deep-rooted feeling emerges in every book I write."

The Defector is about a reticent couple living in Saddlers Hill; he is a scientist who has defected from the Russians, she the author of books critical of the Soviet regime. Their home is burgled and the scientist shoots and kills the burglar. Inevitably there is a trial, with much publicity, and from then on the KGB relentlessly track down the couple.

TIMOTHY SEBASTIAN

British. Born in London, 13 March 1952.

Titles

The Spy in Question. London, Simon & Schuster, 1988.
Spy Shadow. London, Simon & Schuster, 1989.

Biography

Tim Sebastian was educated at Westminster School and New College, Oxford, from where he received a BA Hons in Modern Languages. He was the East European correspondent for the BBC, 1979–82, the European correspondent for BBC TV News from 1982 to 1984, and the Moscow correspondent from 1984 to 1985. He has been the BBC Washington correspondent since 1986. Sebastian has published two non-fiction works entitled *Nice Promises* (1985) about Poland, and *I Spy in Russia* (1986). This author is an accomplished journalist and was chosen as TV Journalist of the Year in 1982.

Critical Analysis

Sebastian witnessed the rise of Solidarity and its aftermath. He was also the BBC's first television correspondent in Moscow, but was expelled in 1985 in a round of retaliatory expulsions between Britain and the Soviet Union. He was later accused by the Soviets — quite falsely — of working for British Intelligence. He uses his experience in journalism and his knowledge of the country and Soviet politics in his novel, *The Spy in Question*.

The story of this novel begins in 1968, with the seduction of a promising, young Soviet, Dmitry Kalyagin, who is then recruited by British Intelligence. The action then moves forward into the space of nineteen days in the December of 1990. By this time Kalyagin has risen to become a privileged Soviet Minister, who becomes aware that he is under suspicion and wants to be brought out of the country by his British spymasters. The man who is trying to bring him "in from the cold", metaphorically and physically, is George Parker, who has to overcome Embassy politics to accomplish his job.

There are a variety of minor, colourful characters and there are vivid scenes of Moscow life. The picture Sebastian presents of the intelligence world is that each intelligence service is as bad as the other — there are no differences between them. The Russians are cynical and ruthless — as seen by their treatment of Kalyagin and the infighting amongst the political elite. The British are also presented as ruthless, in their lack of instructions to George Parker and their treatment and neglect of Kalyagin.

One of the characters, Anatol, an old Russian agent, who had worked for British Intelligence many years ago, voices the key to intelligence: "It was true, what they'd told him. Intelligence was nothing more than reading the right things. Finding and interpreting, straining and squeezing till you have it all in the pot. Then sifting piece by piece, picking the truth from the lies, the clean from the dirty. After twenty years you could hold it up fresh as the day they'd devised it." Unfortunately people are not so predictable!

His second novel, *Spy Shadow* is set in Poland, and involves a battle between the Russian and British secret services, which centres around the planned visit of a new Russian General Secretary to Warsaw. In a review of *Books*, the critic commented: "The book is well written, the descriptions of Poland and Russia are obviously authentic, and yet somehow it all seems dated. Perhaps we have had a surfeit of novels about the Cold War, and even though this one is up-to-date in its plot, it follows very much in the footsteps of writers like Len Deighton and Ted Allbeury. Please, next time let us have something more original."

RONALD SETH

British. Born in Ely, Cambridgeshire, 1911. Died in February 1985.

Non-fiction Titles

A Spy Has No Friends. London, Deutsch, 1952.
Anatomy of Spying. London, Barker, 1961.
Forty Years of Soviet Spying. London, Cassell, 1965.

The Executioners: The Story of Smersh. London, Cassell, 1967.
Encyclopaedia of Espionage. London, New English Library, 1972.

Fiction Titles

Patriot. London, Peter Owen, 1954; as *Operation Getaway*. New York, Day, 1954.
Spy in the Nude. London, Hale, 1962; as *In the Nude*. New York, Day, 1962.
The Spy Who Wasn't Caught. London, Hale, 1966.
The Spy in Silk Breeches. London, Leslie Frewin, 1968.

Biography

Ronald Seth followed his education at Ely Cathedral School, King's School, Ely, and Peterhouse College, Cambridge, by lecturing in English in Estonia. In the Second World War he joined the RAF and was a Flight-Lieutenant. He volunteered for the Special Operations Executive in 1942 and was dropped into German-occupied Estonia. On landing he lost his radio and equipment, and was betrayed by a Nazi sympathiser.

Seth was tortured before being sentenced to death. However, when it came to the execution the scaffold failed to work, and he was taken back to prison and moved to Berlin where he experienced further torture. Seth himself told the story in *A Spy Has No Friends*, and he says that later he bluffed the German authorities into recruiting him into their own Intelligence Service to be used as an agent in Britain.

He was sent to Frankfurt to the Intelligence HQ of the Luftwaffe and then to the Gestapo. On 14 November 1943, Seth was sent, under guard, to Paris. He was told that the Nazis wanted to use him as one of their own agents in Britain. Meanwhile he was put inside a POW camp for British officers as an "ear" for the Germans. However, the officers suspected him and they threatened to kill him, so he had to be removed. He was taken to Frankfurt, and in 1945, with the Allies advancing on Berlin, Gestapo chief Himmler naively sent him to Switzerland with offers of peace to the Allies. Once he was safely in Berne, he contacted the British Embassy and revealed himself as an SOE officer, but the peace mission failed.

Critical Analysis

Most of Seth's writings have been non-fiction, including several books on the history of Russian spying, as well as general works on the subject of espionage.

He has written a few works of fiction such as *Spy in the Nude* which is about Alex Marceau, a writer of spy fiction but also a secret agent. *Operation Getaway* (1954) tells the story of a British agent who is parachuted behind the Iron Curtain to rescue the young son of an important Communist scientist.

Gerald William Herschel Kean Seymour

British. Born in Guildford, Surrey, 25 November 1941.

Titles

Harry's Game. London, Collins, 1975; New York, Random House, 1975.
Glory Boys. London, Collins, 1976; New York, Random House, 1976.

Kingfisher. London, Collins, 1977; New York, Summit, 1978.
Red Fox. London, Collins, 1979; as *The Harrison Affair*. New York, Summit, 1980.
The Contract. London, Collins, 1980; New York, Holt Rinehart, 1981.
Archangel. London, Collins, 1982; New York, Dutton, 1982.
In Honour Bound. London, Collins, 1984; New York, Norton, 1984.
Field of Blood. London, Collins, 1985.
Song in the Morning. London, Collins, 1986.
At Close Quarters. London, Collins, 1987.
Home Run. London, Collins Harvill, 1989.

Biography

Gerald Seymour was educated at Kelly College, Tavistock, Devon, and University College, London, from where he received a BA Hons in Modern History in 1963. He worked as a reporter for Independent Television News (ITN), London from 1963 to 1978. He says that his earliest literary influences were his father, William Kean Seymour, Chairman of the Poetry Society, and his mother, Rosalind Wade OBE, an author and poet.

Critical Analysis

Gerald Seymour's first novel was *Harry's Game*. This story is about Harry Brown, who does undercover work for the army. A Cabinet-ranking politician is gunned down by an IRA assassin, and neither the police nor any of the normal "sources" have produced any clues. So the Prime Minister orders a special agent (Harry) to be sent to Northern Ireland to find the assassin. In a race against time Harry has to find the assassin before he becomes a target. Eric Ambler wrote of this book " ... one of those rare pleasures, a considerable novel that is also a superb thriller". It was made into a television film, and its screenplay written by the author won Seymour the Pye Television Award in 1983.

   When his second novel, *The Glory Boys*, was published, the *Los Angeles Times* said: "Not since le Carré has the emergence of an international suspense writer been as stunning as that of Gerald Seymour." Each succeeding novel has concerned a topical issue, whether the action has taken place in Northern Ireland, Palestine or Afghanistan. Seymour has the ability to show us the heart of the controversy in his novels which can be attributed to his career as a television reporter, his travels and his talent for writing a good story.

   Seymour's latest book, *Home Run*, is set in Iran. It begins with the execution of a teenage terrorist girl, whose father is one of the Shah's innocent generals. The brother of the girl is out to get revenge for his sister's death, and uses the drug trade to hit back at the guilty men. Douglas Hurd in a review of this novel in the *Weekend Telegraph*, wrote: "Mr Seymour describes two establishments, one familiar, the other new but certain now to come at us in novel after novel. As the traditional Cold War thriller loses credibility we shall certainly be exposed to countless mullahs and ayatollahs, with heroes and villains criss-crossing the Gulf and the Turkish frontier as resolutely as they did the Berlin Wall."

Television

"Harry's Game". Yorkshire Television, 1982.
"The Glory Boys". Yorkshire Television, 1984.

DANIEL MICHAEL SHERMAN
American. Born in Los Angeles, California, 31 July 1950.

Titles
Mole. New York, Arbor House, 1977.
Swann. New York, Arbor House, 1978.
King Jaguar. New York, Arbor House, 1979.
Dynasty of Spies. New York, Arbor House, 1980.
The White Mandarin. New York, Arbor House, 1982.
The Prince of Berlin. New York, Arbor House, 1983.

Biography
Dan Sherman was educated at the University of Oregon and received a BA from the University of California, Northridge. Before turning to fiction Sherman worked as a freelance journalist and a public relations copywriter from 1972 to 1974. He was editor of the *Los Angeles Voice* , 1974–75, and since then he has been a full-time freelance writer.

Critical Analysis
In *Mole* Peter Jaeger, known as Poet, from Secret Operations is assigned to hunt out a deep penetration agent working inside the CIA. The search is triggered by a series of murders set off to protect the identity of the mole or the "Sleeping Beauty" as he is called.

Our hero is a cynic, and a disillusioned cynic at that: "Peter had decided that the CIA and the KGB lived for each other — their insanity was symbiotic, one couldn't be without the other. Warriors like Poet, whatever of themselves they brought to the battle, were far less cause than consequence."

In *Swann*, Sherman's next novel, Josey Swann is a Vietnam veteran and is called in by the CIA to do some dirty work for them. He teams up with a grain company meteorologist to prevent a CIA plot which would cause a world famine. Contrary to popular belief that the CIA does not murder people, this story begins with the assassination of the Agricultural Minister of Brazil because he will not fall in line with US policy. In this book the author implies that the philosophy behind the agency is that the ends justify the means. There is no outside control and therefore any changes that have to be made are done from the inside.

The author writes: "*Swann* is fundamentally a true story, given to me by my father who spent some thirty years in the grain industry. He served in South America on the Meals for Millions project and there ran into all manner of CIA personnel. Much of the material dealing with the Russian wheat deal, the pay-offs, and the grain company's connection with the CIA is based on what I believe to be fact. I can't prove it all, but there is more than passing evidence."

Levin Gale Shreve

American. Born in Baltimore, Maryland, 17 February 1910.

Titles

The Phoenix With Oily Feathers. Grimsby, Moore Publishing, 1980.

Biography

L G Shreve was educated at Johns Hopkins University. He worked as a government employee and in banking from 1932 to 1941 and then in a public relations agency in Baltimore for four years. In 1950 he joined the Central Intelligence Agency and worked as an intelligence officer in Washington DC for twenty years. He has been a full-time writer since 1972.

Critical Analysis

The Phoenix With Oily Feathers is about a retired CIA agent in Nantucket who spots a Nazi war criminal. He trails the Nazi to a band of men interested in the impending attempt to raise the *Andrea Doria*.

This novel was well received by the critics and the general public. For example, a reviewer for the *Library Journal* declared the book to be "credible, well written and surprisingly entertaining." David Atlee Phillips, the former director of the Western Hemisphere Division of the CIA, also praised the work: "Shreve has written, as only an insider could, a chillingly authentic tale of intrigue born in the ashes of the Reich." Reviewer Virginia Leache concluded that the book was more than a novel: "*Phoenix* belongs possibly to the new literary genre *faction*, or the docu-novel, in which a work of fiction is seeded with real life characters and events. The technique is exploited with such skill in the *Phoenix* that the narrative assumes a convincing aura of authenticity, leaving the reader trying to recall headlines of the period."

The author described his work in the following way: "Count me as a disciple of such storytellers as Frederick Forsyth, Morris West, and Helen MacInnes. For all the aura which surrounds him and his works, I find John le Carré precious and obscure."

Shreve's experience in intelligence helped him to write in a technical sense, and also provided background material which he could use later as a writer: "By far the most interesting and rewarding period of my life was my long service with the Central Intelligence Agency (CIA). I started working for the agency early on, surviving the lean years when government salaries were not exactly golden. The psychiatric income was very high, however, and more than compensated for the loss of dollars. Moreover, in a sort of 'Catch 22' situation, the experience provided me with a wealth of background material which would have been denied me if I had set out earlier in life to be a full-time writer. In the CIA a lot of reporting must be done by officers in the field. In the course of twenty years or more I must have written the equivalent of ten novels on the whole range of esoteric stuff attributed, rightly or wrongly, to intrigue and espionage."

Upton Beall Sinclair

Pseudonyms: Clarke Fitch, Frederick Garrison, Arthur Stirling
American. Born in Baltimore, Maryland, 20 September 1878. Died 25 November 1968.

Titles

[Major character: Lanny Budd]
World's End. New York, Viking Press, 1940.
Between Two Worlds. New York, Viking Press, 1941.
Dragon's Teeth. New York, Viking Press, 1942.
Wide Is the Gate. New York, Viking Press, 1943.
Presidential Agent. New York, Viking Press, 1944.
Dragon Harvest. New York, Viking Press, 1945.
The World to Win. New York, Viking Press, 1946.
Presidential Mission. New York, Viking Press, 1947.
One Clear Call. New York, Viking Press, 1948.
O Shepherd, Speak. New York, Viking Press, 1949.
The Return of Lanny Budd. New York, Viking Press, 1953.

Biography

Upton B Sinclair was educated at City College, New York and at Columbia University from 1897 to 1901. He wrote nearly 100 pseudonymous "dime novels" while attending Columbia University. He was a full-time writer from 1898 to1962. Sinclair was a noted American "muckraker", and first came to the notice of the public with the publication of *The Jungle* in 1906. This book exposed evils in the meat-packing industry. After this his aim was to expose social and political evils in both his fiction and non-fiction.

Critical Analysis

Sinclair was noted for his morally simple view of history, a view which is clearly apparent in the Lanny Budd novels. This series consisting of eleven volumes, begun in 1940 and completed in 1953, traces the political history of the Western world from 1913 to 1950. It describes historical change in terms of international conspiracy and conflict, mainly between the forces of progress (Socialism and Communism) and the forces of oppression (Fascism). But as the series moves forward in time, America of the 1930s and 1940s takes up the cause of progress to do battle with both Fascism and Soviet-style Communism. (Sinclair enthusiastically supported Franklin D Roosevelt and abhorred Stalinism.)

These novels reflected Sinclair's personal concern with Communism and Fascism. The hero Lanny Budd acts as the personal agent of President Franklin D Roosevelt, and is concerned with various events of the Second World War. After the death of Roosevelt Budd continues his work for President Truman and takes part in the Nuremberg war trials. In the last book of the series Budd is called out of retirement and becomes involved in the events of 1946-49, including the spy trial of his sister.

WILLIAM MICHAEL HARDY SPICER

British. Born in Bath, 22 January 1943.

Titles

Prime Minister Spy. London, Severn, 1987.

Biography

Michael Spicer was educated at Wellington College and Emmanuel College, Cambridge where he gained an MA in Economics. He has been a journalist writing on financial and political affairs and set up an economic consultancy company. He entered Parliament in 1974 as MP for Worcestershire South, becoming Vice-Chairman of the Conservative Party in 1981 and then Deputy Chairman in 1983; he was made Minister for Aviation in 1984.

Critical Analysis

The author describes his first novel, *Final Act* (1981), as "faction" about Britain in the year 2005, controlled from the Soviet Union. He also writes mysteries: "It depends upon what I want to say... I am more concerned about the relationship between intelligence and the political context."

The story of *Prime Minister Spy* begins in Hitler's bunker at the very end of the Second World War. We are introduced to Hitler and his entourage, one of whom is his cook, Konstanze Manzially, with whom he has a brief affair. After the Nazi defeat, she is protected by a Colonel in Soviet Military Intelligence, and discovers that she is pregnant. When her son is born the Russians insist that she has him adopted by a young British military couple stationed in Berlin. The Soviets know the secret of his birth and it is arranged for Konstanze to become his nurse and his Control until he is old enough to be of use to them.

We follow the life of her son Rupert Higginson, who is an ambitious scholar and sportsman at school and university. He enters the Foreign Office and then begins a career in politics, eventually rising to become Prime Minister. However, throughout his life he is haunted by the origins of his birth and because of it, both British Intelligence and the KGB seek to use him for their own ends. Eventually Higginson rejects both sides and works towards his own goals as a world statesman.

Interestingly enough his popularity as Prime Minister rests upon his pro-European policies and his anti-American stand.

This is an entertaining novel with some fine insights into the British political system, as well as vivid descriptions of Berlin just after the war and of war-torn Vienna. The author is now currently working on a new series of mystery novels.

FRANK MORRISON SPILLANE

Pseudonym: MICKEY SPILLANE
American. Born in Brooklyn, New York, 9 March 1918.

Titles

[Major characters: Mike Hammer, Tiger Mann]
The Girl Hunters [Hammer]. New York, Dutton, 1962; London, Barker, 1962.

Day of the Guns [Mann]. New York, Dutton, 1964; London, Barker, 1965.
Bloody Sunrise [Mann]. New York, Dutton, 1965; London, Barker, 1965.
The Death Dealers [Mann]. New York, Dutton, 1965; London, Barker, 1966.
The By-Pass Control [Mann]. New York, Dutton, 1966; London, Barker, 1967.
The Delta Factor. New York, Dutton, 1967; London, Corgi, 1969.

Biography
Frank Spillane attended Kansas State College where he had intended to study law. While at college he worked during the summers as captain of the lifeguards at Breezy Point, Long Island. He began selling stories in 1935, first to "slicks", then to "pulps". He wrote for radio, television, and comic books to put himself through college.

After the war he continued writing for comics for a while, then worked for a short time as a trampoline artist for Ringling Bros., Barnum & Bailey. In 1969 Spillane and producer Robert Fellows formed an independent film company in Nashville, Tennessee, called Spillane–Fellows Productions, which filmed features and television productions.

Critical Analysis
Spillane is best known as the master of the hard-boiled mystery story, and he has received the life achievement award from the PWA (Private Eye Writers of America) in 1983. At one time he had written seven of the all-time ten fiction bestsellers, and the list did not include just mystery fiction.

The Mike Hammer stories have been criticised for their excessive portrayals of sex and violence, but despite this his novels have always been popular. Mike Hammer is strictly a private-eye, involved in matters of murder and crime, but on occasion he is known to have rubbed shoulders with spies. For instance, in *The Girl Hunters*, Hammer takes on a Communist spy ring and a master assassin known as "the Dragon", to avenge the death of a girlfriend.

Closer to spy fiction is his creation Tiger Mann, a character invented to capitalise on the James Bond cult of the 1960s. Spillane wrote only four books in this series. The plots of these stories range from Tiger Mann saving the world from nuclear holocaust to foiling an assassination attempt on a Saudi Arabian oil king.

TAD SZULC
American. Born in Warsaw, Poland, 25 July 1926.

Titles
Diplomatic Immunity. New York, Simon & Schuster, 1981.

Biography
Tad Szulc was educated at the University of Brazil, 1943–45. He worked as a reporter for the Associated Press in Rio de Janeiro, 1945–46, then as a correspondent for United Press International at the United Nations, 1949–53. Szulc served as a correspondent in Southeast Asia, Latin America, Portugal, Spain, Eastern Europe, the Middle East and with the Washington Bureau for the *New York Times* from 1953 to 1972.

He is a lecturer on foreign affairs at universities, government seminars, for the Peace Corps, and on radio and television. He has been an author and foreign policy commentator since 1973.

Critical Analysis

Tad Szulc has written extensively about the CIA and South America. Much of the background employed in this novel represents his personal feelings and findings on current situations in Latin America.

In *Diplomatic Immunity* the female American ambassador to a South American dictatorship is caught in the middle as the CIA try to keep that government in power while the White House seeks to end it. This story reflects the old hostility between the CIA and the State Department and how their aims often conflict.

After writing more than twelve non-fiction books, Szulc turned his foreign policy experiences into a novel. Although *Diplomatic Immunity* was not a bestseller, it evoked some positive comments from reviewers. Robert Sherrill of the *New York Times Book Review* wrote: "Aside from its other merits, *Diplomatic Immunity* is, because of ... Szulc's expertise, a liberal education in State Department metaphysics." Again, in the *Chicago Tribune Book World*, Michael Hutchinson noted: "The author's firsthand knowledge of how US foreign policy ... works is illuminating, turning this into a first-rate thriller." Both these reviewers emphasised the role of Szulc's own foreign experiences in making the characters and foreign intrigue of the plot believable.

In 1986, when asked if his novel was based on fact, Szulc replied: "It's the usual composite of people. The situation itself is invented, obviously. There never was a US woman ambassador in Central America. There was an American woman ambassador whom I knew elsewhere in the Caribbean, but it was just a dramatic device to use a woman as an ambassador. The mythical country in the book is a composite of Nicaragua and El Salvador, and the leader is modeled to some extent on Somoza. It was kind of fun to do because I'd never done it before, and I enjoyed it very much."

DAVID CRAIG OWEN THOMAS

Pseudonym: DAVID GRANT
British. Born in Cardiff, South Wales, 24 November 1942.

Titles

[Major character: Sir Kenneth Aubrey]
Rat Trap. London, Michael Joseph,1976; New York, Bantam, 1976.
Firefox. London, Michael Joseph, 1977; New York, Holt, 1977.
Wolfsbane. London, Michael Joseph, 1978; New York, Holt, 1978.
Snow Falcon. London, Michael Joseph, 1979; New York, Holt, 1980.
Sea Leopard. London, Michael Joseph, 1981; New York, Viking, 1981.
Jade Tiger. London, Michael Joseph, 1982; New York, Viking, 1982.
Firefox Down. London, Michael Joseph, 1983; New York, Bantam, 1983.
The Bear's Tears. London, Michael Joseph, 1985; as *Lion's Run.* New York, Bantam, 1985.

Winter Hawk. London, Collins, 1987; New York, Morrow, 1987.
All the Grey Cats. London, Collins, 1988; as *Wildcat*. New York, Putnam, 1988.

Novels as David Grant
Moscow 5000. London, Michael Joseph, 1979; New York, Holt, 1979.
Emerald Decision. London, Michael Joseph, 1980; New York, Holt, 1980.

Biography

Craig Thomas was educated at Cardiff High School and University College, Cardiff, where he received a BA in 1964 and an MA in 1967, both in English. He worked as a schoolmaster teaching English for eleven years before 1977. His first novel, *Rat Trap*, was published in 1976, and the success of his second novel, *Firefox*, enabled him to become a professional author.

Critical Analysis

Thomas says: "I write 'espionage adventure' rather than spy novels, but no other form of fiction. I think my talents extend to the creation of tension, drama, exotic background and the conflicts of individuals, but especially to the 'sense of danger' in a story, therefore I continue to be drawn to the 'adventure' novel."

Rat Trap is the story of a hijack of a British Airways airliner at Heathrow, with the sub-plot of a convicted Arab terrorist on the run in the West Country (he is the 'object of exchange' for the hijacked passengers).

Firefox is named after a new plane, the MIG-31, designed by the Russians and far in advance of Western technology, its special feature is that it has a thought-guided weapons system activated by the pilot's brain waves. Western powers are afraid that once this plane becomes operational it will alter the balance of military power in favour of the Soviets. To counter this they devise a plan to steal it, and an American pilot is chosen for the mission. He succeeds in stealing the aircraft and the denouement is a dogfight high over the Arctic Ocean. Newgate Callendar of the *New York Times Book Review* wrote :"This episode, like everything else in the book, will have you sweating bullets. Thomas misses no tricks, and tension is sustained from first page to last. He is a very good writer who has the trick of taking an unbelievable set of circumstances and completely winning over the reader."

Robin W Winks, a critic of spy and detective fiction, wrote in a review in the *Washington Post Book World* that: "Thomas writes far better than Ludlum. He often achieves the economy of words of Adam Hall. He can muster up some of the dulled irony of John le Carré. He knows how to make a chase scene drive the reader from page to page, ... he is only one step behind Geoffrey Household at this kind of thing. Best of all, he gets his geography right ..."

In his latest novel, *All the Grey Cats*, the story follows the events of *The Bear's Tears*, and Kenneth Aubrey finds himself increasingly snubbed and distrusted by his superiors — until he is offered the relatively unimportant job of arranging the defection of an East German civil servant. In an attempt to redeem himself he accepts the challenge and opportunity, disregarding the fact that the defector is the only son of General Brigitte Winterbach of East German Intelligence, his oldest and most bitter enemy. When the defection goes disastrously wrong, Aubrey finds himself the victim of Brigitte's violent revenge.

The author says: "Sir Kenneth Aubrey is my favourite and most consistent 'run-on' character — he is who I might wish I was in my more 'ordinary' moments. I have also used, in tandem with Aubrey, Patrick Hyde as a 'field agent'."

When asked if he thought if the spy fiction hero is now anachronistic, he said: "I imagine the 'World War III' or 'techno' thrillers have a limited shelf life, which is not necessarily a matter of regret, despite the fact that I might well claim to have 'invented' the latter genre with *Firefox*. The 'adventure' that contains a 'spy hero' is, however, likely to remain popular."

Film
Firefox. Warner, US, 1982.

MICHAEL M THOMAS
American. Born in New York City, 18 April 1936.

Titles
Green Monday. New York, Simon & Schuster, 1980; London, Hutchinson, 1980.
The Ropespinner Conspiracy. New York, Warner Books, 1986; London, Bantam, 1986.

Biography
Michael Thomas was educated at private schools and attended Yale University from where he obtained a BA. He has worked at various jobs including an art historian, 1959–61, an investment banker, 1961–73 and a corporate finance consultant, 1973–85.

Critical Analysis
Thomas says that he writes "financial thrillers as 'cautionary entertainments' ". He remarks that his books are about "the blurred, almost invisible line between prosperity and catastrophe, the manipulation of politics and economic systems."

The Ropespinner Conspiracy concerns a Soviet plot to infiltrate the West's banking system and lead it to self-destruction. Their plot is aided by a group of disaffected American bankers and economists who have persuaded the government to sanction huge loans to Third World countries and multinationals, which do not have much of a chance of being repaid. Ted Allbeury commented in a review of this book in the *Sunday Mirror*: "I'm not much drawn to financial thrillers but Thomas, an American, has a background of both journalism and finance, and that makes a difference." Another critic, Bob Watt, remarked: "Unfortunately, the man in the street tends to regard the world of high finance as some vast secret society, but Mr Thomas succeeds in painting a horrifying picture of what would happen to all of us if this society were to collapse!"

Ross Elmore Thomas

Pseudonym: Oliver Bleeck
American. Born in Oklahoma City, Oklahoma, 19 February 1926.

Titles

[Major characters: McCorkle and Padillo]
The Cold War Swap [M & P]. New York, Morrow, 1966; as *Spy in the Vodka*. London, Hodder & Stoughton, 1967.
Cast a Yellow Shadow [M & P]. New York, Morrow, 1967; London, Hodder & Stoughton, 1968.
The Seersucker Whipsaw. New York, Morrow, 1967; London, Hodder & Stoughton, 1968.
The Singapore Wink. New York, Morrow, 1969; London, Hodder & Stoughton, 1969.
The Fools in Town Are on Our Side. London, Hodder & Stoughton, 1970; New York, Morrow, 1971.
The Backup Men [M & P]. New York, Morrow, 1971; London, Hodder & Stoughton, 1971.
The Porkchoppers. New York, Morrow, 1972; London, Hamish Hamilton, 1974.
If You Can't Be Good. New York, Morrow, 1973; London, Hamish Hamilton, 1974.
The Money Harvest. New York, Morrow, 1975; London, Hamish Hamilton, 1975.
Yellow-Dog Contract. New York, Morrow, 1976; London, Hamish Hamilton, 1977.
Chinaman's Chance. New York, Simon & Schuster, 1978; London, Hamish Hamilton, 1978.
The Eighth Dwarf. New York, Simon & Schuster, 1979; London, Hamish Hamilton, 1979.
The Mordida Man. New York, Simon & Schuster, 1981; London, Hamish Hamilton, 1981.
Missionary Stew. New York, Simon & Schuster, 1983; London, Hamish Hamilton, 1984.
Briarpatch. New York, Simon & Schuster, 1984.
Out on the Rim. New York, Mysterious Press, 1987.
The Fourth Durango. New York, Mysterious Press, 1989.

Biography

Ross Thomas was educated at the University of Oklahoma, Norman, from where he obtained a BA in 1949. He was a reporter for the *Daily Oklahoman*, 1943–44. During the Second World War he served in the US Army Infantry in the Philippines. He worked as a Public Relations Director of the National Farmers Union in Denver, 1952–56, and was President at Stapp Thomas & Wade Inc., Denver from 1956 to 1957. He was a reporter in Bonn, West Germany, 1958–59, and a representative for Dolan Associates, Ibadan, Nigeria, 1959–61. He was a consultant to the US government from 1964 to 1966.

Critical Analysis

Thomas is noted as an author of spy fiction or "political thrillers" as they are often described. He has won two Edgars from the Mystery Writers of America, one for his first novel *The Cold War Swap* in 1967, and the other for *Briarpatch* in 1985.

In *The Cold War Swap* we are introduced to Mac McCorkle, a barkeeper in West Berlin, and his partner, Michael Padillo, who uses the job as a cover for his espionage activities. In exchange for two spies the Russians want a live agent — McCorkle's partner.

Newgate Callendar of the *New York Times Book Review*, wrote: "Ever since his first novel, *The Cold War Swap*, was published in 1966, Mr Thomas has consistently proved to be one of the best American storytellers. He handles intricate plots with the ease of a master, he has a smooth and sophisticated prose style, his ear for dialogue is admirable, his characters ring true even when they are idealized." A critic of the *Los Angeles Times* said: "Simply as a dramatist — setting scenes, sketching unique characters, evoking tensions and forwarding the plot through sharp dialogue, describing action and confrontations — Thomas has few peers."

What makes Thomas different from other spy fiction writers is his wit and versatile writing style, described by one *Washington Post Book World* critic as "sharp, colloquial, wry, able to modulate easily from repartee to description to gun-blazing action." These qualities in his prose led one critic, Stephen King, to label Thomas "the Jane Austen of the political espionage story."

In 1984 Thomas published *Briarpatch*, his twentieth novel and second Edgar winner. The book describes the political corruption a government consultant uncovers while investigating the mysterious murder of his sister.

The author says: "Spy fiction offers adventure, romance, intrigue and suspense, which are the essentials of most fiction. I write it because I enjoy reading it. I also write novels about crime, politics and scallawags, which also provide adventure, romance, intrigue, suspense and even mystery. Most spy novels provide neither an accurate nor realistic picture of the intelligence world because they are not written by espionage agents. This does not necessarily mean that they are not good novels. I have never wittingly had any formal association with any intelligence agency. But I have known some agents. Knowing them did not hinder my career as a novelist. Nor did it help any."

ARTHUR LEONARD BELL THOMPSON

Pseudonym: FRANCIS CLIFFORD
British. Born in Bristol, 1 December 1917. Died 24 August 1975.

Titles

Act of Mercy. London,Hamish Hamilton, 1960; New York, Coward McCann, 1960.
The Naked Runner. London, Hodder & Stoughton, 1966; New York, Coward McCann, 1966.
All Men Are Lonely Now. London, Hodder & Stoughton, 1967; New York, Coward McCann, 1967.
The Blind Side. London, Hodder & Stoughton, 1971; New York, Coward McCann, 1971.
Amigo, Amigo. London, Hodder & Stoughton, 1973; New York, Coward McCann, 1973.
The Grosvenor Square Goodbye. London, Hodder & Stoughton, 1974; as *Goodbye and Amen*. New York, Coward McCann, 1974.

Biography

Francis Clifford was educated at Christ's Hospital, Horsham, West Sussex. During the war he served in the Burma Rifles, 1939–43, and as Special Operations Executive from 1943 to 1945. After the war he worked as an industrial journalist for the steel industry.

He started his writing career somewhat late in life, but his world sales topped the five million mark and he was particularly successful in winning awards on both sides of the Atlantic. He won the Edgar Allan Poe Special Award of the Mystery Writers of America for *Amigo, Amigo* and twice received the Crime Writers' Association Silver Dagger, for *Act of Mercy* and *The Grosvenor Square Goodbye*.

Critical Analysis

Outstanding among his spy stories was *The Naked Runner*, which opens in Leipzig with Sam Laker, a successful British businessman, reluctantly agreeing to act as an unpaid agent for the West and ends a few days later with Sam turned into a cold and paranoic killer. Frank Sinatra bought the film rights, and played the leading role.

Not all of Clifford's books were spy stories, but *All Men Are Lonely Now* was about a Special Branch investigation into an East German defector's disclosures about a laser-guided missile. *The Los Angeles Times* described it, perhaps rather too enthusiastically, as "the finest espionage novel of the decade". Clifford won many friends among the critics and Francis Iles, writing in *The Guardian*, said that he was "almost unique in combining a deeply felt philosophical truth with the real excitement of the thriller".

The Blind Side was a spy story with a difference, being a study of two brothers under stress in very separate situations. One brother was a priest in the starving villages of Biafra, the other sat at his desk in Naval Intelligence in London, watching, noting, passing on his only link with trust and affection to a man he rarely met ... and then the link between them snapped. In this work Clifford acquired a mastery of characterisation and he followed this up in *Amigo, Amigo*, which was, however, more of a hunt for war criminals in South America than a spy story.

Film

The Naked Runner. Warner, GB, 1967.

John Stevens Trenhaile

British. Born in Hertford, 29 April 1949.

Titles

[Major character: Stepan Povin]
The Man Called Kyril [Povin]. London, Severn, 1981.
A View From the Square [Povin]. London, Bodley Head, 1983.
Nocturne for a General [Povin]. London, Bodley Head, 1985.
The Mahjong Spies. London, Collins, 1986.
The Gates of Exquisite View. London, Collins, 1987.
The Scroll of Benevolence. London, Collins, 1988.

Biography

John Trenhaile was educated at Magdalen College, Oxford, where he received a BA Hons in 1971, and an MA in 1975. He practised for thirteen years at the Chancery Bar before leaving the law to devote himself to writing full time. He travels frequently to the Far East which contributes to the success of his work.

Critical Analysis

His first novel, *The Man Called Kyril*, is the first of his books in the Russian "Povin" trilogy. David Stafford in his book, *The Silent Game* (1988), has written: "This series too deals with a mole, although here it is the hero himself, Povin, a secret Christian (and homosexual), who is passing KGB secrets to Sir Richard Bryant, head of SIS. And it reflects well, in a sophisticated way, the revived concern of contemporary spy writers with Communism, a trend likely to increase in the era of Gorbachev and *glasnost*. 'The real furnace these days — I won't call it a war,' says Trenhaile, ... 'is the ideological conflict between Communism as practised and capitalism as practised. People simplify this into East vs West, Reds vs Capitalists, and so on. But it's not simple. Until you know who your Communists are, what their grandparents thought and what they had to undergo, you can't really be sure of what you're dealing with today'."

Trenhaile has said: "I write because I have to. My work is based on my own experiences. The books are about spies, written up from the Russian viewpoint in an attempt to show that, for all his many faults, Soviet man derives from the same stock of common humanity. I try to keep my personal views out of my writings as far as possible."

A number of his novels are set in the Far East, including *The Mahjong Spies*, and his latest book, *The Scroll of Benevolence*. The latter is concerned with the fate of Hong Kong and the effect upon it when China's aged ruler dies, an event that seems imminent. In Hong Kong the leaders of the great commercial empires, The Club of Twenty, have made arrangements to have their assets removed to a safer place in a brilliant scheme code-named The Scroll of Benevolence.

But there are people who wish to stop them from carrying out their plan. The plot also involves members of the CIA and the KGB forge an alliance to discover China's true military capabilities.

Television

"Codename Kyril" shown on television as a serial in 1988.

TREVANIAN

(Pseudonym of Rodney Whitaker)
Other pseudonym: NICHOLAS SEARE
American. Born in Tokyo, 12 January 1925.

Titles

[Major character: Jonathan Hemlock]
The Eiger Sanction [Hemlock]. New York, Crown, 1972; London, Heinemann, 1973.
The Loo Sanction [Hemlock]. New York, Crown, 1973; London, Heinemann, 1974.
Shibumi. New York, Crown, 1979; London, Granada, 1979.

Biography

Trevanian is the pseudonym for Rodney Whitaker. The author kept his identity secret for many years and it is only recently that his true name has been revealed. He holds four university degrees, including a PhD in Communications. He was formerly Professor at the University of Texas, at Austin.

Critical Analysis

Miles Copeland has said of Trevanian that his work contains "some of the most shocking, brutal fiction in modern literature, but it's also funny — funny, that is, to those who like their comedy a bit sick. Trevanian's characters are real enough and they constantly drop 'in' jokes to tell readers among the pros they are not acting out fantasies, but caricatures."

His first novel was *The Eiger Sanction*. A critic said it started "unpromisingly in a welter of sex, facetiousness and fantastication, but presently when it comes to the climbing settles down to rationality and achieves real grip." This is an understatement.

The story tells of Dr Jonathan Hemlock, a mountaineer, art historian, collector of rare paintings and assassin-designate to an American intelligence department. The story starts in Montreal where Wormwood, an inept, accident-prone agent of the CII, having been handed a tiny packet of bubble-gum in the park, believes at last he has safely carried out his mission. He is about to enter his room when he is clubbed to the ground. Thinking he is about to lose consciousness, he has the presence of mind to stuff the bubble-gum in his mouth and swallow it. Doubtless he thinks the microfilm in the packet is safe from the villains who have knocked him out. Such thoughts are rudely disturbed as he feels them rip open his stomach to retrieve the bubble-gum ... horrible! but fortunately briefly narrated.

Hemlock wants a huge sum of money to buy himself an Impressionist painting. He is told that the price will be "the life of a man in Montreal", the man who killed the unlucky agent, Wormwood. Then it transpires that there is a second man to be killed, but nobody is sure who he is. Ultimately Hemlock goes to Switzerland, joins the party making a perilous assault on the north face of the Eiger and plans his assassination exercise. One of his three companions is to be his victim, but when the climb starts Hemlock still doesn't know who. To make sure, he decides to kill all three.

There is perhaps as much sex as espionage in Trevanian's novels, but even this is brilliantly economical, refreshingly unlaboured and full of the most delicious humour. One of the best scenes is the seduction of an agent named Ms Felicity Arce (pronounced Arse) by Hemlock. This takes place while Ms Arce is briefing Hemlock on his next assignment; the briefing is beautifully punctuated by her endearing asides, spontaneous verbal reactions to Hemlock's love-making technique and grunts which indicate more or less each stage of intercourse.

Trevanian also has a great gift for choosing apt names for his characters. Apart from Ms Arce, Wormwood and Hemlock, there are Dragon, the CII executive, George Hotfoot (a woman), Randie Nickers (another woman) and Anna Bidet, not to mention some really splendid titles for organisations and safe houses within the various intelligence networks.

The Loo Sanction refers to a section of British Intelligence called the Loo Organisation which "provides protection for MI5 and MI6 operatives by the technique of counter-assassination". It is called Loo because its headquarters are in a room which was formerly a lavatory and washroom. Hemlock, who appears again, is sent by the American Search and Sanction Division (a section which hires and employs professional killers) to liaise with the Loo in England.

The Loo sometimes, in order to protect its own killer agents, pretends to bump them off, discreetly arranging for someone's corpse to be left behind as evidence while the agents go into hiding or change their identities. Thus, Loo is frequently in need of fresh corpses and, for obtaining these and making them suitable, its executives have established a "Feeding Station" in the English countryside. Hemlock inquires why this most "un-safe house" has been given this title. The answer is that on this farm the prospective corpses are specially fed: " ...the Ruskies pump the stomach of a corpse and check its contents. It wouldn't do for a supposed Greek to produce the remnants of a steak and kidney pie."

The Search and Sanction Division of Trevanian's fictional CII is another example of those spy novels that assume that an intelligence organisation does arrange assassinations as part of their ordinary functions.

Trevanian's espionage jargon is an absolute delight to addicts of this kind of thing. Some of it is extremely witty invention, the rest shows an insight into the strange language of real-life spooks.

Film

The Eiger Sanction. Universal, US, 1975.

ELLESTON TREVOR

Pseudonyms: MANSELL BLACK, TREVOR BURGESS, ROGER FITZALAN, ADAM HALL, SIMON RATTRAY, WARWICK SCOTT, CAESAR SMITH
British. Born in Bromley, Kent, 17 February 1920.

Titles

[Major character: Quiller]
The Berlin Memorandum. London, Collins, 1965; as *The Quiller Memorandum*. New York, Simon & Schuster, 1965.
The 9th Directive. London, Heinemann, 1966; New York, Simon & Schuster, 1966.
The Striker Portfolio. London, Heinemann, 1969; New York, Simon & Schuster, 1969
The Warsaw Document. London, Heinemann, 1970; New York, Doubleday, 1970.
The Tango Briefing. London, Collins, 1973; New York, Doubleday, 1973.
The Mandarin Cypher. London, Collins, 1975; New York, Doubleday, 1975.
The Kobra Manifesto. London, Collins, 1976; New York, Doubleday, 1976.
The Sinkiang Executive. London, Collins, 1978; New York, Doubleday, 1978.
The Scorpion Signal. London, Collins, 1979; New York, Doubleday, 1980.
The Sibling. New York, Playboy Press, 1979; London, New English Library, 1980.
Pekin Target. London, Collins, 1981; as *The Peking Target*. New York, Playboy Press, 1982.
The Volcanoes of San Domingo. London, Inner Circle Books, 1984.
Quiller's Run. London, WH Allen, 1988.
Quiller KGB. London, WH Allen, 1989.

Biography

Elleston Trevor's name was originally Trevor Dudley-Smith. He was educated at Yardley Court Preparatory School and at Sevenoaks Public School. He was an apprentice racing-driver for two years before the Second World War. During the war he served in the Royal Air Force as a Flight Engineer. He has been a full-time writer since 1946.

Critical Analysis

His best-known and the first of his spy novels was *The Berlin Memorandum* (better known under its American title: *The Quiller Memorandum*), which was awarded an Edgar by the Mystery Writers of America and the French Grand Prix de Littérature Policière. This book began a series of novels featuring Quiller, and all were written under the name of Adam Hall. Quiller is a British "shadow executive", employed by "the Bureau", a government agency assigned to carry out delicate tasks, and it is so secret it does not exist.

As we follow Quiller's "brain-think" sequences we learn that during the Second World War he was an infiltrator who arranged escapes from Nazi concentration camps. Quiller and others like him with specialised skills, do the jobs that MI5 and MI6 cannot do. Quiller is used only at the authorisation of the Prime Minister. In *The Quiller Memorandum* he exposes a large, well-organised neo-Nazi conspiracy in Berlin. Anthony Boucher, reviewing it in the *New York Times Book Review* said: "This is a grand exercise in ambivalence and intricacy, tense and suspenseful at every moment, with fascinatingly complex characters, unusual plausibility in detailing the professional mechanics of espionage, and a genuine uncompromising tough-mindedness comparable to le Carré's."

This novel was followed by *The 9th Directive* with Quiller in Bangkok, and *The Striker Portfolio*, which is again set in Germany. There have been fourteen stories to date, and Quiller has remained consistent in his behaviour, narrating his actions in a cool detached voice. Trevor's Quiller has remained popular perhaps because of this consistency. These novels continue to be reprinted and have been translated into 18 languages.

In his latest adventure, *Quiller KGB*, Quiller is back in Berlin, this time in the East to be briefed on a new mission by Colonel Yasolev of the KGB. Gorbachev's policy of *glasnost* has made him many enemies, but also unlikely allies. Quiller must work with Yasolev to prevent an attempt on Gorbachev's life.

Film

The Quiller Memorandum. Twentieth Century Fox, 1966.

WARREN STANLEY TUTE

British. Born in West Hartlepool, Co. Durham, 22 February 1914.

Titles

[Major character: George Mado]
A Matter of Diplomacy. London, Dent, 1970; New York, Coward McCann, 1970.
The Powder Train [Mado]. London, Dent, 1972.
The Tarnham Connection [Mado]. London, Dent, 1973.
The Resident [Mado]. London, Constable, 1974.
Next Saturday in Milan [Mado]. London, Constable, 1975.
The Cairo Sleeper [Mado]. London, Constable, 1976.

Biography

Warren Tute was educated at the Dragon School, Oxford and Wrekin College, Shropshire. He served in the Royal Navy, 1932–46, and retired as a Lieutenant Commander. After the war he was contracted to Ted Kavanagh Associates for radio work, 1946–47. He then worked as a Director for Random Film Productions from 1947 to 1952. This was followed by a contract with the US government to make Marshall Plan films in Greece, 1952–54. He worked freelance from 1954 to 1960.

After this he became a Director for Theatrework (London) Ltd. and Kenway Theatre Productions from 1960 to 1968. He was the Archivist and Historian to the Worshipful Company of Cordwainers in London, 1974–83, and a consultant to Capital Radio, London, 1976–84; and now he is a Trustee for the Venture Trust.

Critical Analysis

Tute says that he started writing spy fiction as "a relief from writing naval fiction and general non-fiction books", and he says "I have been a jack of all trades working in the theatre, films, radio and TV. I learned very early on to see how socialist and communist influences infiltrated the media as did a trip as a Literary Agent to Poland, Romania, Bulgaria, Hungary, Czechoslovakia which opened further my already open eyes."

The hero of all Tute's spy fiction, except for *A Matter of Diplomacy*, is George Mado, an ex-spy, who used to work for the security services. His cover was blown by Philby when he defected, but Mado still works for the service, doing odd jobs for them all over the world.

Tute's varied career and his extensive travels have given him plenty of material for his spy novels. In the first of his novels, *The Powder Train*, which introduces Mado, the hero is sent behind the Iron Curtain to stir up student unrest and cause trouble for the Kremlin. One reviewer described the book as a "thoroughly satisfying example of the post-le Carré espionage story, peopled with realistically unpleasant characters, and infused with a sardonic sense of humour."

In his last adventure, *The Cairo Sleeper*, Mado is sent to Beirut to watch out for the interests of an Anglicised Greek millionaire. He soon finds himself involved with the KGB and a long-serving British traitor, with whom he has a score to settle. Meanwhile there is a Russian plot to overthrow the Egyptian President.

Lord Chalfont said of this novel "In his seemingly indestructible 'blown' spy, George Mado, Warren Tute has caught the authentic flavour of the sleazy, disorganised world of intelligence. Although his story has a fair ration of Scotch, karate and luscious women, it has none of the specious glamour of the 'secret agent' genre. Mado's progress through the vividly realised streets and hotels of Cairo is nasty and brutish and the lives of those who get in his way usually short. Although none of it is meant to be taken *too* seriously, it is much closer to the real trade of the spy than all that poppycock about Gucci shoes and very dry Martinis, shaken not stirred."

Leon Uris

American. Born in Baltimore, Maryland, 3 August 1924.

Titles

The Angry Hills. New York, Random House, 1955.
Topaz. New York, McGraw Hill, 1967.

Biography

Leon Uris was the son of a Polish immigrant, who ran away from home at the age of seventeen to join the US Marine Corps in the Second World War where he served in the South Pacific. After the war he joined the *San Francisco Bulletin* as a district manager for the home delivery of newspapers. His first book, *Battle Cry* (1953), was about life in the Marines.

Critical Analysis

It was with *Topaz*, a novel about a Soviet espionage network inside French government circles, that Uris made a sensational impact in more ways than one. This book seemed to be an ultra-realistic spy story, telling how the head of the KGB's anti-NATO bureau defected to the Americans and revealed the existence in Paris of a Soviet spy ring code-named Topaz, of which the two key members were a senior French official and a close adviser — code-name Columbine — of the French President.

Le *Canard Enchaîné*, the satirical French weekly, suggested in its columns that Columbine was an accurate portrait of one of de Gaulle's most trusted intelligence advisers. Shrewd observers of the intelligence game paid rather more attention to *Le Canard*'s allegations than did the general public. They noted that the various spy rings organised by the Russians against NATO were known to use the names of jewels for their code-names. The ring organised against the French was actually not known as Topaz, but as Sapphire. Then it was realised that Philippe Thyraud de Vosjoli, formerly head of French Intelligence in Washington, had been a friend of Uris, and in 1968 de Vosjoli, who had been chief liaison officer between the French Secret Service and the CIA, made some astounding allegations which were highly damaging to French prestige.

Nevertheless, although *Topaz* was undoubtedly based on certain elements of truth, it was a work of fiction in that truth had been gilded out of all recognition except to those in the intelligence game.

When ordered back to Paris, de Vosjoli refused to go and resigned from the Service, claiming that the French Intelligence organisation had been infiltrated by the KGB. This resulted in an investigation which exposed a spy in Georges Paques, a French press attaché with NATO, who was arrested and sentenced to imprisonment for spying.

This is one of the most extraordinary examples in modern times of a novel having such far-reaching effects on trans-Atlantic politics — and it all started from a mischievous, if amusing review in *Le Canard Enchaîné*.

Kurt Vonnegut, Jr.

American. Born in Indianopolis, Indiana, 11 November 1922.

Titles

Mother Night. New York, Fawcett, 1962.

Biography

Kurt Vonnegut went to Cornell University and studied chemistry for three years. In the Second World War, he says: "I was the battalion scout and so I was very easily taken prisoner in Germany." As a result of this Vonnegut endured the terrible ordeal of being "a prisoner in a meat locker under a slaughter-house during the Dresden air raid." When it was over he worked as a "miner of corpses".

After the war he went to Chicago University to study anthropology. Then came the diverse jobs of police reporter on the *Chicago City News* Bureau and work in the research laboratory of the General Electric Company. His first novel, *Player Piano* (1952), was, in fact, a sly dig at GEC.

Critical Analysis

Vonnegut's first spy novel was *Mother Night*, and centres on an American spy in wartime Germany who manages to survive because he plays the role of a Nazi so convincingly and makes such virulent and vile anti-Semitic broadcasts. There is no doubt that Vonnegut has a message in this book and, though the theme would be not unfamiliar to le Carré, Vonnegut turns it into a novel of ideas as well as of spies. His theme is that "we are what we pretend to be, so we must be careful about what we pretend to be." Underlying this thought-provoking message is some judicious satire handed out impartially and directed towards Nazis, right-wing Americans, Jews, Negroes and the American left-wingers.

WALTER HERMAN WAGER

Pseudonym: JOHN TIGER
American. Born in New York City, 4 September 1924.

Titles

[Major characters: Captain Garrison, Merlin]
Death Hits the Jackpot. New York, Macmillan, 1954.
Sledgehammer. New York, Macmillan, 1970.
Viper Three. New York, Macmillan, 1971.
The Swap [Garrison]. New York, Macmillan, 1972.
Telefon. New York, Macmillan, 1976.
Time of Reckoning [Merlin]. New York, Arbor House, 1977.
Blue Leader. New York, Arbor House, 1978.
Blue Murder. New York, Arbor House, 1981.

Novels as John Tiger

I Spy . New York, Popular Library, 1965.
I Spy: Masterstroke. New York, Popular Library, 1966.
I Spy: Countertrap. New York, Popular Library, 1967.

I Spy: Doomdate. New York, Popular Library, 1967.
Mission Impossible. New York, Popular Library, 1967.
I Spy: Death-Twist. New York, Popular Library, 1968.
Mission Impossible: Code Name, Little Ivan. New York, Popular Library, 1969.

Biography

Educated at Columbia, Harvard and Northwestern universities, Walter Wager obtained both Law and Arts degrees. He has had a varied career calling for great versatility of talent. After being an editorial research director of Aeroutes Inc., New York, he was awarded a Fulbright Fellowship in 1947 and went to the University of Paris.

This was followed by a spell as diplomatic adviser to the department of Civil Aviation in Tel Aviv (1951–52). He then worked in the United Nations Secretariat, as a writer for TV documentary films for NBC in New York, as editor of *Playbill*, 1963–66, and in a wide range of other jobs, including at least one in a New York State investigation.

Critical Analysis

His earliest book was a spy story, *Death Hits the Jackpot*, which was about dollars stolen from an OSS courier killed in Madrid in 1944 showing up at a Chicago gambling club in 1953, and the efforts of the CIA to solve the mystery. This was followed by *Operation Intrigue* (1958), *OSS: A Short History* (1963) [non-fiction] and *I Spy*.

Sledgehammer was the story of four ex-OSS men who learn of the death of an old comrade and, determined to avenge him, use the skills they acquired during the war to undermine the rule of a gang boss in a small American gambling town — not quite a spy tale, but not entirely unassociated with it. Wager seems to have a nostalgia for the OSS.

Telefon was a more orthodox novel of this genre, telling how Russian "sleepers", and others acting as undercover agents on the quiet, are planted near key installations in America, waiting for the signal to destroy them. Wager then develops a most skilful and ingeniously constructed plot which provides an entertaining glimpse at life in the CIA. The top Soviet agent takes off with a book of triggering signals and sets the destroyers off one by one. By doing this he hopes that the Americans will retaliate and attack Russia. His efforts to set off World War III bring out the spy-catchers from all sides, like maggots out of cheese: the ensuing three-cornered chase is tersely and competently narrated.

Wager has two favourite characters — Captain Garrison in SWAP, a tough Green Beret, and a very glib and violent CIA man code-named Merlin. The latter is very worldly, wise-cracking and so professional that his real name never emerges. One of the themes that recurs in Wager's spy stories is how headquarters Intelligence bureaucrats meddle and resist field agents. To put it in his own words, he tries to demonstrate "how stuffy and nervous the desk commandos are." And, adds Wager, "I often try to show that The Other Side has some decent people, too."

In the 1960s Wager wrote several screenplays for the popular American TV series "I Spy", which starred Robert Culp and Bill Cosby; these screenplays were novelised. He also wrote screenplays for another well-known TV series "Mission Impossible", which were also published as novels.

Films

Telefon. MGM, US, 1977.
Viper Three was filmed as *The Twilight's Last Gleaming*: produced by Lorimar and released in 1977.

EDWARD RONALD WEISMILLER

American. Born in Monticello, Wisconsin, 3 August 1915.

Titles

The Serpent Sleeping . New York, Putnam, 1962.

Biography

Educated at Swarthmore College, Cornell College and Oxford University, where he was a Rhodes Scholar at Merton College from 1938 to 1939, Edward Weismiller then went to Harvard University where he was a postgraduate student until 1943. He soon gained a reputation as a poet of distinction, his first work including such poems as "Deep Woods in Winter" and "Frog" which were published in *The Deer Come Down* Yale Series of Younger Poets (1936).

From 1943 until the end of the war he served in the US Marine Corps, receiving the Bronze Star and the Médaille de la Reconnaissance Française. "At that time," he says, "things moved very rapidly. I was picked up by a secret intelligence organisation and trained in secret camps outside Washington ... by 3 December I was in London beginning another intensive period of training at the hands of British Secret Intelligence ... The Commandant of the Marine Corps is said to have snapped that 'this is the first time I have ever been asked to commission a god-damned poet in the Marine Corps.' To demonstrate to my superiors such skills as I had acquired I had been set loose in a vast industrial city with instructions to spend two days getting as much specific information as I could that would be of use to the enemy. I was, it might be argued, testing the city's security. I pretended to be a freelance writer, down from New England, his identifying papers in his other suit, intent on collecting material for an article on the magnificent things being done by industry on behalf of the war effort ... The information I managed to pick up still makes me shudder when I think of it. I got with ease into numbers of top-secret places; I got photographs, I got figures; I learned 'off the record' things which in the hands of the enemy could have been used in a matter of hours to set back our war effort for months."

Critical Analysis

Weismiller's one and only spy novel, *The Serpent Sleeping*, is nevertheless one of the most important of the genre and, indeed, should be compulsory reading for anyone making a study of this type of fiction. Norman Holmes Pearson has said of this book that it "is one of the few accounts of the handling and psychology of a turned agent, in this case after the invasion of France, when German agents attempted to operate behind the American lines." Weismiller himself describes it as "a novel of counter-espionage," adding that "all the characters in *The Serpent Sleeping*, French and American, young and old, good and evil, are, I suppose, among my selves. In John Peale Bishop's magnificent poem "Ode", occur the lines, 'I have been as many men, as many ghosts / As there were days', and I have tried to show some of the ghosts."

This may seem somewhat arcane to the uninitiated, but to understand what Weismiller is trying to say it is necessary to study his wartime activities and experiences. In July 1944 he was sent to Cherbourg and in France had to become involved with a Nazi agent, the object being to use him in what came to be cynically called the Double-Cross System. Weismiller explains that the agent in question was used "against the Nazis as though he were working freely, as though he were not under our control. Of course we had to give the Nazis information; of course, though our ultimate purpose was deception, some of the information we sent had to be verifiably true, and this meant that we had to betray our own forces, a little, in the interest of the greater good. Fortunately it was someone at Supreme Headquarters, not I, who had to decide how much betrayal, of whom, was acceptable on any given day. But in order to build up my double-agent so that ultimately he would be able to deceive and damage the enemy as much as possible, I had of course to press constantly to give away as much good information about our own troops as could be thought, in balance, not too unsafe ... In the end we caught most of the spies the Germans had trained and left behind to work for them in France. Many of these I interrogated, or came to know in other ways. One of them all was, I think, an evil person; a few of them were morally empty, had become, somehow, human trash. Most of them were decent men and women — not strong, not heroic, but basically decent — whom the German Intelligence Service had manoeuvred into impossible situations, had subjected to impossible pressures."

This was the background to *The Serpent Sleeping*, a book which germinated gradually over the years in Weismiller's mind. It all started partly out of a story called *The Green Place*, which he began to write. Then, having read Rebecca West's *The Meaning of Treason*, he turned his attention to *The Serpent Sleeping* in which he introduced the same boy and girl, but in different situations.

Morris Langlo West

Pseudonyms: **Michael East, Julian Morris**
Australian. Born in Melbourne, Australia, 26 April 1916.

Titles

The Shoes of the Fisherman. New York, William Morrow, 1963.
The Tower of Babel. New York, William Morrow, 1968.
The Salamander. New York, William Morrow, 1973.
Harlequin. New York, William Morrow, 1974.

Biography

Morris West studied with the Christian Brothers Order from 1933, but he left in 1939 before taking his final vows. He was educated at the University of Melbourne where he received a BA in 1937. He was a teacher of modern languages and mathematics in New South Wales, Australia, and Tasmania from 1933 to 1939. He was secretary to William Morris Hughes, the former prime minister of Australia in 1943, and became the managing director of Australasian Radio Productions from 1943 to 1953. He has worked as a film and dramatic writer for Shell Co. and the Australian Broadcasting Network since 1954, as well as being a writer and a commentator.

Critical Analysis

In *The Shoes of the Fisherman*, a humble Ukrainian pope finds himself the central negotiator in an attempt to prevent the United States and the Soviet Union from starting World War III. During the negotiations, the pope must confront the Russian who once tortured him. The work, a popular and critical success, demonstrates West's concern with modern man's inability to communicate with his brother. "We're not using the same words. We don't understand each other. We are not selecting, we aren't balancing ... simply because life is too risky, too tormenting ... I've been trying, therefore to use what is a very old manner of story telling. To make this conflict of legitimate points of view *clear*, through the medium of the novel," West said in an interview.

"In *The Shoes of the Fisherman*, the idea of the central character was a man who believed that he was — publicly claimed to be — the Vicar of Christ," West continued. "Now, theoretically, this is the man who must look at the world through the eye of God, and try to make some sense out of its complexity. He was therefore a natural character medium through which this hopeless attempt had to be made."

In *Harlequin* sophisticated computers programme humans to acts of assassination, kidnapping and revolution.

The Salamander is about an Italian Colonel, who trying to save his own life and find out who killed a general plotting against the government, has one clue—a card with a crowned salamander code-name signifying survival.

DENNIS YATES WHEATLEY

British. Born in London, 8 January 1897. Died 11 November 1977.

Titles

[Major characters: Roger Brook, Gregory Sallust]
Black August [Sallust]. London, Hutchinson, 1934; New York, Dutton, 1934.
Contraband [Sallust]. London, Hutchinson, 1936.
The Scarlet Imposter [Sallust]. London, Hutchinson, 1940; New York, Macmillan, 1942.
Faked Passports [Sallust]. London, Hutchinson, 1940; New York, Macmillan, 1943.
The Black Baroness [Sallust]. London, Hutchinson, 1940; New York, Macmillan, 1942.

"V" for Vengeance [Sallust]. London, Hutchinson, 1942; New York, Macmillan, 1942.
Come into My Parlour [Sallust]. London, Hutchinson, 1946.
The Launching of Roger Brook [Brook]. London, Hutchinson, 1947.
The Shadow of Tyburn Tree [Brook] ; London, Hutchinson, 1948 ; New York, Ballantine, 1973.
The Rising Storm [Brook]. London, Hutchinson, 1949.
The Man Who Killed the King [Brook]. London, Hutchinson, 1951; New York, Putnam, 1965.
The Island Where Time Stands Still [Sallust]. London, Hutchinson, 1954.
The Dark Secret of Josephine [Brook]. London, Hutchinson, 1955.
Traitors' Gate [Sallust]. London, Hutchinson, 1958.
The Rape of Venice [Brook]. London, Hutchinson, 1959.
The Sultan's Daughter [Brook]. London, Hutchinson, 1963.
They Used Dark Forces [Sallust]. London, Hutchinson, 1964.
The Wanton Princess [Brook]. London, Hutchinson, 1966.
The White Witch of the South Seas [Sallust]. London, Hutchinson, 1968.
Evil in a Mask [Brook]. London, Hutchinson, 1969.
The Ravishing of Lady Mary Ware [Brook]. London, Hutchinson, 1971.
The Irish Witch [Brook]. London, Hutchinson, 1973.
Desperate Measures [Brook]. London, Hutchinson, 1974.

Biography

Dennis Wheatley was educated at Dulwich, but modestly described his education as having been received at "HMS Worcester and Germany." He joined his father's wine business in 1914, but in September of that same year was commissioned in the RFA (T), City of London Brigade. He transferred to the 36th Ulster Division in 1917 and, after being gassed, was invalided from the Army in 1919, when he rejoined his father's firm. In 1926 he became the sole owner of this firm, which he sold in 1931 before settling down to writing.

His first book was *The Forbidden Territory* (1933), which was later filmed. This story was set in Soviet Russia and introduced three of Wheatley's most famous characters, Rex Van Rhyn, an American, Simon Aron, a Jewish financier and the Duc de Richelieu, a French aristocrat. Wheatley's early works included such diverse subjects as *Old Rowley* (1933), a "private life of Charles II", *The Eunuch of Stamboul* (1935) and *They Found Atlantis* (1936). Though a late starter in the writing game, Wheatley soon achieved a prolific output of books which mostly enjoyed enormous sales in several languages.

In 1939 he toured England as a member of Sir John Anderson's team of speakers on the subject of National Service. Then he was invited to join Churchill's secret underground fortress off Whitehall, the only civilian member of the Joint Planning Staff. Later he was re-commissioned as an officer in the RAFVR. He not only worked out his own projects, but provided some of the background details for two such successful intelligence coups as "The Man Who Never Was" and the creating of General Montgomery's "double" to put in an appearance at Gibraltar to fox the Germans. After the war Wheatley put together his wartime papers and published an account of his work in *Stranger than Fiction* (1959).

Critical Analysis

Wheatley turned his attention to spy fiction just before the war, introducing two recurring characters, Gregory Sallust and Roger Brook. The former was based on an Army friend of Wheatley's and first appeared as a lone wolf British Secret Service agent in *The Scarlet Imposter*, then in *Faked Passports*. Wheatley made the Sallust stories topical by dramatising the 1939–45 war up to the end of the Russo–Finnish campaign and then in *The Black Baroness* covered the period from the Norwegian campaign to the fall of France.

In the post-war period Wheatley created a highly popular new character, another British secret agent, and a series of spy stories set in the Napoleonic era. In this kind of a setting Wheatley was much more at home and totally uninhibited. His first book of this series was *The Launching of Roger Brook*.

Wheatley was one of the first spy story writers to introduce uninhibited sex as an underlying theme. He sustained a faithful readership over more than forty years, an undoubted tribute to his cynical humour and quick brain. He was said to be King George VI's favourite novelist.

ALAN WILLIAMS

British. Born in 1935.

Titles

The Tale of the Lazy Dog. New York, Simon & Schuster, 1971.
The Beria Papers. New York, Simon & Schuster, 1973.
Gentleman Traitor. New York, Harcourt, 1974.
Shah-Mak. New York, Coward McCann, 1976.
The Widow's War. New York, Rawson Wade, 1980.

Biography

Son of the actor and playwright Emlyn Williams, he was educated at Stowe, Grenoble and Heidelberg universities and King's College, Cambridge. While still a student at Cambridge, attending a world peace conference in Warsaw, Alan Williams helped to smuggle a Polish refugee out of the country. He also witnessed the Hungarian Revolt of 1956 and, among other adventures, had to masquerade his way into and out of East Germany. Williams is no stranger to the intelligence game; he worked for a period for Radio Free Europe, the anti-Communist radio station at Munich which had close links with American Counter-Intelligence, and which was eventually infiltrated by and unmasked by Soviet Intelligence through a Polish agent, Captain Andrzej Czechowicz in 1971.

Later Williams entered journalism in Britain, working for the *Western Mail* and then the *Daily Express*. He covered the wars in Algeria and Vietnam, as well as the revolt in Czechoslovakia and the civil war in Ulster. Some measure of his diligence and objectivity as a war correspondent may be gleaned from the fact that, when in Algeria, both the Algerian and French forces complained about him and suspected he was a spy!

Critical Analysis

Williams, who is still a freelance journalist, has been praised for his spy novels, all of which are topical, relevant to today's problems and have strong, factual backgrounds. *The Tale of the Lazy Dog* was a para-military thriller set in Laos,

Cambodia and Vietnam and about a roving Irish journalist who learns of an American shipment of a billion and a half used dollars out of Saigon.

It was *The Beria Papers* which first attracted the attention of a wider readership. This book postulated the discovery of a diary belonging to Lavrenti Beria, former head of the Soviet secret police from 1938 until his execution in 1953.

The diaries told of Beria's seductions, intrigues and rapes and, in concocting this item of fiction, Williams certainly kept close to the truth, for after Beria's death a great deal of evidence of his sinister habits was provided by those who had previously been too frightened to talk. Alan Williams's book describes how an American publisher was worried about the authenticity of the Beria Papers, and indeed it transpires that the papers are fake, their authors an unsuccessful English novelist, Mallory, and Boris, a temperamental fat Russian exile who works in Munich for Radio Free Europe.

More unusual and intriguing was Williams's *Gentleman Traitor*, which had for its hero none other than Kim Philby. This imaginative twist to a spy thriller was based, says Alan Williams, on a friend's interview in Moscow with a drunken but still cunning Philby who said he was "fed up with Russia and wanted to leave." In the novel he did just this and, bored, drunken and embittered in Moscow, agreed to accept a seedy job in Rhodesia for British Intelligence (still apparently riddled with old traitor chums of his willing to lend a helping hand). So he escaped from Russia and appeared again on behalf of the SIS on a special mission to Rhodesia, having "lost" his identity as part of the bargain. Philby himself was vividly portrayed in this exciting and highly intelligent story. In the end he died of a heart attack when on the point of letting all sorts of inconvenient information out of the bag.

One of the most important lessons of Alan Williams's ultra-realistic spy novels is that they are not just mere entertainment, nor are they, like some of this genre, mischievous realism. Each book takes a slice of history and builds around it with real and fictional people a credible story that really could have happened. It is the making of the incredible credible that is Alan Williams's great talent as a spy story-teller.

GEORGE VALENTINE WILLIAMS

Pseudonym: DOUGLAS VALENTINE
British. Born 20 October 1883. Died 20 November 1946.

Titles
[Major character: Dr Adolph Grundt (Clubfoot)]

Novels as Douglas Valentine
The Man with the Club Foot. London, Jenkins, 1918; New York, McBride, 1918.
The Secret Hand: Some Further Adventures by Desmond Okewood of the British Secret Service. London, Jenkins, 1918; as *Okewood of the Secret Service.* New York, McBride, 1919.

Novels as Valentine Williams
The Return of Clubfoot. London, Jenkins, 1922; as *Island Gold.* Boston, Houghton Mifflin, 1923.

Clubfoot the Avenger. London, Jenkins, 1924; Boston, Houghton Mifflin, 1924.

The Three of Clubs. London, Hodder & Stoughton, 1924; Boston, Houghton Mifflin, 1924.

The Red Mass. London, Hodder & Stoughton, 1925; Boston, Houghton Mifflin, 1925.

Mr Ramosi. London, Hodder & Stoughton, 1926; Boston, Houghton Mifflin, 1926.

The Crouching Beast. London, Hodder & Stoughton, 1928; Boston, Houghton Mifflin, 1928.

The Gold Comfit Box. London, Hodder & Stoughton, 1932; as *The Mystery of the Gold Box*. Boston, Houghton Mifflin, 1932.

The Spider's Torch. London, Hodder & Stoughton, 1936; Boston, Houghton Mifflin, 1936.

The Fox Prowls. London, Hodder & Stoughton, 1939; Boston, Houghton Mifflin, 1939.

Courier to Marrakesh. London, Hodder & Stoughton, 1944; Boston, Houghton Mifflin, 1946.

Biography

Valentine Williams was educated at Downside School and privately in Germany. He joined Reuters as a sub-editor at the age of nineteen and in 1904 became Reuters' correspondent in Berlin. It was in this period that he gathered much of the material that was later to form the basis of so many of his spy stories. In 1909 he resigned to become Paris correspondent of the *Daily Mail*, a post he held for four years before covering the Balkans as a war correspondent.

In 1915 he was appointed as the first accredited correspondent at British GHQ in France and later in the year was commissioned in the Irish Guards. He was wounded twice and won the MC. He represented the *Daily Mail* at the Versailles Peace Conference and was afterwards made Foreign Editor of that paper.

During the Second World War Williams was engaged in confidential work for the British Government in Britain and America. Eventually he was included in the ranks of the PWE (Political Warfare Executive) at their "black propaganda" sanctum at Woburn Abbey.

Critical Analysis

His first novel, *The Man with the Club Foot*, introduced his German Secret Service character and was an instant success. These were followed by many more in the series.

Some of his later spy stories he based on the subterranean intrigues which in the 1920s fermented beneath the ruins of European ex-monarchies. A secret society known as "the Three of Clubs", for example, intends to proclaim the Archduchess Valerie as Queen of Hungary. In *The Crouching Beast* Clubfoot was again brought back, this time into the period of that summer of 1914 immediately preceding the war.

A new spymaster was introduced in *The Fox Prowls*, in which Don Boulton, of the British Intelligence, is detailed to pick up the trail of Alexis de Bahl, known in Rumania as "The Fox".

EDWARD HENRY WILLIS

British. Born in Tottenham, Middlesex, 13 January 1918.

Titles

The Left-Handed Sleeper. London, Macmillan, 1975; New York, Putnam, 1976.

Biography

Ted Willis was educated at Tottenham Central School, which he left at the age of fifteen, and became in turn an office boy, delivery boy and baker's roundsman. Later, while unemployed, he tramped the country working on farms and doing other casual labour. During the Second World War he served in the Royal Fusiliers, achieving the rank of Lance-Corporal. Subsequently he paved the way to success as a scriptwriter for films and television by working as a writer of War Office films and documentaries.

His most notable and long-lived success in the sphere of television films was undoubtedly that of the "Dixon of Dock Green" series. Eight of his plays have been produced in the West End of London and many of his films have won him international fame. A stalwart supporter of the Labour Party, he was created a life peer in 1963 as Lord Willis of Chislehurst.

Critical Analysis

His only spy novel is *The Left-Handed Sleeper* which the author describes as "an attempt to write a spy thriller from the point of view of the woman involved. I first got the idea when I read that Philby had gone out to dinner in Beirut one evening with his wife and en route to the restaurant he stopped the car and made a telephone call. Later that evening he disappeared and, of course, he turned up in Moscow a week or so later ... I then began to imagine what it would be like for a fairly ordinary woman to wake up one morning to find that the man she had been living with had, in fact, been leading a double life — that part of his life was completely hidden from her.

"From this I evolved the idea of a rising young MP who is caught up by the KGB and who eventually defects. However, instead of going to Moscow he goes to a neutral country where he is pursued both by the KGB and British Intelligence. His wife persistently refuses to believe that he is a spy and she follows the trail until she meets up with him. It is only then that he confesses."

DIANA WINSOR

British. Born in Belfast, Northern Ireland, 10 April 1946.

Titles

[Major character: Octavia (Tavy) Martin]
Red on Wight. London, Macmillan, 1972.
The Death Convention. London, Macmillan, 1974.

Biography

Diana Winsor went to school in Hong Kong, Bath and Dunfermline before moving to Portsmouth with her Service family. She published her first story at the age of fifteen and a year later she wrote her first novel. Success in writers' competitions in the *Sunday Times* and *Daily Telegraph* encouraged her to try to write seriously.

At nineteen she joined the *Times Educational Supplement* and after two years in London spent a year on Bath local newspapers and then worked in a magistrates' court and ran a company magazine for IBM.

Critical Analysis

Her father was working in the Navy Department at Bath when Diana's first novel was published, *Red on Wight*, about espionage in the Royal Navy. "I wrote it when my father was with the Admiralty in the weapons department in Portsmouth and I got a lot of information from him. But he's not worried. He is a very untypical civil servant and he does not have access to top secret information. Anyway, I had the book unofficially vetted to make sure I wasn't giving anything away."

Red on Wight was about a KGB plot to immobilise the NATO fleet when the Russians invade Africa. But it is an attractive heroine, Tavy Martin, who comes to the rescue of the Royal Navy when ships at Portsmouth start blowing up in mysterious fashion.

Diana Winsor's new approach to spy fiction suggests that much else that is good is still to come from her pen.*The Death Convention* again brought forward the heroine Tavy Martin for further adventures. Maurice Richardson in the *Observer* described the book as "ultrareadable". It told the story of how Tavy, the girl from the MOD, went to Amsterdam to keep an eye on a convention of conservationists. The chief attraction was a defecting Soviet physicist who appeared to know rather more than was good for him or anybody else.

Paul Winterton

Pseudonyms: **Andrew Garve, Roger Bax, Paul Somers**
British. Born in Leicester, 12 February 1908.

Titles

No Tears for Hilda. London, Collins, 1950; New York, Harper, 1950.
No Mask for Murder. London, Collins, 1950; as *Fontego's Folly*. NewYork, Harper, 1950.
Murder in Moscow. London, Collins, 1951.
A Press of Suspects. London, Collins, 1951; as *By-Line for Murder*. New York, Harper, 1951.
A Hole in the Ground. London, Collins, 1952; New York, Harper, 1952.
The Cuckoo Line Affair. London, Collins, 1953; New York, Harper, 1953.
Death and the Sky Above. London, Collins, 1953; New York, Harper, 1954.
The Riddle of Samson. London, Collins, 1954; New York, Harper, 1955.
The End of the Track. London, Collins, 1956; New York, Harper, 1956.

The Megstone Plot. London, Collins, 1956; New York, Harper, 1957.
The Narrow Search. London, Collins, 1957; New York, Harper, 1958.
The Galloway Case. London, Collins, 1958; New York, Harper, 1958.
A Hero for Leanda. London, Collins, 1959; New York, Harper, 1959.
The Far Sands. New York, Harper, 1960; London, Collins, 1961.
The Golden Deed. London, Collins, 1960; New York, Harper, 1960.
The House of Soldiers. New York, Harper, 1961; London, Collins, 1962.
Prisoner's Friend. London, Collins, 1962; New York, Harper, 1962.
The Sea Monks. London, Collins, 1963; New York, Harper, 1963.
Frame-Up. London, Collins, 1964; New York, Harper, 1964.
The Ashes of Loda. London, Collins, 1965; New York, Harper, 1965.
Murderer's Fen. London, Collins, 1966; as *Hide and Go Seek*. New York, Harper, 1966.
A Very Quiet Place. London, Collins, 1967; New York, Harper, 1967.
The Long Short Cut. London, Collins, 1968; New York, Harper, 1968.
The Ascent of D-13. London, Collins, 1969; New York, Harper, 1969.
Boomerang. London, Collins, 1969; New York, Harper, 1970.
The Late Bill Smith. London, Collins, 1971; New York, Harper, 1971.
The Case of Robert Quarry. London, Collins, 1972; New York, Harper, 1972.
The File on Lester. London, Collins, 1974; as *The Lester Affair*. New York, Harper, 1974.
Home to Roost. London, Collins, 1976; New York, Crowell, 1976.
Counterstroke. London, Collins, 1978; New York, Crowell, 1978.

Biography

Paul Winterton was educated at the London School of Economics, from where he received a BSc in 1928. He was a staff member at the London *Economist* from 1929 to 1933. He worked as a reporter, a Leader writer and a Foreign correspondent for the London *News Chronicle*, 1933–46, during which time he spent three years in Moscow. He was a Founding Member and first joint secretary of the Crime Writers' Association in 1953.

Critical Analysis

Paul Winterton uses the pseudonym of Andrew Garve for most of his suspense/adventure novels. He is very prolific writer and has written over forty books altogether, which cover a variety of characters and stories. The settings of his books also vary from English villages to Australia and the Gulf of Finland. Not all the books listed above are spy fiction — they include stories of adventure, romance, detective and mystery as well, and sometimes a combination.

Winterton's experience as a Foreign correspondent in Moscow during the Second World War inspired several of his books, such as *Murder in Moscow*, *The Ashes of Loda*, *The Ascent of D-13* and *The Late Bill Smith*. As one critic remarked: "His knowledge of the Russians and the Soviet government lends these tales an unusual authenticity."

DAVID WISE

American. Born In New York City, 10 May 1930.

Titles

Spectrum. New York, Viking, 1981.
The Children's Game. New York, St. Martin's Press, 1983.

Biography

David Wise was educated at Columbia College from where he graduated in 1951. He worked for the *New York Herald Tribune* , 1951–66, starting as a reporter in New York City. He became the White House correspondent in Washington DC, rising to become bureau chief in the Capitol. He was a fellow of the Woodrow Wilson International Center for Scholars in Washington, 1970–71, and worked as a lecturer in political science at the University of California, Santa Barbara from 1977 to 1979.

Critical Analysis

Wise is better known for his non-fiction works about American politics and the intelligence establishment. He came to the attention of the public with the publication of his book *The Invisible Government*, written with Thomas B Ross, in 1964. He was one of the first reporters to investigate the so-called abuses of the CIA. After this Wise wrote another book about the CIA with Ross, *The Espionage Establishment* (1967). He continued to write books on this subject on his own and to contribute articles to national magazines.

In *Spectrum*, the story is about CIA Director Towny Black's efforts to cover up a 1965 theft of uranium which will further damage the reputation of "the Company", and thwart three separate investigations.

In *The Children's Game*, Bill Danner, who has left the agency in disgust, is recalled to solve a long line of compromised operations, and he is brought in to find a suspected high-level penetration of the agency.

Joseph Hosey, a critic of spy fiction and an ex-employee of the CIA, said of this book and the author: "Wise has given us a gelatinous slab of tripe which has nothing to do with either the real CIA or the real world of espionage, but which portrays an agency that never was... The plot of this book is a manifest absurdity both in general outline and in detail. The characters are cardboard cutouts ...Their wooden behaviour demonstrates only the author's intention to perpetuate the most fatuous, popular misconceptions about intelligence activity and the people who conduct it."

PHILIP GORDON WYLIE

American. Born in Beverly, Massachusetts, 12 May 1902. Died 25 October 1971.

Titles

The Spy Who Spoke Porpoise. New York, Doubleday, 1969.

Biography

Philip Wylie was educated at Princeton University from 1920-23. He worked as a staff member of the *New Yorker*, 1925–2, and as the advertising manager of Cosmopolitan Book Corp. Wylie was a writer for Paramount Pictures and Metro-Goldwyn-Mayer for several years. For a while he worked for government war information agencies.

Critical Analysis

Philip Wylie was a prolific writer, including hundreds of short stories, serials, articles, syndicated newspaper columns, radio programmes and advertising copy, but only the book above can be classified as spy fiction.

The Spy Who Spoke Porpoise is an intriguing tale about R W Grove — a veteran intelligence officer, who becomes the private spy of a new president who does not trust the CIA, especially when he discovers that certain information is withheld from him.

In this case the CIA stands for the Combined Information Authority, and is concealed 26 storeys below the Federal Computer Building in Maryland. Eaper, the Director of the CIA, is afraid of Grove because of the secrets he might reveal. They had worked alongside each other during the war and shared many experiences as well as secrets. Eaper warns Grove: "It wasn't 1942 any more. Or '48. The business of information gathering had changed. Cloak and dagger stuff was now a minor factor. And where it had to be used, it was highly mechanized and technical, demanding young men, with the reflexes of youth and years of training behind them."

Grove proves the Director wrong: while apparently enjoying a quiet retirement in Hawaii he discovers a Russian plot — Project Neptune — to establish a secret Russian base for submarines. He uses his expertise to expose them.

This story has the familiar situation of the lone intelligence officer solving a problem on his own, working outside the bureaucratic morass of the organisation. However, it is a highly original story despite this old technique, and is an enjoyable read.

Chapter 1
A Brief History of American Spy Fiction: before and after 1945

The first spy novel was written by American author James Fenimore Cooper. However, this early success of *The Spy* (1821) did not herald a surge of spy fiction from American authors. Indeed, it is only recently that a good collection of spy novels has begun to emerge. Few of them are at present published in Britain.

There have been several recent publications on the subject of British spy fiction, but the American side has been neglected or ignored. And yet British spy novels are exported to America — authors such as le Carré and Deighton are just as well known in America as they are in Britain. The reasons for this neglect is due in part to various factors in American history — events that have contributed to the unpopularity of the spy as a national hero. These events have influenced the evolution of the American spy novel and dictated the timing as to when the spy became a popular hero in fiction.

There were very few American writers of spy fiction before the 1940s because the spy, it was believed, did not have the stuff that heroes are made of, and also because the political context of the spy novel held no interest in a nation that had cultivated its geographical and political isolation since the turn of the century. The examples of international intrigue which dominated the colonial empires of Britain and other European powers did not inspire the American republic to follow suit.

Although two distinguished American writers — James Fenimore Cooper and Edgar Allen Poe — had chosen the subject of the spy for some of their stories, the spy novel was not taken up again at a popular level until two world wars had changed social attitudes towards the spy and made him an acceptable hero for an adventure novel.

Eric Ambler in the introduction to his *To Catch a Spy* (1964), claimed that "it is impossible to find any spy story of note written before the twentieth century." He dismissed Cooper's story as unreadable and mainly concerned with conflicting loyalties during the American War of Independence. Contrary to this opinion, John Welcome, in his *Anthology of Best Spy Stories* (1967), commends this novel as "the real tap-root of the modern story of espionage". These conflicting views reflect the difficulties in assessing a spy story and defining its qualities.

Nevertheless, Cooper saw the spy in strictly military terms and the behaviour of his hero, Harvey Birch, was tolerated because he was in fact acting as a double-agent for George Washington. Cooper's book was an early example of the way in which a spy in war could be used as a fictional hero. Also it is the earliest example of the use of a double-agent in spy fiction.

Edgar Allen Poe wrote two stories, *The Gold Bug* (1843) and *The Purloined Letter* (1845), which could loosely be defined as spy stories. The first tale was inspired by Poe's interest in cryptography, and may have encouraged future practitioners of spy fiction. The second story contained many elements that make up the classic espionage story such as the search for a missing document containing government secrets, the ineptness of the police in this situation, and the necessary intervention of an intelligence expert.

Henry James was another author that ventured into this murky territory with his novel, *The Princess Casamassima* (1885). Ronald J Ambrosetti, a student of spy fiction, cited this book as another nineteenth-century prototype of the spy novel. Again this book is not what we would regard now as a classic spy story, but it is concerned with international intrigue and political assassination. Henry James blamed the novel as being partly responsible for his waning popularity in the late 1880s. In 1883, James wrote to his friend, William Dean Howells, that he feared that his own reputation had suffered because of his last two novels, *The Bostonians* and *The Princess Casamassima*. These early works reflected the limited appeal of espionage, as well as the threat to popular authors embarking upon this subject in their literature.

With the examples of Cooper, Poe and James, it is surprising that so few writers tried to imitate their spy stories in the nineteenth century. This was because of the attitude of the American people to espionage in general. The unpopularity of the spy in American history and its corresponding absence in fiction was due to various events in the late 1800s and early 1900s. There has been a long and close relationship between the spy and the detective in American history, particularly in the formation, or rather the destruction, of their labour unions. The labour spy was employed by many detective agencies in this period and they were responsible for a great deal of violence which resulted in virtually destroying any power that the labour unions had managed to attain.

The detective and his activities as a labour spy was so unpopular by the late 1870s that Allan Pinkerton, the founder of the Pinkerton Detective Agency, turned to fiction — writing stories showing the detective in an heroic light, to change his popular image as a bogeyman. The main function of these stories was propaganda, as they bore no relation to reality, but they succeeded as a number of writers imitated Pinkerton's idea and established the detective as an attractive representative of law and order, at a time when society felt a need for such a protector. Thus the detective became an acceptable hero, and one that has continued to flourish in American fiction ever since.

However, the spy, in particular his job as a labour spy, retained his rather tarnished image. He was still so unpopular in the late nineteenth century that many states were persuaded to act by the Knights of Labor, the Populists and the American Federation of Labor, to pass "anti-Pinkerton" laws, in the hope that this would curtail their activities. But this did not solve the problem, and by 1914 there were about 270 agencies supplying these labour spies to break up unions. The problem continued to grow as industrial espionage was one of the main topics investigated by the La Follette Civil Liberties Committee of the 1930s.

Another domestic influence which affected the American public's perception of espionage was the treatment of Intelligence by successive administrations in time of war.

Spies were used in the American War of Independence and the Civil War, but their adventures were not well publicised, and people did not become fully aware of the existence of espionage until 1898 and the Spanish –American War. At this time many innocent people were subjected to the patriotic zeal and undemocratic methods of the Secret Service men, which further undermined the image of the Intelligence professional.

When Intelligence came under the control of the State Department in 1915, espionage activities were given a low profile and most Americans were only dimly aware of its development and increased professionalism. This situation changed when America entered the First World War in 1917. Then the American public was suddenly confronted with the impressive exploits of their own secret agents, who succeeded in rounding up a large number of German and Austrian spies operating on American soil. This provided excellent propaganda and served to perpetuate the myth that espionage was employed only in times of war.

This myth of peacetime demobilisation of Intelligence was cultivated by succeeding administrations. Politicians were aware that spying was an occupation frowned upon by most Americans — it smacked of empire-building and European intrigues. These administrations made no effort to educate the public into believing that Intelligence was a necessity, unless the nation was at war. This policy also prevented public scrutiny of government espionage operations. It seems to be no coincidence that after both world wars the American government reverted to a policy of domestic surveillance and the persecution of radicals and communists, which erupted in the Red Scare of 1919– 20 and the era of McCarthyism in the 1950s.

Thus ambivalent attitudes have been held about the spy throughout American history. It was not until American citizens felt threatened, economically and politically, that people recognised the need for espionage in times of peace as well as war. The Second World War and the Cold War opened the way for the fictional spy to become a popular hero.

There were a few writers who made tentative inroads into the spy story; they included Frederick Faust, Francis Van Wyck Mason and John P Marquand. Tentative, because the heroes of these stories were usually amateurs (apart from Mason's Colonel North, who started as a detective and changed into a professional counter-intelligence agent), who became unwilling spies in an adventure which usually took place in Europe, where that kind of behaviour was more acceptable.

In Britain the spy was accepted sooner because she had grown to become a world power by building an empire that needed an Intelligence organisation in order to survive. Consequently the British people learnt to accept the existence of the spy, especially when he was seen as acting in the interests of patriotism. It was not until 1945 that America found herself in a similar position with responsibilities and obligations to protect weaker nations that a peacetime Intelligence organisation was even contemplated. This was eventually recognised with the formation of the Central Intelligence Agency in 1947. However, it was not until the 1960s that the spy fiction hero began to compete with the detective.

In the American post-war world of international tension there was scope for the spy and the counter-intelligence agent to become the new folk hero. The situation called for a superman, who could maintain the tenuous balance in a world overshadowed by the possibility of nuclear war. America did not produce a significant volume of its own indigenous spy novels until the 1960s. One reason for its resurgence at this period was the appearance of Ian Fleming's *Casino Royale* in 1953, which provided a new hero while inspiring a large number of American authors to imitate him. Bond seemed to possess all the attributes of a superhero, a character who was to dominate the spy novel in Britain and America for at least two decades.

Allan Dulles remarked in his *Anthology of Great Spy Stories* (1969): "World War II and the Cold War served to elevate the reputation of spying in the public mind and to make it socially acceptable because a more attractive and more highly motivated type of individual appeared to be engaged in it."

A number of books were written during and after the war about the exploits of the Office of Strategic Services (OSS), the forerunner of the CIA, and the adventures of its members. Some of these were in the guise of autobiography, but read more like fiction. Whatever their literary pretensions they had the same effect — glamorising the spy as a romantic hero. Although espionage was accepted by the end of the Second World War, the spy himself was not totally assimilated in a cultural context until the 1960s.

Spy fiction in this decade made an important contribution in making the occupation appear more attractive — with exotic locations, high living and abundant sex. The archetypal spy novel expressed a simple view of the world divided between the good (the Western democracies) and the bad (the USSR and the Communist satellites). This picture was strongly supported by both American novelists and their reading public until the late 1960s, when the changing world situation could no longer be seen in such simple terms. Spy fiction also celebrated man as an individual, with free choice and the ability to change situations. This was a refreshing view in an age when technology threatened to supplant the human element in espionage. For these reasons the spy was the perfect hero at this time and increased the demand for spy fiction in America, which authors hastened to supply.

In the absence of major wars the spy had become the hero of the post-war world, giving rise to the Cold War spy novel. Ronald J Ambrosetti described this form as the classic spy story representing the height of its development: "The 'cold war' spy story grew out [of] the isolationalism and international Cold War of the 1950s and early 1960s. This formula depicts the peacetime secret agent in his function to *prevent* the final disaster — total global destruction through nuclear proliferation."

While the British had tired of Fleming's Cold War fantasies and turned to the more cynical novels of le Carré and Deighton, the Americans were still immersed in the philosophy and outlook of the Cold War. The character of James Bond supplied the hero that had been absent from American fiction since the golden age of the detective in the 1930s. Bond provided the bridge between the traditional private-eye of American literature to the new spy hero of international politics, who could roam the whole world and was not confined to the dirty back streets of Bay City. Authors such as Philip Atlee, Edward S Aarons, Michael Avallone and E Howard Hunt, developed series characters based on James Bond andsent him on missions against the Russians, and later the Chinese, to restore the political balance of the Cold War.

Although British and American spy fiction have shared common roots as well as the same enemies, its development in each country has reached certain stages at different times. For instance, the James Bond cult ended in Britain sooner than in America, but also its influence was far greater in the latter country as the Fleming imitators perpetuated the sensational approach in spy fiction until the late 1970s. It lasted longer in America partly because of the lack of an alternative. The realistic approach to spy fiction has emerged gradually and is only now reaching proportions that outnumber the sensational variety.

One reason for this increase in realistic spy fiction is a tradition these authors share with their British cousins. In the 1970s a series of books were published by men who had worked for the Central Intelligence Agency, such as Victor Marchetti, E Howard Hunt and William F Buckley. These novels were written for various reasons, but they brought a new authenticity to the spy novel, an aspect that had been lacking in American spy fiction.

This tradition had existed in Britain since the beginning of the twentieth century and during the two world wars a number of writers were employed by the Secret Service. This did not happen in America until the early 1940s when a number of writers, intellectuals and actors, amongst others, were employed by the OSS. These people brought fresh ideas into the formerly closed world of espionage, and were particularly useful in the field of disinformation.

As readers tired of the Cold War theme the form of the spy novel changed and in the late 1970s and 1980s it began to focus on other subjects, such as terrorism and conspiracy theories. In America it began to be more sophisticated with more technical details, backed by extensive research, and in some cases, first-hand experience.

The stages in development of British and American spy fiction can be found in the change of the hero. For instance in the early stories the hero was always an amateur as in Erskine Childers' *The Riddle of the Sands* (1903) and *The Phantom Spy* (1937) by Frederick Faust. After 1945 the amateur was replaced by the professional agent, epitomised by James Bond in Britain and heroes like E Howard Hunt's Peter Ward in America. In the last twenty years this protagonist has been ousted by the professional maverick or vigilante agent who is not employed by any particular secret agency, but works for them as a freelance, or simply for personal reasons. Two examples can be found in W T Tyler's *The Man Who Lost the War* (1980) and *The Judas Factor* (1984) by Ted Allbeury.

Another characteristic which marks the evolution of the spy novel is that in the early stories the hero's job was relatively minor in importance — to recover a secret document from the enemy or rescue an innocent hostage. The outcome of the mission did not necessarily affect the state of nations. As the open conflict of war was replaced by the secret war of espionage after 1945, the fictional spy hero took on more responsibility and his adventures became of vital importance — the fate of the world depended on his abilities and the successful outcome of his mission.

The Cold War theme is no longer a viable backdrop to spy fiction, a reflection of the changing political world. Instead of directing its "energy" towards the enemy, the spy novel of today is preoccupied with its own Intelligence organisation and the constant fear that it has been penetrated from the outside, as well as the bureaucratic infighting within the secret world. The overwhelming feeling in these novels is that the Intelligence organisations have got out of control; not only are the personnel unaware of what is going on around them, but the politicians who should be directing espionage activities seem to have no say in the matter. At the moment British and American spy fiction has reached the same stage of development, but we will have to see if the age of *glasnost* inspires a new direction in the spy novel of the future.

Chapter 2
Fiction from Fact: the treatment of real events in the spy novel

The use of real events is one of the characteristics of the spy novel which has increased the general realism of its modern form. A growing number of authors now use real events to inspire their fiction and offer new interpretations of events in the light of espionage activities. For instance, in Ken Follett's novel *The Eye of the Needle* (1978) the story was based upon the actual deception plan created by the British in 1944 to persuade the Germans that they would launch their offensive from Calais, rather than Normandy which was the real location. From this basis Follett added the ingredient of a German spy in Britain who discovered that it was indeed a deception operation, and traced his efforts to try to get this information and the proof required to show the Germans that they were being misled.

There are many other examples in British and American spy fiction which show that more and more authors are returning to the past — in particular the Second World War — as in the spy novels of Ib Melchior, or using current newspaper headlines for inspiring their stories.

One specific event which has affected people all over the world, but particularly Americans, was the assassination of President Kennedy in November 1963. It was an event which had an extraordinary psychological impact upon a whole generation and has inspired a whole sub-genre of fiction in its own right — shared by British and American authors alike, although most of the authors dealt with here are American.

America has had a long history of assassinations of its political leaders, which began with the murder of Abraham Lincoln. But the death of Kennedy seemed to overshadow all these past assassinations because he was so young and ambitious and was regarded by many as a leader who could accomplish so much more than his predecessors. Whether this was due to the good publicity Kennedy and his administration received or whether he could have achieved all that he wished to do will remain unanswered. His death is seen in retrospect as so tragic because of events which took place after it — the escalation of the Vietnamese war, the race riots and civil unrest at university campuses. Many people believed that if Kennedy had still been around these things would not have happened.

The date of 22 November 1988 marked the 25th anniversary of the

Kennedy assassination. This event is still shrouded in mystery and the examination of the facts surrounding it still provoke controversy. The tragedy not only haunts Americans but thousands of people all over the world. Many still do not believe that Lee Harvey Oswald was the only gunman involved in the shooting and yet the 26-volume report of the 1964 Warren Commission concluded that Oswald was responsible and was acting alone. Because this explanation did not satisfy the majority of Americans the House of Representatives set up the Select Committee on Assassinations in 1978. After two years of investigation it arrived at the conclusion that in contrast to the Warren Commission, their 12-volume report stated that the President "was probably assassinated as a result of a conspiracy". But a conspiracy by whom? Many members of the committee believed that the Mafia were responsible for his death as they had strong motives and the means to accomplish it.

The controversy surrounding Kennedy's death has inspired a number of authors to write books, fiction and non-fiction to air their own views. Many of these books were written after 1963 but the 25th anniversary of the incident has provoked a new flurry of publications on this subject. Of the non-fiction variety, one persuasive study is *The Mafia Killed President Kennedy* by David E Scheim (London, W H Allen,1988). In great detail this author documents the large number of political assassinations initiated by the Mafia in the past, as well as the determination of the President and his brother, the Attorney General, to wipe out organised crime, which Scheim believes prompted the Mafia to act. Kennedy's policies had made him many enemies in the FBI, the CIA, the anti-Castro Cubans, the munitions-makers and the oil kings. All these groups included powerful people who could have been responsible, particularly if they had worked together.

Conspiracy theories about the assassination continued to develop mostly because, extensive as it was, the Warren Report left a lot of doubt in people's minds and did not tie up all the loose ends. New witnesses and information continued to provide fuel for these theories. Other recent non-fiction publications on this topic include *One Brief Shining Moment: Remembering Kennedy* by William Manchester (Boston, Little Brown, 1988); *The Web: Kennedy Assassination Cover-Up* by James R Duffy (Alan Sutton Publishing, 1988); *The Kennedy Legacy: A Generation Later* by Jacques Lowe and Wilfrid Sheed (London, Viking, 1988) and *Life in Camelot: The Kennedy Years* (Boston, Little Brown, 1988), edited by Philip B Kunhardt.

There have been many non-fiction books on this subject, such as those listed above, which have set out to prove that a conspiracy existed, but just as facts can be manipulated to emphasise certain details, these books are no more reliable than some of the fiction that has embraced the same facts and presented a number of theories over the years.

For instance, five months *before* President Kennedy's assassination, British solicitor Michael Eddowes was approached by the FBI for information on political sabotage in New York and London, about which he had inside knowledge. After this he wrote *The Oswald File* (non-fiction) on the Kennedy affair, having travelled thousands of miles tracking down people who could give him information and studying the Warren Commission's 26 volumes of testimony.

In his book Eddowes not only claims that the Warren Report was a whitewash job, but he contends that the Commission ignored evidence as well. He makes these points:

1 Why was the original warning from Hoover that Russian agents might well be planning to use identification papers of Lee Harvey Oswald for their own purposes ignored by the Warren Commission?

2 Why was the testimony of both Oswald's mother and brother regarding eight differences they noted in Oswald's appearance and manner upon his return from the USSR ignored by the Warren Commission?

3 Why did Oswald give two different biographies to two different FBI agents and why were these discrepancies never dealt with in the investigation?

4 Why was the true nature of the assassin's highly secret work in the war map room at Jaggars-Chilese-Stovall not revealed in the Warren Report? Why was no mention made of his spy equipment?

5 Why were no notes of any kind taken either by the Dallas police, the FBI, the CIA, or the Secret Service when the assassin of the President was interrogated? — routine procedure on any criminal case.

6 Although seven physical characteristics of the assassin's corpse differed significantly from Oswald's original medical records, no inquiries on the matter were made. Why?

Eddowes's points raise a number of questions which have not been adequately explained and which perhaps point to why so many authors have been drawn to speculate in fiction.

Eddowes himself works on the theory that the Soviets slipped a well-trained operator into America and gave him an American identity — that of an eccentric 22-year-old marine, Lee Harvey Oswald. He tried to show how the imposture took place and how the authorities collaborated in what he claimed was surely one of the most monstrous and successful examples of criminal deception in history. [1]

The mystery surrounding Kennedy's assassination has inspired a number of spy novelists to recreate events to show different motives for the murder. These authors include Wilson McCarthy, Richard Condon, Charles McCarry, Jim Garrison, Robert Littell, George Bernau and Don DeLillo.[2]

One British spy fiction writer who has explored this subject is Ted Allbeury. Sometimes when reading his books it seems like reading something out of the newspapers, such is his talent for creating a real-life situation. *Pay Any Price* (1983) takes as its theme, not only that the assassination of President Kennedy and his brother were the result of a strange alliance between the CIA and the Mafia, but that mind-bending techniques had been employed to manipulate both Lee Harvey Oswald and Sirhan Sirhan. Therein perhaps lies a very real risk for the author who continues writing "factional" spy novels. No writer can allow himself to be imprisoned by the apparent facts: sooner or later imagination must take over, and the danger is that it can occasionally take over completely. For the reader there is the risk that, having relied on the authenticity of the novelist in his attention to detail and facts, he begins to believe the imaginative parts are also factual. Most authors who have tackled this subject are quick to point out that their books are fiction, and their explanation is a purely personal interpretation of events. However, it can be argued that non-fiction books on the Kennedy assassination can also only offer theories based upon facts which are freely available to the novelist and the historian.

Another author, Richard Condon, was also interested in brain-washing and its uses as a political weapon. His two novels *The Manchurian Candidate* (1959) and *Winter Kills* (1974), both explore the theme of political assassination. *Winter Kills* is a thinly disguised story about the Kennedy assassination, and the relationships between the members of the Kennedy family. It does not present a flattering portrait of any of them. The hero of the story is Nick Thirkield, the half-brother of Tim Kegan, the young President who was shot. Nick takes up the investigation fourteen years after the event, when a man on his death-bed confesses that he was the second gunman.

Nick is led around in circles, chasing up clues and different leads which finally baffle and confuse him, which he discovers is the object of the exercise. He is offered various explanations by his father, which gives the author the opportunity to air most of the popular conspiracy theories which surround the assassination. For instance, he says that the President was killed because he failed to pay back the Mafia for their campaign contributions, or that a jilted lover killed him out of revenge. As with all lies they have to contain elements of truth in order to be plausible. Tom Kegan employs a Professor Cerruti to create possible explanations.

At the end of the book, when Nick confronts Cerruti, the Professor replies: "We were prepared to go on weaving scenarios until we had exhausted you. Fictionalized facts. Fantasized facts. Those are the steady cultural nourishment of the American people, forcefed down their throats through the power hoses of the most powerful and pervasive overcommunications design ever dreamed of by man to enslave other men ... And that is where our collective genius really lies — in the extraordinary American ability to perceive only when we are told to perceive and to believe only when we are told to believe. Not before. All the facts of your brother's murder have been there to be examined for fourteen years, Mr Thirkield. It is only now that you have been told to disbelieve them." [3]

Another author who has taken this topic and transformed it into spy fiction is Charles McCarry. His second novel, *Tears of Autumn*, was set in 1963 after the assassination of Kennedy. The hero of the book, Paul

Christopher, believed that he knew who had organised it, and for what reason. He set out to prove his theory that the CIA had arranged the murder of President Ngo Dinh Diem of Vietnam, and three weeks later Diem supporters sent their agents to shoot Kennedy in revenge. President Lyndon B Johnson believed in this theory, but the Castro revenge motive was perhaps more credible. However, these examples were still speculative explanations of Kennedy's assassination.

This novel was published in 1974, at a time when several CIA apostates, like Victor Marchetti, were voicing their criticisms of the Agency. A number of people believed that McCarry had joined their ranks as he had government officials alike hopping around like scalded cats wondering what new revelations were going to emerge. The book caused such a stir because of its subject matter and the explanation McCarry provided for the Kennedy assassination, which not unnaturally irked those officials whose main purpose in life seems to have been trying to stop the case from being reopened. The author himself said about his novel "Maybe the Vietnamese did kill Kennedy. But they sure didn't tell me."

George Grella, a critic of spy fiction, remarked: *"The Tears of Autumn* is one of the post-Kennedy assassination thrillers, a sub-genre that has flourished since the event and remains an important index to the cultural paranoia of the country and the time." [4]

Robert Littell's novel *The Sisters* (1986) is the story of two veteran CIA operatives, Francis and Carroll, who are continuously working on new covert plots. Carroll thinks up a "beautiful operation" in which they will activate a KGB sleeper agent and get him to commit an act — the assassination of the President — which will be traced back to the Soviets. The plot is further complicated by the Russians discovering (through a hidden mole in the CIA) what they are up to and their attempts to deactivate their agent.

Peter Andrews in a review of this book in the *New York Times Book Review* commented: "Mr Littell's suspenseful fiction surrounding the Kennedy assassination is fascinating and strains credulity to the breaking point, but no more than the Warren Commission report did. Do you really believe that Lee Harvey Oswald acted alone and two days later, while in police custody, was shot and killed by a grieving nightclub owner? And what about those puffs of smoke from the grassy knoll? Mr Littell has provocative answers to all those questions and more." [5]

A more recent example of this sub-branch of fiction can be found in Don DeLillo's *Libra* (1988). This is the author's ninth novel, and in a number of interviews DeLillo talked about the haunting effect the event has had upon his own life and why he needed to write the book. The story is told on three levels: that of Oswald's life — up until the moment he is shot; the machinations of a group of disaffected members of the CIA, involved in the Cuba invasion, who devise a plan to bring a resumption of hostilities towards Castro back into the foreground; and the meanderings of Nicholas Branch, a retired senior analyst of the CIA, who has been hired on contract to write the secret history of the assassination of President Kennedy. The latter parallels the author's task to a certain extent, except that in the case of Branch, if he eventually finishes the investigation and writes it up, it will never be published.

Because of this haunting effect of the assassination it has cut through the boundaries of literature and its practitioners — although DeLillo cannot be described as a spy novelist, this book reflects the rather morbid attraction this subject holds for many writers. One critic described *Libra* as "both a culmination and a departure for the acclaimed writer".

In the Author's Note at the end of the book, DeLillo makes it quite clear that "This is a work of imagination. While drawing from the historical record, I've made no attempt to furnish factual answers to any questions raised by the assassination." He does not want his novel to be regarded as just "one more gloom in a chronicle of unknowing. But because this book makes no claim to literal truth, because it is only itself, apart and complete, readers may find refuge here — a way of thinking about the assassination without being constrained by half-facts or overwhelmed by possibilities, by the tide of speculation that widens with the years."

In an interview in *Publisher's Weekly* DeLillo stated that it took him three years to write the book and "It had never occurred to me before to base a novel on an historic event ...". DeLillo did extensive research for the book, but it was important to him not to confuse fact with fiction. He says that he "felt a very strong responsibility to fact *where we knew it*. And I made up the rest because we don't know it. If there was a conspiracy, we don't know how it evolved. Oswald is as close as I could make him to what I perceived to be the real person. I really didn't take liberty with fact so much as invented fresh fact, if you can call it that. I tried very hard to create a unified structure with no seams showing. That was my major technical challenge."

As with all events that have no satisfying explanation, the author remarks that Kennedy's murder was no exception: "I think we see different things in the assassination at different periods in our history. We feel a bit differently about it today than we did in the '60s and then in the '70s. But we still don't know what happened, that's the core of it." In some ways the mystery offers a continuous object of fascination because it reflects contemporary fears and paranoias.

The author goes on to say that for some obtuse reason a conspiracy is a more attractive concept psychologically than belief in a random act: "Believing in conspiracy is almost comforting because, in a sense, a conspiracy is a story we tell each other to ward off the dread of chaotic and random acts. Conspiracy offers coherence." In conclusion he comments: "I am suggesting that it is possible to make up stories in order to soothe the dissatisfactions of the past, take the edge off the uncertainties. Perhaps we've invented conspiracies for our own psychic well-being, to heal ourselves." This belief suggests that theories to explain the Kennedy assassination will continue to proliferate because people affected by the event will continue to write stories to exorcise the experience, as in the case of this author, but also people will continue to be fascinated by these explanations because they cannot reconcile themselves to the inconclusive facts. [6]

One example of a film, not based upon a book, but written purely as a cinematic story was *Executive Action* (1973). The story was written by Dalton Trumbo, and Leslie Halliwell described the film as "An imaginative version of the facts behind the 1963 assassination of President Kennedy. Interesting but rather messy mixture of fact and fiction; makes one sit up while it's unreeling." [7]

Leonard Rubenstein, another film critic, wrote: "John F Kennedy's assassination was ready-made for a spy film; there was a complex net of circumstances surrounding the actual event and a whole series of rumors that had not been stilled by an official investigation, as well as the drama of an attractive young president shot in front of his wife during a ceremonial motorcade. If only a portion of the rumored conspiracies did exist, the ramifications were both ominous and widespread. The distrust of government and the idealistic hope that something could be done to effect change united with the popular attachment to spies and melodrama in *Executive Action*." [8]

The plot presented the assassination in the light of a conspiracy organised by multi-billionaires and former government officials who agreed to co-operate because they disagreed with Kennedy's policies. Made ten years after the event the film incorporated many of the theories about the assassination (for instance that Oswald was not the only gunman), and it hinted that the plotters had help within the government itself to ensure the success of their mission. The film used a variety of techniques to add authenticity such as newsreels, voice-overs and simulated events to convey the drama. The climax was not so much the successful execution of the President but the presentation of eighteen faces at the end of the film, all these people had been witnesses of the incident and had since died within the last ten years. Thus the film ended on a menacing note.

"Fiction is both a haven from chaos and a mirror-image of conspiracy", [9] and as the spy novel becomes more realistic with the increasing use of historic events, it is likely that a number of people will regard the spy novel as a possible source of historical interpretation. The uniqueness of the spy story lies firstly on its ability to entertain but as Don DeLillo also said it can sometimes offer a refuge for those people who were effected by a traumatic event, by reflecting predominant fears and paranoias.

Chapter 3
Role of the Mole: and the treatment of treachery

Increasingly in modern spy fiction the emphasis in most plots has been on the mole and the traitor rather than the straightforward spy-agent of his own country. To a large extent this trend has been due to what has been happening in the real world rather than any preference of the writers. They have instinctively felt that the new reading public is more interested in the mole and the traitor than in the Buchan–Fleming secret agent heroes.

This may be the case to some extent, but the problem is (and it is one in which readers are deeply interested) what lies behind the treachery, what makes the mole behave the way he does. In this respect what has occurred in real life has not made the solution of this problem any easier for the authors. It should be stressed that in real life the moles who most interest people are not the agents who betray their homelands for money, but those whose real motives are wrapped in mystery. This particularly applies to such people as Blunt and Philby. Not even their most diligent biographers have satisfactorily explained why they acted and behaved as they did: neither was a typical ideological Soviet-type communist by any means.

Graham Greene, who knew Philby well over many years and corresponded with him after his defection, would seem to have used this intimate knowledge in shaping two of his minor characters in *The Human Factor* (1978). Yet it could not be said that his major character, Maurice Castle, the agent who defects, resembles any of the principal moles of recent years and certainly not Philby. Castle defects not through belief in a cause, but solely because he is intensely in love with his black South African wife. "Greene has expressed dissatisfaction with *The Human Factor*," writes Dr David Stafford. "He had wanted, he claims, to write a novel of espionage free of the conventional violence of the James Bond type, one which showed that the daily routine of the secret service was like that of any other profession. It is odd that he should have expected to accomplish this given his strong liking for melodrama. Of course, he fails. Dr Percival, the SIS doctor who poisons the initial suspect in the case, Castle's colleague Davis, is a fairly melodramatic figure, and the violence of his intervention is quite consistent with the aim that Greene sets himself. As Philby himself wryly told Greene after he had read the novel, the doctor must surely have been imported from the CIA." [10]

One of the sometimes forgotten aspects of the life of the secret agent (and this applies even more so when he is a mole and a traitor) is the feeling of isolation and loneliness which it generates. While they tend to shy away from widespread social contacts, they cling to their clubs like a dying person stays in a hospice he has come to understand. There is a good example of this in the estranged figure of the spy hero in Adam Hall's *The Quiller Memorandum* (1965).

It is illuminating to note which of the real-life moles has most frequently been borrowed for fictional characters. Blunt, a somewhat unsympathetic character in any case, and Guy Burgess (far too much of a comedian) have been eschewed. Philby, however, has not merely been used as the basis of a fictional character, but has even been introduced into spy fiction under his own name and as himself! This is a considerable feat. Ted Allbeury, Frederick Forsyth and Alan Williams have all brought Philby into their books. As Forsyth has done recently in *The Fourth Protocol* (1984), released as a major film in 1987, it is of special interest. In this book Philby, from the safety of Moscow, gives advice to the General Secretary of the Soviet Union on how to manipulate a Labour victory at the British polls so that Neil Kinnock could be overthrown shortly afterwards and a hard-left Marxist–Leninist put in as Prime Minister. The essence of the plot was a Soviet scheme to put Labour back into power in Britain by means of a mini-atomic explosion. A basic atomic bomb was to be constructed, small enough to fit into a suitcase and simple enough to be assembled from a dozen prefabricated components. Plan Aurora was to infiltrate such a bomb into the United Kingdom and to cause enough damage to appear like a nuclear accident close to an American Air Force base in East Anglia. The idea was to "panic the ten per cent floating vote into supporting unilateralism and the Labour party."

To put such an idea into fiction would, of course, help to destroy the effectiveness of any such plot which the Russians might put into operation in the future. If they had such a plot in mind, this might well be a means of warning them that the news of it had leaked, and the counter-measures were being prepared. It might cause them to scrap their project. But if such an operation should be put into operation, the fact that the story had already been told in fiction might destroy the desired psychological effect on the floating voters. Psychological warfare can be waged as easily in fiction as in fact — sometimes more effectively so. Indeed, it has been suggested in some quarters that this idea was submitted to Forsyth by someone in the intelligence game.

This suggestion, whether true or otherwise, is perfectly feasible and opens up the whole question as to whether spy fiction writers can be, or are, used by intelligence services. What we do now know is that such services eagerly read the books of such writers as they are published, especially those compiled by ex-Secret Service officers. Mostly what they are looking for is the inclusion of real-life operations and personalities wrapped up in fiction. This has resulted in some writers receiving letters warning them to be more careful in future.

One author, André Jute, tells me of an "hilarious episode when a man from ASIO [Australian Secret Intelligence Organisation] and a monkey from Special Branch (or so he said; he wore a belted double-breasted trenchcoat in the middle of an Australian summer) confiscated manuscript copies of my book *Reverse Negative*." Eventually a warrant was produced and Jute handed over three copies of his manuscript, luckily retaining a photocopy which was hidden under some letters. About two years before this Jute claims that he sent letters to MI5 and MI6, putting forward certain facts and conclusions regarding Philby, asking for confirmation or denial. Not surprisingly he received no reply. Jute's comment was: "The fact is that I had blended published information and extremely credible conclusion so closely that I may have stumbled on a number of explosive truths."

The late John Bingham (Lord Clanmorris), was one writer of this genre who studiously avoided trying to puzzle his readers, as so many of the modern spy fiction practitioners seem to do. There is a certain love of obscurity for its own sake in le Carré and Deighton, though this shows more in the films and television adaptations made out of their stories than their books. Bingham felt that the latest electronic gadgets in espionage only contributed to obscurity and left readers guessing. His wife reported him as saying: "Nothing beats an agent in the right place. Bugs can't tell you who is sleeping with whom, who is jealous of his superiors and fed up with his job — and who is drinking." [11]

Clandestineness and its links with treachery tend to create a different morality and even a different kind of dialogue as well. Le Carré and Eric Ambler understand this perhaps best of all. They more than almost any others grasp the one vital characteristic of moles and traitors, what Professor Marcello Truzzi of Michigan University calls "the sociology of secrecy". A cult of secrecy, whether in personal life or in one's work can easily produce treachery of one kind or another, often without being intentional.

One remarkable example of a novel which explores the theme of treachery and betrayal is Rebecca West's *The Birds Fall Down* (1966). It is a great work of literature and its inclusion may seem surprising, but the themes she embraces are relevant to our discussion. Rebecca West was fascinated by espionage and from her knowledge of Russian emigrés she created a comprehensive picture of their preoccupations and torments at the turn of the century. This novel serves as a fictional companion to her book *The Meaning of Treason* (1949).

As Victoria Glendinning remarks in her introduction to the novel: "*The Birds Fall Down* is first and foremost a mystery story; it is also a family story, a political thriller, and a philosophical drama." [12] The main character of this book is Laura, who is young and naive, but as the story progresses she becomes torn between her conservative, staid English roots, and the Russian world of conspiracy and violence into which she is plunged. She accompanies her Russian mother to Paris to visit her mother's father Count Nikolai Nikolaievitch Diakonov, who lives in exile with his sick wife. He was banished from his beloved homeland by the Tsar because he was (wrongly) suspected of treason.

Laura is instructed to travel with her grandfather on a journey to a sea resort in northern France. On the train they are joined by Chubinov, a young revolutionary who persuades the Count to hear his long story about a police spy working amongst the revolutionaries, a man who is close to the Count. As the drama unfolds Laura finds that she has to sacrifice some of her principles in order to protect herself and her family, and eventually ends up being protected by this man who has betrayed her grandfather and his revolutionary colleagues.

The theme of treachery explored in this novel is not only political, but also personal. The double-agent in the story was based upon a Russian Jew named Ievno Aseff, or Azeff, who by 1909 had become the head of the largest and most powerful terrorist organisation in Russia, and had operated as a spy for the Tsar's police for at least six years. As in this story, the existence and identity of the double-agent was revealed during a conversation on a train.

The conversation as recorded by historians took place in 1910 on the Eastern Express between its departure from Berlin and its arrival at Cologne. As Rebecca West has put it in her foreword "The real participants differed from my characters in many respects, but not in their interests and emotions; and their exchange in information had the same effect on the Russian political scene." The author has changed a few details, for example setting the story at the turn of the century, but her interpretation of this occasion is perfectly credible, and her characters are magnificent portraits of men and women caught up in such momentous events.

At one point in the book the double-agent, without revealing himself, explains to Laura the principle of the dialectic and the Hegelian philosophy of thesis, antithesis and synthesis, to justify his behaviour. He explains that by moving on from one concept to another "in the hope that it will complete the first or annul its contradictions ... The most profitable type of second concept which we can choose is the exact opposite of the first, for it covers the same field. Thus we can fruitfully compare them, and discard what is false in both, and lo! that gives us a third concept, which brings us a step nearer reality."

The double-agent in this case believes that by carrying out both functions, in his capacity as a spy and an agent, he is, in himself, performing an act, and its negation, thereby achieving a union of opposites, or synthesis. By working for both sides this character feels that he is doing something commendable, but it also reveals the man's compulsion to strive for individuality and his belief that he can metamorphose into a superior human being by his acts.

Victoria Glendinning remarks of Rebecca West: "The strength of her novel indeed lies in the fact that she understands treachery every bit as fully as she understands loyalty." "All men should have a drop of treason in their veins," Rebecca West wrote in *The Meaning of Treason*, "if the nations are not to go soft like so many sleepy pears. Men must be capable of imagining and executing and insisting on social change if they are to reform or even to maintain civilisation, and capable too of furnishing the rebellion which is sometimes necessary if society is not to perish of immobility."

The author emphasised that nations must move forward in order to progress. In this novel she shows that men and women are capable of enormous treachery, but also great loyalty. But she also implies that you cannot have one without the other for life to have any meaning. Although politics and society may change, people's emotions and motivations remain the same.

Having digressed into the past we will now return to the modern phenomenon of the double-agent in spy fiction. The straightforward villainous mole — ideological or for monetary gain — is increasingly unpopular today. Not only does he bore the average reader, but they actually prefer mystery and obscurity, a psychological puzzle. Whereas the intellectuals may become irritated with the occasional deliberate obscurity in le Carré's work, the great mass of readers when questioned pretend they lap it up and understand it. They would never admit that they didn't understand it. Thus the writer concerned with moles and treachery must create a figure who, for the greater part of the book, remains a mystery, one whose behaviour is a constant puzzle, even one who occasionally looks like a hero ("a goodie", if you like), at other times highly suspect.

It is thus that le Carré decided that in Britain's post-imperial phase it was time for the Bond-style and Buchan-eering epics to give way to self-questioning and self-criticism. Many older Britons disliked this aspect of le Carré's work, but it was perhaps enjoyed rather more in America.

Le Carré once said of James Bond: "You could take James Bond and given the prerequisites of the affluent society, given above all an identifiable villain of whatever kind — and weak people need enemies — you could dump him in the middle of Moscow and you would have a ready-made Soviet agent ... the really interesting thing about Bond is that he would be what I call an ideal defector. Because if the money was better, the booze freer and women easier in Moscow, he'd be off like a shot. Bond is the ultimate prostitute." [13]

What Fleming's reply to this would be is doubtful. Certainly Bond deteriorated from book to book. Whereas Fleming had a talent for writing with tongue in cheek, sometimes spoiling his work in exploiting it, le Carré never forgot what he had learned in real life in Intelligence service. He has remained the perpetual realist and earnest questioner for the truth. He is always concerned with what he sees as the moral corruption — inseparable from espionage — and how this can infect the good just as much as the weak and devious. "It's an old illness you suffer from, Mr Smiley," says Elsa Fennan in *Call for the Dead* (1961), " ... and I have seen many victims of it. The mind becomes separated from the body; it thinks without reality, rules a paper kingdom and devises without emotion the ruin of its paper victims."

Sometimes le Carré seems more interested in what he sees as the totally unscrupulous methods used by his (or our) own side than in the creation of a mole. What he does bring out again and again is how such methods tend to disgust intelligence officers so much that occasionally a few react by turning over to the other side. In *Tinker, Tailor, Soldier, Spy* (1975), the mole, Bill Haydon, is based at least in part on Philby, a traitor protected by a conspiracy of class and the "old boy" network.

A much earlier, but less realistic mole in fiction was Wilhelm Oerter in R Wright Campbell's *The Spy Who Sat and Waited* (1975). Wright took a German wartime propaganda story as the basis for his own tale of a "sleeper" mole.

Curiously enough two other books on a similar theme and more or less set in the same area were published in 1938 and 1939, just before the Second World War broke out. These were *Operation MO* and *The Shetland Plan*, both by "Taffrail" which was the pseudonym of Captain Henry Taprell Dorling, RN, who, having retired from the Navy in 1929 settled down to a career as a writer.

The first of these two books was about a spy discovering an Admiralty secret, while the second was set among the fishermen of the Shetland Isles, adjacent to the Orkneys. The story showed how the fishermen became involved with spies and a plot to seize one of the islands when war was declared.

William Hood is particularly effective in his fictional treatment of both moles and defectors, and his book *Spy Wednesday* (1986) provides some remarkably apt insights as to how intelligence services recruit and evaluate defectors, not least fake defectors. For this last reason alone *Spy Wednesday* is almost a guide on how to spot the fakes. His character, a Soviet defector named Boris Kudrov, bears some resemblance to Vitaly Yurchenko, a real-life KGB officer, who, in 1985, defected to the Americans and shortly afterwards claimed to identify several CIA employees as Soviet agents. The US Justice Department denied this, but his defection was nevertheless hailed as a body-blow for Soviet espionage. Then in November 1985, Yurchenko re-defected to the Soviet Embassy in Washington DC and at a press conference protested that he had been kidnapped, tortured and drugged until he did not know what he was saying. Later he returned to Moscow.

Professor Douglas Wheeler, who from 1984 to 1985 was a Richard Welch Fellow in Advanced Research on Intelligence CFIA at Harvard, was so impressed with *Spy Wednesday* that he wrote: "I recommend it without hesitation to students in the field of intelligence studies, past and present."[14] The reason for this advice is the skilful and analytical picture which Hood gives of an agent brought out of retirement, Trosper, who has to decide who is a genuine defector and who is a fake.

In recent years there has been an overemphasis on technology in both real-life intelligence circles, and among practitioners of spy fiction. Hood would appear to put this into proportion when he says of Trosper's mission to Budapest: "There were no gadgets to fall back on, no experts to consult, and no reams of printout, spun fresh from a computer chip. There was only a case man on his own at the end of the line."

Possibly American Intelligence has for many years been confronted with the problem of fake defectors, this theme is more frequently developed by American writers than any other. That it is a serious problem, not least when sometimes the doubts about a defector last throughout his entire life-time, is apparent from the creation of a special study group at Jamestown University on the whole subject of defectors and how they should be treated. Meanwhile the fiction writers continue to play around with this theme. Apart from Hood there is E Howard Hunt's *The Hargrave Deception* (1980), which takes up the improbable theme that Kim Philby was, a defector who pretended to be a traitor to fool the KGB. Charles McCarry also touched on the fake defector in his first novel, *The Miernik Dossier* (1973).

There are some writers who seriously question whether moles are any more than of limited value to their masters. One such is Ted Allbeury, who served in Military Intelligence in the Second World War. Allbeury keeps a sense of balance: he gets his mixture right — the correct amount of thrills, excitement, accurate background, dialogue and know-how. With Len Deighton the details, the new technology, the gimmicks are all paraded for his own amusement. John le Carré becomes too wrapped up in his own opinions, his own private battle with the world of Intelligence. But All-beury wishes to convince, not to dazzle or pontificate. He is one of the few writers who have made "faction" a clean, rather than a dirty word.

One of his most remarkable books was *The Special Collection* (1975) which, in effect, adopted the theme of the creation of large numbers of moles intended to create chaos through subversion. His theme was the infiltration of communism into Britain, a swiftly moving story of a gigantic subversive operation planned by the KGB and aimed at reducing Britain to industrial and social chaos by means of selective blackmail, strikes, student riots and murder. It was in fact so realistic that Lord Chalfont, former Minister and specialist on defence and foreign affairs, said of it: "the whole story has an immense topical significance ... I hope that people who read it will not regard it entirely as fiction." This was perhaps the supreme accolade for Allbeury's work.

It also shows that molery — to coin a new word — has many forms and that treachery can be induced in large numbers of people without many of them being aware of it. Nevertheless in dealing with the single mole the biggest problem for the author must inevitably be the interpretation of his character in a manner which holds the attention of the reader until the very last moment.

Chapter 4
Writers of Spy Fiction Worldwide

To define exactly who can be rated as a foreign writer of spy fiction in a guide which is essentially concerned with such books written mainly in English is less easy than it would seem. Some of the best of such writers, neither American nor British by birth or parentage, have made their names entirely through writing in the English language. A typical example is Joseph Conrad, a Pole who became a naturalised British subject. After Polish, French was Conrad's first and natural language before he studied English and there are examples of the French influence in his English prose. Nevertheless, Conrad does not qualify as what, for the purpose of this chapter, can be described as a "foreign writer".

There are, of course, a number of examples of foreign writers who have ultimately made their reputations in the English language, but here we are mainly concerned with the influence spy fiction writers have had in other languages in other lands. In France there had been at least twenty talented writers of this genre prior to World War I, including such names as Léon Sazie (1870–1920), whose best known work was *Zigomar au service de l'Allemagne* (1916) and Paul d'Ivoi who wrote under the pen-name of P Deleutre (1856–1915).

Realism in French spy fiction can be dated to the approach of the Second World War in the late 1930s and perhaps the most notable author in this period (and indeed for many years afterwards) has been André Léon Brouillard, whose pseudonym has usually been Pierre Nord. Since his first and highly commended book, *Terre d'angoisse* (Librairie des Champs-Elysées) in 1937, he has produced two notable spy thrillers, both translated into English as *Double Crime on the Maginot Line* (1967) and *The Thirteenth Suicide* (1970). The latter was so popular that it was made into a successful film by Henri Verneuil, entitled *Le Serpent* (1972). It was about a defector, Vlassov, from the USSR to the USA who revealed to the CIA a list of spies operating in Western Europe for the Kremlin. The suspense derived from whether Vlassov could be an agent of the KGB, for in this book he made allegations of treason among high personages in the celebrated Sapphire Ring affair of the 1960s.

"Pierre Nord" has written other espionage books, and eight of his novels have been adapted for the French cinema, including *Deuxième Bureau contre Kommandantur*, *Intelligences avec l'Ennemi*, *La Bigorne* and *Caporal de France*.

Other outstanding French spy fiction writers of this latter period include Gilles Perrault (especially for his *Le Dossier 51* (A Fayard, Paris, 1969)) and Vladimir Volkoff, whose work, *Le Retournement* (Julliard/L'Age d'homme, Paris, 1979), has been rated by one critic as "excellent as a novel quite apart from its realistic portrayal of espionage." Volkoff has also used the pen-name of Lavr Divomlkoff.

There are some who deny that Hubert Monteilhet is a spy fiction author. Most of his books, it is true, are concerned with crime, mystery and detection, but he is worthy of mention for the special quality which he brings to bear in what little spy fiction he has written. Educated at the Sorbonne, his prose has a touch of the *matoufan* or mischievousness of which de Maupassant wrote, a subtle hint of *les dégringolades*. Of his admittedly unusual style of spy fiction *Le Cupedevil* is perhaps unique and its originality sets it apart from the run-of-the-mill stories of espionage. The novel seems to reveal a peep at the mind of an author who, during the years of the war, was himself an adolescent living in a strange, unreal world. The "Cupedevil" was a catalytic evil genius named Arnaud. He started out as a normal adolescent until he became the pawn of his own game and the games of others. The name of the game was Diane. Arnaud loved her, but didn't get her; Jacques didn't love her, but got her. Count Daspect wasn't sure, but he never refused a gift. The Maquis didn't even know that they, too, were involved in the game of Diane. There was also a French officer who actually invented the game. It is all rather mysterious until the story is gradually unwrapped and then it becomes stylish entertainment — a comi-tragedy of studied depravity. Monteilhet, who lives in Tunisia, lists as his recreation the somewhat surprising subject of theology! He has been awarded the Grand Prix de Littérature Policière as well as the Inner Sanctum Mystery Award.

One of the most powerful and at the same time curious spy novels coming from a German pen in recent times has been *No Man's Land* by Martin Walser (translated into English by Leila Vennewitz, Henry Holt & Co., New York, 1989). Walser is also a playwright and this particular novel has something of the intensity and directness of drama. At the same time it is an accurate picture of a divided Germany and how one man copes with the problem of becoming a spy. Born in East Germany, Wolf moves to West Germany and marries Dorle, who works in the Ministry of Defence. Through her, he meets Sylvia, whom he seduces into obtaining various NATO secrets. It is the story of a German spying for Germany on Germany, which Wolf tries to tell himself can hardly be called genuine betrayal! "To what extent may one's thoughts contradict one's actions?" is a question posed by the author. "How much irreconcilability can one bear within oneself? Whenever Wolf went down to the 'phone booth at the edge of Popelsdorf he had to ask himself why he didn't make these 'phone calls from his home although he was sure his line wasn't tapped."

It is noticeable to any detached and objective critic, however, that other German and, indeed, East European dissident writers, share Walser's obsession with the problem of a divided nation. While such an obsession gives their novels a semblance of reality, it tends on occasions to slow down the actual story, even to spoil the plot. Zdena Tomin, another dissident, tells such a story in *The Coast of Bohemia* (translated into English, London, Hutchinson,1987). Marese Murphy in reviewing the book said that it told "the tale of oppression and resistance ... heatedly, and with an emotional involvement that at times rocks the strength of the narrative. The narrator, a woman, develops a fierce possessive relationship with a mentally sub-normal girl and puts both of them at risk by her obsession ... Though her own basic integrity remains unimpaired, by the end of the novel it is clear that her services to the ideal of Czech freedom are better employed from the safe distance of refuge in England." [15]

In the Soviet Union it was policy for many years to totally deny that they had anything whatsoever to do with espionage: that was something which was only practised by the capitalist states of the West. Then in the early 1960s it was decided that in the light of revelations of Soviet espionage being made in the Western media and of the number of novels being written on the same subject, a change of policy was needed. The new aim was to glorify the deeds of Soviet agents and to improve the image of the USSR in this respect, popularising the KGB and GRU officers as noble heroes who protected their fatherland.

This policy was launched by Vladimir Semichastny, who had been appointed head of the KGB in 1961, when he contributed an article to *Izvestia* on this very subject. He told the story of a young man serving in a Soviet mission abroad who was compromised by a foreign intelligence service. Because the young man still had "old ideas" about the KGB, he was afraid to inform the Soviet authorities of what had happened and agreed to work for the foreign service. However, in due course he regretted his action, confessed it and did not lose his job. One can smile somewhat cynically at the idea of the KGB retaining the services of anyone who had even temporarily served a foreign power.

While the USSR put the emphasis on real-life stories of such of their own spies as Colonel Rudolf Abel and Richard Sorge, the powers-that-be encouraged spy fiction, again encouraging those works which might show the Western world in a bad light and tell of heroic Russian agents. Such books were strongly sponsored by the KGB under Semichastny's regime, relatively short-lived though this was. One Bulgarian novelist who re-sponded to the KGB's request for the services of writers who would turn out such work was Andrei Gulyashki. He invented an ace Soviet spy named Avakum Zakhov, whose main mission in life seemed to be to destroy James Bond, described as "this supreme example of imperialistic espionage." It was the USSR's answer to Ian Fleming, whose success worried the KGB, some of Semichastny's colleagues believing that Britain had scored a major propaganda success in the Cold War by producing James Bond!

Gulyashki's book, *Zakhov Mission* (1966), was an instant success and was serialised in *Komsomolskaya Pravda*, the Soviet youth paper under the title of *Avakum Zakhov versus 07*. The Bulgarians were unable to get copyright permission to use Bond's name or "007", so they got around this difficulty by deleting one zero from the code name. The book was then translated into English by Maurice Michael and published in Britain in 1968. Avakum Zakhov was, understandably, a much more proletarian figure than Bond; instead of the fastidious culinary tastes of Bond, the Soviet hero gulped down large quantities of cabbage and noodles.

By the 1980s spy fiction had become almost as popular in the USSR as in the West. The chief writer of this genre in Russia is Julian Semyonov, now one of the richest men in the USSR, with a large apartment in Moscow and two other homes, one a villa on the Black Sea. He is said to have sold more than 30 million copies of his fifty plus books, the best known of which is *Tass Is Authorised to Announce*, which has also been turned into a Soviet television series. This book, also now translated into English, is most significantly set in an African country where the KGB assists a Marxist government to foil a CIA plot to bring it down. Dr David Stafford writes that Semyonov "has close KGB contacts (and is rumoured to be one of its colonels), and, like some of his American counterparts, exploits similar obsessions: at the centre of the plot of *Tass Is Authorised* is a CIA mole passing information to Washington." [16]

Sometimes European writers who venture into spy fiction tend to become bogged down in the trivialities of espionage and this tendency becomes almost exaggerated when their work is translated into English. They seek far too often to portray the feelings of a spy, his private thoughts and his fantasies. One such is Antonio Tabucchi, who was born in Pisa in 1943. *Little Misunderstandings of No Importance*, a collection of short stories, is the first of his fictional works to be translated into English. [17]

The author divides his time between Portugal and Tuscany, writing in Italian. In this book there is the story of an agent waiting to make contact with someone his masters have sent to meet him. "She was the contact, no doubt of it," runs the narrative. "'Good evening, would you like a drink?' 'No thanks, I'd rather do business right away; I imagine you left a box of chocolates at the cloakroom. Shall we exchange tickets? If, on the other hand, you've the money on you, let's go to the telephone booth, where I can use this big evening bag. I had to look all over to find this size.'" And so it continues, undoubtedly less effective in English than in Italian, especially the dialogue, as somehow the absurdity of such trivialities, apart from the lack of professionalism, tends to make the whole story little more than an exercise in fantasy.

Steadily, the Japanese spy novel is coming into favour. Their leading spy novelist is Eisuke Nakazono, whose book, *A Secret Message*, is regarded as what one critic called "the trailblazer for Japanese spy novels". He has also written another ten such works in which, not unlike some European writers of the genre, he describes the emotions and conflicts within the mind and between persons rather than the wider geopolitical issues. It is interesting to contrast the approach of Nakazono in *A Secret Message* with that of Kazuo Ishiguro, the Nagasaki-born novelist who came to Britain and won the Booker Prize with his work, *The Remains of the Day*. [18] Ishiguro is neither a spy novelist, nor a Japanese writer, his work being entirely in English, but in his story of an elderly English butler who ponders on the age of the great country house in Britain, he reveals something of this same preoccupation with emotions and mental conflicts. Suddenly he begins to have doubts about his former master and a feeling that he has been deceived. Was old Lord Darlington really such a great gentleman, or just a dangerous supporter of the Nazis? Should he have kow-towed to such men and such a class? Not quite a spy story, but the elements of characters who would fit into such a tale are all there.

One Japanese writer who writes only spy fiction is Yoshio Takayanagi, whose masterpiece is *Jesters from Prague*, a work not perhaps up to the standard of Nakazono, but hailed as being "eminently realistic and authentic". Other notable Japanese authors of this school are Shoji Yuki (*The name of Gomez is Gomez*), Toru Miyoshi (*Dusty Zone*), Ro Tomono (*Sun sets at the Mekong*) and Yoshiaki Hiyama (*Assassination Plot Against Stalin*).

Sometime in the not-too-distant future one must look to China for books such as these and it will indeed be fascinating to see what form they take and how they seek to develop the genre. All the more so because China supplied some of the earliest examples of spy fiction. Mao Tse-tung was known to pay tribute to the inspiration he received from studying the *San Kuo* (*The Romance of the Three Kingdoms*), written by Lo Kuan-chung of the Yuan dynasty (1260-1341).

This is an extremely long historical novel which tells how the spies and spymasters of those days operated. Dennis Bloodworth, a distinguished student of Chinese affairs over many years, has written that "American military analysts now pay serious attention to *The Romance of the Three Kingdoms*, for it has gradually dawned on the West that the inspired trickery practised by that legendary third-century slyboots of a strategist, Chuko Liang, remains as subtly influential among the Chinese as an early mother's-knee sermon. Recognised as a worthy preceptor by Mao, carefully studied by the Vietcong guerrillas in South Vietnam, Chuko Liang was a 'Sleeping Dragon', a sage in retreat who never wielded a sword, for the essence of the great Chinese military tradition has always been that brains baffles brawn." [19]

Chapter 5
Future Directions of the Spy Novel

A question frequently asked today in some literary circles is whether the human spy is redundant in the face of technological developments in espionage. Has the new era of satellite espionage, which is now vital to all national security systems, somehow made the human spy an anachronism at the worst, or a feeble substitute at the best?

Certainly satellite spying will continue to become extended increasingly to outer space probes, and in wartime, as the Falklands War demonstrated, the intelligence it produces can be all-important. Obviously satellite spying is a subject about which spy fiction writers will need to keep themselves closely informed, particularly on new developments and the lessons learned from its operation. There is also the useful ploy for plots that already some nations are transmitting disinformation for the satellite-spotters to pick up. But the short answer to the query made in the first paragraph is that the spymaster has to be a human being, one who can analyse the material received and even spot the disinformation, and that only the human spy can find out the real motives behind certain people's actions, or learn what is inside their minds.

In any event even satellite spying has provided some admirable real-life subjects for plots worthy of a fictional pen. There was the case of Christopher Boyce, who was sentenced to forty years' imprisonment in the USA in 1977 for passing on to Soviet agents "documents and a package containing the KH-11 manuscript." KH-11 is the CIA name for the "keyhole" satellite, a device capable of making observations on Russia as if through a keyhole. Boyce had worked in the code-room of a Southern California firm which supplied and operated top-secret satellites for the CIA.

There have been many pessimists who have prophesied the doom of spy fiction. As long ago as 1972 Julian Symons, a discerning critic, in his book, *Bloody Murder From the Detective Story to the Crime Novel* (1972), predicted that the prospects for the spy novel were exhausted. Yet it was in the years immediately following this appraisal that the popularity of spy fiction increased enormously and production of the genre grew at a corresponding pace. During recent years there has been a new reason put forward as to why the spy novel is on its way out — *glasnost* and *perestroika*. However, it is unlikely that either East or West will regard the other with anything other than at best a cautious, if benevolent realism for a long time to come, even with the opening of the Berlin Wall.

But apart from this it is surely obvious that there is ample scope for the spy novel of the future against the background of widespread terrorist organisations such as the world has never seen before in such profusion. Similarly, it can be said that whereas it is highly unlikely that either a NATO power or the USSR is likely to start a nuclear war as long as the one matches the other in armament capability, the possibility of a terrorist organisation using a nuclear bomb is an increasing danger. This in turn could provide the novelist with a variety of new settings in which to place his story, ranging from Northern Ireland and the Irish Republic to Cyprus, the Lebanon, Israel, Iran, Pakistan, Afghanistan, Sri Lanka and even in such remote places as some of the islands of the Pacific and Mediterranean.

What is true, however, is that as the practice of disinformation and the sophisticated use of the agent of influence is more highly developed so these techniques become much more practical than much conventional espionage. One of the problems which the writer of the future will need to overcome will be to explain to the reader just what all this involves, and what it means and, above all, how to put it over in a comprehensible story. The agent of influence in real life is often a person well known for his devotion to charities and good causes, a highly respected figure. To prove that he is a subtle exponent of subversion can be wellnigh impossible. Indeed, the spy novelist could probably point the way for people to study this enigma in real life.

"Peacetime spy organisations normally develop their reputations when an empire's going downhill ... That's what happened with the British, and now that we're getting screwed up the CIA's getting important just like the British spies did ...", writes Taylor Branch in his work *Empire Blues*. [20] The relevance or indeed the truth of this allegation is questionable. Only when a nation feels seriously threatened by another does it start to develop its security and espionage services. This was the case with Britain in the early part of this century in view of the threat from Kaiser Wilhelm's Germany, and again in the USA when the Cold War started. One reason why, for its size, Israel has one of the finest intelligence services in the world is that it has been surrounded by enemies for most of its existence.

Events in the Soviet Union in recent years have certainly caused spy writers to take a new look at life behind the Iron Curtain. It is said to have caused le Carré to work longer and harder on his new book, *The Russia House* (1989), in order to take heed of them. If the creator of Smiley and Karla has had to come in from the Cold War, exactly what front will he now fight on? "We will have to find a new evil," said Eric Major, head of his publishers, Hodder & Stoughton. "In the spy novels of the thirties, it was Germany. But all novelists reflect their contemporary world and, in my view, le Carré does in *The Russia House*. But others may not think so." [21]

Certainly le Carré left no stone unturned in his research both for facts and atmosphere in his new novel: he accepted an invitation to visit Moscow for the first time and he was said to have been somewhat puzzled by the new openness he found there. Hence perhaps the reason for the somewhat curious blurb announcing the book, stating that *The Russia House* was "a spy story and an anti-spy story, a story of Cold Warriors who continue to dance in their grey cellars after the music has ended ... a cast of characters on both sides of the rusting Iron Curtain."

Lars Sauerberg, author of *Secret Agents in Fiction* (1984), and a diligent student of le Carré, has said that "I do not see him opening up toward something that would change his mind. I doubt very much whether he will be able to handle the end of the Cold War. Thriller writers have had to find new evils in these hard times. The classical resort of the *genre*, when foreign possibilities dry up, is to turn inwards, in this case to the British Establishment, as Len Deighton has done in his new trilogy, *Hook, Line and Sinker*."[22]

On the other hand, the spy writer who has himself worked in British Intelligence (as has le Carré) is to some extent inhibited in tackling this approach to the subject. Those who have signed the Official Secrets Act agreement are always liable to be challenged on some point or other, albeit one they have easily missed. Le Carré himself has had one example of this when, without being aware of what he had done, he used the name of a real-life agent as one of the characters in his novel. The authorities asked him to change the name, which he did.

When Eric Major spoke about spy writers having to find a "new evil" to tilt at, he had a swift response in a letter from Elspeth Huxley. "I don't think Mr Eric Major will have to look far," she stated. "I have been wondering for some time what he and his fellow spy-men will do now that their horses have been shot under them by Mr Gorbachev. Muslim fundamentalists are the answer, the bookburners of Bradford. Nor should we forget that their ancestors conquered all Spain and Portugal and were only turned back from the rest of Europe at the gates of Vienna." [23]

Already Frederick Forsyth has produced his own example of what can be called a forerunner of the future spy novel. This is *The Negotiator* (1989), which is set in the near future, and its background is the struggle for peace by Gorbachev and the President of the United States and the elements on both sides who want to destroy it. What is of rather more interest to the student of current affairs, however, is Forsyth's picture of his character, Marshal Koslov, who had organised the withdrawal of Soviet forces from Afghanistan and who has vowed never again to lead the Soviet army in retreat. The key to his mood, wrote Forsyth, "lay in a report on his desk. It ended: *The point therefore is not that the planet is forecast to run out of oil in the next twenty or thirty years, it is that the Soviet Union will run out of oil in the next eight.*"

This, of course, immediately brings the whole subject of *perestroika* into question. As Koslov muses, "If the Soviet Union could take control of a ready-made source of ample crude oil in territory presently outside her borders ... He could even suggest that territory — Iran. And if that peace-lover in the Kremlin with his precious *glasnost* flinched at the word 'invasion', then there were others in Russia who understood their duty better."

What other options are open to writers of the future in this sphere, and what else are they likely to probe in a restless quest for new horizons? It may be that one such lies in more adequate explanations of the psychology of the spy. True, a writer can create the psychology of his character and at the same time provide the evidence and reasons for his spy behaving the way he does. But this is a little too easy and in the light of many famous real-life spies the lesson is only too — obvious that rarely, if ever, is their behaviour satisfactorily analysed. In none of the biographies of such people as Blunt, Burgess and Maclean has this been achieved. One would, for instance, like to know whether the fact that his father gave Philby the nickname Kim after Kipling's boy-spy had any influence on his views of life. A skilled psychologist writer could turn any of the aforenamed into superb fictional psychological studies. Ralph Harper in *The World of the Thriller* (1974) takes the view that the spy story enables the reader to realise some of his secret desires and fears, in order to relate these to conscious ideas and values. "More than any other genre, the thriller invites us to spread the untidy contents of our subconsciousness on the same floor with our approved attitudes, and decide which we want to take seriously," he writes with considerable perspicacity. [24] One has the feeling that with Blunt and Philby this was abundantly true, perhaps more so in the case of the latter, and it may explain his mesmeric fascination for the works of Graham Greene.

Harper would appear, however, more interested in the effect of the spy story on the reader than of the author's attempt to explain psychological puzzles. He suggests that "experience of the self as empty, nameless, rudderless is for some people precisely what impels them to read thrillers. In that reading they will be given one more, and a very special, chance to choose themselves." [25]

This theme brings us to the question of the medical man, the psychologist or physiotherapist as a suitable type for writing spy fiction. There have been a number of such who have succeeded admirably in the past, not only as writers, but as workers in the intelligence and security services. Perhaps the most outstanding example was Somerset Maugham. It should also be remembered that Dr Harold Dearden acted as a psychological adviser to MI5 at Camp 020, the highly secret detention centre for captured German spies at Ham Common, near Richmond, England, in the Second World War. Dr Dearden was admirably suited as an adviser on how best to "turn" enemy agents to work for the British cause. He had taken a lifelong interest in criminological mysteries from Jack the Ripper to the Siege of Sidney Street and the strange case of "Peter the Painter". His task was difficult, not so much in assessing how reliable a captured German agent would be, or if he could be persuaded to be turned, but how quickly this could be achieved. Speed in "turning" these agents was absolutely essential. The psychologist and his various medical colleagues are more vital to such "Double-Cross" operations today than ever they were when Dearden operated.

Not only the psychologist, but also the student of the paranormal has a part to play in the spy novel of the future. However, the introduction of aspects of the paranormal into spy fiction is not without difficulties: the harsh facts are that in Britain and some other countries, the paranormal is not only disregarded by most people, but it is regarded as being boring as well. To create the "medium spy" or the "PSI spymaster" might sound an attractive and original idea, but one discerning publisher is "for the immediate future, at least," inclined to think such work could be an "absolute sales flop".

But he cautiously adds: "For God's sake don't use my name, for I may be proved wrong sooner than I wish. What is more, some author who has written such a book might not offer it to me, while another publisher could make a killing!" So even he is not quite as sure as he at first suggests!

Except in technical journals and books, very little has been published on the study made by various intelligence services into aspects of the paranormal — ESP, parapsychology, psychonkinesis and Kirlian photography, so to the average reader such subjects are wrapped in total obscurity. But in Bulgaria there is an Institute of Suggestology, while in the USA parapsychology laboratories are increasing in numbers. One day the PSI spy will come into his own.

One day, too, we may have the astrological spymaster coming into the foreground, for there is a wide readership who are not only interested in astrology, but actually know quite a lot about it. It should be remembered that the late Sir Maurice Oldfield, former head of MI6, who studied Chinese astrology when he was serving in the Far East, declared that "from the point of view of character assessment it was better than positive vetting."[26]

To strike a flippant note, there is yet another future possibility — the privatisation of security and intelligence services! In his latest book, *Tango* (1989), this is just what Alan Judd has done. It tells how British Intelligence has been privatised as "Special Information Services, plc".

Nor is this quite such a far-fetched theme as some might imagine. Even the Soviet Union of all nations has in one sense gone in for what is almost a form of privatisation of intelligence in the last few years. A retired KGB officer, Yevgenny Pitovranov, now a distinguished businessman, has master-minded an ultra-secret service which is called Special Reserve, and is outside the KGB. Its officers are businessmen, bankers and commercial travellers who circulate around the world, gathering intelligence and extending the influence of the USSR in a variety of fields.

I expect that one day dividends will come from any author fortunate enough to be able to spend time at Lund University in Sweden. It is here that Professor Stefan Dedijer has established a small independent institute attached to the university's faculty of social sciences for the study of intelligence services. It is sometimes referred to as the Lund Spy School. Professor Dedijer, a Yugoslav, who was a parachutist with the American forces during the Second World War, says: "Two hundred countries have intelligence organisations, yet nobody studies them. These services know enormously more about each other than the public know about any of them. I think that it is time that politicians and ordinary citizens learn how these things function." [27]

Finally, it is worth taking a look at some authors' opinions on the spy story of the future. Charles Robertson, an American author, says "There will always be spy novels. The spy novel is one of the few ways in which a writer can discuss the great geo-political conflicts of our time without being overtly didactic." To some extent this view is upheld by Gavin Lyall, who states that the spy story has "got a future as long as spies crop up in the headlines, but my guess is that it will become more political, with spying as an everyday element more than being stories of an enclosed and isolated world."

In the opinion of a British novelist, Melvin Bolton, "The future of the spy novel will presumably reflect that status of the Cold War but there are obvious ways of perpetuating the conventional spy story. The nationality of protagonists can be changed, for instance. Bear in mind, though, that the popularity of war stories/films long outlasts wars!" He goes on to say, "In my own work I have been particularly interested in plots that show how secret intelligence work can lead the secret organizations/agencies into areas of operation outside the world of spies and espionage. In this connection the future of 'the spy novel' rather depends on how narrowly one defines the genre. For example the line between terrorism and hostile acts from foreign governments is already blurred — some governments assist terrorists. It follows, then, that the work of intelligence officers and special police units/anti-terrorist forces will be equally interrelated. Intelligence-gathering is as necessary as ever in maintaining national security especially at the terrorist level of operations. Technology has moved most spying into the air waves and, as in warfare, this calls for fewer, more highly technical, operatives. There is, nonetheless, fertile ground here for 'spy novels' for a long time to come. It will not disappear with *glasnost*!"

The best answer to the query raised at the beginning of the chapter probably comes from John Gardner who writes: "Recently, I heard an author, who should know better, say espionage is all satellites now, so the days of espionage fiction are numbered. He was either jesting, ill-informed, or lacking in imagination ... While it is true to say that the number of field officers in intelligence has now dropped to an eighth of the number employed on field work in the 1960s, intelligence is not merely left to SATINT and ELINT — information gathered by satellite or electronic means. A large percentage of serving officers do indeed have to interpret SATINT and ELINT, though the field officer is still a very necessary part of intelligence work. The interpretation of SATINT and ELINT must have back-ups through HUMINT — human intelligence; bodies on the ground."[28]

Chapter 6
Cross-Fertilization: the relationship between writers and the world of Intelligence

A number of people from different professions have been attracted to the spy novel as a vehicle of expression for a variety of reasons. For instance there are many journalists, British and American, who have written spy fiction, among them are Tim Sebastian and Nik Gowing, David Ignatius and Tad Szulc. There is also a surprising number of politicians from both countries, who have ventured into this field of fiction, for example, Douglas Hurd and Michael Spicer, William F Buckley and Gary Hart.

However, the strongest recurring link is that between spy fiction (most notably among the English-speaking writers) and real-life espionage and intelligence work. Fact begets fiction and fiction begets fact. Fenimore Cooper may well have undertaken some espionage missions himself while serving in the Great Lakes area as a midshipman on patrol in the US Navy. A E W Mason tells us quite frankly that, when on an espionage mission for the British NID (Naval Intelligence Division) in the Second World War, he borrowed an idea for disguise from a story by Conan Doyle. There is an astonishingly long list of authors who have actually been involved at some time or other in intelligence work and who have produced spy stories.

On the British side there is Somerset Maugham, A E W Mason, Compton Mackenzie, William Le Queux, Graham Greene, Dennis Wheatley, G K Chesterton, Ian Fleming, Sydney Horler, Sir John Masterman, John Buchan, John le Carré and David Mure. The list of spy writers who have been engaged in intelligence is not merely extensive, but impressive. Those above are only a sample of writers who have acknowledged their association with intelligence, there a probably many more who are disguised by pseudonyms or have kept their association a secret. While some, like Sydney Horler, may have merely been on the fringes of "the game" (attached to the propaganda section of Air Intelligence in the First World War), others have held key posts and may even have influenced vital events in history.

In Britain a majority of those spy fiction authors listed above have been responsible and have contributed to the more authentic portrayals of intelligence in their fiction, as compared to the more sensational examples of the genre. In America the number of authors who have been engaged in intelligence work and have then turned to spy fiction is now growing. Again some of these authors, such as Ib Melchior and Edward Weismiller, have been involved in intelligence work only during the Second World War, but most of them — Joe Maggio, Victor Marchetti, David Atlee Phillips and Howard Hunt and others — have been career officers in the CIA, over long periods of time.

Unfortunately there is not the space here to explore all the known writers who have been involved in intelligence, therefore in this chapter the area will be confined to a selection of British authors to show how their experience has influenced their fiction - if it has at all. Another question raised by this connection is whether these authors give us a more accurate picture of the secret world. Are these authors using the form of the spy novel for personal or political reasons? These are just a few of the questions that will be explored in this chapter.

Erskine Childers' novel, *The Riddle of the Sands* (1903), was important not only because it is now regarded as the first modern spy novel with literary pretensions, dealing with the subject of espionage in a serious and plausible manner. Its significance at the time of writing was that it focused attention on a problem that was of current paramount importance, and had a far-reaching influence upon British politics.

The book actually proved to a horrified Director of Naval Intelligence that Admiralty charts of the Frisian Isles off the German coast were out of date compared to those of the German High Command. In the 1903 edition of Childers' novel there is the following note on page ix: "The fragment of charts (Charts A and B) are reproductions on a slightly reduced scale, and omitting some confusing and irrelevant details, of British and German Admiralty charts. Space precludes the insertion of those bulky engravings in full, but the reader who wishes for fuller information is referred to Charts Nos.406 and 407 of the British series and to No.64 of the German series."

Not only had Childers sailed around the coasts of Germany and Holland in his yacht *Vixen*, but he had done some spying on his own account into the machinations of German agents. His book sought successfully to create the propaganda of fear. Churchill remarked that this novel was greatly responsible for Britain's decision to establish naval bases at Invergordon, Firth of Forth and Scapa Flow.

If nothing else it prompted the Naval Intelligence Division to act and by so doing proved the difficulties involved in the task that Childers himself actually accomplished. NID sent two officers to spy on the Frisian Isles and German coastal defence. Lieutenant Brandon, RN and Captain Trench, Royal Marines, were told to do this while on holiday, with the churlish but strict understanding that this was an unpaid jaunt and that, while the Admiralty would be delighted if the pair succeeded, they could expect no help if they failed and were caught. They carried out the assignment, took various photographs and made sketches, but they were caught and sentenced to four years' imprisonment. It was not until 1913, some 17 months before the expiry of their sentence, that they were pardoned by the Kaiser on the occasion of King George V's visit to Berlin.

Childers was but one of the many authors who alerted the British public and the politicians to the unpreparedness of the British Navy and the threat of Germany. William Le Queux and E Phillips Oppenheim also wrote novels on the same theme; the difference between these authors was that Childers did not inject unnecessary sensationalism into his novel — it was informative, well researched and the story was entertaining and plausible. Le Queux claimed to be in the employment of the British Secret Service and was the first to pronounce that his stories were based on his own adventures in the Secret Service, and his research: "As I write I have before me a file of amazing documents which plainly show the feverish activity with which this advance guard of our enemy is working to secure for their employers the most detailed information." [29]

Childers was one of the earliest writers in Britain to treat espionage as a serious subject in fiction, and give an accurate portrayal of the secret world. This tradition was followed later by Somerset Maugham with the publication of *Ashenden* in 1928. Here was another author who had been involved in the intelligence business.

Maugham's experience in Switzerland during the First World War, as an agent of the British SIS, after he had served with the Red Cross in France, undoubtedly provided him with the material for the character of Ashenden. However, it was later on that he was given a less boring and uneventful job when he was sent to Russia in 1917. He was the chief agent in Russia for Sir William Wiseman who was in control of the British Secret Service in America at the time. Maugham used his cover as a writer to gain information about the political situation in Russia. The Wiseman Papers in the E M House Collection, Yale University provide abundant evidence of Maugham's career in the Secret Service.

In a letter from Maugham to Wiseman dated 7 July 1917, he wrote: "I do not know whether it is intended that I should have any salary for the work I am undertaking. I will not pretend that I actually need one, but in Switzerland I refused to accept anything and found afterwards that I was the only man working in the organisation for nothing and that I was regarded not as patriotic or generous but merely as damned foolish. If the job carries a salary, I think it would be more satisfactory to have it." On 18 July Maugham signed a receipt for the sum of $21,000 from Wiseman.

Maugham had in his possession a long list of code names for various people and institutions. The British Government was "Eyre & Co.", Trotsky was "Cole", Lenin was "Davis" and the American Government was "Curtis Co." Maugham himself was "Somerville".

His reports from Russia were detailed and covered individuals and organisations. Reporting on the Czech organisation (which was being used by the Americans as an agency for spying on the Bolsheviks) he said it "has

1,200 branches and a membership of 70,000. The whereabouts and activities of each member is controlled by a card system." He named the chief German agent in Russia, one Max Warburg, and he warned that the moderate Kerensky, the Russian leader, was "losing popularity and it is doubtful if he can last." He didn't! "Murders of officers continues freely. Cossacks are planning a revolt."

In October 1917, according to Maugham, Kerensky wanted Maugham to pass on to Lloyd George personally a secret message. Afraid that his stammer might ruin his delivery of the message verbally, Maugham wrote out the report and many years later blamed himself for the Prime Minister's lack of response to Kerensky's request.

Maugham himself remarked in 1951: "The work of an agent in the Intelligence Department is on the whole monotonous. A lot of it is uncommonly useless. The material it offers for stories is scrappy and pointless; the author has himself to make it coherent, dramatic and probable." [30]

Many critics and writers have praised *Ashenden* for the way in which it presents the sordid world of intelligence, and a number of writers have acknowledged their debt to Maugham, including John le Carré. It may be argued that in this novel Maugham anticipated the work of Ambler, Greene and le Carré. The highest praise came from Raymond Chandler: "There are no other great spy stories — none at all. I have been searching and I know. It's a strange thing. The form does not appear so very difficult. Evidently it's impossible. There are a few tales of adventure with a spying element or something of the sort, but they always overplay their hand. Too much bravura, the tenor sings too loud. They are as much like *Ashenden* as the opera *Carmen* is like the deadly little tale that Merimeé wrote." [31]

Compton Mackenzie turned to spy fiction for different reasons, he was the first British author to make an exposé in fiction of some of the nonsenses of our own British Security and Intelligence Services in their pre-World War II days. Mackenzie was prosecuted under the Official Secrets Act, not because he wrote of his experiences in intelligence work in his book *Athenian Memoirs* (1932), but because he "revealed the mysterious consonant by which the Chief of the Secret Service was known". In the end Mackenzie was fined £100. The charge was a ridiculous farce and Mackenzie's solution was to answer in kind by writing his novel *Water on the Brain* in 1933.

At one point in the novel, the hero, Arthur Blenkinsop, makes the mistake of referring to his chief, N, by his real name, Colonel Nutting. He apologises quickly and is told: " 'I know you won't do it again. Of course, in one way, it doesn't matter in my room at the War Office. But it's against the principles of the Secret Service. You do it once in private, and then before you know where you are you'll go and do it in the middle of Piccadilly. After all, the whole point of the Secret Service is that it should be secret.' 'Quite, quite, sir, I'm very sorry.' 'Of course, I wouldn't go so far as to say that the secrecy was *more* important than the service, but it's every bit *as* important. Well, it stands to reason that if the Secret Service was no longer secret, it would cease to be the Secret Service. After all, we're not Cabinet Ministers. We can't afford to talk.' "

When the Americans were creating the Office of Strategic Services during the Second World War, they used *Water on the Brain* as a textbook for their trainees, which must have given Mackenzie much quiet satisfaction. Such farcical court actions as that brought against Mackenzie only served to show the British Secret Service in a ridiculous light and became unthinkable in the 1960s following such Secret Service blunders as those of Commander Crabb diving under a Soviet cruiser in Portsmouth harbour, and the revelations of Kim Philby's treachery. Not only was "C" mentioned in the press, television, radio and books, but the names of recent MI6 chiefs were also published, much to the annoyance of Whitehall.

Graham Greene is another author who joined the SIS in the Second World War. He was stationed early in 1942 in Freetown in West Africa and was later posted back to London where he worked with Philby in the SIS Section V. When Philby's book was published in Britain in 1968, Greene wrote a foreword to it in which, far from condemning Philby, he compared his loyalty to the Soviet Union with that of the English Catholics who secretly worked for the Spaniards in the reign of Elizabeth I. Philby's defection gave Greene the idea for *The Human Factor* (1978), yet Maurice Castle in this book, though inspired to some extent by Philby, is a rather more likeable character.

Like Compton Mackenzie before him Greene saw the British Secret Service as an object of ridicule, providing material for comedy as well as tragedy, which was marvellously portrayed in *Our Man in Havana* (1958). Although Greene preferred to call his espionage novels "entertainments", they provided him with an outlet to explore the themes of treachery and betrayal, as well as a canvas to display the foibles of human nature.

In the introduction to *Our Man in Havana* written in 1970, Greene wrote: "I had the idea of writing a Secret Service comedy based on what I had learned from my work in 1943-4 of German Abwehr activity in Lisbon. Those Abwehr officers who had not been suborned already by our own service spent much of their time sending home completely erroneous reports based on information received from imaginary agents. It was a paying game (and a safe one), especially when expenses and bonuses were added to the decipherer's salary.

"I had sometimes thought, in the course of my work, of how easily in West Africa I could have played a similar game, if I had not been content with the more modest profits suited to the parsimony of my office. I had learned that nothing pleased the services at home more than the addition of a card to their intelligence files." [32]

Ian Fleming is another figure who features prominently in the history of the British spy novel and British Intelligence, but unlike his predecessors he chose the sensational path in spy fiction. His experience as a journalist, and as Personal Assistant to the chief of the Naval Intelligence Division during the Second World War, provided him with ample material for his novels. However, the figure of James Bond was more of an outlet for his frustrated ambitions as a writer and an intelligence desk-man, rather than an opportunity to impress upon his audience his intimate knowledge of the workings of an intelligence service.

Fleming may also have been drawn to sensationalise his fiction because the realities of the Intelligence world were too unpleasant. This can be seen in his portrayal of the Anglo-American relationship in his stories. In the early novels Fleming was keen to emphasise the close relationship between the two nations, but this arrangement soon soured as Britain could no longer be regarded as an equal political or economic partner — she was now the poor relation, dependent on the generosity of her richer cousins. This was reflected by a developing feeling of resentment and envy that Bond showed in the later novels, notably in *You Only Live Twice* (1964), when Bond goes to Japan to get Soviet cryptographic secrets because the CIA won't pass them on to the British. Also Fleming did not explore the theme of treachery and betrayal that le Carré was to enlarge upon. It was mostly because of the spy scandals in the 1950s that the Americans came to distrust the British Secret Service, and so were disinclined to share information so freely with the British. It is interesting to note that Fleming reveals more about the political situation by what he leaves out in his novels rather than by what he chooses to disclose.

David Mure served in the Second World War in A Force in the Middle East. This was the organisation headed by Brigadier Dudley Clarke, whose role it was to deceive the enemy in the Mediterranean and the Near and Middle Eastern areas. Its headquarters were in Cairo, with strategically placed stations throughout the Middle East. The main deception was practised through agents thought by the Germans to be under their control. They were in fact under the British, feeding false information to the enemy. Secondly, to lend credence to the agents' transmissions, Dudley Clarke, with the help of Jasper Maskelyne, the master magician, gave apparent verification to these reports by fabricated invasion flotillas, tanks, aircraft etc., and built up a system of displaying false divisional signs converting non-operational to "operational" formations.

Mure should certainly have been able to produce a most factual and original novel based on his wartime experiences in the deception game through which the Germans were constantly misinformed about Allied plans and movements. Instead he confined such material to factual books such as *Practice to Deceive* (1977) and *Master of Deception* (1980), but made his one novel out of completely different material. In researching wartime deception tricks for these two books, he came to the conclusion that there was a mole in a key position inside the British Security Service who had never been unmasked. Every time he raised the question or sought to investigate this subject he was met with extraordinary hostility and even threats if he dared to write anything factual on the matter.

In the end he decided to turn his investigations into a novel entitled *The Last Temptation* (1984), which his publishers describe as follows: "Rooted in fact, this novel follows the parts played by the central character and his colleagues in the shadowy world of intrigue, during the Second World War with their involvement in the complexities of the Double-Cross System, and then in the duplicities of Anglo-American post-war relations with Soviet Russia ... A blend of fact and fiction, with fascinating insights into the strange and sometimes sinister lifestyle of Guy Burgess and his fellows, *The Last Temptation* surely comes closest to the truth in explaining the phenomenon of senior British Intelligence officers exposed in the end as traitors to their own land — the reader is left to make the final judgement."

True, the average reader would not easily be able to make a final judgement because he would not be able to identify all the characters in the novel. Mure listed the real names of the characters he had called the Duchess (Burgess), Pig Baby (Maclean), Humpty Dumpty (Churchill), Red Queen (Blunt), etc., but he had also listed White Rabbit and the First and Second Unicorns as "censored", while cunningly calling the villain of the story "I" and listing him as "myself". Of course this should not be taken to suggest that Mure was the villain, and it is quite clear from the narrative that they are not one and the same. Those of us who have researched his story in depth in real life are in no doubt that the first person narrator of this piece of fiction is intended to be Captain Guy Maynard Liddell, former Deputy Director of MI5, who died in 1958.

Last but not least in this gallery of writers, there is David Cornwell, better known under his pseudonym John le Carré, who admitted only a few years ago his involvement in the British Secret Service. His approach to spy fiction owes much to his predecessors, in particular Childers, Maugham and Greene, and in his work he has continued the tradition of a more cynical and critical view of the world of espionage.

Le Carré said in an interview that he had followed the tradition of the "realistic" school in spy fiction, in contrast to Fleming, who sensationalised the spy story: "whereas there were many precedents for writing realistic stories about espionage which ... indicated the spy was like a rider on a historical horse." He mentions Conrad's *Under Western Eyes* and *The Secret Agent*, as well as Maugham's *Ashenden*. "...but for some reason ... it wasn't getting through and ... I think the explanation was that really we wouldn't look at reality." [33]

Le Carré's experience in the British Secret Service provided him with much raw material for his novels, and he often expresses his delight that much of his invented descriptions and words such as "lamplighter", "babysitter", "pavement artist", "shoe-maker" and others, have now allegedly entered the vocabulary of the "real" Secret Service. One clear example of the transference of fiction into fact.

One characteristic le Carré pointed out is the related nature of the work between the writer and the intelligence officer: "The writer's life is so similar to that of the spy's: He's dependent on the people he deceives for reprocessing to serving up to his rather remote masters, the readers. There is always that feeling that you must withdraw from society to report on it, which is exactly the spy's condition, the feeling that you live on occupied territory." [34] This is probably one of the main reasons why writers with intelligence experience have been attracted to spy fiction.

David Stafford in his book, *The Silent Game*, pointed out that Graham Greene in his first autobiography, *A Sort of Life* (1971), also remarked upon these similarities: "he says that he supposes every novelist 'has something in common with a spy: he watches, he overhears, he seeks motives and analyses character,' and in his attempt to serve literature he is unscrupulous.' In Greene's case, it is difficult to know when the writer stops and the spy begins. Nor does Greene really want us to know, for he has followed the trail blazed by Le Queux, and deliberately drawn smokescreens across his tracks." [35]

In conclusion we may say that although there has been a close relationship between writers and those who have had experience in Intelligence this does not guarantee that the fiction will convey an accurate picture of the intelligence services, as can be seen in the case of Fleming and the flamboyant James Bond.

Also one cannot categorically state that having had intelligence experience makes for a better writer. In fact, if the object of the writer is not to give away secrets, it may well hinder the development of the writer's imagination. We have seen how the spy novel can be used as a powerful propaganda weapon in the hands of a writer like Erskine Childers. Spy fiction also has the potential to become an effective exposé of intelligence matters, whether unintentionally, as in the case of Compton Mackenzie, or intentionally, as David Mure set out to do in *The Last Temptation*. Then there are those writers like Maugham, Greene and le Carré who have continued the tradition of the "realistic" spy novel from a knowledgeable standpoint, and although the British Secret Service may inwardly refute the portrayal of themselves in these writers' hands, their readers have enjoyed the benefits of their experience and the pleasure of their stories.

Chapter 7
Adaptation to the Screen

Very few spy novels have adapted well to the screen or television. The only true and lasting success has been the James Bond films which have become a cult unto themselves. For various reasons the spy novel does not adapt well visually, and even if it is a success commercially it is more likely to be due to a complete change in the plot or the introduction of new characters. The problem of adaptation is similar to that of the translator, whose aim is not so much to make a literal translation of the work (sometimes language can be obscure and may not have the equivalent form in the target language), but to capture the spirit of the literary work — a harder task if the work is a classic in the country of origin. Similar problems arise for the film or television director; his task is not so much to make a literal copy of the story from print to screen, but to give a visual interpretation of the story which incorporates the spirit of the book, while entertaining at the same time. For various reasons this has not been achieved very successfully in the past.

   This chapter discusses books which have been adapted to the screen and the problems that have arisen. There are also recent examples of spy novels having been adapted for television series which raises other issues. There is very little material on this subject but most of the information has been found in newspaper articles and three source books — Leslie Halliwell's *Film Guide*, Leonard Rubenstein's *The Great Spy Films* and Eric Rhode's *A History of the Cinema*.

   The cinema has a great potential as a propaganda weapon and this aspect was exploited shamelessly in the 1930s and during the Second World War. One prime example of propaganda on the screen can be seen in the Secret Service films of Ronald Reagan. He made four movies featuring Brass Bancroft during 1938 and 1939. Stephen Vaughn, who has written an interesting article on this subject, states: "In addition to publicizing the 'Brown Scare', these pictures formed part of a campaign to enhance the image of government agents in their battles against counterfeiters, illegal aliens, and international spies and saboteurs. In the films a youthful, heroic Reagan, then under contract to Warner Bros. Pictures, Inc., dramatically set forth concerns about law and order and national security to an international audience." [36]

   In the 1930s the cinema was the main source of public information and entertainment. This was the age before television, and although the radio had made its mark as a great communicator (proved by the "fireside chats" of Franklin D Roosevelt, which had brought the voice of the American President to millions of people), the screen was unique because not only did it reach a wide audience of every age and background, it was also the main form of entertainment.

The bad image of the law enforcement officer made him an ideal target for propaganda. Too many films like *Little Caesar* (1930) had portrayed the gangster and criminal in an heroic light, and the police or G-men as stupid and incompetent. The FBI and its Director J Edgar Hoover were keen to co-operate with the film industry to improve the image of the law enforcement officer. Warner Brothers was one of the first studios to change its approach to the gangster movie and reverse the roles of the gangster and the law man. The first film to witness the change of roles was *G-Men* (1935). "This picture has been regarded by film historians as a turning point in the way movies portrayed government agents. It shows a highly efficient FBI that needed bright, well-educated, and well-armed agents... After the appearance of *G-Men* it became common for movies to make heroes of government agents and other law men." [37]

In those days the movie studios felt a great responsibility for screening the "right" entertainment, and various organisations were created to enforce a code of practice to which the film directors were meant to conform. The Hays Office, formed in 1922, was established to monitor Hollywood films, but it was not until the formation of the Production Code Administration (PCA), created in 1934, that these codes of practice were enforced effectively.

"Reagan's Secret Service films reflect at least three movie industry concerns in the late 1930s. First, they treat federal agents in an attractive manner. For years, controversy had raged over the often all-too-favorable portrayal of crime and criminals. The Brass Bancroft series constituted part of a larger effort to use motion pictures to improve the public's understanding of government agents and law enforcement agencies. Second, these movies reveal how, by the end of the decade, Hollywood had become troubled by international espionage and the presence of Nazi spies in America. The Warner brothers in particular worried about this problem and called attention to the threat. Finally, some of the Brass Bancroft films promoted military preparedness. Most Hollywood studios staunchly opposed Nazi Germany and such resistance to Hitler was especially strong at Warner Bros., where films often emphasized the need for stronger national defense." [38]

Just as Erskine Childers with his novel, *The Riddle in the Sands* (1903), had alerted the British public to the lack of naval defence around the British Isles, and the threat from the "German menace", in the early part of the twentieth century, many of the films made in Hollywood in the 1930s were used to promote a certain direction in American foreign policy, namely to support President Roosevelt in his wish to help Britain and the other European powers against the advance of Hitler's armies.

Each of the four Secret Service films (in which Reagan was the hero), was concerned with some contemporary aspect. In all these pictures he played a Treasury Department operative. In the first one, *Secret Service of the Air* (1939), the hero had to infiltrate a ring of criminals who smuggled illegal aliens into America from Mexico. The next two films, *The Code of the Secret Service* (1939) and *Smashing the Money Ring* (1939), dealt with counterfeiting. It is the last film which is of interest — *Murder in the Air* (1940) — which carried a thinly disguised warning about Nazi saboteurs, and featured a death-ray weapon called "the Inertia Projector".

In promoting the films Warner Brothers tried to give them an aura of authenticity by saying that the stories were "but thinly disguised dramatizations of actual adventures" taken from the files of William H Moran, a former chief of the US Secret Service. The studio had employed Moran as a consultant on a salary of $250 a week. Warner Brothers also encouraged a close relationship with the FBI and other law enforcement agencies, to promote better understanding of these organisations and enhance the authenticity of the films.

The movie industry's concern with the problem of internal subversion culminated in the film *Confession of a Nazi Spy* (1939) made by Warner Brothers. It was written by Milton Krims and John Wexley, and was based on material collected by a former FBI agent, Leon G Turrou. He had written a best-selling book about the counter-espionage work of the FBI in seeking out active Nazi spies and their networks in America. Turrou and Krims had written a series of stories on the same theme for the *New York Post*. Their stories were published in the *Post* in December 1938, after the spy trial USA vs. Otto Herman Voss *et al.* in November. These spy scandals had been widely publicised by the press so that it was familiar material to many movie-goers. This film provided an excellent opportunity to bring entertainment, propaganda and topicality to the masses. One critic remarked about this film: "The Warner brothers have declared war on Germany with this one ... with this precedent there is no way any producer could argue against dramatizing any social or political theme on the grounds that he's afraid of domestic or foreign censorship. Everybody duck." [39]

Leonard Rubenstein also commented on the political impact of this film: "A commercial and critical success, this film not only confirmed Warner Brothers as the pre-eminent socially oriented studio in Hollywood, but also introduced American feature film audiences, *the* mass of moviegoers, to the topical drama rewritten from actual events and employing newsreel footage within its staged sequences. Part of the film's success had to do with reality, since a year before its release there had been a series of federal investigations and trials of Nazi sympathizers and organizers. *Confessions of a Nazi Spy* triggered a German diplomatic counter-offensive which succeeded in having the film banned in some eighteen countries." [40]

The Secret Service films of Ronald Reagan are but one example of the many films which were used as effective propaganda by the film industry, at a particular time in history. In the 1950s Hollywood became a major target of McCarthyism precisely because its films were regarded as so influential. A number of actors and film directors were accused unjustly of Communist affiliations, and as a result many careers were destroyed by these accusations. To a certain extent, Hollywood has never recovered psychologically from this political attack and has tried to cultivate a less controversial and more conservative image since then.

Dilys Powell, who was a member of the Board of Governors of the British Film Institute, and has been a film critic for the *Sunday Times* since 1939, believes that the spy film has stagnated: "The trouble with spy films is that like thrillers they are wearing out — the reader begins to unravel things for himself. Periodically cinema is obsessed by some particular theme — teenage tales, horror movies, and now espionage; spy fiction looks like a good easy way of shaping an exciting narrative, but with the years the novelty wears off, situations are repeated and the enemy shifts but not his tactics.

"And now one has to reckon with another element: fact. The spy used to belong to fiction. Today he is part of daily life, he is there in every newspaper, he outdistances fiction. The fantasies of real-life defection and betrayal challenge the screen; it becomes impossible to outdo the stories of our own agents and counter-agents and traitors. Only one or two writers from television and the cinema are gifted enough to survive competition with fact, and they often enough turn out to have worked in the real anti-spy business." [41]

The film is a visual medium: the camera directs the audience to focus on particular details, therefore the plot is more prone to predictability than the novel (which at least leaves something to the imagination). It is harder for the spy film to convey subtlety, and yet one film which succeeded in portraying brutal sentiments in a subtle form was *The Spy Who Came in from the Cold*, which marked a watershed in spy film history. It was directed by Martin Ritt, who was one of the film-makers blacklisted during the 1950s. The harsh reality of espionage was something rarely seen in the cinema, and in Paul Dehn's screenplay, like the novel, the plot is only partially revealed to the audience. It is not until the end that we learn the extent of the betrayal through the eyes of the disillusioned hero, Alec Leamas.

Another unusual ingredient in this film was the character of the enemy agent, Fiedler, who was given a sympathetic treatment. As Leonard Rubenstein has remarked: "Throughout the film Fiedler was characterized as a curious combination of idealist and functionary who rebuked Leamas as the 'lowest currency of the Cold War' and then asked what motivated Leamas to be a spy in the first place, what grand ideal. Fiedler was, of course, shocked at Leamas's total indifference to ideology. Mundt, on the other hand, was depicted as the brutal secret police officer familiar from wartime films. The audience's sympathy was divided between Leamas and Fiedler, particularly since the only times when the camera veered away from Burton was when Oskar Werner spoke."

Rubenstein concluded: "*The Spy Who Came in from the Cold* was a landmark in film history; not only was it a seriously honest and grim portrayal of modern espionage, but it also avoided many of the hallowed traditions of the spy film. There were no car chases, fist fights, hidden bombs or extended shoot-outs, only the businesslike machine gun bursts at the Berlin Wall. There were no excessive scenes of torture nor long-winded explanations of the strategic importance of Leamas's assignment. Besides focusing on the moral ambiguity surrounding espionage work, the film also depicted an ostensible enemy agent in a sympathetic light. Despite the thematic innovations, *The Spy Who Came in from the Cold* was a conventional narrative."[42]

This film shows that by subtle changes of emphasis a spy novel can be successfully adapted to the screen as a powerful drama. It could be argued that the film had a greater impact than the book because it was so harsh in its photography and in the views it expressed. This harshness may have been influenced by the fact that the director, Martin Ritt, had been the victim of political attack, which lead him to be critical in his interpretation; Paul Dehn, the writer of the screenplay, was himself a veteran of Intelligence, and the combination of these elements may have contributed to this particular portrayal of espionage.

The spy film continued to be used for propaganda purposes long after the war had ended. In some cases the express purpose of the author was ignored to serve political ends. For instance, in Graham Greene's *The Quiet American* (1957), the film completely reversed the political message of the book, changing it from anti-American to anti-Communist.

In the 1960s Hollywood films became more critical of authority, just as the spy novel did in the 1970s; some became more paranoid as the Cold War and the threat of nuclear holocaust seemed to permeate all forms of popular culture. The manifestation of this paranoia was reflected in some of the films made at this time, in which man was seen to be no longer infallible, and that perhaps he was unable to control the world around him. Eric Rhode, the author of *A History of the Cinema* (1976), commented on how these films reflected the changing values of the Hollywood film industry: "*The Manchurian Candidate* contains an attack on the electorate's trust in its politicians; and the value of this criticism has been confirmed by the mystery that still surrounds the assassination of John F Kennedy, or the revelation of the Pentagon Papers and the Watergate Affair. But, just as importantly, its debunking typified a distrust of politicians that the old Hollywood would never have allowed, an awareness of how inadequate human beings may well be in controlling the technological power that Kubrick was to play with in *Dr Strangelove* and Sidney Lumet to embroider on more solemnly in *Fail Safe* (1963), where a terrible dream about nuclear destruction is acted out in reality." [43]

Having seen how spy films were used as a propaganda weapon, we will now take a closer look at some of the technicalities involved in adapting a spy novel to the screen. Sometimes the book may need considerable alterations before it is suitable material for a visual drama. For instance, Pat

Barker, a British author, has just had her book, *Union Street*, bought by Hollywood's MGM to be made into a film called *Letters*, starring Jane Fonda and Robert de Niro. She comments: "Of course any novel adapted for the screen has to be stripped down and reinvented. Novelists who don't know this are naive. Scriptwriters who don't do it are incompetent." Although they have made changes to her book she is not criticising their adaptation. She says: "I don't intend to join those novelists who bank the film money and then traipse round after producers and directors asking, in effect, 'Please may I have my virginity back?' Film is a different medium, which has to reach its own solutions. The message for the novelist has to be: if you can't take the consequences, don't sell the rights." [44]

One author who learned the hard way is Ken Follett, who stated: "I did not write the screenplays for the movie of *Eye of the Needle* or the miniseries of *The Key of Rebecca* and *On Wings of Eagles*. In each case the producers sent me the screenplays they had commissioned, and I gave my comments. In no case did they take any notice of what I said! In each case the adaptation was less successful commercially than the original book, and I suspect that was because the screenplay was not up to scratch. I have now adopted a policy of refusing to sell screen rights unless the producer also commissions me to write the first draft screenplay. This has happened with *Lie Down with Lions*, which has been optioned by British producer Geoff Reeve, but has not yet been shot." [45]

The spy novel can be adapted easily if the story is an action-adventure story, or a sensational drama rather than a realistic one, but problems can arise if the book contains a lot of description or analysis, chunks of this material may well be left out.

In contrast, Robin Winks, a critic of spy and detective fiction, argues that "Unlike mystery fiction, spy fiction adjusts to the motion-picture screen superlatively well, and no one ever did it better than Alfred Hitchcock, even when he changed utterly Buchan's own book. To *The Thirty-Nine Steps* Hitchcock added what he called a MacGuffin — a word he stuck with through all his pictures. A MacGuffin is visually essential; on the printed page it is valuable though not indispensable." [46] It is essentially a red herring or a diversion in the plot that has no relevance whatsoever, but keeps the viewer "on his toes".

The Thirty-Nine Steps has been filmed three times, in 1935, 1959 and 1978, and it is fascinating to see how each of them differs. Hitchcock's version filmed in 1935 is a classic and the two later versions are poor renditions of the book or the original film. Leslie Halliwell describes it as a "marvellous comedy thriller with most of the gimmicks found not only in Hitchcock's later work but in anyone else's who has tried the same vein. It has little to do with the original novel, and barely sets foot outside the studio, but it makes every second count, and is unparalleled in its use of timing, atmosphere and comedy relief."

One reviewer, Sydney W Carroll, said of it: "A narrative of the unexpected — a humorous, exciting, dramatic, entertaining, pictorial, vivid and novel tale told with a fine sense of character and a keen grasp of the cinematic idea."

While another, George Perry, remarked in 1965: "Such is the zest of the Hitchcock plot that the original point of the title was totally forgotten, and half a line had to be added at the end by way of explanation."

In the next version, filmed in 1959 and directed by Ralph Thomas, Halliwell comments: "Just to show that stars and story aren't everything, this scene-for-scene remake muffs every opportunity for suspense or general effectiveness, and is practically a manual on how not to make a thriller." [47]

It is extraordinary that one film can be treated so differently and shows the dilemma for the director in deciding whether to stick to the story or to disregard it to make a good film.

Most of the James Bond films have been popular and they are still being produced today. All of the Bond stories have been made into films, but they bear little resemblance to the original titles. The plots have been reconstructed and gadgets have been added which were largely absent from the novels; the scriptwriters have rewritten the dialogue and created a stable image of the hero which does not exist in the books. But this is probably why Bond is such an adaptable hero on the screen, for the films are pure, sensational entertainment, inclined to parody themselves, but they seem to have a timeless appeal even though at times the plots are outrageously unrealistic. We are now onto the fourth actor to take up the mantle and each one has brought something different to the character.

In a recent article, Philip Zeigler referred to the vividly described scene of the threatening scorpion in *Diamonds Are Forever*: "Tautly written, scrupulously observed, the action cries out to be filmed. Sadly, it is typical of the Bond films that when this episode was actually put on the screen, it was vulgarised by the addition of a gratuitous and senseless murder. Indeed, most of those who denounce Fleming's sadistic violence have in mind the crimes that the cinema has perpetrated in his name." [48]

Just as there has been a close connection between British and American spy writers and Intelligence, there have been parallels too between those involved in film and espionage. For instance, Paul Dehn was a very successful producer of films after a wartime career in the SOE (Special Operations Executive) in the Second World War. He wrote screenplays for three of the best known post-war spy films — Fleming's *Goldfinger*, le Carré's *The Deadly Affair* and *The Spy Who Came in from the Cold*. Much of his know-how in the world of spying in real life proved useful in this work. During the war he spent some time at the SOE training camp, Camp X, in Canada. Philby wrote of him that "he bubbled and frothed like a trout stream" and "his tomfoolery at the piano shortened the long summer evenings" (that was when he was at a similar training camp at Beaulieu). [49]

Dehn was an instructor at both camps, and he had also served in the Intelligence Corps. *The International Encyclopaedia of Films* suggests that his best screenplays drew upon his experiences as a Major in the SOE. His screenplay of *Orders to Kill* (1958), which won him awards, was described by Bosley Crowther in the *New York Times* as follows: "The point is made very clearly that only the toughest, most cold-blooded and emotionally stable people were used to perform the critical assignments of counter-espionage in World War II. Then it [the film] goes right ahead to show us a completely soft and unstable guy being given the task of destroying a treacherous member of the French underground." [50]

This film tells the story of an American airman trained to kill a traitor. But he discovers that he likes his prospective victim, a gentle little man who likes cats, and he actually believes the man is innocent and not a traitor. Urged on by an underground woman, he kills the man, but as a result becomes a guilt-ridden alcoholic.

Another example of the close relationship between espionage and the film industry can be found in the career of the Hungarian-born film director Alexander Korda, whose films included *The Third Man* (1949). He was never a British agent, but worked closely with MI6 for several years before the Second World War. According to a newspaper article in the *San Francisco Chronicle*: "Korda's film company, London Films, was used as a cover for British agents going abroad to such an extent that, according to one report, the MI6 deputy director, Sir Claude Dansey, was eventually given a seat on the company board so that he could keep track of his men."[51]

On the whole American intelligence officers do not like spy films, mainly because they are unrealistic in their portrayal of the intelligence officer. In particular, they dislike the fact that the spy hero in the movies is as conspicuous as the beautiful women he seduces, and gives a false image which bears no relation to reality.

According to William Colby, former director of Central Intelligence, or America's top spy, a real spy has to be "a gray man who has a hard time catching the eye of a waiter in a restaurant. As a result, I still have a hard time catching a waiter's eye in a restaurant." Leslie Gelb of the *New York Times* found that in his survey of what American intelligence agents think of spy movies: "It is not that the real spies object to spy movies as entertainment; it is just that they are not entertained. To Walter Pforzheimer, who has 42 years in the intelligence business and is one of the men who helped bring about passage of the 1947 Act that established the CIA, their careers are 'too serious' for the screen or even most books."

Intelligence officers are also critical of spy films because they are old-fashioned, as far as their conception of espionage is concerned: "Spy movies haven't caught up to the fact that modern intelligence has little to do with people, the lifeblood of drama, and much more with technology. Human intelligence-gathering has been largely replaced by machines and by organizations and people who know how to run them." Just as the sensational spy writers tend to exaggerate the importance of the spy hero, the spy movie follows suit.

A critic complained recently in *The Spectator* that "more and more films, and television programmes whose techniques derive from films, and which purport to contain sequential narrative, 'a story', no longer bother to make narrative *sense*." [52]

This critic was talking generally, but it is an appropriate description of many of the spy novels which have been adapted into long-running series for television.

Success in the adaptation of a novel can be very tenuous and sometimes the director can make terrible mistakes, in which the spirit of the book is completely lost. For instance, Andrew Hislop commented in *The Times* in 1987, when the first part of le Carré's *The Perfect Spy* was broadcast as a television series: "The BBC and the script writer Arthur Hopcraft had served le Carré brilliantly in the past and again the acting (Ray McAnally splendid as the father), direction and dialogue was admirable. But the decision to progress chronologically through Pym's childhood was an unforgiveable error — the more so if it was done to make things 'easier' for the viewers."

"Mystery is an essential ingredient of the genre (How many completely understood 'Tinker Tailor' on television?) and avoiding the opening confusions of the spy-story framework which permeates the personal exploration lessened our entertainment without making us the wiser.

"We may all plod on chronologically but only understand our progress through flashbacks and competing narratives."

When a spy novel is well adapted, the critics take note; for example Richard Last, in a review of one episode of *Storyboard* (written by Philip Broadley, and made by Thames Television), commented: "Most TV spy stories work so hard at being inpenetrable that they give you a headache. This one just lets you sit back and wonder whether lines like 'The Official Secrets Act is not mocked, Blair,' are unconscious humour, or genuine wit." When they are adapted to the screen the directors seem to forget that they are trying to entertain.

Len Deighton's three books, *Berlin Game*, *Mexico Set* and *London Match* have recently been serialised on television as "Game, Set & Match" by Granada. This ITV company has had great success in the past with its impressive adaptations of other novels, such as *Brideshead Revisited* and *The Jewel in the Crown*. It is also the first time that one of Deighton's stories has been adapted for television.

The series consists of 13 hour-long episodes and it took a year to film, with a budget of £5 million. Charles Spencer in the *Daily Telegraph* wrote that the adaptation of so long a story into thirteen cohesive episodes presented a number of problems. A lot of Deighton's dialogue had to be cut and new material added to establish the central character of Bernard Samson (the background of which consisted of explaining his experience in a badly organised mission to Poland which causes him to lose his nerve), which tells us why, when we encounter him, he is deskbound. Spencer writes: "The series producer, Brian Armstrong, is unrepentant about the alterations to the original. When he first discussed the project with Deighton, he warned that changes would have to be made for television and the author gave him a free hand. 'I think we serve the books best by sticking to the spirit and that may occasionally mean breaking the letter,' he says."

Spencer's view is that the adaptation worked reasonably well, and is a good example of one that comes across as a drama and entertainment, without too much obscurity for its own sake. "From what I've seen so far, I believe Armstrong is probably justified in his approach. Much of Deighton's distinctive tone and bleak humour survives intact, though I regret the loss of so much dialogue."

The series was filmed on location in Mexico and West Berlin. Granada was also the first television company to be allowed to stage dramatic action at Checkpoint Charlie, although they also built a studio set of Checkpoint Charlie which can be found next to the set of "Coronation Street". They were not allowed to film in Eastern Europe, but "Manchester and Bolton double convincingly as Eastern bloc settings", which does not say much for Bolton or Manchester! [53]

Now that satellite television is available to anyone with a satellite dish (or a dustbin lid if you prefer), these lavish productions may decline in number and quality. Television adaptations have some major advantages over the cinema, especially now that television is the most dominant source of entertainment, but more time can be taken in a series, which increases the chances of a more faithful rendering of the story. Lastly, these television series have boosted the publishing industry as many of these books have been re-published at the same time that the series is being broadcast, which should encourage viewers to return to the written word.

Chapter 8
State of the "Art": the modern spy novel

Although the age of detente eased the tension between the superpowers, it had little effect upon the espionage operations of the CIA or the KGB — in fact or fiction. Similarly, the period of *glasnost* and the opening of the Berlin Wall will probably have little consequence upon the secret war which continues to fester. There is a momentum attached to the gathering of intelligence that reaches beyond politics, and which involves all secret services in a competition for new sources of information. This factor alone virtually guarantees the survival of espionage, but apart from this most countries would no more voluntarily contemplate dismantling their intelligence organisations than they would their military arsenals, unless, of course, they were forced to dismantle them due to political pressure.

The modern spy novel discussed in this context will include those written in the 1970s and 1980s in Britain and America. This fiction displays various characteristics which distinguish it from its Cold War predecessors. As the spy novel is a reflection of our contemporary world it is an interesting exercise to look at the spy novel in its current state to show our present preoccupations and concerns.

Various themes discussed in these chapters, such as the role of the mole and terrorism in the spy novel, have now lost their innovative appeal. The USSR is no longer a viable or realistic enemy in this kind of fiction and certain authors are making a bid to find new sources of conflict and intrigue within our community. There is plenty of scope as far as material is concerned especially as the spy novel has become more realistic — it can draw upon real events and newspaper headlines for inspiration.

Apart from a change of themes which characterises the modern spy novel there are other features which distinguish it from its past. For instance, the locations of these stories has gradually changed from the traditional battlegrounds of the superpowers — Europe — to the new settings of the Far East, the Middle East and the Third World countries in Asia and Africa, thus reflecting contemporary economic and political concerns.

To a certain degree the Cold War-sensational spy novel has been replaced by a more sophisticated approach to the subject of espionage which can be seen in the plots, the characters, the spy hero and the settings. This change has resulted from the presence of readily available information about espionage, politics, places, and other details which the author can no longer gloss over if he wants to be regarded as a credible writer.

Paul Henissart, an American spy writer, remarked upon this new awareness in his reading public: "Today's spy stories undoubtedly require a high degree of realism and precision. Readers to whom they are addressed are better informed than in the past, a fact which an author should look upon with satisfaction: it is no challenge to write for the uninformed."[54]

To show how the modern spy novel has developed it is necessary to return briefly to the Cold War spy novel of the 1960s to point out the differences. A vivid example can be seen in the development of the spy hero and how his role has changed. One novelist writing in this period and who still writes today is Howard Hunt, a man who worked for the CIA, although this fact has little bearing upon his novels as far as realism is concerned. His series of books about Peter Ward (written under the name of David St. John) show the hero as a superman with a talent for getting out of tricky situations and saving the world.

Although the spy novel is rooted in politics, the spy novels of this period, which can be seen in the Peter Ward series, tended to put the political situation in a subordinate role and elevate the status of the hero, just as Fleming did with James Bond. Authors of this literature in Britain and America have shown a consistent tendency since the Second World War to show the spy as the defender of the political status quo. The Cold War offered a clear battleground in which the American or British agent could be shown defending the world against the aggressive actions of the Soviet Union and its satellites. The maintenance of this political equilibrium was the ultimate goal of these heroes, no efforts were made to come to a better understanding of nations with a different political colouring. These novels reflected a stance that perpetuated fear, aggression and misunderstanding.

As Grant Hugo, a student of spy fiction, has confirmed: "Subversion of the established political order, whether the villains are domestic or foreign, has long been a traditional theme for the thriller.

"Most writers handle it on the fairly simple assumption, which could be a reflection of the views of the readers rather than an attempt to influence them, that the status quo is acceptable and its subversion a crime. Complications arise when the powers that be are infiltrated by the enemy or otherwise incapable of right action, so that the hero must actually struggle against authority to restore the just equilibrium ... It is striking how often, nowadays, this father-figure turns out to be some kind of secret policeman." [55]

Samuel J Hamrick, an American author of spy fiction, who writes under the pseudonym of W T Tyler, noted this political stagnation in the spy novel: "The spy novel is very much a recitative of cold war clichés. Ian

Fleming, a great favorite of John Kennedy, is probably the best example of that. Spy novelists like Fleming did little to help us understand the Russians or the Soviet bureaucracy, did little to help us better understand ourselves or our times. (As George Kennan points out in a recent article in *The New Yorker*, the genre has probably contributed to our gross ignorance of the Soviet Union and heightened our paranoia.)" [56]

Hunt is one example of an author who has moved on from the Cold War theme, as portrayed in his Peter Ward series, to the more modern topics of terrorism, such as the agent of influence and the mole. To a certain extent, with the departure of the Cold War spy novel, the focus has been taken off the spy hero — as the novels have become more realistic he has been given an increasingly subordinate role — he has fallen from the heights of the superman to the depths of the human state. This change is reflected in a number of features that characterise the modern spy novel which include: an increase in the preoccupation with the hero's personal problems, which impinges on his profession; a more profound assessment of the political situation in which the story takes place; and the effects of the bureaucracy of the intelligence organisation and the corresponding behaviour of its members. The authors and the reading public are more interested and better informed about politics, hence the increase in the spy novel being labelled as a "political thriller".

Readers now expect to be educated as well as entertained when they pick up a spy novel. If the author does not present an informed picture to the reader he is liable to lack credibility. As John Atkins, a literary critic of British spy fiction, expressed it: "The modern spy writers refer constantly, not only to the sovereign states by name, but to their actual policies, their leaders, their espionage organizations, their successes and the failures. Sometimes historical personages appear as characters in the novels — spies like Philby particularly, but also Prime Ministers and Presidents. Every effort is made to create an impression of actuality." [57]

A number of novelists introduce historical figures into their fiction. One example comes from William F Buckley's *Who's On First* (1980), which contains conversations between Allen Dulles, when he was the Director of the CIA, and Dean Acheson, Secretary of State. Notorious characters such as Nixon and Kissinger feature prominently in the novels of John Ehrlichman. He knew both these men personally, a fact which makes his portraits of them all the more alarming! These characters are brought in to the story to create an authentic atmosphere and to add conviction to the plot.

Another example of the new "realism" in the spy novel is the close attention paid to the location of the story, which often involves a great deal of research by the author. Robin Winks, a critic of spy and detective fiction, admits that although the spy and detective novel is concerned with urban violence, the scene can be set anywhere: "Having admitted to the falsity of the scene as often set, I must insist that some of the best travel writing done today occurs in the midst of spy and detective fiction." [58] Because of the vicarious quality of the spy novel the authors employ considerable skill in conveying the atmosphere of a particular setting.

Some very good examples can be found in such books as Joseph Hone's *The Private Sector* (1971), in which we are given a wonderful picture of the changing face of Cairo in the 1950s and 1960s. There are many other examples in which the descriptions of the location are so vivid that they threaten to smother the plot. But this accuracy of detail is all part and parcel of the modern spy novel, adding a further dimension of interest for the reader.

As well as the introduction of "real" people the spy novelists have become adept in their ability to reconstruct history. LeRoy L Panek, a critic of British spy fiction, argues that the early novels of Frederick Forsyth (*The Day of the Jackal* (1971), *The Odessa File* (1972), *The Dogs of War* (1974) and *The Devil's Alternative* (1980)), met the expectations of the new, more sophisticated and knowledgeable reader of spy fiction: "In these novels Forsyth takes the traditional techniques of the thriller, of which he has a high level of mastery, and combines them with the principle of that other popular genre, the historical novel, creating the perfect entertainment for the seventies." [59] One of the enduring qualities of the spy novel is its adaptability to the contemporary world and its flexibility in its incorporation of different genres.

The spy hero in fiction has moved on from the early examples of the amateur at the beginning of this century: reaching the status of the professional intelligence officer after the Second World War, especially in the 1960s, to become the freelance professional or vigilante hero as in Howard Hunt's *The Hargrave Deception* (1980) and Alan Furst's *Shadow Trade* (1983). In the latter the hero operates his own clandestine agency in competition with the official government security organisation, thus illustrating the general competition for secret information whether it is intelligence about the enemy or one's friends. The question explored in many of these novels is not what the "enemy" is going to do, but who he is — is he on your side? working for himself? or some group enterprise?

This new kind of spy hero can be found in W T Tyler's *Rogue's March* (1982). Here we are presented with an experienced CIA officer at his post (in this case a small state in Africa), who knows the country and its political leaders, showing the clash of interests between the officer in the field and his spymasters in Washington, both trying to interpret events in their own way. The hero of this story, Andy Reddish, is not a fantasy figure like James Bond — plunged into a conflict with no knowledge of the problem or the protagonists. Reddish is a veteran intelligence officer who has been stationed in one place for several years, with an intimate knowledge of the country and its people. In contrast to James Bond and his fellow agents, this hero is a bureaucratic agent — unable to alter the situation by his own efforts, he is a victim as much as any other character in the book.

The modern spy novel has introduced a moral ambiguity into espionage and questions the previous conviction of the sanctity of the political status quo. This change is reflected in the vigilante spy hero who does not take orders from any bureaucrats in an office but makes his own decisions and judgements in a given situation. He relies upon his professional experience to take action and therefore has only himself to blame if anything goes wrong.

With the development of the spy hero the cult of the professional has been introduced. One example of this is Adam Hall's Quiller, who works for a British Intelligence agency, but he will only work alone — he rejects the organisational back-up that he is entitled to call upon. He prefers to work alone as there is less risk to himself and to his colleagues. This kind of protagonist could also be described as a variation on the vigilante spy hero, except that he is still employed by an intelligence service.

Frederick Forsyth's Jackal is another example of the professional hero, and even though he is a "baddie", he is presented in such a way that readers almost want him to succeed, and respect him for his professional abilities. Bruce Merry, a critic of spy fiction, comments: "This professionalism is a distinguishing mark of the 'second generation' of thriller writers, and can be contrasted directly with the dashing amateurism of the 'first generation': John Buchan, Sapper, Somerset Maugham, Graham Greene and Eric Ambler." [60]

Readers of spy fiction are tremendously fickle and quickly tire of repetition. This presents a challenge to authors for they must find new subjects and themes to explore. Some have resulted in failure and others have succeeded, but success breeds its own problems as a popular theme is in danger of being copied — just as the theme of the mole has lost a great deal of its appeal through exploitation.

Imitation of the same theme is one of the dangers in spy fiction — with repetition a theme can lose a great deal of its originality, and it is a fault that both authors and critics have noticed. For instance, Alan Furst, an American author of spy fiction, wrote: "I'd like to see an evolution into complexity, with demands of good fiction elevating the form. I'd like to see British and American novels less instinctively prone to condemning their national services, not so quick to fall back on 'betrayal' and 'conspiracy' etc. as literary devices — that's much too easy and fairly dishonest. The future depends on the form improving, but I believe it will." [61]

In a recent review by Ted Willis, an author and critic of spy fiction, in the *Daily Telegraph*, he lamented the fact that so many writers had overdone this particular theme: "On the evidence of 1986 and the early entries for 1987, the spy-thriller seems to be declining rapidly into the sere and yellow. The rich seam that was opened up so brilliantly by John le Carré and Len Deighton has now been hijacked by too many inferior imitators who, reversing the role of the old alchemist, spend their time turning gold into dross."

One example of a failure in spy fiction was that of industrial espionage, tried at one point by Ken Follett in the mid-1970s. His first two books, *The Shakeout* (1975) and *The Bear Raid* (1976), made inroads into this topic.

Follett wrote in 1977: "The spy story has been done by so many authors that it seems difficult to produce anything fresh. My solution was to write about industrial espionage. To the best of my knowledge my character Piers Roper is still the only industrial spy in fiction. Roper is a high-powered marketing executive who takes posts with a series of companies purely to steal their secrets. To move unsuspected in the boardrooms he has to be a member of the upper class, and he is (Eton and Cambridge and an Army commission), but why should such a man betray his background by becoming a snoop? He is withdrawn and inhibited, hopelessly incompetent to deal with an emotion stronger than casual friendship and fastidious about etiquette, food and clothes. He was the first character of my creation who would not let me do as I liked with the plot: I took this to be a good sign."

But unfortunately it was not, and the author said recently that "These books were not very successful. They have never been published outside the UK and are probably no longer available here." Perhaps the subject did not provide enough scope for an exciting story; certainly the world of industry does not have the same glamour that is attached to international intrigue. There is always a risk in trying something new, which may be one of the reasons why spy writers hung on to the Cold War theme for so long, and why the search for the mole has continued. But until an established writer branches out and makes a success of something new, it is unlikely that others will follow his example. The mole and the theme of treachery and betrayal has inspired some good fiction in Britain and America, but now it is in danger of becoming stale and boring.

A successful theme is a gamble, but one that has paid off is Clive Cussler's Dirk Pitt and NUMA. He always uses the theme of underwater exploration in his stories, but his hero is really a vigilante and becomes involved in espionage incidentally, or for personal reasons, which was the case in the story *Deep Six* (1984).

The author explains how he achieved this success: "When I decided to develop a series hero I looked around the field and studied everyone from Sherlock Holmes to James Bond to Travis McGee. I figured the last thing the adventure arena needed was another private detective, spy or CIA agent. So I created a guy by the name of Dirk Pitt who is Special Projects Director for NUMA (the National Underwater & Marine Agency). Fortunately, I stumbled onto a good thing. The mysteries that can be expanded upon in and around the water are as boundless as the oceans themselves." [62]

There are still many more subjects for the spy writer to explore and a few which have been neglected, as Reg Gadney points out: "The one influence upon stories of the secret life that still, incredibly, goes almost ignored is that of the computer and especially electronic surveillance and information retrieval. I dealt with such matters in *The Champagne Marxist* some twelve years ago. More recently I have dealt with the new generation of MI5 and MI6 officers in *Nightshade*." [63]

One of the reasons why computers and spy technology are not more prominently featured in espionage fiction is because they threaten to eliminate the spy hero. This fiction has a vested interest in promoting the benefits of human espionage, otherwise it would have to admit to the supremacy of technology in espionage, which may be true in fact, but will never happen in fiction. However, spy novels compensate for this by the use of high-tech gadgets to help the hero and with the occasional appearance of the analyst spy hero. So far there are very few examples of this kind of hero, but he may grow in stature if the agent in the field declines in popularity. After all someone has to analyse all the information collected by agents and sophisticated machines. [64]

John Atkins argues that the introduction of domestic problems into the modern spy novel is "a human compensation for the dramatic loss imposed by the new situation." In the face of competition from technology in espionage, these personal details add a human dimension to the story as well as an added interest in the hero. He goes on to say "Ronald Seth in his *Encyclopaedia of Espionage* makes the same point. The American NSA (National Security Agency — officially — but some call it Never Say Anything) engages in top-secret cryptography and electronic espionage. Seth says their work has little interest for novelists because it is too technical and backroom to have mass appeal. The NSA lacks the glamour of some other agencies, such as the CIA, which at least conducts its politics with reference to human beings and individuals, if only on the best way to get rid of them."[65]

David Stafford, in his book *The Silent Game*, concludes that: "The end of the Reagan years in the United States and the ascendancy of Gorbachev in the Soviet Union may herald a new era of *detente*. But this will not dry up the torrent of spy fiction, merely divert it to new channels. *Detente* will remain fragile, the nuclear armouries well-stocked, and humanity will continue hostage to the whims of national rivalry, ideological passion, and its own innate capacity for folly. Civilization, as John Buchan put it on the very eve of the First World War, will remain precariously poised on the brink." [66]

Notes

1 Michael Eddowes, *The Oswald File*. New York, Clarkson N Potter, Inc., 1977.
2 Authors who have written fictional stories concerned with the assassination of President Kennedy, or deal with a similar theme, include: Wilson McCarthy, *The Fourth Man*. London, Hutchinson, 1972; Richard Condon, *Winter Kills*. New York, Dial Press, 1974; Charles McCarry, *The Tears of Autumn*. New York, Saturday Review Press, 1975; Jim Garrison, *The Star-Spangled Contract*. New York, McGraw Hill, 1976; Robert Littell, *The Sisters*. New York, Bantam, 1986; George Bernau, *Promises To Keep*. New York, Warner Books, 1988; Don DeLillo, *Libra*. London, Viking, 1988.
3 Richard Condon, *Winter Kills*. London, Book Club Associates, 1975, pp.249-250.
4 George Grella's criticisms of Charles McCarry's novels in *Twentieth Century Crime and Mystery Writers*, (ed.), John M Reilly, New York, Macmillan, 1980, p.1038.
5 Peter Andrews' review of Robert Littell's *The Sisters*, in the *New York Times Book Review*, 2 February 1986, p.9.
6 Quoted from an interview with Don DeLillo in *Publisher's Weekly*, 19 August 1988, p.56.
7 Leslie Halliwell, *Film Guide*, 6th edn, London, Paladin, 1987, p.321.
8 Leonard Rubenstein, *The Great Spy Films*. Secaucus, NJ, The Citadel Press, 1979, pp.63-64.
9 Martin Cropper's review of Don DeLillo's *Libra*, *Daily Telegraph*, 3 December 1988, p.x.
10 Cited by David Stafford in *The Silent Game*. London, Viking, 1989.
11 *Times* obituary of Lord Clanmorris, 9 August 1988.
12 Rebecca West, *The Birds Fall Down*. London, Virago Press, 1986.
13 BBC interview with le Carré.
14 "A Case Man on His Own", Douglas L Wheeler's review of *Spy Wednesday* in the *Intelligence Journal of Intelligence and Counter-Intelligence*, Vol.1, No.2, 1986.
15 Review in the *Irish Times*, 14 November 1987.
16 Cited by Stafford.
17 Antonio Tabucchi, *Little Misunderstandings of No Importance*. London, Chatto & Windus, 1988.
18 Zazuo Ishiguro, *The Remains of the Day*. London, Faber, 1989.
19 Dennis Bloodworth, *The Chinese Looking-Glass*. London, Secker & Warburg, 1967; New York, Farrar, Straus & Giroux, 1970.
20 Cited by Stafford.
21 *Sunday Telegraph*, 29 January 1989.
22 Lars Ole Sauerberg, *Secret Agents in Fiction: Ian Fleming, John le Carré and Len Deighton*. New York, St. Martin's Press, 1984.
23 Letter from Elspeth Huxley, entitled "A 'new evil' for Mr Le Carré", to the *Sunday Telegraph*, 5 February 1989.
24 Ralph Harper, *The World of the Thriller*. London and Baltimore, Johns Hopkins University Press, 1974.
25 Ibid.
26 Richard Deacon, *"C": A Biography of Sir Maurice Oldfield*. London, Macdonald, 1985.
27 *The Times*, 19 December 1975.
28 The comments of the authors in this paragraph come from their replies to questionnaires sent out by the authors of this book.
29 Quoted in Philip Knightley, *The Second Oldest Profession*, London, Deutsch,1986, pp.17-18. Originally from the Introduction to Le Queux's *Spies of the Kaiser: Plotting the Downfall of England*. London, Hurst & Blackett, 1909, p.xi.
30 Quoted in Bruce Merry, *Anatomy of the Spy Thriller*, Dublin, Gill and Macmillan, 1977, p.47.
31 Quoted in John Atkins, *The British Spy Novel*, London, John Calder, 1984, p.165, from the Maugham Papers in Humanities Research Center, University of Texas, Austin, 13 January 1950.
32 Graham Greene, from the Introduction to *Our Man in Havana*, London, Heinemann,1970, p.vii, first published in 1958.

33 From the transcript of an interview with John le Carré from a programme broadcast by PBS in America in 1981, introducing the televised series of *Tinker,Tailor, Soldier, Spy*.

34 Stephen Hunter, "Under the Spyglass" — an interview with John le Carré, *Espionage Magazine*, May 1987, p.76.

35 Quoted in Stafford, p.137.

36 Stephen Vaughn, "Spies, National Security, and the 'Inertia Projector': The Secret Service Films of Ronald Reagan", in *American Quarterly*, part 3, Vol.39, 1987, p.355.

37 Ibid. p.358.

38 Ibid. p.356.

39 Pare Lorentz's comments on the film, *Confessions of a Nazi Spy*, cited in Halliwell, p.210.

40 Rubenstein, p.114.

41 Letter from Dilys Powell to the authors of this book.

42 Rubenstein, pp.57-58.

43 Eric Rhode, *A History of the Cinema*. New York, Da Capo Press, 1976, p.622.

44 Pat Barker, *Sunday Times* Book Section, 26 February 1989, p.G4.

45 Letter from Ken Follett to the authors of this book.

46 Robin Winks, *Modus Operandi - An Excursion into Detective Fiction*. Boston, David Godine, 1982, pp.49-50.

47 Halliwell, p.1039.

48 Philip Zeigler, "Shaken, not interred", in the *Daily Telegraph*, 18 March 1989.

49 Cited from Kim Philby, *My Silent War*, New York, Grove Press, 1968.

50 Quoted from *New York Times*, 18 November 1958.

51 Tyler Marshall, *San Francisco Chronicle*, 1 June 1986, p.18.

52 P J Kavanagh, *The Spectator*, 4 February 1989, p.32.

53 Charles Spencer's television criticism of the series *Game, Set & Match*, *Daily Telegraph*, 1 October 1988.

54 Paul Henissart, "Of Spies and Stories", in *The Writer*, May 1978, p.16.

55 Grant Hugo, "The Political Influence of the Thriller", in *Contemporary Review*, December 1972, p.287.

56 Letter from S J Hamrick to Katy Fletcher, 30 October 1984.

57 Atkins, p.119.

58 Winks, p.61.

59 LeRoy L Panek, *The Special Branch*. Bowling Green, Ohio, Bowling Green University Popular Press, 1981, p.272.

60 Bruce Merry, "The Spy Thriller", in *London Magazine*, April 1976/77, Vol.16, p.10.

61 Answer from Alan Furst in reply to a questionnaire sent out by the authors of this book.

62 Clive Cussler, "Writing the Suspense-Adventure Novel", in *The Writer*, February 1978, Vol.91, No.2, p.14.

63 Answer from Reg Gadney in reply to a questionnaire sent out by the authors of this book.

64 There are several examples of the spy novel with an analyst as a spy hero, and they include: *Talon* by James Coltrane; *Six Days of the Condor* by James Grady; *The Amateur* by Robert Littell; and *The Kremlin Watcher* by Will Perry.

65 Atkins, p.110.

66 Stafford, p.229.

Glossary

Ag & Fish Refers to the British Ministry of Agriculture and Fisheries which, in the Second World War, was sometimes used as a cover address for "resting" Intelligence operatives. Alexander Foote, the double agent who worked for Russia and Britain, had a desk there for a period. "Ag & Fish" came to mean "gone to ground" in the early 1950s.

Agent of influence An agent who is employed to change and influence opinion in the country where he operates.

Agent provocateur An agent employed to stir up trouble, create chaos and generally make mischief.

Apparatchik In the West this has come to mean a secret agent or unit of such agents. In the USSR it simply means an official who has administrative powers.

ASIO Australian Secret Intelligence Organisation

AVB (Allami Vedelmi Batosag) The Hungarian Intelligence Service, formerly known as the AVH.

Bfv (Bundesamt fur Verfassungsschutz) West German Federal Internal Security Office.

Biographic leverage CIA jargon for blackmail. Used by Trevanian in *The Eiger Sanction.*

Black-bag jobs Agents' work, which ranges from bribery to burglary.

Black operations This covers several illegal operations such as murder, blackmail, extortion and kidnapping carried out by intelligence agencies.

Black trainees The nickname given to foreigners recruited for CIA undercover training at the hush-hush "Farm" in Virginia. These trainees were at one time allegedly not supposed to know that they were on American territory.

Bleep-box Used by some agents for both telephone tapping and obtaining calls to anywhere in the world without paying. In its primitive form this has been extensively used by agents in Europe and especially in Britain. The Chinese have developed a more sophisticated device called a multi-frequency-simulator, a machine for generating tones or frequencies used on various telephonic networks by which they have cracked the secret numbers of many organisations around the world — and so gained much useful information.

Blown The phrase used to describe an agent whose cover has been broken, or a network of spies which has been infiltrated. When an agent deliberately gives away to the opposition details of his sub-agent, wife or mistress for some devious reason, he is said to have "blown his own strumpet".

BOSS Bureau of State Security of the South African Government. This has been a favourite with some writers, probably due to the wild tales told about it and the mysterious but unsubstantiated innuendoes made by Sir Harold Wilson in the 1970s. It has since changed its name to the National Intelligence Service (NIS).

Boyeva gruppa KGB squads trained to kill and kidnap.

BPR A joke reference for many years to CIA headquarters in Langley, Virginia. The only indication as to the address in that area was a signpost bearing those initials which were supposed to signify Bureau of Public Roads. Eventually the signpost was replaced by one stating "Fairbanks Highway Research Station". But the CIA has many establishments in Washington DC, New York, Chicago, San Francisco, New Orleans and other American cities.

Bugging All manner of eavesdropping, from telephone tapping to electronic devices.

Burnt The word applied to an agent who has either been discovered or so severely compromised that he is no longer useful.

C The initial given to denote the head of the British Secret Service. The full initials are CSS.

Cacklebladder Secret Service slang for the method of disguising a live body to look like a corpse after having induced an enemy agent to hit or shoot the "dummy". As a general rule, the blood of poultry is used for smearing over the corpse. Though this may sound more like spy fiction than fact, it is a ploy adopted more often than would be supposed in real life, usually for blackmail purposes or forcing a confession from an agent.

Cannon Name given to a professional thief, employed by an intelligence agency, for the sole purpose of stealing back from an enemy agent or target some object given to him or her by another agent in order to make a deal or buy information. Often practised by intelligence units short of funds, especially in wartime.

CASMS Abbreviation for Computer-controlled Area Sterilisation Multi-Sensor System, a highly sophisticated area of modern intelligence and a revolutionary development of electronic eavesdropping which was tried out in Vietnam. Hundreds of small, self-contained bugging devices are dropped by aircraft in a certain area. They can pick up the movements of troops or individuals hidden in the jungle, or tanks and armoured cars.

CAT Civil Air Transport, the CIA's private air service. Founded in 1946 in China and later based in Taiwan from when it supported clandestine air operations in Korea, Vietnam and other Asian states.

CELD Central External Liaison Department, an important branch of the Chinese Secret Service which is concerned with the analysis of foreign intelligence.

Centre Refers to KGB headquarters in Moscow.

CESID (Centro Superior para la información de la Defensa): Spain's Intelligence service.

CHEKA (Chrezuvychainaya Komissiya po Borbe s Kontr-revolutisnei i Sabottazahem): Extraordinary Commission for the Struggle against Counter-revolution and Sabotage, predecessor of the KGB.

CHEKIST Derived from the **Cheka** and sometimes used to describe KGB members.

Cheng Pao K'o Chinese counter-espionage service, employed against foreign agents and to keep watch on the Chinese overseas. Not to be confused with *Chi Pao K'o*, the Internal Security Section.

CIA Central Intelligence Agency (US). South Korea also has its own CIA.

Circus Le Carré's name for the British **SIS** headquarters.

Cobbler A forger of false passports.

COMINT Official term (US) for Communications Intelligence. It is officially defined by the National Security Council Intelligence Directive No. 6 as "the interception and processing of foreign communications passed by radio, wire, or other electromagnetic means, and by the processing of foreign encrypted communications, however transmitted ..." Uncoded written communications, press reports and propaganda broadcasts are not included in this category.

Company Nickname for the CIA.

Condemned spy A Chinese Secret Service term which has sometimes been wrongly interpreted into English. Literally, it means: "Ostentatiously doing things calculated to deceive our own spies, who must be led to believe that they have been unwittingly disclosed. Then, when these spies are captured in the enemy's lines, they will make an entirely false report, and the enemy will take measures accordingly, only to find that we do something quite different. The spies will thereupon be put to death."

Control questions A system of checking used by the KGB. These questions are known to the **Centre**, the **Resident Director** and the agent concerned, and are employed to verify his identity should he appear in an unexpected place.

Counter-spy An agent put in place where he can betray or mislead opposing spies.

Cousins British **SIS** members' nickname for the CIA.

Covert action CIA jargon for attempting to influence the affairs of another country.

Cut-outs These are intelligence officers who come directly under the area Chief Intelligence Officer (or, in the case of the Russians, the **Resident Director**). They are talent spotters and recruiters, and act as go-betweens for agents and the Resident Director or Chief Officer.

Defectors There is, of course, the genuine defector from one side to another; more complicated are the forced, or kidnapped defector and the bogus defector. The **Walk-in Defector** is the person who arrives unannounced, bringing information with him. The **Defector-in-Place**, is one who stays on ostensibly as a defector, but in reality as an undeclared agent who sends back information as and when he can.

Demote maximally To purge by killing. Trevanian mentions this phrase as an example of the CIA's bureaucracy's "new-speak".

DGI (Dirección General de Intelligencia) Cuba's Secret Service.

DGSE (Direction Général de Sécurité Extérieure) This is the new title for the French Secret Service, replacing the **SDECE**. Many writers have fallen into the error of calling the *Deuxieme Bureau* the French Secret Service, and Ian Fleming even described it as the French counter-intelligence agency — wrong again. The *Deuxieme Bureau* began as a branch of military intelligence within the French Army. Today it is still a military service, but one which co-ordinates all intelligence services concerned with national defence.

DI5 The new title for MI5, though even old hands in the Intelligence world still use the old title.

DI6 The British Secret Service, controlling overseas agents, formerly known as MI6. Also known as the SIS.

Dirty tricks Usually applied to the "black operations" of the CIA and covering a wide range of espionage and counter-espionage skulduggery. It is a phrase sometimes applied to breaking into premises illegally to install bugging devices, also called "dirtying".

Disinformation The technique of discrediting one's opponents by manufacturing evidence, or smear tactics. Forged documents are used to discredit opponents. The KGB actually have a department of disinformation, known as Department D. But some other powers also use forgery on occasions, the notorious Zinoviev Letter being an example.

Doctor The police.

D of I Director of Intelligence (RAF).

DMI Director of Military Intelligence.

DNI Director of Naval Intelligence.

Double-agent In the past a double agent was usually a freelance intelligence agent working for two sides without either knowing about the other. He could be working for two powers who were allies, or two at war with one another. In recent times it often means an agent who appears to be working for two sides, but in fact is deliberately and knowingly used as a double-agent by one side, both to obtain information and to fob off false information on the opposition. Sometimes, though more rarely, there are treble and even quadruple agents, but their careers are normally brief. The exception was the Englishman Sidney Reilly, who worked for at least four powers during more than thirty years in Intelligence.

Double-cross system This is the system by which one country either plants her agents on the enemy, or captures enemy agents and "turns" them (converts them to their side), with the object of misleading the opposition. This system was adopted by the British in the Second World War with great success.

Drop This word has two meanings. In CIA ranks it denotes success in a "black operation". Inside the KGB it refers to a "letter-box", or hiding-place for secret messages, sometimes a crevice in a wall. See also **Dubok**.

DS (Darjavna Sugarnost) Bulgaria's State Security Service.

DST (Direction de la Surveillance du Territoire): The French Internal Security organisation.

Dubok Name given to secret hiding-places for agents' messages inside both the GRU and KGB. Curiously, for a nation so sophisticated in espionage, Soviet agents sometimes adopt the kind of hiding-place used by schoolboys for their secret notes. For example, a Soviet sub-agent in the Colonel Abel case told the Americans that he had been using a hole in a flight of steps in Prospect Park in Brooklyn. Park workers had noticed the hole and filled it in with cement.

Ears The antenna of an agent's radio rig.

Earwig Listening in to others' conversations.

ECM Electronic-counter-measures. Special gear for producing these measures is installed in NATO power submarines engaged in round-the-clock anti-submarine warfare watch — which used to be the front line of espionage, now it could be argued that special satellites provide the front line of defence.

E & E Escape and Evasion. Specialist agents in the CIA are used for these tasks — e.g. sending a man in to rescue a captured agent, or preparing an escape route.

ELINT Official term (US) for Electronic Intelligence. It is defined officially by National Security Council Intelligence Directive No. 6 as "the collection (observation and recording) and the processing for subsequent intelligence purposes of information derived from foreign, noncommunications, electromagnetic radiations emanating from other than atomic detonation or radioactive sources." Including information obtained by planes, ships, submarines, space satellites, electronic intercept stations and radars. This is handled and interpreted by **Squawk Hawks**, officially known as substantive intelligence analysts. Within ELINT there is a further category called **TELINT**.

Etsivakeskus Former name of Finland's Secret Police (now *Suojelupoliisi*).

FBI Federal Bureau of Investigation, the American counter-intelligence organisation.

FIA NATO power Intelligence Agencies' name for the West German Federal Intelligence Agency, known in Germany as the *Bundesnachrichtendienst*.

Field "In the field" means an agent actually on assignment in foreign territory.

Firm (the) Sometimes used by British agents to describe their Secret Service.

Fix This is a word used in CIA phraseology, usually relating to a situation where somebody is singled out for being compromised or blackmailed, or possibly just conned. Those seeking out the possibilities of employing such tactics talk of a "low-key" fix or an OK fix; the latter is actual blackmail.

Fluttered To be examined by a polygraph lie-detector.

Footwarmer A linear amplifier used in radio transmission.

FORTRAN Formula Translation Language. This is an abbreviation used both by Ted Allbeury and Len Deighton and it refers to computer language with special reference to engineering and scientific matters.

Friends, The The Hon. Monty Woodhouse, in his book Something Ventured, wrote: "MI6, a department in the Foreign Office politely, but not very sincerely, known as the Friends".

Fumigating Checking premises suspected of having been planted with listening and other devices and de-bugging those which actually have been so treated.

Fur-lined seat cover This is an oblique reference to an agent who has a female passenger.

Game (the) A person who works in Intelligence is said to be "in the game". Not to be confused with "on the game" (prostitution), though sometimes the two are combined!

GCHQ Government Communications Headquarters. The communications monitoring and listening post of the British Government, stationed at Cheltenham. It is linked to a worldwide network of spy bases, ships, planes and satellites and part of the four-nation UK-US network (including Britain, America, Canada and Australia) which shares out intelligence and divides the world into different areas to be monitored by each participant.

Large listening stations with more than 1,000 staff are operated in Cyprus, Hong Kong and Berlin, but there are also smaller station links in the Ascension Islands and Oman, while British GCHQ bases are to be found at various places in Britain, from Brora in Scotland to Morwenstow in the south-east. GCHQ itself operates from two large sites at Oakley and Benhall on the outskirts of Cheltenham. See **HMCC**.

Going private Leaving the Secret Service — this applies both to DI6 and the CIA, but not, of course, to the KGB!

GRU (Glavnoye Razvedyvatelnoye Upravlenie) Founded by Trotsky as the Fourth Department of the General Staff of the Red Army, a highly professional military intelligence-gathering organisation.

Harmonica bug A tiny transistorised eavesdropping gadget which can be placed inside an ordinary telephone.

Hauptverwaltung Aufklarung East Germany's Intelligence Service (part of MfS).

HMCC Her Majesty's Government Communications Centre. A separate organisation from **GCHQ** sited at Hanslope Park, north of Milton Keynes, which is responsible for the British Government's own communications. It brings into Britain all radio signals intercepted at small listening posts throughout the world. These are transmitted directly to GCHQ at Cheltenham.

Hospital Prison.

HUMINT Official term (US) for Human Intelligence, i.e. Intelligence gathered by spies and agents, as opposed to intelligence obtained from technological sources. See **ELINT**.

Illegals Soviet espionage élite agents sent, usually on false passports, into foreign countries where there is a death penalty for espionage. They are mainly deployed by the GRU. Referred to in Intelligence circles as "singles" or "doubles", the latter meaning married couples who are illegals.

JIC Joint Intelligence Committee (GB), a body comprising representatives of all Intelligence Agencies.

Joe Originally an American OSS euphemism for a spy or agent, and used by le Carré in *The Perfect Spy*.

Joe-houses In the Second World War this expression was used for places where agents were accommodated.

KGB (Komitet Gosudarstvennoy Bezopasnosti) An organisation of vast ramifications covering both espionage and counter-espionage on behalf of the Soviet Union.

KISS Korean Intelligence and Security Service.

Ladies A euphemism for female members of an intelligence team out to compromise one of the opposition. They set out to ingratiate themselves with the male **Target** for treatment, sometimes, but not always, seducing him. Often the Ladies are, as implied, out of the top drawer of society.

Lamp-lighters If you hear this phrase used by somebody claiming to be "in the game", suspect him at once. It is a spy fiction title for a certain type of agent, used (and probably invented) by John le Carré.

Legend The faked biography of a spy to provide him with a cover.

Lion-tamer When an agent is sacked, he sometimes goes berserk and makes threats. One of the Agency's muscle men is then called in to soften him up.The Lion-Tamer is also used to cope with recalcitrant or double-crossing **Ladies** or **Sisters**.

M The initial used to denote the head of the British Secret Service in the James Bond series. This gave rise to the mistaken idea that the initial denoted the surname of the chief, because Mansfield Cumming (First World War) had been known as "C" and in the Second World War Sir Stewart Menzies was the head. Probably Fleming's Service training made him jib at using the true initials for the head of the SIS, which had been "C" for more than seventy years. The head of the **SOE** was known as "M" for a brief time.

Magpie board A small board or pack of keys, wire, knives and other odds and ends for aiding escape. In more sophisticated packs benzedrine tablets, compasses, maps and even miniature radio transmitters are included.

Measles The term applies to a murder carried out so efficiently that death would appear to be due either to natural causes or an accident.

MfS (Ministerium fur Staatssicherheit) East Germany's Ministry for State Security.

MGB (Ministerstvo Gosudarstvennoy Bezopasnosti) The Soviet Ministry of State Security.

MI 1C The original initials of the British Secret Service before this was changed to **MI6**; hence the use of "C" for the head of the Service.

MI5 The old title for **DI5**, Britain's counter-intelligence service, operating primarily at home.

MI6 Initials of the British Secret Service, which operates abroad, after discarding its original title of **MI 1C** and before it was changed to **DI6**.

MI8 Entirely an American organisation -set up after the First World War by the cryptographer, Herbert O Yardley. It was, in effect, the cryptographic bureau of military intelligence and was the precursor of the National Security Agency. See **NSA**.

MI9 Initials of the Second World War organisation set up by the British for planning escapes and escape routes for Allied prisoners of war and others. Its most celebrated executive was the late Airey Neave, M.P., who paved the way by escaping from the German prisoner of war camp at Colditz in 1942.

Misinformation Baffling and misleading the opposition by planting false information. The technique was brilliantly employed by the British in the Second World War through the **Double-cross system** and in modern times has been effectively employed by the Russians in creating mistrust and ill-feeling between the Western allies.

MIS T/O The somewhat obscurely named Military Intelligence Systems Table of Organisation, which was set up by the Americans at Camp Ritchie, Maryland, in the Second World War. American Indians were trained there for use as combat radio operators because, by speaking their own native tongue, they were said to be able to baffle the Japanese radio monitors.

Mokrie dela In Russian this means literally "wet or bloody affairs" and refers to espionage missions actually involving bloodshed, violence or death. The CIA refer to a killing in the course of business as "wet work".

Mole Agent ordered to infiltrate the services of the enemy in order to send back information. This is, however, practised as much between powers at peace with one another as in wartime.

Mossad (Mossad Le Ailiyah Beth) Israel's Institute for Intelligence and Special Services.

Mozhno girls Mozhnos or "permitted girls", are recruited and trained by the KGB to seduce Western officials and agents and to report back what they learn from them. This practice was somewhat curtailed after Stalin's death because a fewMozhnos actually married the person they had been told to seduce. One such Mozhno was Nora Murray, who wrote a book called *I Spied for Stalin*.

Mukhabarat Libya's Intelligence Service.

Mukhararat El-Aam The General Intelligence Agency, Egypt's secret service.

Music box A wireless transmitter.

Musician A radio operator. A network of such people is sometimes called an **Orchestra**.

MVD (Ministerstvo Vnutrennikh Del) The Soviet Ministry of Internal Affairs.

M-20 A meeting place, often used on Citizens' Band radio, as well as in espionage.

Naked Operating entirely alone and without any assistance from outside.

Nash A person belonging to one's own side. This is a horrible corruption of a Russian word used by Western operatives.

Neighbour Soviet operatives use this phrase to refer either to the local Communist Party or one of its members. Westerners would call a neighbour a "fellow traveller".

Neighbours Warsaw Pact Powers.

News News in the intelligence game is usually bad, and this term is used for passing the word to a contact or a **Target** that he is on the spot — i.e. that he must either deliver the goods (which can mean anything from revealing information to carrying out a mission) or face exposure or blackmail. The "news" is usually conveyed subtly and not directly so that it will slowly sink in and the victim can ponder the alternative. Occasionally this is done merely to keep a **Target** on ice, that is, to hint that he may eventually be required to perform a task for his mentors or tormentors — in CIA language be "re-activated".

NID British Naval Intelligence Division. Once the equal of MI6, but now deplorably reduced in size.

NIS National Intelligence Service of the South African Government, which was formerly called **BOSS**.

NKGB (Narodnyi Kommissariat Gosudarstvennoi Bezopasnosti) The Soviet People's Commissariat for State Security.

NKVD (Narodnyi Kommissariat Vnutrennikh Del) The People's Commissariat for Internal Affairs.

NSA The National Security Agency (US). Established by presidential order in 1952, the Agency has two main functions: to conduct signals intelligence (**SIGINT**) operations and activities; and to ensure the communications security of eighteen federal agencies involved in national security matters.

Ochrana The Tsarist Intelligence and Security Service, succeeded by the **Cheka**.

OKW (Ober Kommando Wehrmacht) German military intelligence organisation in the Second World War.

One-man Bay of Pigs This was the nickname given to the unlucky and incompetent agent in Trevanian's *The Eiger Sanction*, Wormwood, who was killed in Montreal. It refers, of course, to that catastrophic CIA operation against Castro during Kennedy's presidency, and no doubt has been used in real-life Intelligence about any disastrous and accident-prone agent.

ONI Office of Naval Intelligence (US).

Orchestra A term coined by Lenin to refer to the creation of a team of potential long-term agents, people selected without being told but allowed to remain dormant until ultimately they could be bullied, blackmailed, cajoled or compromised into collaboration. Usually the people chosen were those who had access to secret information or to important individuals or offices (this would apply as much to cleaners as to people inside the Establishment or a high-level social clique) and had weaknesses which could be exploited — perversions, homosexuality, alcoholism, marital infidelity, etc. Sometimes the term is applied to a network, though this is mainly because in the Second World War the Germans nicknamed the Soviet espionage network in Belgium Rote Kapelle (Red Orchestra), when they discovered that a radio-operator in Soviet espionage terminology was a **Musician** and a transmitting set was a **Music Box**.

OSS Office of Strategic Services. On 13 June 1942, the Office of the Co-ordinator of Information became the Office of Strategic Services, under General "Wild Bill" Donovan. The forerunner of the CIA.

Pavement artists A surveillance team or an agent keeping watch on a house. It is used by le Carré, but does not appear to be employed outside fiction.

Peep The name given to both an espionage photographic specialist who can take good (useful) pictures in conditions of great difficulty, and a planter of secret cameras.

PFIAB President's Foreign Intelligence Advisory Board (US).

PHOTINT Official term (US) for Photographic Intelligence.

Piano concerto Message, e.g. "See my 43rd concerto".

Piano study Radio operating.

Piscine Nickname of the French Secret Service headquarters because it was situated close to a large swimming pool.

Place of conspiracy A Soviet term for a secret meeting-place, usually in a nearby country where an agent may in certain circumstances make contact with his "side" on fixed days.

Playback This occurs when an agent is captured and forced to continue transmitting back home, usually including false information. His aim will always be to try to indicate what is happening without his controllers knowing.

Plumbing The work undertaken to prepare for a major operation, though it can also refer to reconnaissance of a building and the planting of **Bugging** gadgets. This work is undertaken by "plumbers".

Pudding A sarcastic term applied by intelligence agents in the West to the United Nations. "In the pudding club" means inside UN headquarters.

Puzzle palace A nickname for the NSA headquarters at Fort Meade, Maryland, derived from James Bamford's book about the Agency called *The Puzzle Palace*.

PZPR Polish Secret Police and Intelligence Agency.

Quick trip around the Horn An agent-radio operator's check on activity in communications.

Queen Anne's Gate Many say fiction writers have referred and still do refer knowingly to Queen Anne's Gate. Allbeury, for example, writes of "one of those beautifully panelled little set-ups that MI6 finds so necessary to its trade in Queen Anne's Gate". An Intelligence Branch of the War Office was started at Queen Anne's Gate in 1871. It was moved to Adair House in Pall Mall in 1874 and then returned to its original location in 1884. DI6 developed out of this and for many years its principal address was at 21 Queen Anne's Gate and the telephone number was listed under a sub-branch of the Ministry of Land & Natural Resources.

Questors Investigators of Section Q of the CIA.

RABCOR A system of "worker-correspondents" (*rabcor* in its abbreviated Russian form) was one of the first forms of Soviet espionage and was set up in France before the Second World War and revived afterwards. It began with the development of a system of industrial espionage in factories and elsewhere. During the early 1950s there were said to be more than 800 rabcors in France, all supplying information to Soviet Intelligence.

Radar button A gadget which can pinpoint its carrier's position back to base at any given time. The agent can be shadowed by the controller and aided if he is in trouble.

RADINT Official term (US) for Radar Intelligence i.e. intelligence collected through the use of radar. For instance, foreign missile tests might be observed by tracking the test vehicle by radar; strategic installations might be observed by air- or spaceborne side-looking aircraft radar.

R-12 Sometimes called the "Buzby Bug", this can be inserted into a telephone and then called up from anywhere in the world to eavesdrop on conversations. The bug was invented by the Special Investigations Divisions of the Post Office — code-named R-12, and based at Martlesham Heath, near Ipswich, Suffolk.

Raven A male agent employed to seduce men or women who could be of value to his agency.

Resident Director In the Soviet Secret Service the Resident Director of a spy network does not as a rule live in the country against which the network is directed, but in an adjacent or nearby territory. He usually has diplomatic status, but not always.

Residentura Refers to the spy network controlled by the **Resident Director**.

Safe-house A hide-away, where agents and **Defectors** can be accommodated. More often the term is applied to a place where agents and suspects are interrogated.

Sanctification An American term, bluntly described by Miles Copeland as "blackmail for the purposes of extracting political favours from a victim, not money". A Russian translation of this word is applied to tactics of the KGB and GRU in winning defectors from the Roman Catholic priesthood. When they secure a priest as an agent, the KGB say he has been "beatified".

Sanction To "sanction" a man means that his killing (usually for revenge or other countermeasures) is sanctioned by an intelligence Agency. Trevanian makes use of this word in the titles of his two books, *The Eiger Sanction* and *The Loo Sanction*. The phrase is used sometimes in CIA circles. Trevanian has given it a special department — the Search and Sanction Division of CII — which is a counter-assassination organisation aimed at removing the opposition's killers.

SB (Sluzba Bezpleczentstwa) The Polish Intelligence Service. See also **PZPR**.

Scalp-hunters Specialists in the whole subject of defection and experts in telling who is genuine and who is a fake defector. Their job is to keep their ears open for news of any diplomat or priority **Target** in the enemy camp who seems anxious to defect. They are given top priority in such instances over other intelligence operators.

SDECE (Service de Documentation Extérieure et de Contre-Espionage) Formerly the French Secret Service. See **DGSE**.

Setting-up The jargon used for framing or trapping an individual by secret agents. A diplomat, for example, is said to be "set up" when he is lured into a bedroom, fitted with hidden cameras and microphones, to be seduced by one of the **Ladies** or **Sisters**. The KGB are past masters at "setting up", but these tactics have been used by Western Intelligence Services as well.

Shoe A false passport.

Shopped This word has been used by British Intelligence to refer both to assassinations and betrayals.

Sifar The Italian counter-espionage service.

SIGINT Official term (US) for Signals Intelligence. This is a general category of intelligence which includes any intelligence collected from intercepted communications (e.g. microwave, landlines, secret writing) or electromagnetic emanations (e.g. foreign radar signals or telemetry) from an object of intelligence interest. There are two main categories within SIGINT — COMINT and ELINT.

SIS Secret Intelligence Srvice. (GB). Another title for DI6, but sometimes wrongly used as a blanket term for DI6 and DI5.

Sisters The lower ranks of the **Ladies**, they usually get the tougher assignments and invariably find themselves bedding down with the opposition regardless of their inclinations.

Sleeper A deep-cover agent planted in opposition territory with orders to lie low and work up contacts over a period of years. Gordon Lonsdale (Konon Molody), the Soviet spy caught by the British in London in 1961, was a typical sleeper, having been planted in Canada in the 1930s.

SMERSH An abbreviated combination of two Russian words, *Smyert Shpionam* (Death to Spies), used to describe the Soviet organisation James Bond was fighting. In fact, Fleming (writing in the late 1950s), was somewhat out of date talking of SMERSH. An organisation of this name existed in the 1940s, but was incorporated into the OKR (*Otdely Kontrrazvedki*) counter-espionage service in 1946.

Soap Nickname for the truth drug, specially treated sodium pentathol, known for short as SO-PE.

SOE Special Operations Executive. Second World War British-sponsored organisation for aiding and collaborating with Resistance movements in Occupied Europe.

Software Official jargon for the programming and designing of systems for use on computers in intelligence.

Son et lumiere This is the amusingly apt phrase used to cover the obtaining of evidence from a **Setting-up**. It means that the seduction of the victim by a **Lady** or a **Sister** is recorded by hidden cameras and microphones.

Special Forces Club Mentioned by a number of spy fiction writers, notably by Allbeury in *A Choice of Enemies*: "It's quiet and friendly and, unless we have another war soon, it's going to run out of members." The club actually exists at 8 Herbert Crescent, London SW1, and membership is open to those who have been "in the game" — SIS, SOE, SAS, etc.

Special projects CIA jargon for the tougher and more unpleasant side of Intelligence, including anything from murder to paramilitary operations, but sometimes this covers illegal **Bugging** as well.

Spoofing Post-Second World War aerial reconnaissance. The name was conjured up by the British when they sent out planes skirting the borders of the USSR, sounding out radar installations and collecting intelligence. "Spoofing" was usually limited to flying across the Soviet borders and back again, occasionally provoking intervention by Soviet planes. It was eventually replaced by the U-2 operations, which were launched by the Americans in 1956.

Spook A professional intelligence executive or agent. Also covers spy-catchers.

Spook's club A somewhat esoteric club, whose members, if elected, must not only be recognised writers of spy fiction, but have other qualifications, one of which is to have been "in the game". They operate internationally and have "drops" on both sides of the Atlantic, but are London-based. Their meeting-place is known as "The Safe House", but the address is not normally publicised.

Spookspeak The language of the Intelligence fraternity.

SQP One character in William Hood's *Spy Wednesday* says: "It will be SQP all right ... business as usual." "SQP?" "*Sauve qui peut*" [Every person for himself].

SSD (Staatssicherheitsdienst) The East German Intelligence Service.

Stable The list of **Ladies** and **Sisters** available for **Setting-up** operations in an allotted territory. This sometimes included **Taxis** or "Fairies".

Station chief Top CIA official under diplomatic cover in an American Embassy.

Stepped on Signal and radio interference.

Stroller An agent operating with a walkie-talkie set.

STB (Statni Tajna Bezpecnost) The Czech Intelligence Service.

Stucen According to Len Deighton (doubtless with tongue in cheek) this is the War Studies Centre, London, and situated in Hampstead — see his war-gaming, nuclear submarine-cum-espionage book *Spy Story*. For more sober inquirers there are the Royal College of Defence Studies, 37 Belgrave Square, London SW1, the Institute for the Study of Conflict 12/12A Golden Square, London W1, and the International Institute for Strategic Studies, 23 Tavistock Street, London WC2.

Sweetener Any method used for softening up a **Target** either by gifts or inducements.

Target Someone selected for **Sanctification** by the Americans and, in British parlance, for "special treatment" — in other words, a person usually in the enemy camp on whom incriminating evidence is needed so that a hold on him (or her) can be acquired. But it can also refer to someone marked out as a likely **Defector** who needs just that last push to be lured across.

Taxi Cover word for "Jacksie", a homosexual member of the **Stable**, but now somewhat dated as even "Taxis" tend to be called **Ladies** or **Sisters**. As one SIS executive told a British Minister during a sex scandal involving another Minister: "we are all bisexual these days and when our Stablemates say that they have 'got the whips on', they aren't talking in parliamentary language."

TELINT Official term (US) for Telemetry Intelligence, a subcategory of **ELINT**. This would include information on foreign missile tests obtained by intercepting telemetry sent by the test missiles while in flight.

Thermal detector A gadget which makes it possible to discover where people have been sitting or lying and even how many clothes they have been wearing.

Thirty-threes An emergency.

Tiger-in-the-tank A linear amplifier.

Toby (doing a) An "in" word in **NID** and some other British Intelligence circles in the Second World War, meaning to be involved in devious procedures. It originated from Lieutenant-Colonel "Toby" Ellis, an intelligence executive in Tangier, notorious for his sometimes incomprehensible imbroglios.

Turned agent An agent of an enemy power who is either captured or comes over voluntarily to the other side to feed false information to the enemy and obtain Intelligence from them.

Twisted balls Originally a Russian expression to indicate an agent who had previously been given electric shocks in the genitals. Such a man was considered a relatively easy subject for further interrogation.

Walk-in One who volunteers information or offers his services.

War of diversion This is a Soviet term for carefully calculated sabotage of Western installations and factories. This is hardly ever indulged in on a large scale, but is intended mainly as a "diversion" and a probe, and occasionally is done under cover of such terrorist movements as the IRA. It used to be controlled by the 9th Section for Terror & Diversion of Soviet Intelligence.

WEB West European Bureau of the Comintern, USSR.

What's your twenty? Where exactly are you?

XX Committee The Double-Cross (usually referred to in code as "The Twenty") Committee, set up in the Second World War to control and exploit double agents by BI A Section of **MI5**.

Y Service Wireless deception.

ZE-2 Polish Military Intelligence.

Zeta men Name given in some circles to graduates from St. Antony's College, Oxford, who have joined **DI6**.

Zoo Police Station.

Bibliography
and Acknowledgements

Before listing works and sources consulted in compiling this book it should perhaps be made clear that, in the case of living authors, a great deal has been supplied by the authors themselves, occasionally in interviews, sometimes in their own response to questionnaires. Where appropriate, their own comments have been given in direct quotation. Various authorities on espionage in real life have also been consulted: many of them are so impressed by the spy fiction of today that they have sometimes said that the fiction very often puts on paper what they themselves think. A great deal of research on earlier writers has been done at the British Library and we would like to record our appreciation to the London Library for helping to provide a detailed catalogue of spy fiction from 1900 onwards.

We are especially indebted to Hodder & Stoughton for supplying all their catalogues from 1900 to the present time, and to Miss Livia Gollancz of Victor Gollancz for assistance in tracing some pre-war authors; to the late Mr Gerald Austin of the Century Hutchinson Group for all manner of help and answering of queries over several weeks; to Miss Marian Babson, of the Crime Writers' Association; to Mr Simon Wood for his contribution to the entry for John Gardner; to the staff of the following publishing houses who have assisted us with information: Century Hutchinson, Transworld, Simon & Schuster, Severn House, Headline, Grafton Books, Robert Hale, The Bodley Head, Jonathan Cape, WH Allen, William Heinemann, Hamish Hamilton, Constable and Macmillan London Ltd. We would also like to thank the helpful staff of West Sussex County Libraries and the Book Information Service of the Book Trust in London; and finally all the authors who supplied information about themselves.

Books specially consulted and which can be recommended to any student of the genre are listed below:

Agee, Philip, *Inside the Company: CIA Diary*. Harmondsworth, Middlesex, Penguin, 1975.

Ambler, Eric, *To Catch A Spy*. London, Bodley Head, 1963.

Ambrosetti, Ronald J, "A Study of the Spy Genre in Recent Popular Literature", Bowling Green State University, Ph.D., 1973.

Amis, Kingsley, *The James Bond Dossier*. London, Cape, 1965.

Andrew, Christopher, and Dilks, David (eds), *The Missing Dimension: Governments and Intelligence Communities in the Twentieth Century*. London, Macmillan, 1984.

Andrew, Christopher, *Secret Service: The Making of the British Intelligence Commnity*. London, Heinemann, 1985.

Atkins, John, *The British Spy Novel: Styles in Treachery*. London, John Calder, 1984; New York, Riverrun Press, 1984.

Atlee Phillips, David, *The Night Watch*. New York, Ballantine, 1977.

Atlee Phillips, David, *The World and I*. November 1986, pp.61-63.

Atlee Phillips, David, "American Espionage Writers", undated, *c*.1984, as yet unpublished, title provisional, supplied by kind courtesy of the author.

Aydelotte, William O, "The Detective Story as a Historical Source", in Irving and Harriet A Deer (eds), *The Popular Arts — A Critical Reader*. New York, Scribner's, 1967.

Ball, John (ed.), *The Mystery Story*. London, Penguin, 1978.

Bamford, James, *The Puzzle Palace: a report on NSA, America's Most Secret Agency*. Boston, Mass., Houghton Mifflin, 1976.

Barley, Tony,*Taking Sides: The Fiction of John le Carré*. Milton Keynes and Philadelphia, Open University Press, 1986.

Barzun, Jacques, and Hertig Taylor, Wendell, *A Catalogue of Crime: Being a Reader's Guide to the Literature of Mystery, Detection, and Related Genres*. New York, Harper & Row, 1971.

Barzun, Jacques, "Meditations on the Literature of Spying", *American Scholar*, Vol.XXXIV, 1965, pp.167-178.

Benson, Sumner, "The Historian as Foreign Policy Analyst: the challenge of the CIA", *The Public Historian*, Vol.3, 1981, pp.15-25.

Blackstock, Paul W and Schaf, Frank L (eds), *Intelligence, Espionage, Counterespionage, and Covert Operations: A Guide to Information Sources*. Detroit, Gale Research Co., 1978.

Blaufarb, Douglas S, *The Counterinsurgency Era: US Doctrine and Performance 1950 to the present*. New York, The Free Press, 1977.

Breen, Jon L (ed.), *What About Murder: A Guide to Mystery and Detective Fiction*. Metuchen, NJ, Scarecrow Press, 1981.

Bryce, Ivar, *You Only Live Once: Memoirs of Ian Fleming*. London, Weidenfeld & Nicolson, 1975.

Buranelli, Nan and Vincent, *Spy/Counterspy — An encyclopedia of espionage*. New York, McGraw Hill, 1982.

Campbell, Iain, *Ian Fleming: A Catalogue of a Collection*. Iain Campbell, Liverpool, 1978.

Cawelti, John G, *Adventure, Mystery and Romance: Formula Stories as Art and Popular Culture*. Chicago, University of Chicago Press, 1976.

Cawelti, John G and Rosenberg, Bruce A, *The Spy Story*. Chicago, Chicago University Press, 1987.

Cline, Majorie *et al.* (eds), *Scholar's Guide to intelligence Literature*. Baltimore, Md., University Publications of America, 1983.

Cline, Ray S, *Secrets, Spies and Scholars — Blueprint of the Essential CIA*. Washington DC, Acropolis Books, 1976.

Colby, William E, *Honorable Men: My Life in the CIA*. New York, Simon & Schuster, 1978.

Constantinides, George C, *Intelligence and Espionage: An Analytical Bibliography*. Boulder, Colorado, Westview Press, 1983.

Copeland, Miles, *Without Cloak and Dagger*. New York, Simon & Schuster, 1974.

Corson, William R, *The Armies of Ignorance*. New York, Dial Press, 1977.

Craig, Patricia and Cadogan, Mary, *The Lady Investigates: Women Detectives and Spies in Fiction*. London, Gollancz, 1981.

Cussler, Clive, "Writing the Suspense-Adventure Novel", *The Writer*, February 1978.

Davis, Earle, "Howard Hunt and the Peter Ward–CIA Spy Novels", *Kansas Quarterly*, Vol.X, Fall 1978, pp.85-95.

Deacon, Richard, *The Truth Twisters*. London, Macdonald, 1986.

Dulles, Allen (ed.), *Great Spy Stories in Fiction*. New York, Harper & Row, 1969.

Dulles, Allan (ed.), *The Craft of Intelligence*. London, Weidenfeld & Nicolson, 1963.

Dulles, Allan (ed.), *Great True Spy Stories*. New York, Ballantine, 1968.

East, Andy, *The Cold War File*. Metuchen, NJ, Scarecrow Press, 1983.

Eddowes, Michael, *The Oswald File*. New York, Clarkson N Potter, Inc., 1977.

Farago, Ladislas, *The Game of Foxes: The Untold Story of German Espionage in the United States and Great Britain during World War II*. New York, Bantam, 1973.

Felix, Christopher, *The Spy and his Masters: A Short Course in the Secret War*. London, Secker & Warburg, 1963.

Fitzgibbon, Constantine, *Secret Intelligence in the Twentieth Century*. New York, Stein & Day, 1977.

Fletcher, Katy, extracts from an article entitled "American Spy Fiction before World War II", *Red Herrings*, September 1985, pp.4-5. *Red Herrings* is the monthly bulletin of the Crime Writers' Association.

Fletcher, Katy, "Evolution of the Modern American Spy Novel", *Journal of Contemporary History*, Vol.22, No.2 (April 1987).

Frye, Northrop, *Anatomy of Criticism*. Princeton, NJ, Princeton University Press, 1957.

Gid Powers, Richard, "J Edgar Hoover and the Detective Hero", *Journal of Popular Culture*, Fall 1975, Vol.IX, pp.257-278.

Greene, Graham, and Greene, Hugh, *The Spy's Bedside Book*. London, Rupert Hart-Davis, 1957.

Grella, George J, "The Literature of the Thriller: A Critical Study", University of Kansas, Ph.D., 1967.

Hagen, A Ordean, *Who Done It? A Guide to Detective, Mystery, and Suspense Fiction*. New York, Bowker, 1969.

Hall, Stuart and Whannel, Paddy, *The Popular Arts*. London, Hutchinson, 1964.

Halliwell, Leslie, *Film Guide*, 6th edn. London, Paladin, 1987.

Harper, Ralph, *The World of the Thriller*. Baltimore and London, Johns Hopkins University Press, 1974.

Haycraft, Howard (ed.), *The Art of the Mystery Story*. New York, Simon & Schuster, 1946.

Henissart, Paul, "Of Spies and Stories", *The Writer*, May 1978, pp.15-18.

Hubin, Allen J, *The Bibliography of Crime Fiction 1749-1975*. San Diego, University of California Extension, 1979.

Hugo, Grant, "The Political Influence of the Thriller", *Contemporary Review*, December 1972, pp.284-289.

Jeffreys-Jones, RJ, *American Espionage*. New York, The Free Press, 1977.

Jeffreys- Jones, RJ , "The Historiography of the CIA", *Historical Journal*, Vol.23, No.2, 1980.

Johnson, Timothy and Julia (eds), *Crime Fiction Criticism: An Annotated Bibliography*. New York, Garland, 1981.

Kahn, David, *The Codebreakers: The Story of Secret Writing*. New York, Macmillan, 1967.

Keating, HRF, *Whodunnit? A Guide to Crime, Suspense, and Crime Fiction*. New York, Van Nostrand Reinhold, 1982.

Knightley, Phillip, *The Second Oldest Profession: The Spy As Bureaucrat,Patriot, Fantasist and Whore*. London, André Deutsch, 1986.

Landrum, Larry N, Brown, Pat and Brown, Ray B, *Dimensions of Detective Fiction*. Bowling Green, Ohio, Bowling Green University Press, 1976.

Laqueur, Walter, "Le Carré's Fantasies", *Commentary*, LXXV, June 1983, pp.62-67.

Marchetti, Victor and Marks, John, *The CIA and the Cult of Intelligence*. NewYork, Dell, 1975.

Masterman, Sir JC, *The Double-Cross System in the War of 1939-45*. New Haven, Yale University Press, 1972; see foreword by Norman Holmes Pearson.

McCormick, Donald, *Who's Who in Spy Fiction*. London, Elm Tree Books, Hamish Hamilton, 1977.

McGarvey, Patrick J, *CIA: The Myth and the Madness*. New York, Saturday Review Press, 1972.

McGehee, Ralph W, *Deadly Deceits: My 25 years in the CIA*. New York, Sheridan Square, 1983.

Merry, Bruce, *Anatomy of the Spy Thriller*. Dublin, Gill and Macmillan, 1977.

Merry, Bruce, "The Spy Thriller", *London Magazine*, XVI, April 1976, pp.8-27.

Milward-Oliver, Edward, *The Len Deighton Companion*. London, Grafton, 1987.

Monaghan, David, *The Novels of John le Carré: The Art of Survival*. Oxford, Blackwell, 1985.

Monaghan, David, *Smiley's Circus: A Guide to the Secret World of John le Carré*. NewYork, St. Martin's Press, 1986.

Morgan, Ted, *Somerset Maugham*. London, Cape, 1980.

Most, Glenn W and Stowe, William W, *The Poetics of Murder*. New York, Harcourt Brace, 1983.

Murch, Alma, *The Development of the Detective Novel*. London, Peter Owen, 1958.

Mure, David, *Practice to Deceive*. London, Kimber, 1977.

Mure, David, *Master of Deception: Tangled Webs in London and the Middle East*. London, Kimber, 1980.

Nevins, Francis M, Jr, (ed.), *The Mystery Writer's Art*. Bowling Green, Ohio, Popular Press, 1971.

Newman, Bernard, *The World of Espionage*. London, Souvenir Press, 1962.

Orlov, Alexander, *Handbook of Intelligence and Guerrilla Warfare*. Ann Arbor, University of Michigan Press, 1963.

O'Toole, GJA, *The Encyclopedia of American Intelligence and Espionage—from the Revolutionary War to the Present*. New York, Facts On File, 1988.

Page, Bruce, Leitch, David and Knightley, Philip, *The Philby Conspiracy*. Garden City, NY, Doubleday, 1968; see introduction by John le Carré.

Palmer, Jerry, *Thrillers: Genesis and Structure of a Popular Genre*. London, Edward Arnold, 1978.

Panek, LeRoy L, *The Special Branch: The British Spy Novel 1890-1980*. Bowling Green, Ohio, Popular Press, 1981.

Penzler, Otto, *The Private Lives of Private Eyes, Spies, Crime Fighters, and Other Good Guys*. New York, Grosset and Dunlap, 1977.

Philby, Kim, *My Secret War*. London, MacGibbon and McKee, 1968.

Pick, JB, "Through a spy glass darkly", *The Scotsman*, 3 March 1984.

Powers, Thomas, *The Man Who Kept the Secrets : Richard Helms and the CIA*. New York, Pocket Books, 1981.

Pronzini, Bill and Muller, Marcia, *1001 Midnights — The Aficionado's Guide to Mystery and Detection*. New York, Arbor House, 1986.

Ransom, Harry Howe,*The Intelligence Establishment*. Cambridge, Harvard University Press, 1970.

Rausch, G Jay and Diane K, "Developments in Espionage Fiction",*Kansas Quarterly*, Fall 1978, pp.71-82.

Reilly, John M (ed.), *Twentieth Century Crime and Mystery Writers*. London, Macmillan, 1980.

Reilly, John M (ed.), *Twentieth Century Crime and Mystery Writers*. London, St. James' Press, 1985.

Rhode, Eric, *A History of the Cinema*. New York, Da Capo Press, 1976.

Rockwell, Joan, "Normative Attitudes of Spies in Fiction", in Rosenberg, B and Manning-White, D, *Mass Culture Revisited*. NewYork, Van Nostrand Reinhold, 1971.

Rodell, Marie F, *Mystery Fiction : Theory and Technique*. London, Hammond, 1954.

Rubenstein, Leonard, *The Great Spy Films*. Secaucus, NJ, The Citadel Press, 1979.

Sauerberg, Lars Ole, *Secret Agents in Fiction: Ian Fleming, John le Carré, and Len Deighton*. New York, St. Martin's Press, 1984.

Schlesinger, Arthur, *A Thousand Days — John F Kennedy in the White House*. Boston, Houghton Mifflin, 1965.

Seth, Ronald, *Encyclopedia of Espionage*. Garden City, NY, Doubleday, 1974.

Skene Melvin, David, "The secret eye; the spy in literature: the evolution of espionage literature — a survey of the history and development of the spy and espionage novel", *Pacific Quarterly*, Vol.III, January 1978, pp.11-26.

Skene Melvin, David and Skene Melvin, Ann, *Crime, Detective, Espionage, Mystery, and Thriller Fiction and Film*. Westport, Connecticut, Greenwood Press, 1980.

Smith, Bradley F, *The Shadow Warriors — OSS and the Origins of the CIA*. London, Deutsch, 1983.

Smith, Joseph B, *Portrait of a Cold Warrior*. New York, Putnam's, 1976.

Smith, Myron J, *Cloak and Dagger Bibliography: An Annotated Guide to Spy Fiction 1937-1975*. Metuchen, NJ, Scarecrow Press, 1976.

Smith, Myron J, *Cloak and Dagger Fiction: An Annotated Guide to Spy Thrillers*. Santa Barbara, California, ABC-Clio Inc., 1982.

Smith, R Harris, *OSS*. Los Angeles, California, University of California Press, 1972.

Snelling, OF, *Double O Seven: James Bond — a report*. New York, Signet, 1964.

Snepp, Frank, *Decent Interval*, 2nd edn. Harmondsworth, Middlesex, Penguin, 1980.

Snyder, John R, "The Spy Story as Modern Tragedy", *Literature/Film Quarterly,* S u m m e r 1977, Vol.V, pp.216-235.

Stafford, David, *The Silent Game: The Real World of Imaginary Spies*. London, Viking, 1988.

Stafford, David, "Spies and Gentlemen: The Birth of the British Spy.

Steinbrunner, C and Penzler, O, *Encyclopaedia of Mystery and Detection*. London, Routledge, 1976.

Symons, Julian, *Bloody Murder: From the Detective Story to the Crime Novel, A History*. London, Faber & Faber, 1972.

Symons, Julian, *Bloody Murder: From the Detective Novel to the Crime Story, A History*. London, Viking, 1985.

Usborne, Richard, *Clubland Heroes: A Nostalgic Study of Some Recurrent Characters in the Romantic Fiction of Dornford Yates, John Buchan, and "Sapper"*. London, Constable, 1953.

Vaughn, Stephen, "Spies, National Security, and the 'Inertia Projector': The Secret Service Films of Ronald Reagan", *American Quarterly*, part 3, Vol. 39 , 1987.

Watt, Ian, *The Rise of the Novel*. London, Chatto & Windus, 1957.

Weismiller, Edward, *Serpent's Progress: The Writing of a Novel*. Center for Advanced Studies, Wesleyan University, 1968.

Welcome, John (ed.), *Best Spy Stories*. London, Faber & Faber, 1967.

Winks, Robin W (ed.), *Detective Fiction: A Collection of Critical Essays*. Englewood Cliffs, NJ, Prentice Hall, 1980.

Winks, Robin W (ed.), *Modus Operandi: An Excursion into Detective Fiction*. Boston, David R Godine, 1982.

Winn, Dilys, *Murder Ink*. New York, Workman Publishing, 1977.

Wise, David and Ross, Thomas B, *The Espionage Establishment*. NewYork, Random House, 1967.

Wiseman, Sir William, *The Private Papers of Sir William Wiseman*, in the EM House Collection, Yale University Library, New Haven, Connecticut.

Yardley, Herbert O, *The American Black Chamber*. New York, Ballantine, 1981.

York, Andrew, "Thriller Writing", *The Writer*, February 1979.

Index

Pseudonyms are listed in this index, followed by *see* and the author's real name. Authors, books (in *italic*) and films (in *italic*) have entries only if they are referred to in the Introduction or Section 2. The rest of the authors appear in alphabetical order of surname in the A-Z section.